SATHER CLASSICAL LECTURES

Volume Thirty-six

POIESIS

Structure and Thought

POIESIS
Structure and Thought

by H. D. F. KITTO

UNIVERSITY OF CALIFORNIA PRESS
BERKELEY AND LOS ANGELES 1966

UNIVERSITY OF CALIFORNIA PRESS
BERKELEY AND LOS ANGELES, CALIFORNIA

CAMBRIDGE UNIVERSITY PRESS
LONDON, ENGLAND

LIBRARY OF CONGRESS CATALOG CARD NUMBER: 66-15665
PRINTED IN THE UNITED STATES OF AMERICA

Preface

It is as long ago as 1960 that the University of California paid me the compliment of inviting me to deliver the Sather Lectures. My apologies are certainly due to the University Press for my slowness in preparing the book; also my gratitude for its forbearance. However, I do not plead guilty to idleness. In one of the lectures, discussing the Greek feeling for eloquent structure, I devoted one and a half minutes to Thucydides: the almost unavoidable reference to the juxtaposition of the Melian Dialogue and the Sicilian War. But since one cannot decently *print* half a page on a writer like Thucydides, I had to decide whether to leave him out or try to deal properly with his ideas on how a book should be written. Wisely or not, I decided not to leave him out. And one thing leads to another.

A kind reviewer of an earlier book of mine suggested that there is room for a "grammar of dramatic technique". This book is not that, but I shall be happy if some of its readers think that it makes some contribution towards a grammar of critical interpretation. I have certainly made no secret of my view, that something of the kind is needed.

I might add that the translations in the text are all my own except when a translator's name is stated.

An earlier version of the *Tyrannus* section of chapter 4 appeared in the *Drama Survey* for October, 1961 (vol. 1, no. 2, pp. 133–148).

Like every occupant of the Sather chair, I wish to express

as best I can my deep gratitude for the warm and sustained welcome that my wife and I received on that most friendly campus at Berkeley. Where so many names might be mentioned, I will mention none; only reëcho what was so well said by one of my predecessors, A. W. Gomme: "To leave, even in order to go home, was difficult".

Bristol
July, 1965

H. D. F. KITTO

Contents

List

OF CHIEF WORKS REFERRED TO

Abbott, G. F. *Thucydides: A Study in Historical Reality.* London, 1925.

Anonymous. "Interpretating Greek Tragedy," *The Times Literary Supplement*, February 6, 1959.

Bowra, C. M. *Sophoclean Tragedy*. Oxford, 1944.

Broadhead, H. D., ed. *Aeschylus: Persae*. Cambridge, 1960.

Burnet, John. *Early Greek Philosophy*, 4th edition, reprinted. London, 1945.

Cornford, F. M. *Thucydides Mythistoricus*. London, 1907.

Microcosmographia Academica. Cambridge, 1922.

Dodds, E. R. *The Greeks and the Irrational.* Berkeley and Los Angeles, 1951.

Drachmann, A. B. "The Composition of Sophocles' Antigone," *Classical Review*, XXIII, 1909, pp. 212–216.

Farnell, L. R. "The Paradox of Prometheus Vinctus," *Journal of Hellenic Studies*, LIII, 1933, pp. 40–50.

Finley, M. I. *The Greek Historians*. New York, 1959.

Gomme, A. W. *Essays in Greek History and Literature*. Oxford, 1937.

The Greek Attitude to Poetry and History. Berkeley and Los Angeles, 1954.

A Historical Commentary on Thucydides. Oxford, 1945, 1950–1956. 3 vols.

Granville-Barker, H. *Prefaces to Shakespeare* (*Fifth Series*). London, 1947.

Guthrie, W. K. C. *The Greek Philosophers*. London, 1950.

Jebb, R. C. All references are to his editions of the plays of Sophocles. Cambridge, various dates.

Kamerbeek, J. C., ed. *Sophocles' Trachiniae*. Leiden, 1959.
Kitto, H. D. F. *Greek Tragedy*. London, 1961 (1st edition, 1939).
Form and Meaning in Drama. London, 1964.
Knights, L. C. "Shakespeare's Politics," *Proceedings of the British Academy*, XLIII, 1957, pp. 115–129.
Knox, B. M. W. *Oedipus at Thebes*. New Haven, 1957.
Kuhns, Richard. *The House, the City, and the Judge*. Indianapolis and New York, 1962.
Lattimore, Richmond. *Classical Studies Presented to W. A. Oldfather*. Urbana, Ill. 1943.
The Poetry of Greek Tragedy. Baltimore, 1958.
Letters, F. J. H. *Life and Work of Sophocles*. London, 1953.
Lloyd-Jones, Hugh. "Zeus in Aeschylus," *Journal of Hellenic Studies*, LXXVI, 1956, pp. 55–67.
Lucas, D. W. *The Greek Tragic Poets*. London, 1959.
Méautis, G. *Sophocle: Essai sur l'héros tragique*. Paris, 1957.
Page, D. L., ed. *Aeschylus: Agamemnon*. Oxford, 1957.
de Romilly, Jacqueline. *Thucydide et l'impérialisme athénien*. Paris, 1947.
Saintsbury, George. *Shakespeare*. Cambridge, 1934. (Reprint of chapters in *Cambridge History of English Literature*, Vol. V, 1910).
Spencer, Theodore. *Shakespeare and the Nature of Man*. New York, 1949.
Thomson, George, ed. *Aeschylus: Oresteia*, Cambridge, 1938. 2 vols.
Whatmough, Joshua. *Poetic, Scientific and Other Forms of Discourse*. Berkeley and Los Angeles, 1956.
Wright, B. A. *Milton's Paradise Lost*. London, 1961.

I

Criticism and Chaos

Let us contemplate Chaos, beginning with a severe judgment made by Professor Hugh Lloyd-Jones in his article, "Zeus in Aeschylus." It is an important article, and we shall be concerned with it for some time.

> Scholars have expended much learning and ingenuity in tracing a gradual development in ethical profundity from Homer to Hesiod, from Hesiod to the lyric poets and early elegists, from lyric to Aeschylus, from Aeschylus to Sophocles. Much of their work has no relation to what is in the texts, but is simply a product of the nineteenth century's insistence upon progress in all matters, and its conviction that the power of poetry must reside chiefly, if not wholly, in the ideas, and especially the ethical ideas, which it expresses.

"Much of their work has no relation to what is in the texts": if this is true—and surely it is—then it is a fact which classical scholars should strive to keep secret, lest some interested layman should ask: "To what purpose do you people spend so much time and erudition upon the purification of Greek texts, if then you cannot be trusted to read them properly, and to report with reasonable accuracy what their authors were saying?" We ourselves know well that where the plain purport of a text has been distorted, or where scholars have given irreconcilable accounts of the same play, the reason is very rarely carelessness, and not often wantonness; but if not that, what is it?

Lloyd-Jones has suggested one reason: the sheer pressure of local or temporary ideas—in this case, belief in progress. Elsewhere in the same article he suggests another:

After a hundred and fifty years of controversy, the interpretation of the *Prometheus Vinctus* is still the subject of debate. To the romantic poets of the revolutionary era, the Titan tortured by Zeus for his services to mankind appeared as a symbol of the human spirit in its struggle to throw off the chains which kings and priests had forged for it. But to the distinguished Hellenists who after the fall of Napoleon laid the foundations of the great century of German scholarship, no such naïve and one-sided view seemed tolerable. It was partly, perhaps, that the political atmosphere discouraged an interpretation so adverse to authority . . .

Here we must make a distinction, that between the myth and the play. Of course romantic poets made out of the tortured Titan a symbol of revolt against Tyranny—but why not? Doing this, they were doing just what their Greek predecessors had done: refashioning the myth in order to say through it something that they wanted to say. We can have no quarrel with Goethe or Shelley on that score; but an existing play is another matter. Aeschylus, constructing *his* play out of the myth, meant *something*, and if an interpreter, for whatever reason, makes him to have said something else, then he has failed in his duty as critic; for the major task of criticism is to promote the meeting of minds—the reader's with the writer's.

But is it not both officious and impertinent to say this? Will not any sensitive and sensible reader make that contact himself, without the help of any critic? If Lloyd-Jones is right, the answer is at least not an unqualified Yes. If it is true that "much of their work has no relation to what is in the texts", then they certainly did not establish full contact with the mind of Aeschylus—in which case, I must admit, the unassisted plain reader might not have done worse. Lloyd-Jones implies—correctly, as I think—that they were making contact with something more familiar, namely their own minds, or the collective mind of their own age.

The *Prometheus* is indeed a special case, being only one-third of a complete work; though I doubt if that makes much difference, in view of what has happened to Euripides, for during the same century and a half he has been represented as a deplorable atheist, as the daring and noble critic of an immoral and effete Olympian religion; as a "botcher", as the contriver of infinitely subtle plays that meant one thing to the simple and something much more exciting to the clever; as the preacher of a philanthropic liberalism and rationalism, as a total irrationalist; as a sour misogynist, as the first Greek to recognise that women too are of the human race.

> —Do you see yonder cloud that's almost in shape of a camel?
> —By th' mass, and 'tis like a camel indeed.
> —Methinks it is like a weasel.
> —It is backed like a weasel.
> —Or like a whale.
> —Very like a whale.

But in fact, much more like a chameleon. Is the age one of religious fervour or of scepticism? liberal or authoritarian? assured and complacent or disillusioned and uneasy? Greek tragic drama, it seems, will unfailingly assume the corresponding colour. "Chaos" is not too strong a word. It is no very impressive tribute to this part of classical scholarship that, contemplating a body of poetic literature which does not make a point of being private, allusive, obscure, and is written in a language which, after all, we know fairly well, it then issues a different report about the plays every twenty-five minutes or so.

Naturally, this is no new complaint. One of my predecessors in the Sather chair, Professor Whatmough, dismissed literary criticism as "a mere exchange of opinion", and himself took refuge in a kind of literary mathematics; which is like studying the inward parts of a clock but renouncing all hope of ever telling the time. Why should we be in so unprofitable a situation?

Perhaps we can take a hint from that prince of satirists Plato—if indeed we know how to read Plato. He has been here before us, with the malicious passage on the interpretation of poetry that occupies the middle part of the *Protagoras*. Simonides' poem is expounded to a distinguished company of scholars by Protagoras; then Socrates, tongue in cheek, gives a highly sophistical and quite different interpretation of the same poem. No discussion follows, no objections, criticism, questions. Hippias compliments Socrates on his brilliant exposition, and adds: "I also have a good lecture on this poem. Would you like to hear it?" "Very much," says Alcibiades, "but not today". In his typically Hellenic fashion Plato has made his point: this kind of thing has no τέχνη, no discipline; a poem is whatever you choose to make it: camel, weasel, or whale.

Questions arise. First, does it matter very much? In some cases it matters a great deal, even to Hellenists whose interest in Greek poetry may be less than passionate. This will be illustrated in the next chapter: briefly, Attic drama, like the Church arts in the Middle Ages, was a very public art, responsible beyond anything that we know today; misunderstanding of it, therefore, has wider implications than would misunderstanding of, say, Browning or Joyce. An audience is involved, and so far as we can judge a solidly popular one, not a coterie.

Another question: is it not inevitable, poetry being what it is? We will say (if only to hear what it sounds like): "Tastes always differ; judgment is always personal. Further, it is normal that what one generation admires, the next will reject. Interpretation will therefore always be in a state of flux".

This, maybe, sounds like sense, but it needs examining, from more than one point of view. We will begin with an interesting and recent illustration of chaos, one in which taste and judgment play no part at all, since the point at issue is one of dramatic fact.

Everyone will agree that to Aeschylus, in the *Agamemnon*, the killing of Cassandra was of importance; at least, for one-fifth of the play he makes her dominate the stage, and thereafter keeps her body before our eyes and does not leave it off-stage, as Sophocles does Antigone's. He also makes it clear to us, the audience, that although Clytemnestra does the physical killing, Cassandra is being destroyed by Apollo too. Therefore it is of importance to our understanding of the play, and of Aeschylus' mind, that we should understand what Aeschylus meant by it. We may have our own ideas of what a Greek or an Aeschylean god would or would not do. If we are omniscient, that settles the matter; if we are not, we should do well to hold our ideas in abeyance and attend carefully to what is in the play. Now, it happens that within the last three years there have been published two scholarly books, each seriously concerned with the *Oresteia:* Dr John Jones' *Aristotle* and Professor Richard Kuhns' *The House*. What Aeschylus is saying to Dr Kuhns about Cassandra and Apollo is that "the terrible punishment meted out to Cassandra is the result of yet another violation of the marriage vows and female duty . . . In breaking her word and denying her duty Cassandra has violated the covenant of marriage . . . Apollo's experience both with Coronis and with Cassandra is that of a man whose right to be a father has been denied" (pp. 40 f.). What Aeschylus is saying to Dr Jones is that "gods and men alike are assailed by the erotic feeling, by the same blend of physical itch and more exalted elements which assail humans"; and it was this that "caused Apollo to attempt the rape of Cassandra" (p. 175).

Of these two explanations, one must be wildly wrong—which is not to say that the other must be right. It is simply not possible that Aeschylus should have entertained both ideas, and if he left his audience halting between them, he was inconceivably incompetent. This is not a case where one generation thinks differently from another, and if we take refuge in the statement that one man will naturally respond to a work of art differently from another, then we must add that at least one of these responses would have been incomprehensible to Aeschylus. But there is another point. If a man is by profession an industrial chemist, or a banker, and is in Greece only as an interested visitor, then the response that he makes to a work of Greek art is his own private concern; but if we are scholars and critics, and our responses are as contradictory as these, then something is wrong. If there is no discipline, no τέχνη, to control such aberrations, then Whatmough is right, criticism is only an exchange of opinion, and chaos is inevitable and everlasting.

Yet these facts may be relevant. Dr Jones writes his exposition of the *Oresteia* without mentioning Cassandra, except once, incidentally; the remark about eroticism turns up in a chapter on Sophocles. Professor Kuhns' argument does indeed begin, as it should, with *Agamemnon* 1202–1213, in which the chorus asks: "Did you come together [or 'lawfully', for the text is disputable] to the child-making business?" and Cassandra replies: "I first agreed, and then refused him"; but thereafter he writes several pages about Coronis. She—as we shall recall, if we do not mind absenting ourselves for a few minutes from what is happening on the stage—was made pregnant by Apollo, eloped with Ischys "though bearing the pure seed of the god" (Pindar—and we have all read Pindar), and was burned on a pyre for this sin; but Apollo, unwilling that his child should perish unborn, snatched it from the mother's body.—But Aeschylus never mentions Coronis!—True, but he does mention her brother Ixion twice, though not in the *Agamemnon* (*Eumenides* 440 f. and 716 f.); but in each case the point is that Ixion, who like Orestes had murdered, was forgiven by Zeus. Coronis does not come into the picture at all. But there is something else: twice Aeschylus mentions Asclepius, once in the *Agamemnon* (*Agam.* 1019 ff., *Eum.* 645 ff.)—each time as one who had violated the finality of death, by raising a man from the dead, and was punished for it. Perhaps it would hardly occur to the lazy-minded reader of the play, or the enthralled spectator in the theatre, to ask who was Asclepius' mother. Who indeed was she? Why, Coronis! So there we are, led straight back to Cassandra—though not by Aeschylus. Cassandra, too, frustrated Apollo's paternity, and is being justly punished exactly like the Coronis whom unaccountably Aeschylus forgot to mention.

But if we may extrapolate into the blue like this, we can find our way almost anywhere. Meanwhile, what Aeschylus is laying before us is that Apollo, in his wrath (v. 1211), punished Cassandra once, and is now punishing her a second time by having her conveyed to this palace, a charnel-house, a haunt of the Erinyes, to be murdered by Clytemnestra. Further, this murder is most firmly welded, by Aeschylus, into the whole chain of murders that began with Atreus and will end with Orestes. These matters we do not notice, though they are inside the play, because we are chasing Coronis, who is not.

I would not like to suggest that these two critics are in any way exceptional; merely *infelices opportunitate*. We shall meet the like again.

Our argument so far has been: (*i*) it is of importance to Greek studies as a whole that our interpretative criticism should, if possible, stop short of being ridiculous; and (*ii*) that however much allowance it may be thought proper to make for different sympathies and insights in different critics, we are so often confronted with disagreement on matters of fact that only one conclusion is possible—Plato's: either criticism has no discipline, or, if there is one, it is not sufficiently understood.

Continuing the argument, we will consider another possible objection, namely that there is no sense in speaking of the "meaning" of a play, even under proper restrictions. We will put it like this: "It is not in the nature of a work of art to make a definite statement. Not only does it reveal new facets of truth to successive generations (if it remains alive), but also, at any moment, it has meaning on different levels; not 'a meaning', therefore, but multiple meanings." It sounds so impressive, and is so convenient, especially to psychoanalytic interpreters of the present day, that it deserves discussion. Some elementary history may be helpful.

Today, in musical composition and analogously in the other arts (except architecture, which at least has to keep out the rain), we are passing through a period in which it is one accepted theory that the non-composer sets down what used to be called a theme, and instructs the performers to do with it this, that, and the other thing, as they like and in what order they like. The non-composer agrees with Iocasta, in the *Tyrannus:* chance rules; forethought is useless. (Iocasta, we remember, committed suicide.) Such a theory obviously implies that no statement is possible, or that the non-composer has none to make. There is nothing to say; the human mind must do obeisance before the fortuitous. Your guess is as good as mine.

This may be regarded as an extreme development of an aesthetic which for some time we have not unreasonably regarded as valid: the artist hardly makes a "statement"—as for example the nowadays unpopular Milton did; rather, he first awakens, then satisfies, our sensibilities. He sets up resonances; he works in ambiguities. What he creates has in it something elusive; what we make of it depends very much on ourselves. The theory has validity within its own confines, but we should not try to universalise it; in particular, we should not apply it to Greek poetry without considering the simple historical fact that down to about the middle of the fifth century Greece had no prose literature. The implications of this we will discuss more fully later; here it will be enough to point out that our more elusive, suggestive, individual conception of poetry is natural in a culture that has an abundance of prose forms for the public communication of ideas which are important to the community and the human race, but is not natural to one in which poetry is the only medium. In a society that had no prose literature, poetry naturally attracted, and discharged, a wider and heavier responsibility than it does today. Painting, today, can perhaps afford the luxury of being only fascinating—"All painting aspires to the condition of wallpaper"—but those who painted for the Medieval Church, though they could indeed be fascinating, had as their first responsibility the duty of saying simple and important things, about simple and important things, to a people that was largely illiterate. It was a Greek doctrine that the poet was a teacher. Our response to that outmoded idea should not be "How naïve!" but "How obvious!" When poetry stood alone, it could not afford to be only an aesthetic luxury.

With that introduction we will return to our question of meaning, statement. We will put the opposing views in an exaggerated form: a work of art means (a fairly definite) *something;* or, a work of art means *anything.* The status of poetry in Greece being what it was, one to which the last few centuries afford no parallel, it seems probable from the start that we should be ready to move decisively away from *anything* toward *something.* That is, if one modern critic finds Euripides a wicked blasphemer, and another an enlightened reformer, the explanation of the difference will lie not in the indefinite and ineffable nature of the dramatic art, but in bad criticism. The first-rate dramatists will have been those who had something of weight to say—and we must remember that none but poets would have given it public utterance—and could say it excitingly and memorably; the inferior dramatists will have been those who could do no more than what Wilamowitz innocently supposed they all did: merely transfer Greek saga to the stage; or what the younger Wilamowitz, just as innocently, thought Sophocles did: put together one effective scene after another, without much caring if they made cumulating sense or not. If we speak of "the Aeschylean meaning" of a play (as distinct from Mr So-and-so's brilliant exposition), or for that matter of "the Shakespearian meaning", we may not be positing something that does not exist.

Next: what about the new aspects of truth which great works of art are said to reveal to successive ages? They seem usually to be less important than the old aspects of truth that they no longer reveal. We have a native illustration that is well enough known: the history of Shakespearian tragedy in criticism and in performance. As far as the Tragedies are concerned, it seems not too much to say that the late seventeenth and the eighteenth centuries hardly understood what Shakespeare was talking about. He was of course admired; critic after critic wrote of his great humanity, his wonderful truth to nature, and the rest—though often deploring his grave lapses from the immutable principles of Taste that had not yet been revealed to his rude age. But there was more than this to deplore: an Age of Reason, it seems, cannot endure tragedy, whose reason seems too big for Reason. It was intolerable that Shakespeare (as Dr Johnson put it) should have allowed Cordelia to perish in a just cause; and the same qualms were felt over Juliet. If Shakespeare was still to be played—and this was very much desired—these matters had to be seen to. And they certainly were: Davenant remodelled the one play to save Juliet from death, and Nahum Tate, to Johnson's great satisfaction, not only reprieved Cordelia, but also rewarded her virtuous constancy by arranging for her a happy marriage with Edgar.

Then came the nineteenth century, with its romantic introspection, its admiration of the Tragic Hero and—a natural corollary—its admiration of the grand actor. On the stage, the plays were romanticised; in criticism, there was the concentration on individual character, which produced, for example, the long series of contradictory Hamlets, each critic (as a cynic has said) turning Hamlet into his private portrait of himself.

That brief history suggests one or two reflections which may be germane to our subject. We will say, in the first place, that it proves the enduring vitality of Shakespeare. No doubt; but what does that mean? It means that his genius could transmute his tragic thinking into dramatic forms which were so dramatic that they remained alive and still gave delight even when much of that thinking was misunderstood and neglected. The same could not happen to Ben Jonson: an age that does not relish keen satire can do nothing with his plays; take away the satire, and not much is left. Here, incidentally, lies the answer to the impatient question sometimes heard: "Why can't you critics leave the plays alone, and let us enjoy the plays in peace?" The answer is another question: "How much pleasure do you want, and of what quality?"

There is another point. In the eighteenth century the public wanted Shakespeare—as it still does—and, naturally, it wanted its Shakespeare to be intelligible. But by this time the mental world of the sixteenth century had vanished, so that some things in Shakespeare had become unintelligible. Yet, oddly enough, the form of the plays had a certain relationship with the old-fashioned ideas which they contained; for which reason, as we have seen, the form had to be changed, here and there. Now, it would be silly, and certainly futile, to reprobate the successive rehandlings and reinterpretations to which Shakespeare has been subjected in the theatre. The plays will be produced on those terms that will make them acceptable to audiences; all that one can demand of the theatre is that the presentation of the plays be sincere and not exhibitionist. But this has nothing to do with the scholar and critic; he is in a different position from the theatre-man and playgoer. His business is to see the plays, as best he can, not through eighteenth- or twentieth- but sixteenth-century eyes; to promote contact with the mind of Shakespeare, to seek the Shakespearian meaning of the play; and in fact, in our own time, such critical effort has had a marked effect on the theatre too.

Our thesis that there is such a meaning—or by all means let us say instead a central area of meaning—is now strengthened by the observation that some of the plays resisted, to the point of amputation, the meaning that the eighteenth century desired to find in them. It is then true that a play cannot mean *anything*. Since the days of Davenant and Tate we have become less heroic with the plays, but the moral is the same. Do we want Hamlet to be a paralysed intellectual, or—a newer fashion—a soft homosexual? If so, we can have it—but at the cost of playing down, omitting, or leaving incongruous, those parts of the play which make him by nature a resolute man of action. Again, since most of us have read *Pickwick Papers*, it may take our fancy to represent Polonius as a genial buffoon: such we can certainly make him—but we had better leave out the Reynaldo scene, which shows him as a nasty and treacherous old man. But then, the play is too long anyhow, and we can easily persuade ourselves that the scene is unnecessary; besides, if we took it seriously, it might upset our ideas of the play; we should be in danger of having to substitute the Shakespearian meaning for our own. The man in the street may have good reasons for doing this kind of thing; the critic can have no justification at all. If he is content merely to "respond" to his author, as the lay public is entitled to do, then let him join the lay public, and really work for his living.

Now let us return to our own private chaos, perhaps consoled a little by the discovery that it is not the only one of its kind. We have been arguing that it does not arise from the nature of drama itself; we have been on the verge of suggesting that at least there are certain controls that can be used. We may now consider an interesting passage by Cornford, in his *Thucydides Mythistoricus* (p. viii). Explaining the title of his book, he writes:

I mean history cast in a mould of conception, whether artistic or philosophical, which, long before the work was even contemplated, was already inwrought into the very structure of the author's mind. In every age the common interpretation of the world of things is controlled by some scheme of unchallenged and unsuspected presuppositions; and the mind of every individual, however little he may think himself in sympathy with his contemporaries, is not an insulated compartment, but more like a pool in a continuous medium—the circumambient atmosphere of his time and place. This element of thought is always, of course, most difficult to detect and analyse, just because it is a constant factor which underlies all the differential characteristics of many minds.

As time passes, the "circumambient atmosphere" changes. Slowly, sometimes quickly, what had been taken for granted is replaced by other things that are taken for granted. The new generation is now in its own pool; the author, of course, remains in his. As we look out of our pool, our view may suffer considerable diffraction. Johnson illustrates the point well: it had become unintelligible and unendurable—*μιαρόν*, as Aristotle said—that Shakespeare should have allowed Cordelia to perish. He was living in an atmosphere of Reason, Natural Justice; Shakespeare lived and wrote in a very different one. Diffraction here amounted to distortion, and no eighteenth-century writer, least of all the confident Johnson, could even imagine that a corrective technique might be necessary: was not Philosophy beginning to reveal the whole truth about the Universe?

But does this help *us*, in the gloomy puzzle with which we are confronted, namely why we give such apparently random reports on ancient plays, and why some of the best of us can be accused, after the lapse of a few years, of not having read the texts properly? We are by profession earnest students of Greek literature and Greek ways of thought; we ought not to be deceived by so obvious a phenomenon as diffraction. Yet, if Lloyd-Jones is right—and he is—some of the ablest of our predecessors were incapacitated, here and there, from reading the texts aright by so local an event as a belief in Progress.

It seems helpful to point out that such aberrations do not seem to affect the other Greek arts. Certainly, as the years pass, different periods of Greek art seem to be held in the highest esteem: that is another matter. A Greek sculptor fills a pediment with, say, a representation of the war between the gods and the giants. We, contemplating his work, derive pleasure from its purely sculpturesque virtues, a pleasure that will be deep or superficial in the degree to which we are able to respond to the visual arts. At the same time we shall understand that the sculptor is "saying" something; he is expressing an idea. This idea we shall not try to verbalise except in the most general way, but if we say to ourselves that he is presenting the idea of order triumphing over disorder, of harmony over violence, of civilisation over barbarism, we shall certainly find that others have received the same impression, and if a man told us that on the contrary the sculptor was representing hopeless resignation in the face of the inevitable, or the superiority of the agricultural over the commercial way of life, we should conclude at once that he was out of his mind. Why should there be a general agreement here, continual disagreement there? Does the explanation lie in a difference between the two arts, or between their respective interpreters, or in both? The answer is, in both.

In the first place, we are under no temptation to regard the pediment as anything but what it is: a work of art, a *mimesis* in stone, as Aristotle would put it. We know that it is not a kind of photograph of a real and particular event; we know, without being told, that a certain man, the sculptor, set to work with lumps of stone, his tools, his skill, and with a certain idea or subject in his head. We know that these are solely responsible for everything that we can see in the pediment. Further, it has an unmistakable frame, which nothing but the most childlike naïveté would tempt us to disregard. If in a landscape painting we notice a figure trudging through the middle distance, we do not try to determine who he is, where he is coming from, where he is going, and why; nor, if a portrait displays the sitter holding a book, do we debate whether it is a copy of Shelley or of Mill on *Liberty*, knowing that the painter would have made that clear had he thought it of any significance.

Drama, we sometimes assume, is different. Not always has it seemed manifestly insane to turn it face-about, as it were, in the hope of finding more on the back, or just outside the frame—to enquire, for example, what Hamlet studied at Wittenberg, and under which professors—the kind of folly ridiculed by L. C. Knights in his essay "How Many Children Had Lady Macbeth?" The scholar-critic will not infrequently do this kind of thing; he will confuse the situation within the play with a situation in actuality; it happens often enough for A. J. P. Waldock to have coined for it the term "documentary fallacy". There is for example the double burial in the *Antigone*—a feature of the play which certainly gives the critic (not the spectator, who will not notice it) something to think about. One explanation that has been gravely offered is that the first burial was performed by a scrupulous passer-by—which leaves us wondering if Sophocles himself knew of the inconvenient interloper, and if so why he did not mention him. The hypothesis would be an intelligent one to entertain if one were the detective put in charge of the case by Creon; entertained by a critic, it shows only that he has forgotten the nature of the material he is dealing with. Even Jebb, puzzled by Antigone's return to the body, confessed that he could see no better explanation than that on her first visit she had forgotten the libation. Yet if on looking at a pediment we noticed that one warrior had no spear, we should not think of asking where he had dropped it, or whether he had forgotten it; we should at once ask ourselves why the sculptor had represented him spearless. Our thinking would be done entirely within the frame of the pediment. We know that the sculptor began with the rude stone, and that everything we see there was designed by him, presumably with intelligence; we do not find it so easy to remember that the *Antigone* began with a pile of clean paper on Sophocles' table. In effect, the documentary fallacy eliminates the only thing that really counts: the dramatist sitting at his table, with his paper—probably tearing up a lot of it before he is satisfied with his work; for the waste-paper basket is one of the author's indispensable tools, and its existence is sometimes overlooked, as when a critic will cheerfully assume that a fairly careful craftsman like Sophocles changed his mind half-way through a work and left beginning and end unreconciled: see Drachmann on the *Antigone*, for example. The documentary fallacy substitutes for the constructive imagination of the dramatist the imagination, constructive or not, of the interpreter.

Another difference. If we look at a pediment with any attention at all we cannot help but see what is there: all of it, without addition, subtraction, or substitution. Moreover, the component parts are grouped in one unalterable way; the composition has what the Greeks called *rhythm*, and it never occurs to us that we should mentally recompose it. Stone is unaccommodating stuff, and the pediment is defiantly present to our gaze, all at once; it forbids us to add bits and pieces of our own imagining, to neglect something that is visibly there, to alter the proportions of its parts.

Drama, being more fluid than stone, does not so sternly impose its own discipline—unless we are watching it in the theatre. We do, habitually and quite unconsciously, subtract and alter to an alarming degree, in our reading. We have just seen Coronis added to the *Agamemnon* and Cassandra subtracted; here is another instance of posthumous collaboration between playwright and interpreter, from Professor G. Méautis' *Sophocle*. Méautis argues that the Sophoclean Hero is rather like the Christian Saint: he is made of altogether finer stuff than ordinary mortals; he may have sinned greatly, he certainly suffers greatly; he passes through "la nuit obscure" and emerges purified and triumphant. An attractive idea perhaps, but it can be substantiated only by neglecting some of what Sophocles put into the plays and adding things that he failed to put there. For instance, in order to see that Oedipus is such, we have to believe that Sophocles thought out the three Theban plays as a connected trilogy, and that Creon is not only the same figure in each of them but also the same character. In reading the *Tyrannus* we must understand that Creon bitterly resented Oedipus' accession to the throne, has been nursing his resentment ever since, and has been waiting for his opportunity of satisfying it. When he says, upon his last entrance, "I have not come, Oedipus, to exult over you", we are to understand the opposite. He, the exact opposite of Oedipus, is the man of mean soul; it is a sign of his essential baseness that when he finds, in the *Antigone*, that he has been defied, he immediately suspects bribery, as the man of vulgar mind will. Therefore, having added to the *Tyrannus* something that is not there, namely Creon's resentment, we now have to take away something that is there, namely that as soon as Oedipus hears about the murder of Laius, he instantly suspects bribery, as again later, when he is confronted by Teiresias. Since Oedipus is not of mean soul, this must be passed over.

I take a rather different example. Professor D. L. Page, in his edition of the *Agamemnon*, makes this comment on v. 1607, where Aegisthus declares that his share in the vengeance was "just":

It is indeed the strength of his case: nobody could deny that the surviving son of Thyestes was bound by law, human and divine, to take the life of Atreus' son in return for the murder of Thyestes' family. His position is stronger than Clytemnestra's, whose case leaves a loophole for argument. Here as elsewhere Aeschylus goes out of his way to stress that the conflict is between right and right, not between right and wrong.

Certainly somebody goes out of his way, but it is not Aeschylus, who is pursuing a quite undeviating course. The critic, for the moment, is forgetting the frame; he is bringing in what he knows, from outside—a very natural temptation indeed—and not really looking at what is there, in the play. For what "nobody could deny" the chorus at least gives no sign of admitting, and what Aeschylus is laying before us is this: that Thyestes committed adultery with Atreus' wife, that Atreus took his bloody revenge; that Thyestes' son, described as a skulking coward, has committed adultery with Agamemnon's wife and shared in his murder; that he now makes himself the lawless tyrant of Argos, to the intense indignation of the Chorus of Argives. Aeschylus does indeed put the word *Dike*, "Right", into Aegisthus' mouth, but in circumstances which, when we look at them, raise in us the suspicion that his "right" was, in the estimation of the poet, intolerable wrong. Surely it would not occur to us, considering a work of art in any other medium, so to remove one detail from its surroundings and look at it against a background of our own devising. Not so shall we make our contact with the mind of the author.

I am tempted to add, from the same source, what seems to be a yielding to the documentary fallacy. Clytemnestra prays, or hopes, that the gods will now leave her in peace (vv. 1567–1576). The editor comments: "A cool, practical, and thoroughly sensible suggestion for solving the problem to the satisfaction of both parties". This is not the way in which we look at a pediment or painting. Aeschylus has just made his chorus to restate the law "which abides while Zeus remains on his throne: the doer must suffer"; he has also arranged that Clytemnestra shall be the latest of a series of "doers", of whom her predecessors—Paris, the sacrilegious army, Agamemnon—have already suffered. Clytemnestra thinks, as many another criminal must have thought, "Wouldn't it be nice, now that I have had my turn, if there were no consequences?" It is indeed interesting, that what Aeschylus makes Clytemnestra say here seems to his editor a sensible suggestion; but it seems clear that Aeschylus himself thought otherwise, and our first concern is with what *he* thought, and we do not arrive at that by detaching Clytemnestra from her dramatic surroundings and converting her into an actual person who may, perhaps, just have been consulting the family solicitor.

A common assumption underlies all the interpretations that we have been considering: it is that we are entitled to decide for ourselves what parts of play count, and what parts do not count. If Clytemnestra's suggestion is cool and sensible, then what the chorus has just been singing does not count; if Cassandra is getting her just deserts, or if, alternatively, we can penetrate to Aeschylus' thought without taking any particular notice of her part in the play, then the long and moving scene in which she is being done to death by a murderess and adultress—at the instance of Apollo—is a scene that does not count. But if we can leave out what we choose, and even supply what we need, is it surprising that the result is a certain amount of chaos?

But not only can we fall into the temptation of adding or subtracting: we can even make sheer mistakes, such as we would never make looking at a pediment, still less at a document. For instance, in his Introduction to the *Electra*, Jebb discusses anxiously and at length the "moral problem" of the play; he speaks repeatedly of the "god-commanded matricide", not having taken notice of the fact that Orestes plainly says (vv. 32 ff.) that it was he himself that took the decision. He notes too that Sophocles leaves out the pursuit of Orestes by the Erinyes and tries to explain why he could do such a thing; he did not notice that Sophocles does much more: at vv. 1386–1390, he actually identifies the avengers with the Erinyes. These two facts, clear enough in the text, both unobserved by a careful editor, at once invalidate his whole argument; but if Jebb can do this, certainly the rest of us are in some danger.

Another instance. It is the usual report on the trial-scene in the *Eumenides* that the human jury, of twelve, is equally divided, whereupon Athena gives what is often called her casting-vote, a "tie-breaking vote", as Professor Kuhns puts it. It is a long tradition; it seems to have influenced Professor Lattimore's translation, in which Athena is made to begin and end her speech thus:

> It is my task to render final judgment here . . .
> And if
> The other votes are even, then Orestes wins.

A gnat-strainer might point out that the adjective in the first line, *λοισθίαν*, does not mean quite as much as "final", only "last of a series"; but it is a little more than a gnat when we notice that there is nothing in the Greek of the last verse that corresponds to the word "other". The words *κἂν ἰσόψηφος κριθῇ* mean simply "if the voting proves even".

A man whose recollections of the play were a bit faded might recall the outline of the scene in this fashion: Aeschylus writes twelve couplets for the Chorus and Apollo, alternating, to cover the movements of the twelve jurors to the voting urn; then Athena declares that if the votes are found equal she is going to give her vote for Orestes. The votes are counted, they are even, and the goddess' casting-vote comes into operation. There we are: human wisdom is baffled; divine wisdom decides the issue; everything is as we should expect.—Everything but the text; for Aeschylus does not write twelve couplets. He writes ten, followed by one triplet. Then he makes Athena say: "It now devolves on me to give the last vote. I am going to vote for Orestes, because . . . And Orestes gets the verdict, even if the votes are equal. Now, you whose task it is: empty the urns without delay." The stage-business of counting is covered with some dialogue; then Athena speaks again: "He is acquitted: the votes are equal."

This may not be what we should have expected; it is certainly what we get. Athena has already voted, among the twelve, unless upon her simple verb *προσθήσομαι* we are prepared to unload the sense, "I will vote if the other votes are equal"—which would break its poor back. Her vote is among the twelve and cannot be a thirteenth, as thirteen is, and always was, an odd number. Moreover, it is impossible to make stage-sense of the ten couplets and the triplet if the human jury consists of twelve; no playwright could have devised such a lopsided arrangement. But what the text clearly implies, that Athena is one of the twelve, also explains the unsymmetrical dialogue: each of the ten couplets gives time for one juryman to come to the urn, drop his pebble, and go back to his station; the triplet gives time for the eleventh to do the same, and then for Athena to come forward in her turn; and there she is, at the urn, ready to drop her pebble and to make her little speech. The "casting-vote" "has no relation to what is in the text".

We ask then: Why did Jebb fail to see what the text says,

on two points that directly bore on his argument? Why has one scholar after another imputed to Aeschylus, at a critical moment in the trilogy, a casting-vote that the text will not tolerate? The explanation is simple: we come to the play with settled convictions of our own, what Cornford called "unchallenged and unsuspected presuppositions". If there is a conflict between one of these and the text, it is the text that must give way. We read the words, but they do not bite into our minds; the temptation to make the text accord with what we *know* that the dramatist must have meant is irresistible.

Jebb begins the exposition of his own perplexity by saying that Apollo is "the supreme arbiter of purity". This may be true, but because Jebb took it to be the whole truth, not to be modified or extended by anything that Sophocles might say, he found that the plot "labours under a disadvantage which no skill could quite overcome". What the poet himself says or implies is not evidence—except for his own mistakes. Similarly, when a god and a man are acting, as we may say, in concert, it is of course the god who does the directing; anything else is inconceivable. It is so obvious that when the text says something else we genuinely do not take it in; at a pinch, we will assume that Orestes, in the *Electra*, had got it all wrong—for the documentary fallacy is never out of reach. So in the *Eumenides:* we know enough about Greek religion to be absolutely certain that Athena must be the Divine Judge, sitting apart from and above the human jury; nothing else is conceivable—except to Aeschylus and, I suppose, his audience. In this case we have a further and respectable excuse: elsewhere in Greek literature when human jurors are mentioned in this connection they are regularly twelve. (The references are assembled in Professor George Thomson's note to the passage.) But "elsewhere" means "outside the frame of *this* play". The fact does indeed instil caution, and caution never comes amiss; but what other writers imagined is not evidence for what Aeschylus imagined; our sole authority is his text. The old fable of the Irish defendant seems apposite: when the prosecution produced two witnesses who had seen him do it, he produced forty-seven who hadn't.

Our analogy with the pediment further suggested that the critic should not only avoid adding or subtracting, in the interests of his own prepossessions, but should also respect proportion—as we are almost bound to do when we see a play for the first time in performance. If I do not abuse the forbearance of Professor Kuhns, I will illustrate the point—one that is perpetually turning up—by referring again to his disagreement with Dr Jones over Cassandra and Apollo: attempted rape, or grave offence followed by condign punishment?

One knows that in actuality—in a murder case for example—an apparently insignificant detail can prove all-important; but we are concerned with works of art, not actuality. In a picture or pediment, a minor figure remains a minor figure; we neither can nor wish to alter its stature, and if we do, in an interpretation, we are virtually asserting that the artist made a bad mistake, and that we know better. Apollo and Cassandra: what in fact does Aeschylus lay before us? What are the proportions in the whole scene? The passage in which he deals with Cassandra's offence against Apollo, or his against her, as the case may be, is limited to about half a dozen verses, in fairly dry stichomythia (vv. 1203–1212). The passage, as it seems to me, is neutral in tone, though another might so far agree with Dr Jones as to say that it throws no particular credit upon Apollo, and yet another might so far agree with Professor Kuhns as to think that Cassandra, having accepted Apollo's gift, should have paid his price. If it could have been a historical event, we might argue about it, as we can argue about the justice of Roger Casement's execution. It is not a real case; it is something that Aeschylus devised and wrote down as part of a play. It may be fun to argue about it, but arguing takes us outside the frame. The only real question is: what did Aeschylus mean? Like a detail in a pediment, it is part of a considered whole, one moment in a continuing rhythm. What we must do, if we would seize the artist's intention, is to watch what he is doing; anything else can only be a distraction.

We watch, therefore. First, the playwright contrives the long scene in which Cassandra is visible but silent. Then, the strange scene—very strange, until we understand what is going on—between Clytemnestra, Cassandra, and the chorus, Cassandra still silent. Then Cassandra's first outburst, the substance of which is that Apollo is destroying her for a second time, conveying her to this house of blood, seat of so many crimes, haunt of the Erinyes, to be murdered with Agamemnon by his wife. Then comes the brief stichomythia. Next, we hear more about Thyestes' children, Clytemnestra's treachery, her own coming death—and here the unseen god strips her of her prophetic insignia—until at last she goes into the palace that to her smells like a tomb.

This, briefly, is what we are shown. It is not for us to disregard any of it because it does not help the conception of the play which we have already formed, nor is it enough to respond emotionally and not mentally too—to say, for example, that it is one of the most strangely beautiful and terrible dramatic scenes that exist, and then to grapple with Aeschylus' thought without any more reference to it. The first critical question to ask surely is: To what is the dramatist directing my attention?—the question that we instinctively ask ourselves on looking at a work of graphic art, or of architecture. In the theatre, as I have said, there is no difficulty; our attention automatically goes in the direction intended by the dramatist—unless something has gone wrong, as when a cat walks across the stage. In reading, just because we can hold up the rhythm of the play as we choose, we simply have to take our elementary precautions. Is it not abundantly clear that throughout this whole passage the weight is thrown not on the justice or otherwise of Apollo's revenge, or punishment, not on the culpability or otherwise of Cassandra, but on this: on the manner in which Apollo is punishing her, on the place, on the agent—namely both Clytemnestra and the presiding Erinyes—on the conception that the killing of Cassandra is one more link in the whole chain?

But if the proportions and therefore the effect of the whole scene are like this, how do we resolve the disagreement over attempted rape or just punishment? Quite simply: these are rival answers to a question that does not exist. It is like asking whether the warrior had forgotten, or had accidentally lost, his spear. Aeschylus might have brought the question into the foreground, as by making Cassandra say much less about Clytemnestra and the Erinyes and a great deal about the amorousness of gods, or by making the chorus say that when a god wishes to father a child, the chosen mother should agree. He shows no interest in these matters. The short stichomythia is no more than is necessary to explain why Apollo is destroying her; if we try to expand it into significance, changing the proportions of the design, we shall inevitably reduce to relative insignificance what the poet is really trying to put before us. Is it our aim to make contact with the author's mind, or to work out ideas of our own within what he has created? If the latter, there are no rules, no limits. If the former, we should try not to add, not to subtract, not to alter proportions. It may be thought that our analogy with the other arts is not valid. In that case we will follow the well-tried principle: Quote Aristotle when he agrees with you, and when he does not, explain why he went wrong.

Turning then to Aristotle's general theory of the arts, or at least of *poiesis*, we note the following points: that it is not concerned with "poetry" but with certain kinds of poetic composition and with a certain kind of prose literature too; that it firmly associates such "mimetic" literature with other kinds of mimesis such as painting and dancing; and that when Aristotle comes to consider drama, he is by no means hypnotised by the verbal or discursive element, but on the contrary is emphatic that of the six "parts" he finds in tragedy the most important is *mythos*, which we translate "plot" and he immediately explains as ἡ σύνθεσις τῶν πραγμάτων, "the putting together of the events", the disposition of the material, the ordering of the stuff. Let us briefly consider this.

The first point he makes very clear by his firm distinction between a Homer and an Empedocles, the one being a *poietes* and *mimetes*, the other not. Empedocles, for Aristotle, may have been a magnificent "poet", but the fact is immaterial. He may use highly imaginative language, but he does it in order to give direct expression to his ideas; the voice that we hear is always the voice of Empedocles, just as, in the *Poetics*, it is the voice of Aristotle. Homer, on the other hand, imitates or represents personages who speak and act; we do not see or hear Homer: we hear his personages speak, and what they do is described to us in entirely objective narrative. I think we do no violence to Aristotle if we say that, for him, Homer creates a picture, for he certainly does class Homer with painters and sculptors, but calls Empedocles not a *poietes* but a φυσιολόγος, a "natural philosopher". A remark that he makes later is entirely consonant with this: Homer surpasses the other (epic) poets in nothing more than in this, that he knows how much a poet should say αὐτός, in his own voice, namely as little as possible. The other poets, he says, are continually taking a part in the game themselves: αὐτοὶ δι'ὅλου ἀγωνίζονται. That is, because their constructive and mimetic powers were not good enough, they had to *talk*—to comment, to explain, to underline, like the comic strip artist who uses balloons. "Because," he continues, "while they talk, they are not being *mimetai*." The inference is that Homer, for Aristotle (as for us), succeeds in putting everything into his *mimesis*—and that of course is what a painter or sculptor necessarily does. That the same is true of the dramatist as well as the epic poet needed no saying: the dramatist cannot literally speak in his own voice, though he does the dramatic equivalent, and resembles the inferior epic poet, if he invents a dummy character to talk for him, or makes a personage "speak out of character", as occasionally Euripides will.

This distinction between Homer and Empedocles is perfectly

sound, and accords with experience: we do not in fact listen to both in the same way. When we make all allowance for the poetic splendour of Empedocles, it remains true that our response to him is basically an intellectual one, while Homer, like a dramatist or painter, invites us to exercise something like a coöperative effort of the imagination. These give us not a direct statement but a picture.

Further, what is most important in dramatic *mimesis* is "the disposition of the material". The dominating element is what happens rather than what is said. What we call the "text" is, after all, only a part of the whole—no justification indeed for neglecting it in any single particular, but we deceive ourselves if we think that it *is* the whole. *Mythos* Aristotle directly compares with design in a painting (*Poetics*, 1450A 29 ff.): as in drama *mythos* is more significant than *ethos*, *lexis*, and *dianoia* (character, diction, and the rhetorical or discursive element), so in painting is design more important than colour.

It is agreeable indeed to have Aristotle on one's side, though that does not prove the truth of one's own case. Yet it would follow from Aristotle's theory that if we wish to understand the mind of a dramatist, as expressed in a given play—not of course that Aristotle was at all interested in the dramatist's mind, at least in the *Poetics*—we must give to the work the same kind of attention that we do to the work of any other artist, fully understanding what it is that separates him not only from an Isocrates but also from an Empedocles, namely that he expresses himself in a *mimesis*, and that the most important element in that is the *mythos* or disposition of the material.

This comes hard, it seems. With a text, we know where we are; for the most part, we are sensitive lovers of poetry. But Aristotle makes his sharp distinction between *poiesis* and "poetry": Empedocles is not a *poietes*, though he is a poet, since what distinguishes the *poietes* is that he ποιεῖ, "makes", "constructs", a *mimesis*, and the better *poietes* he is, the less does he speak in his own *persona;* and in the *mimesis* the first thing, "the ἀρχή and as it were the ψυχή", the foundation and the life and soul, is the σύστασις τῶν πραγμάτων, the disposition of the material. It seems sensible; one might have believed it even without Aristotle's authority. But, as it seems to me, we are reluctant to believe, or at least to apply, it, and look about for means of escape.

The most efficient is the heroic idea that what Aristotle says has nothing to do with fifth-century tragic drama, whether because he, not being an Athenian, did not quite understand the Attic spirit, or because those dramatists, being dead, were unable to practise what he was the first to preach. Wilamowitz preferred the former explanation when he simplified life by propounding that the fifth-century dramatists had no conception of the specifically dramatic and undertook nothing more exhausting than the task of representing Greek saga on the stage. If this were true, we could discount altogether the "constructive" element in the plays; that would have been given, by saga; it would have had little or nothing to do with the poet's mind and purpose. Since to most readers and spectators the plays *are* specifically dramatic, one might allow this idea to sleep in peace, especially since if we ask "What *was* Greek saga?" a substantial part of the answer must be that it consisted of myths as they had been developed by a long succession of Greek poets, not least by the tragic poets. In Platonic language, there "was" no such thing as Greek saga; it was always "becoming".

But there has been at least one recent attempt to revive the idea, if one may rely on reports in *The Times* and the *Manchester Guardian* (August 13, 1958) of a paper read to a Classical Conference in Cambridge, but not (so far as I know) published. The argument, as reported, restated that the dramatists of the fifth century had little notion of what a tragedy ought to be, except "a piece of saga complete in itself" (Wilamowitz' phrase), because theories of the true nature of tragedy did not begin before the time of Aristotle, "whom the tragedians of the great period had not the advantage of having read". This is a desperate business indeed. It assumes that theory comes before practice; it would give us a situation surely unique in the long history of the arts, if the most admired masters in the tragic art did not know what they should have been doing, nor how, because the philosopher and scientist had not yet arrived who was going to explain what were the possibilities and the principles of the art. No less remarkable would it be that the dramatists who could learn from Aristotle were by common consent greatly and uniformly inferior to those who could not; and the same goes for the epic poets: if only Homer could have waited until Aristotle had explained the principles of the epic! Aristotle himself was more modest: twice he remarks, almost going out of his way to do it, that long practice, *συνήθεια*, or natural ability, *φύσις*, can work the same effects as *τέχνη* or trained skill. There is only one reason why we should accept this view of the matter: the well-known fact that animals did not know how to move properly until Aristotle wrote for them *De Incessu Animalium*.

But there are quieter ways of escape. We can reject a theory like that one and yet retain powerful weapons which, used with determination, will put the dramatist at our mercy and enable us to make him say what we already know he must have meant.

One is the assumption that the dramatist will inevitably make mistakes, great or small. Fallibility is the human lot; it is unreasonable to suppose that a dramatist, even a Sophocles or Aeschylus—for we are not concerned with apprentices—could always do what he really intended, or really intended what he did. Therefore, if something in a play does not accord with our explanations, we can make ourselves comfortable by invoking this uncertainty principle. I admit that it seems to me like the innocent presumption of the amateur who has not realized what professional standards of competence are, especially among Greek craftsmen. It would be much more plausible, if we knew that Athenian potters, masons, painters of repute fairly often marred their work through clumsiness or inattention. Is there any reason to suppose that the dramatist, sitting down at his table to work at a play, should prove any less competent as a craftsman than his fellow artists? This is where a second weapon comes into play. Yes, we are told, there is: the Greek painter or sculptor, like the composer of music today, was in complete control of his material; the composer actually invents all of it; the tragic poet could not exercise such complete control, since he could not—or at all events did not—invent his plot but found it in existing Myth, and therefore to some extent was controlled by it; sooner or later he found himself doing not what he wanted, but what he had to.

This myth about Myth should be exploded. It does us little credit, since all the evidence points the other way, and it renders us no service beyond that of exempting us from taking seriously all that we find in a play. The extreme of naïveté in this matter of the plot we glanced at in discussing the documentary fallacy. When this has been committed, the critic has unconsciously allowed himself to think that the event actually happened, and that all the poet has done is to put it into poetry; he is forgetting that it was the dramatist who, as it were, caused it to happen. (It is for this reason that Aristotle wisely says that even if the *poietes* happens to represent an actual event, he is none the less its *poietes*.) What we are considering now is of course not naïve in that way, but not much less mistaken. It is true, as Aristotle remarks, that a dramatist could not alter, for example, the Orestes myth to the extent of having Clytemnestra killed not by Orestes but by someone else; but this means no more than that certain myths were not suitable for the expression of certain ideas: if you are possessed by the conviction that man is master of his destiny, you will not choose the Oedipus myth for your play but a more suitable one, for you would have to alter the myth so radically that it would lose all authority, and your play would at best be a mere *tour de force*. But where is the evidence that a dramatist ever allowed the existing state of the myth to deter him from altering it as he wished? We have at our disposal several versions of the Orestes myth, and Dio Chrysostom's abstract of the three Philoctetes plays: none of these gives the idea that the dramatist sitting at his table was ever hampered by intractable material. Did myth assert that the Erinyes pursued Orestes? Sophocles represented the contrary. That Artemis held up the fleet because Agamemnon had offended her by shooting a stag? Aeschylus invented something quite different—and when a recent editor, Page, explains (p. xxiii) that Aeschylus would have made his meaning clearer by *not* altering the myth, one can only envy the feeling of certainty which can correct the evidence. Euripides invented a marriage for Electra, kept Iocasta alive for years after the discovery, and arranged that Medea's children should be killed not by the angry citizens of Corinth but by their mother. The Prometheus of Aeschylus is a totally different god from Hesiod's—and so one might continue. There was a tradition that Orestes was tried before the Twelve Gods; since that would have signified nothing in the *Eumenides*, Aeschylus invented something quite different—so original that hardly anybody believes it. The one instance known to me where a dramatist flies in the face of mythic fact and then has to make good is the *Philoctetes*—and there, Sophocles is quite unconcerned about it: he simply brings in a *deus ex machina* to put things right.

But if this weapon fails, as I maintain it does, then the situation is that we have no more reason to suspect faulty construction in a first-rate Greek dramatist than in a first-rate sculptor or potter: he was, effectively, in control of his material; certainly he regularly behaves as if he were. And why should he have been more careless or incompetent? If we say that the Theseum is inferior to the Parthenon, we do not mean that the architect of the Theseum, being only human, committed errors or oversights; we mean that his whole conception was less exciting, not that he carried out his design imperfectly. If we had preserved to us a second-rate play by Sophocles, it is not likely that it would prove to be technically inferior; much more likely that it would be beautifully tailored, but with no very interesting body inside.

The opposite view is naturally popular: it seems natural,

until one takes the trouble to look into it, and it is much more comfortable. The dramatist does something that we do not expect; he does something that does not accord with our ideas of dramatic beauty: he clearly made a mistake. The great Tudor composers of England put in sharps and flats where their Victorian editors knew there should be none, for which reason they removed them, so demonstrating to their less provincially minded successors that their self-confidence and ignorance were evenly matched. Sophocles does not bring back Antigone's body: it used to be said sometimes: "This was a mistake; it impairs the unity of the play." Complacency was not disturbed by the reflection that the man to whom so elementary an error was attributed was one of the best three or four of the world's dramatists; and another thing that was not disturbed was the popular and slightly romanticised interpretation of the play. If Sophocles' ideas were rather different from those current at the time (which is possible), the ready invocation of incompetence threw away one chance of discovering what that difference was. Our interpretations must have respectful regard not only to the text, but also to "the disposition of the material".

Cornford's simile of circumambient atmospheres is worth keeping in mind. Inevitably, we are all children of our own age, and on top of that, some of us have new and powerful ideas of our own. But there is cause for mistrust. There is that grave charge, not easy to rebut, that "much of their work had no relation to the texts". Setting aside some few examples of sheer willfulness, we should all maintain, stoutly and rightly, that the cause was not lack of scholarship nor carelessness; but if the cause was not sin, it must have been ignorance: ignorance of the means, if any exist, whereby atmospheric distortion can be corrected, partly if not wholly; probably indeed ignorance that there is such a phenomenon.

Aristotle did regard the dramatist, and the epic poet too, as an artist of the same general kind as the painter and sculptor; he may not have been mistaken. He did not treat the dramatists as grand poets; he surely thought they were, but then, he surely thought the same of Empedocles, whom he puts firmly on the other side of his dividing line. If Aristotle is talking sense, as he does sometimes, the implication is that we do not necessarily reach our dramatist's mind by contemplating only what he says; what he says, or what he gives his personages to say, is only one part of his complete mimesis, and we must attend to the whole. The *lexis* (by which I shall mean the "poetry") is very important, and in no detail is to be neglected or fudged, but the foundation of the whole, the governing element (if Aristotle is right) is the choice and disposition of the material.

I hope that the idea is worth following up, especially since we are inclined to think of the material as fixed beforehand, and to judge "plot" by only aesthetic standards. The main argument of this book is that Aristotle was right; further, that classical Greek literature differs from modern literature in nothing more than the reliance it places on the choice, disposition, articulation, of its material. If the argument is a good one, then we have one control at least over diffraction and individual enthusiasms. There is however one serious matter to be attended to first: the promised demonstration that what we are talking about is of general importance to Greek studies at large.

II

Aeschylus

We have been considering what may be among the causes of the chaos that so many deplore. It has been suggested that we do not always think clearly enough about the differences between a play and an actual event; that we are reluctant to believe that the dramatist's mind took charge of the material that is in the play, selecting and shaping it according to his own fairly specific idea; that the dramatist did do this, so anything we may add, from outside the play, does not further elucidate the purpose of the dramatist, but is more likely to be an obstruction, even a defacement; that we do not always recognise that the text of a play is not coextensive with, but smaller than, what the dramatist designed and presented. In short, we rarely apply to our interpretative criticism a considered critical method, with the result that we have nothing—no Rules of Evidence, as it were—with which to control our procedures; so that we are too much at the mercy of our own inevitable prepossessions; and these can have the effect that here and there we read the text without really assimilating it, and can attribute to the author ideas which are ours, not his, and may even be in direct conflict with what he says or clearly implies. However, we have it on good authority that things have recently taken a decisive turn for the better; Chaos is on the way out.

The authority on which I make this cheerful announcement is a very well-informed article, "Interpreting Greek Tragedy", which appeared in *The Times Literary Supplement* on February 6, 1959. Since this periodical follows the maxim *omne ignotum pro magnifico*, the article was unsigned; for brevity therefore I will refer to the author as Ignotus.

He begins by observing that in this field, as nowhere else, interpretative imagination outruns academic discretion:

Every age can find a new facet of truth in the plays of Aeschylus, Sophocles and Euripides; but equally, every age can, and does, overlay them with a top-dressing of contemporary *idées reçues*, literary, ethical, social, political or religious. It is only within the past few years that a determined effort has been made to scrape away all the modern accretions and to take a (comparatively) objective look at what lies beneath.

Consequently, Ignotus believes that "the 1950's look like marking a watershed in the criticism of ancient drama":

One by one the old shibboleths are being knocked down; perhaps the most important discovery is that the so-called "theology" of Aeschylus and Sophocles is a great deal more primitive and Hesiodic than most nineteenth-century commentators would allow. Jane Harrison and Professor Dodds pointed the way; and two years ago Mr. Hugh Lloyd-Jones, with obvious relish, stripped Aeschylus' Zeus of the quasi-Christian mask clamped on him by the Oxford Movement and put him firmly back in his crude ritual setting. Zeus, we perceive, was the Homeric paterfamilias writ large, an angry authoritarian of peculiarly arbitrary whims, one who could be defeated only by Fate (Moira) or vulgar blackmail, as in the case of Prometheus. This clarifies the *Oresteia* and *Prometheus Vinctus* considerably; but—and this is vital—it makes not the least difference to their poetic validity. Only those who commit the fallacy of identifying poetry with ethical content (having first set up their own scale of ethical values) could argue that any depreciation of Aeschylus' creative genius was here involved.

The discovery, if that is the right word, is clearly important; more is involved than merely an assessment of the mind of

Aeschylus. It is important because in Athens tragic drama was the popular art, and we know that for Aeschylus the Athenians had great admiration. Therefore our assessment of their mental calibre, in general, will vary considerably according as we decide whether they were admiring something glorious as poetry but crude in content, or something that was glorious as poetry and made good sense too. Since nobody has ever suggested that the Athenians received Aeschylus' plays with impatient ridicule, what we think of him we must also think, in some degree, of them. However, it is comforting to know that it makes no difference to the poetic validity of the plays whether their mental content is crude, on the level of "vulgar blackmail", or vigorous enough to engage our attention even today.

There is another achievement of the decade now safely past which Ignotus welcomes—rightly: "the serious analysis of poetry as such". Of the traditional way of handling poetic texts he writes:

> Bold metaphors and pregnant symbolism are obelised as corrupt, or emended into comfortingly commonsense prose; and much time and ink are wasted in arguing whether Aeschylus meant A or B, when he probably implied both—with C, D and E thrown in associatively. Recently however there has been a welcome change in the wind.

Whereupon Ignotus refers with an approval that is fully shared by the present writer to Professor Richmond Lattimore's *The Poetry of Greek Tragedy*, Mr Robert Goheen's *Imagery of Sophocles' Antigone*, and the third chapter of Professor F. J. H. Letters' book on Sophocles. This livelier interest in poetry for its own sake is all to the good. We need no longer feel unscholarly if we dismiss as pedantry a long note that seeks to prove that the genitive case in a given phrase is neither possessive nor ablatival but indubitably a genitive of reference; and this remark implies no disrespect for the science and discipline of grammar, but on the contrary more respect for the human mind and human speech.

The point has been made too by Mr William Arrowsmith, in

an article which appeared in the *Tulane Drama Review* (Vol. III, no. 3). He too rejoices that at last the New Criticism has begun to makes its impact on classical studies, "delayed both by the addiction to cultural lag which is almost a point of pride among classicists, and by the extreme penetration of classical studies by the austere and quasi-scientific methodologies of the German *gymnasium*"; though he has to admit that even the New Criticism can become pedantic in the hands of pedants, and that its methods have been applied to Greek plays with bizarre results by Kenneth Burke, Edmund Wilson, and some others. Perhaps we classicists, with our long historical perspective, shall be on our guard lest our new liberators play the traditional role of liberators and become the new tyrants. Aristotle saw that speech is only part of drama. The sensitive analysis of poetry as poetry may not be enough; we still may have to enquire what is the relation between poetry and *poiesis*.

Meanwhile, still guided by Ignotus, we learn that the two great achievements of the 1950's, scrutiny of the foundations, and the proper study of the poetry of Greek drama, have led to much the same conclusions: Aeschylus' thought was quite primitive, and "Sophocles' thought is far less saturated with sweetness and light than we had supposed"; on which we might as well say at once that since tragedy rarely has a high sugar content, the banishment of sweetness from Sophocles need cause neither alarm nor incredulity. Ignotus quotes Lattimore on the *Tyrannus:*

> "Like Oedipus again and again through the ironies of the play, the Chorus say more than they know. All meanings are combined: the civic violence that breeds the tyrant, the tyrant's violence which makes him tyrannical in action, with the violence of lust breeding the tyrant, the child who never should have been born and who, born in defiance, lays hands on secret places and defiles his mother, the wife who is no wife."

again,

The *Trachiniae*, as Mr Letters pointed out, is riddled with primitive magic. To understand the *Antigone* in full we have to take account of archaic vendetta and burial customs . . .

Ajax's death—especially in the superstitious handling of Hector's sword—is [and here Ignotus is quoting Lattimore] "enacted, like the blinding of Oedipus, in an atmosphere of unreason, barbarism, primitive passion, where logic cannot reach, whose force we feel but can never quite account for nor understand. This is the dark substrate of Sophoclean tragedy . . ."

If Sophocles was endeavouring to bring Apollonian light into these dark places (and the point is at least debatable) he was working nevertheless within a far more archaic framework than has been generally supposed.

So there we are, on the right side of the watershed at last. The gallant 1950's have cast aside the delusions of those romantic and inaccurate people our own grandfathers (except apparently the delusion that the better we understand what Sophocles did not bring into the *Antigone* the better we shall understand what he did bring in), and have begun to look at the foundations and at the poetry itself. The results attained so far would have astonished a long line of Hellenists, from Winkelmann to Gilbert Murray, but our concern is not with them but with the truth, and first with the methods by which the truth, in these matters, is most likely to be found. Admittedly, elderly gentlemen, on being assured that a New Age has just begun, have a deplorable tendency to grin, but sometimes elderly gentlemen are mistaken. We must look objectively first at the foundations, then at the superstructures—though perhaps entering one *caveat* before we begin. Those distinguished anthropologists Jane Harrison and Professor Dodds discovered certain facts about early Greek culture which our grandfathers did not know, and perhaps would not have wished to know; but are they also to be held responsible for "pointing the way"? And if they are, can we be certain that Aeschylus and Sophocles, before them, had been so complaisant as to follow it? This we may not take for granted.

We will begin with Aeschylus. Our purpose will be, in this chapter, to examine the critical assumptions or principles which underlie these new discoveries—merely to assure ourselves that they are unassailable, or at least reasonable, since it would be a pity if there should be put into circulation a new Aeschylus and a new Sophocles who rested on nothing but bad literary criticism. Aeschylus it will be convenient to examine under two heads which I present as questions: How intelligent was Aeschylus? and How intelligent were the Athenians? It will not be my fault if a third question gradually emerges: What did Aeschylus think about on week-days?

1. How Intelligent Was Aeschylus?

Not very, according to the impressive sponsors of the new Primitive Aeschylus, supported by Ignotus. They are Professor D. L. Page and Professor Hugh Lloyd-Jones. I must not suggest that they agree with each other at all points, but a few citations will show that they are of one mind in believing that Aeschylus was not a man of reason. To quote from Lloyd-Jones' article "Zeus in Aeschylus":

> The so-called "Zeus-hymn" seems to me to yield no evidence whatever in favour of "advanced conceptions", let alone an "Aeschylean Zeus-religion". On the contrary, it is set entirely within the primitive framework of the theology of the *Works and Days* of Hesiod. (p. 65)

> Aeschylus' conception of Zeus contains nothing that is new, nothing that is sophisticated, and nothing that is profound. (p. 64)

> If Aeschylus had ever heard of Heracleitus or Xenophanes and their attempts to inculcate a more refined notion of divinity, there is nothing in his works to prove it. Further, there is little doubt that the view of Zeus and Dike that we find in Aeschylus is not materially different than that of Hesiod. (p. 65)

In like vein, Page writes, in the Introduction to his edition of the *Agamemnon* (p. xv):

Innumerable superstitions darkened and dominated the lives of men, even among the most intelligent; and in this respect Aeschylus was certainly not in advance of his time. For him, the ministers of the divine will are a diverse and jealous brood, and Zeus appears indifferent to the conflict of their claims. The crime of Orestes was enjoined by Apollo at the command of Zeus, who authorised the Furies to exact retribution . . .

which last statement, we will note in passing, takes no notice of the fact that in the *Choephori* (298–305) Aeschylus makes Orestes explain that he would have to exact the vengeance anyhow, for personal and political reasons of his own, even if Apollo had not enjoined it; nor of the fact that Zeus did *not* authorise the Furies to exact the retribution: they do it because it is their ancient privilege, and they are extremely angry with Zeus when he interferes (as he does) with their procedure.

There is much that is crude, much that is confused, in these conceptions; there is no possibility of deducing a coherent theology, let alone philosophy, from the diversity of demons revealed in only seven plays. There may be light within Aeschylus, and light at the end of the path along which he struggles; but around him is still darkness, or twilight at most . . . Nowhere is there any awareness of what profounder thinkers had been preaching for many years: reading the meagre fragments of Xenophanes and Heracleitus, we should naturally suppose that Aeschylus must have lived long before them, so much more penetrating is their insight into the nature of the world and the nature of man. Aeschylus is first and foremost a great poet and a powerful dramatist: the faculty of acute and profound thought is not among his gifts. (*Ibid.*)

I would say once more, and quickly, that I would agree entirely when Lloyd-Jones rejects an earlier Zeus, "the beneficent monarch of the *Supplices* and *Agamemnon*", whom scholars credited with "the purpose of perfecting men in goodness through the discipline of suffering". It would have been edifying had Aeschylus promulgated such a Zeus; I find no evidence that he did. But as for "advanced conceptions", since neither I nor anyone else cares twopence whether or not we find them in Shakespeare, I see no reason why we should expect them in Aeschylus, or be impressed either by their presence or by their absence. Who is concerned to know whether Shakespeare shows any advance on the thought of Abelard or Aquinas? Who is depressed that he is backward in comparison with Copernicus? Certainly not astronomers, who read Shakespeare for other reasons.

As we have seen, it devolves here upon literary criticism to decide a question important enough to interest that austere race of men, historians of Greece: in admiring Aeschylus, were the Athenians of his time admiring mental confusion, or good sense? The rest of this chapter may, I fear, seem a little combative here and there, but there are occasions when to be combative appears to be a duty, as well as a pleasure.

It will be clear from the outset that the new Aeschylus, the important new discovery that so much impresses Ignotus, depends in no small degree on the proposition that the divine or supernatural or superhuman powers whom he presents are irrational Beings, Demons. Page is quite explicit: we must not imagine them to have represented laws or forces of a spiritual kind (p. xv). If this is true, if when Aeschylus mentions Ate, Hybris, Peitho, and the like he is not using terms that have to do with intelligent thought but is referring to irrational Demons, then the proof is complete already: what mind Aeschylus may have been born with was paralysed by superstition. Therefore, naturally, we ask on what evidence so important an assertion rests. Page offers two proofs. The first is borrowed from a rhetorical and inaccurate passage in Walther Krantz' *Stasimon* (English translation, p. 37):

In our land there dwell no more immortals, such as were adored on the heights and in the caverns of Aeschylean Athens. Unlike the people to whom the poet belonged, we have no faith in the thousand various phantom powers above and below the earth, gods and goddesses, heroes and demons and holy serpents. We build them no temples to house their images, celebrate no festivals at which they are our invited guests. Their sublime portraits are not everywhere before our eyes in cult-statue or holy frieze. We do not encounter in the streets their priests and priestesses, processions and sacrificial trains. We have no trust in oracles, mysteries, soothsayings and dreams; we do not pray at sunrise and sunset, before we drink, at departure and homecoming. We make no libation of wine, no sacrifice to the souls of our dead; we do not give the god his share at each success in battle, in the games, in the theatre, in the work of our hands.

I have transcribed the passage at length becauses it raises an important question: to borrow a phrase from *The New Yorker*, how scholarly can you get? Enough, it seems, not to be aware of what goes on under one's own eyes; enough to imagine that differences in outward form imply a total difference in content.

Passing over the fact that these tokens of superstition catalogued in Aeschylean Athens were to be found also in Platonic Athens, we observe that Krantz appears not to have known that many people today do pray morning and evening, before and sometimes after meals—especially in College dining-halls; that though we do not make libations of bread and wine, communicants use them, even more mystically, in the central Christian sacrament; that although we do not offer sacrifice to our dead, Roman Catholics do say masses for the repose of their souls. We do not thank the gods for successes in the games or in the theatre (we take neither so seriously as did the Greeks), but Elgar inscribed A.M.D.G. at the head of his printed scores, and when a music recital is given in a church, it regularly begins and ends with prayer; but what Krantz says about success in battle and the work of our hands is simply not true, and he should have known it: in Great Britain at least it is the invariable custom to hold a solemn service of thanksgiving in

St. Paul's, with the βασιλεύς and βασίλισσα present, for success in war; every church and chapel, at Harvest Festival, returns thanks to the gods for the harvest, and one hears of priests blessing ploughs and fishing-nets. Krantz may not be blamed for not being a constant reader of *The Times;* if he had been, he must have noticed very often, in its Personal Column, testimony gratefully given (and paid for, at advertisement rates) to help received from St. Jude or some other Phantom Power; and though not all Christians believe in the efficacy of a multitude of saints, very many do, and would hotly resent the imputation of dark superstition—as they would also if they were called unintelligent because they believe in three Gods who are also one, and in one who is also three.—It is a good example of Cornford's "circumambient atmosphere"; but must we be so provincial in outlook?

Page continues: "Innumerable superstitions darkened and dominated the lives of men, even among the most intelligent"; but if comparable observances in our own time do not prove darkness, why must they prove it in ancient Athens? It is not a very impressive start, but there is a triumphant supporting argument which Page borrows from Lloyd-Jones, and I believe that it is intended seriously:

> We must be on our guard against the temptation to believe that his [Aeschylus'] gods and demons are represented as being laws or forces of a spiritual kind; in truth he gives them human shape and many human qualities. All, except Zeus, may walk on earth, and all may be manifest to human sight. We are told that they have eyes to see and ears to hear; what clothes they wear, and by what means they travel. Zeus himself has human shape, is seated on a throne in a palace like a mortal tyrant; has bows and arrows, weighs in actual scales.

Lloyd-Jones, in a parallel passage (p. 65), mentions further that these Demons have special means of transport; and that sets one thinking of what Cowper wrote, in the unenlightened eighteenth century:

God moves in a mysterious way,
His wonders to perform;
He plants his footsteps in the sea,
And rides upon the storm.

Obviously a Demon—unless we take refuge in the explanation that Cowper, unlike Aeschylus, was a poet. And if the observed possession of physical attributes proves demonism and disproves any spiritual reality, what of Milton's horrific description of Sin and Death in the second book of *Paradise Lost?* Must we maintain that these, to Milton, were Sin and Death, Demons, and by no means the two realities sin and death? Or shall we undertake to prove that what is natural imagery to poets of all other ages was, somehow, impossible for the poets of a few decades in Athens?

We must concede to Krantz and Page that we do not find, in the streets of Cambridge or Berlin shrines to Fury, Ruin, Imprecation, Temptation, and the like—but then, has one never been inside a Gothic church and seen representations of the Devil and the Seven Deadly Sins? These had legs good enough to enable them to walk and function upon the Medieval stage; does that prove that they were not spiritual realities? How one could present such realities in dramatic art except in physical shape, it is difficult to see; but if, again, the unlucky Athenians were in this respect unlike other people, are we condemned to believe that the normal representation of Victory on Attic vases demonstrates that they thought victory to be a kind of dickey-bird? We today, being much less superstitious and much more intelligent, have abolished such crude conceptions as Greed, Sloth, Pride, Wrath, Lechery, with their arms, legs, and ugly noses; in our clear-headed way we worship real abstractions like National Prestige, Historical Necessity, Economic Determinism, Psychological Maladjustment, powers that do not lend themselves to pictorial representation on Banks or Chambers of Commerce. Which of the two sets has the greater reality is perhaps an open question.

If the theory is true, it will bear a certain amount of investigation and extension; Demonism, like Sin, has its consequences. It raises at once a practical question: on the Athenian stage, how did the actors distinguish, in their pronunciation, between a capital and a small initial letter? If there were no distinction, then it is not surprising if the Athenians were a bewildered people. For consider the two pairs, *kratos* and *bia*, very common nouns meaning "might" and "violence", and Kratos and Bia, Demons. When the latter pair walk upon the stage at the beginning of the *Prometheus*, they are "manifest to human sight" and have the usual supply of limbs (though one of them apparently cannot speak); therefore they qualify as Demons. They also have capital letters in our texts. We, obediently, are on our guard against the temptation to believe that they are laws or forces of a spiritual kind; Zeus is by no means applying might and violence to Prometheus, but torturing him with Demons. But when the leader of the chorus in the *Agamemnon* says to the Queen: ἥκω σεβίζων σόν, Κλυταιμήστρα, κράτος, he must surely have had some vocal device for indicating that the word, here, is *kratos* and not Kratos; not Might, a Demon, but *might*, the common noun. Still more so a little earlier, when the chorus sang of the ὅδιον κράτος, where the adjective ("wayside" *kratos*) so naturally would have suggested that this "might" had legs and was therefore a Demon. The difficulty is not one to be taken lightly.

There are others. In *Agamemnon* 744 we hear of the νυμφόκλαυτος, Ἐρινύς, "the Erinys who brought lamentation to the bridegroom". Page comments, in his note on the passage: "It is of course the Fiend of Wrath, Ἐρινύς, who was sent by Zeus Xenios in pursuit of Helen". This indeed is exactly what Aeschylus does say, here; but is the Fiend as "actual" as the scales in which Zeus weighed the souls of the dead, or as his bows and arrows, or as the crowbar which he lent to Agamemnon (on the evidence of the Herald, who apparently saw it) wherewith to batter down the walls of Troy? Or after all is a measure of poetic imagery to be allowed to creep in—not a totally irrational Demon, defiant of meaning, but something like Wrath—that Wrath which a later age was to see as one of the Seven Deadly Sins? As if to help us, in our extreme perplexity, Aeschylus has just made the chorus say that Μῆνις or μῆνις, Wrath or wrath, drove an *army* against Troy. Now, unluckily we have no means of finding out whether this Mênis is a Demon or plain wrath; no limbs, dress, or special means of transport are mentioned, and we cannot know how the singers were instructed to pronounce the initial *m* or *M*; but why Zeus should have thought it necessary to send the Erinys, a Demon, when Wrath or wrath had already sent an army, that is difficult to see, unless perhaps, knowing that these Demons are "a jealous brood", he thought it wise to give them both a chance. But there is something else that makes it even more difficult: earlier in the play the same Zeus Xenios despatched, on exactly the same errand, the two sons of Atreus, "like an Erinys" (v. 60).—It was Alice who said: "I think I would understand, if only you wouldn't explain".

This Erinys will bear looking into—which is more than one can say for that exceptionally fierce Demon Ares, disliked even by the other Demons (who therefore were not wholly irrational); for in the *Persae* (v. 85), Xerxes mobilises, ἐπάγει, this Demon with his bow, τοξόδαμνον Ἄρη, against "men renowned for the spear"—and gets a sound drubbing. The demonic armory, apparently, had been allowed to get out of date, unless perhaps the Demon had meanwhile deserted Xerxes, A.W.O.L., as at *Agamemnon* 78, Ἄρης δ' οὐκ ἔνι χώρᾳ.

But we were really considering the Erinys, as a Demon or Fiend. Towards the end of the second ode of the *Agamemnon*, 437–470, there is an apparently clear sequence of thought. Ashes of the dead begin to return to Argos from Troy; people are enraged at the wanton loss of life and murmur angrily against the kings. Anger like this, the chorus remarks, amounts to a public curse; they fear some dark deed perpetrated on Agamemnon under shadow of night. If common sense has any status in these matters, the chorus are afraid that some maddened Argive or Argives may try to assassinate Agamemnon in revenge. "Because", they continue, "the gods do not overlook men of blood; the black Erinyes get him." In the imagined case, furious Argives will have murdered Agamemnon, and at the same time he will have been destroyed by the Erinyes—the colour of whose dress, we note, has been observed and recorded. But for the powerful edict against supposing that the Erinyes might mean something intelligible, like vengeful wrath, all would be clear; as it is, things have become very difficult, to be explained only by the assumption that Aeschylus, though a great poet and a powerful dramatist, was practically incapable of consecutive thought.

What makes it the more baffling is that Heracleitus, who did not have the excuse of being a poet, and was so much more advanced in thought than Aeschylus, can say (fr. 94): "If the Sun should transgress his limits, the Erinys, helper of Dike, will take note of it"—and we understand at once that he is talking sense, though (regrettably) in metaphor. But we can go backwards in time, past Heracleitus and that Demon of his that would, if need be, bring the Sun back to his orbit; we can go back to the end of *Iliad* XIX, where a demonic Erinys reduces to proper equine behaviour Achilles' horse Xanthos. Parity of reasoning would have us imagine that Homer, or one of the Homers, believed in a "actual" horse, as actual as the scales of Zeus, who broke not only into human speech but even into Greek hexameters, until this Demon intervened. Parity of reasoning, in fact, enables us to acquit this poet at least of the charge of lunacy: this Erinys bears a startling resemblance to that of the advanced thinker Heracleitus, as being something like a guardian of the established order, a corrector of abnormalities. It seems that it was only among Athenian poets and their audiences, and only during this one strange period, that personification, metaphor, and the like were unknown. It would be an interesting enquiry, how long this particular paralysis lasted in the dear city of Cecrops, but it would take us too far from our subject.

If the reader is not by now terrified out of his wits by these Demons, we will consider another, Peitho. Again the question of pronunciation besets us, for *peitho* as a common noun is simply "persuasion" or "temptation" as the case may be, while Peitho is a Demon: "No connection with the firm across the road." Page assures us (*Agamemnon*, p. xxix, and note on vv. 374 ff.) that Paris was "compelled" by the Demon Peitho, "the intolerable daughter of Ruin" (Ate, another Demon), to run away with Helen. It was planned beforehand by Peitho; there was no remedy. "Paris is driven to his crime by supernatural powers against his better judgment"; "It is particularly to be observed how strongly, with what emphatic words, the poet insists on the helplessness of the human victim" (p. 103). If this is what Aeschylus meant, we must hope against hope that Ignotus is right when he says that the quality of the ideas expressed makes no difference to the validity of the poetry.

It would help us to believe what Page says here if Aeschylus had made it clear that the other criminals who meet their doom in the trilogy—Clytemnestra and Aegisthus, for example—were likewise helpless victims compelled against their better judgment to commit their crimes. So far as Agamemnon is concerned, it is made clear that what he did, in leading so many men to their death, was, if not his better judgment, at least his judgment—and when he returns from Troy the chorus frankly tell him what they had thought about it (vv. 799 ff.). But where is the "better judgment" of Paris ever mentioned, apart from Page's note? Aeschylus himself was so remiss that he said not a word about it. The first stanza of the ode in question, textually difficult though it is, certainly compares Paris to the man who is corrupted by wealth, and ends by saying that wealth is no defence to the man who has kicked over the altar of Justice. Continuing, the chorus does not say that Paris was *compelled* (Page's italics) by Peitho; the Greek for that would be ἀναγκάζει. They say that Peitho, Temptation, βιᾶται, "assailed him", "pressed violently upon him". In this there is nothing unusual; Paris is not singular in having been violently tempted, nor in having given way. But Peitho is the offspring of Ruin, and Ruin has her plans ready, *πρόβουλος*; there is no remedy.—And why not? Shall we listen to the poet, who makes sense of it, or to his editor, who cannot? Aeschylus says: "The blemish, *σίνος*, is not hidden; it glares like a baleful light. Brought to the test, the man shows up, as bad bronze shows up under a hammering.—A boy tries to catch a bird on the wing!—This man brings his infection upon his city. Prayers? No god will listen. Such was Paris, who shamefully stole the wife of his host."

Where is the helplessness of the human victim on which the poet insists? Paris was no good—a rich play-boy; he was violently tempted, and could not stand up to it. Remedy? It is too late, now; things must take their course. And what about crafty Ruin, who lays her plans beforehand? I suspect that we have become far too clever to understand this kind of thing; what would have been simple in an age of religion can be very difficult in an age of plastics. For example: it used to be thought that there was a Devil; that his business was to seek our ruin, which he did by laying temptation in our path; that our business was not to oblige the Devil by giving way. The simple imagery was of the kind that we, quite incorrectly, call "supernatural"; in truth, what it reflects is natural to the core, a stark reality. Among the Greeks there was indeed no Devil, but there were efficient substitutes. The Greeks too were capable of seeing that Ruin is a present menace, and Temptation one of its chosen instruments. Our own times afford apt illustrations in plenty, if we care to think for a moment about the murkier side of politics or high finance, for instance. A man is not necessarily out of his mind if, instead of writing like an earnest sociologist in words of not less than seven syllables each, he draws a picture of Ruin waiting for a man like Paris, visiting him with a fierce Temptation, and getting him.

If Peitho must always be a Demon, certain foolish results ensue, as in the *Eumenides* when Athena describes It as "the sweet enchantment of my tongue" (v. 886), and cherishes Its eyes (v. 970). Once a Demon always a Demon, obviously—at least, in the same trilogy: to deny it would be to admit that the Athenian audience had some discrimination and intelligence. However, since the reader may by now be tired of Demons and anxious to return to the subject (which is chaos), it must be left for future scholars to investigate the fascinating fact that one Demon, Dike, was phosphorescent, since she could be seen in the dark: *Δίκα δὲ λάμπει μὲν ἐν δυσκάπνοις δώμασιν* "Dike shines out in smoky cottages"; and to clear up, if possible, the confusion of Demonic agriculture whereby (*Persae* 821) the Demon Hybris came into flower and reaped the full ear of another Demon, Ate: *ὕβρις γὰρ ἐξανθοῦσ' ἐκάρπωσεν στάχυν ἄτης.*

We find our way into this fairy-land by an unusual route: not by giving way to unrestrained fancy, but on the contrary by being as flatly literal as possible. Yet how literal must we be? Not literal enough to read everything that Aeschylus wrote about these irrational Beings; that would be decidedly inconvenient. We had better take no notice of the *Persae* (as we shall see later), nor the fragment of Aphrodite's speech in the *Danaides*. She, if anybody, ought to be irrational; yet Aeschylus makes her say:

> The Sky loves to impregnate the Earth; love seizes the Earth to take the Sky in wedlock. Rain causes the Earth to swell, and she nurtures sheep for men and the living corn; from this rainy espousal the fruits of trees come to ripeness. In all this, I am the present cause.

Had Aeschylus not been so unlucky as to write in Greek, and during these gloomy decades, one would infer from such a passage that both he and his audience were positively intelligent.

All this, of course, needs diagnosis rather than refutation, and in truth the case is not a very difficult one. Modern researches have disclosed one aspect of the total life and thought of the Greek world which hitherto had been discreetly ignored. Ignotus can assert that "Jane Harrison and Professor Dodds pointed the way", but their way was to assemble evidence and elicit facts; they must not be held responsible for an indiscriminate stampede of this kind, one which takes two things for granted: that what was true of one part of Greek life was true of the whole, and that poetic literature is incapable of producing evidence and facts from itself.

Let us look still further, bearing in mind Ignotus' happy confidence that we are at last learning to look at the foundations and so learn the truth.

The discoverer of the crude, Hesiodic Zeus asserts, as one step in the argument, that in the *Septem* "we are repeatedly told that Zeus and Dike are on the side of Eteocles and the defenders; this is implied at vv. 443–6, 565–7, and 630, and is clearly stated at 662–71, where Eteocles calls Dike the maiden daughter of Zeus and affirms that Polyneices, from his earliest years, has had no part in her" (p. 59). If Aeschylus did hold that the supreme god, and Dike, took sides in a local conflict, however distinguished in tradition, then one would be disposed to agree that his thought was hardly as deep and philosophic as that of Heracleitus—but did he? The phrase "we are repeatedly told" surely implies that Aeschylus, possessed of a certain idea, did what he could to pass it on to his audience. He is said to do this four times. The first time he misleads that audience by making them suppose that Capaneus is being discussed. The Spy has described the arrogant device and language of this Argive assailant; then Eteocles speaks at length of his wild blasphemy, and opines that Zeus will surely destroy such a man. Unless the Athenians were not stupid, but on the contrary had something like second sight, they would certainly draw the conclusion that, in the dramatist's opinion, Zeus on the whole dislikes blasphemy. In the second of the four passages Capaneus is still the subject: the women of the chorus are praying that Zeus may quell their wicked foe with a thunderbolt. What Aeschylus is telling us here seems to be that the women are terrified, and that since Capaneus is so blasphemous, they think it not unreasonable to offer this prayer. In the third passage, the chorus, again, is praying—that the gods may listen to their "just petition", save the city, and smite its assailants—and here too a different foundation-examiner might have thought it relevant that Aeschylus described all the assailants, except Amphiaraus, as morally reckless, and all the defenders, with the exception perhaps of Eteocles, as men of prudence and moderation. In the fourth passage, Eteocles is preparing to meet his brother in single combat. He does indeed assert that Dike is on his side—but what happens? If Dike acts at all, and presumably she does, she causes Eteocles and Polyneices to kill each other. Therefore, if it is true that Aeschylus was really "telling us", the audience, that Zeus and Justice were on the side of Eteocles and the defenders, he is also telling us something else, though under his breath: "For goodness sake, do not be so simple as to imagine that I have devised any connexion at all between what I am really telling you and what you are actually hearing with your ears and seeing with your own eyes." Those abbreviated remarks that we find in the margins of our printed texts—ET, XO, and the like—are to be entirely disregarded by those who would know what Aeschylus really thought about Zeus.

But this is only an extreme example of what has been not an uncommon assumption in classical criticism: what *happens* in a play, such as the mutual destruction of the two brothers here, has nothing to tell us about what the dramatist was thinking; only the text can do that. (Being in these matters an extreme pessimist, I foresee the objection that Eteocles and Polyneices *had* to kill each other in any case, because it was in the myth; the answer to which is that Aeschylus had already taken that into account in writing Eteocles' last speech.) For instance, we have been told many times that the first ode in the *Supplices* is Aeschylus' firm confession of faith in Zeus—as if Aeschylus were not beginning a play but writing an anthem: Zeus is the supreme god, and he protects the suppliant; *Zeus verlässt die Seine nicht*, as Pohlenz once put it, in truly Lutheran accents. So too does Lloyd-Jones write, on Zeus the Hesiodic champion of Dike: "At *Supplices* 145 f. the chorus appeals to Dike as the daughter of Zeus . . . Zeus holds the balance and dispenses injustice to the wicked and holiness to the law-abiding (403 f.); the power of Zeus is just (437); Zeus is implored to look with hostile eye, 'in accordance with justice', upon the violence of the pursuers." And are we to suppose that when we have card-indexed these four passages we have exhausted the evidence at our disposal about the poet's ideas of Zeus? Being a less discriminating reader of plays I add two more passages to the list: vv. 29–39 and 528–530. In each of these Aeschylus causes the Suppliants to pray to Zeus, explicitly, that he drown their wicked pursuers at sea. How edifying it would be, how exquisitely "in accordance with justice", if Zeus had obliged! He would have been protecting *die Seine*, and all would be well. What then did Aeschylus expect his audience to think when, after these two prayers, the wicked oppressors turn up in Argos, undrowned, quite dry, and very violent? Or was it the case, and one perfectly understood by his astute audience, that Aeschylus could exercise control over the words he wrote, but none whatever over the other parts of his plays?

In this instance I am in the happy position of being able to record an anecdote, though unluckily I have lost my reference to its ancient authority. It concerns a man from Acharnae who had brought his son to Athens to see the first production of this very trilogy. As they were trudging homeward through the gathering dusk, having set out before dawn, the boy suddenly asked—for he was an intelligent lad, as intelligence went in those benighted years—"Father, is Aeschylus a wicked man?" The father smiled. "Why do you ask that?" "Well", said the boy, "he made those poor girls pray to Zeus to save them from the wicked Egyptians, and Zeus did nothing at all. Did Aeschylus mean that Zeus doesn't care *what* happens to us, and that it is no use to pray to him?" "Ah", said the father, "that's what comes of falling asleep half-way through a trilogy."

This charming little tale has its bearing also on the Hesiodic Zeus of the *Oresteia*. On the Hymn to Zeus of the *Agamemnon* Lloyd-Jones writes (pp. 60–61) that it shows little trace of an advanced conception; rather it recalls the crudest myths of Hesiodic cosmogony. Ouranos ruled first until Kronos overthrew him; then Kronos ruled until he was overthrown by Zeus; sing to Zeus a hymn of victory, and you will have managed to attain good sense. . . . To sum up, the so-called Zeus-hymn seems to yield no evidence whatever in favour of 'advanced conceptions', let alone an 'Aeschylean Zeus-religion'. On the contrary, it is set entirely within the primitive fabric of the *Works and Days* of Hesiod.

Similarly, Page writes (p. 83): "It is vain to search for profound philosophy in vv. 160–183: these simple lines neither say nor imply more than the man in the street might have said—that Zeus alone can give relief from heaviest burdens. Zeus is all-powerful . . ."

Let all these comments be perfectly true, as the first of them certainly is: they are also distressingly irrelevant, unless we can persuade ourselves that Aeschylus had been writing plays all these years without picking up any ideas at all about his craft. We will put it this way: The performance of the trilogy began, we will assume, at 8:00 A.M. At 8:20 or thereabouts we come to the Hymn. Is it very sensible to walk out of the theatre at 8:22 and announce to those who had not been able to get in: "You haven't missed much. Pure Hesiod! Why, you could have written it yourselves." In fact the trilogy is going on until, say, 12:15 P.M. Would it not be wiser to wait and see what happens? The man in the street could perhaps have written the Hymn, though not quite so well; the question is however if that ingenious pedestrian could have gone on to construct all that follows.

But is there any point in waiting until 12:15? None at all, on the assumption which these two critics are making and Ignotus apparently can accept: that Aeschylus is not a dramatist but a metrical lecturer, who diversifies his *dicta* by showing at intervals inconsequent and distracting lantern-slides, as of Capaneus for instance. But if we do wait until the bitter end, we find that the Hesiodic Zeus has receded somewhat; that the thunderbolts, though still in existence, are now under lock and key; that Zeus's daughter Athena has propounded a few ideas which are apparent neither in the Hymn nor in Hesiod; that Zeus prevails this time not by main force, not as the τριακτήρ, but by reason and persuasion, as Zeus Agoraios, "le dieu de la parole", as Mazon translates it.

Having decided not to wait until 12:15 in order to see what Aeschylus was thinking about, we have to guess; for his explanation we substitute our own. Lloyd-Jones contrives the following: The chorus are in a dilemma; therefore they break off the narrative about Aulis in order to appeal to Zeus, for (he says) "Zeus only has the power to stave off the danger of which the prophet has given warning". The reference in the Hymn to good sense, φρενῶν, echoed in σωφρονεῖν, means "the recognition of the feebleness of man in comparison with the gods".

And yet we are to suppose that the Athenians of the time were rather stupid! To penetrate to this meaning they must have been gifted indeed. In the first place, not a word of the text justifies our taking it as an "appeal"; it does not even begin ὦ Ζεῦ. In the second place, this chorus could not appeal to Zeus to stave off the danger without making itself, or the poet, ridiculous, because five minutes earlier it was saying, with emphasis, that in no way at all can one bend the inflexible will of the gods. Further, why assert that the "wisdom" in question is "the recognition of the feebleness of man in comparison with the gods"? No need to say that this was a thoroughly Greek idea. Of course it was, but then, the Greeks had several ideas. The notion of man's feebleness would have no discernible relevance to anything else in the trilogy, in which, time after time, we meet characters, not noticeably feeble, who in one way or another act alongside the gods, as it were, as when the bloody-minded Clytemnestra murders her husband's mistress, and is thereby sating Apollo's wrath against the same girl, or as when Athena declines to give judgment on her own and enrolls a human jury to sit with her. Those who wait until 12:15 may notice that just as the violent Zeus of the Hesiodic hymn contrasts notably with Zeus Agoraios of the end, so the "wisdom" here may connect with what is said at the end by the Erinyes, now the Eumenides: *σωφρονοῦντες ἐν χρόνῳ*, "wise at last". Lloyd-Jones remarks that the law of Wisdom through Suffering "cannot be dissociated from a famous passage in *Works and Days*". Certainly; but Hesiod also said that the knee is nearer than the shin: it is a little daunting to find that what is said in the Hymn can be entirely dissociated from the end of this very trilogy. On the whole, it seems better to do one's rumination about the meaning of the Hymn in the theatre itself, with some help from the dramatist, not in the street outside, with a copy of Hesiod in one's hand.

Modern scholarship, according to Ignotus, has finally disproved two earlier delusions: that Aeschylus was something of a monotheist, and that he could conceive the idea of development in the Supreme Deity. Each point is important in itself, but underlying both is the question of evidence: what it is, in such matters, and how it is to be used.

About the former doctrine, Lloyd-Jones remarks: "Some have gone so far as to detect tendencies to monotheism in Aeschylus", as if it were a mere aberration. Ignotus finds it quite absurd; at least, he writes, of Mr S. M. Adams, "He still believes firmly that Aeschylus was a monotheist"—where I find the word "still" particularly charming. Mr Adams, it seems, is rather like a grown man—one's bank-manager for instance—who "still believes" in Santa Claus, or in phlogiston. But after all, Mr Adams could cite a few shreds of text to cover his shame. The chorus of the *Agamemnon*, even after it has described the indignation shown by Artemis against "the winged hounds of her father", can yet say (vv. 1485 ff.) that Zeus is the cause of all, the worker of all things, for what is accomplished among men apart from Zeus? Mr Adams, in his despair, might quote the fragment from the *Heliades:* "Zeus is the Aether, the Sky, the Earth; Zeus is the Whole, and anything else there may be." This fragment Lloyd-Jones does of course mention, but only to say that without a knowledge of its context it is unsafe to argue from it; which may sound like scholarly caution, but what in fact does it mean? It cannot be denied that one day Aeschylus sat down at his table and wrote the words, for some character to speak, that "Zeus is the Whole". Certainly we cannot deny this either, that he may have written next, for the other character to speak: "What, foolish wight? Art thou not aware that this is an idea that no man will promulgate until some fifty years have run their course and Ionian thought has ruined Athens?" But it seems unlikely. It is a little hard on a poet that when he bequeaths us a statement but with no context we may not consider it, while when we have the complete context (as in the *Septem*) we are at liberty to neglect it entirely.

Even more pertinently, Mr Adams and other such backward people might invoke a play which Lloyd-Jones does not mention, and Page only in a remarkable footnote which will instruct us later—the *Persae*. In this play it is clearly a matter of indifference to Aeschylus whether the Power that works against Persia is called Zeus (vv. 534, 740, 762), or *theos* in the singular "the god" (454, 495, 502, 514), or *theoi* in the plural (216, 362, and 749, where for an obvious reason Poseidon receives honourable mention among "all the gods"), or *daimon* in the singular (601, 725), or *daimones* in the plural (1005). If Aeschylus was both a poet and a sensible man, there is nothing here deserving of comment; if on the other hand he was a bewildered polytheist baffled by "a diverse and jealous brood of Demons", then it is a little odd that in this play they should be neither diverse nor jealous, and that Aeschylus himself should express neither astonishment nor relief.

Lloyd-Jones settles the matter in this way (p. 65): "Aeschylus certainly makes Zeus supreme; so is he supreme in Homer. Numerous passages could be cited to show that Aeschylus, just as much as Homer, believed in the efficacy of gods other than Zeus, of Apollo and Athene, Artemis and Ares, Hera and Poseidon"—besides the many quasi-daemonic beings. The unspoken, perhaps unrealised, assumption is that if Aeschylus had believed the godhead to be One he would have said so, always—thereby debarring himself from the use of Greek myth, which is a lot to ask of any Greek artist. We have noticed already that the same line of argument would reduce to polytheism all Christians. In another way it is even more unlucky, because it proves far too much. The triumphant and impressive conclusion of the whole argument—impressive to Ignotus—is that Aeschylus never got within shouting distance of the advanced thought and real monotheism of Plato; yet what nonsense it is—nonsense surpassed only by Mr Adams'—to call Plato a monotheist! To take only one passage (*Gorgias* 523): Plato believed not only in Zeus, but also in the existence of Poseidon and Pluto, and of three sons of Zeus and in the efficacy thereof: Minos and Rhadymanthus, who were born in Asia, and Aeacus, who was born in Europe. We have only to look at the text; it is there in black and white. If Aeschylus, a poet, must be held to the letter, why should Plato, a prose writer, be allowed to escape? To base an argument on the fact that a poet does not expressly and doctrinally renounce the accepted religious imagery, which not even Plato does, is not to "knock down the ancient shibboleths"; on the contrary, it is to use shibboleths and nothing else.

Still concerned with evidence and method, we turn to the other ascertained fact, that a change in the character of Zeus is impossible. Lloyd-Jones writes (p. 56):

> Is the notion of a god thus changing in character one that Aeschylus could possibly have entertained? Schmidt flatly asserted that it was impossible; the Greek notion of divine growth, he contended, is expressed in Callimachus' address to Zeus:
>
> ἀλλ' ἔτι παιδνὸς ἐὼν ἐφράσσαο πάντα τέλεια
> (Even as a baby thy mind was full-grown.)

The word "flatly" was certainly well chosen. Schmidt was deceived by a not uncommon misconception, that "the Greek mind" was a Parmenidean ἕν—solid, immovable, and dense. Is it so difficult to see that in this hymn Callimachus was thinking —if he was thinking— in terms of pretty and pious mythology: the baby in the bullrushes, the burning bush, the staff that turned into a serpent, that kind of thing? If Aeschylus used the idea of a change in the character of Zeus, his thought would have been as remote from that of Callimachus, here, as is the thought of Deutero-Isaiah from these Biblical legends.

The argument continues (the *Prometheia* being the immediate subject): there is no convincing parallel; "that of the *Eumenides* was exploded by Farnell". Unfortunately, what Farnell exploded, in this connection, was Farnell; and the incident is worth our attention. He, a good scholar indeed, had spent a lifetime researching into Greek myths and cults, and in what was (I think) the last article that he wrote (*Journal of Hellenic Studies*, Vol. LIII, 1933) he confessed that he had found an insoluble dilemma in the *Prometheus*. By the fifth century, as he said, the idea was firmly established that Zeus was the supreme god, "the High God" as he put it. He also found, naturally, that Aeschylus fully shared this idea; he described him in consequence as an "apostle" of Zeus, as Pindar of Apollo. But at this point Aeschylus comes along with a play, the *Prometheus*, in which the High God is portrayed as a cruel tyrant. (Farnell might have mentioned, but did not, that the portrait of Zeus, and of Apollo, in the *Oresteia*, is hardly any better, since Zeus first "sends" Agamemnon to avenge a wrong in blood, and then has him destroyed because he has shed much blood.) As for the *Prometheus*, since he had "exploded" the idea that a god can change in character, and since he had enough literary judgment to reject the idea that the play was written not by Aeschylus but by someone else, at a more convenient date, he was at a loss, and very honestly said so: Aeschylus, writing like this about the High God, must have been prosecuted for blasphemy; he was not so prosecuted. It was inexplicable.

The dilemma, as stated, must be unreal; something must have gone wrong somewhere. Not with the facts: Aeschylus did write the play, and he was not prosecuted. Nobody seems to have minded a bit. Therefore something is wrong in the assumptions. The use of terms like High God and Apostle indicate one assumption that Farnell was making, namely that Greek religious thought of the fifth century was like Christian religious thought of the nineteenth—devotional, pious, and doctrinal. (Aristophanes might have corrected this mistake for him.) If we get rid of this unconscious importation into the Athenian scene, we also get rid of the dilemma. Farnell found his Greek text impossible to understand because he thought the wrong way round: instead of beginning with the text and its obvious implications, deducing from the circumstances that the Athenians in general could not have been offended by this presentation of Zeus, he began with his own knowledge of religious observances and the assumptions that he had added to them, inferred that they must have been shocked, and could not understand that they were not.

So too do Lloyd-Jones and Ignotus find it impossible that Aeschylus should have conceived of a change in Zeus, but the primary evidence is the text, not the fact that there are no parallels outside Aeschylus. In one respect the phrase "change of character" seems to be misleading. One of Lloyd-Jones' arguments against such change is that nowhere do the Erinyes express regret for their earlier persecution of Orestes, therefore they have not changed. Unlike the polite telephone operator, they do not say "I am sorry that you have been troubled". Let us peaceably agree that neither the Erinyes nor Zeus are "characters" in this sense.

The evidence, we have just said, is not what other Greek poets did not write, but what Aeschylus did write. How does it fare?

Our Newest Criticism is not greatly impressed by the *Eumenides*, not enough to read the play with much care. Page, editing the *Agamemnon*, had perhaps no pressing reason to take notice of it—though it might have helped. He does however find room, in a footnote, for the following (p. xx):

> It was evidently Aeschylus' purpose in *The Eumenides* to maintain his audience's interest by an almost continuous display of highly spectacular theatrical effects—the priestess running on all fours; the disgusting exhibition of the Furies; the ghost of Clytemnestra; the pursuit of Orestes to Athens; the arrival of Athena, air-borne; the representation of a law-court, complete with jury; the torch-lit procession at the end. The trial-scene itself is, and surely seemed to its audience, rather weak: but its faults might be excused as congenital to its purely antiquarian purpose, and overlooked in the brilliance of the spectacle it provided. . . . Such pantomime was put away in the age of enlightened decadence.

It must certainly be admitted that Aeschylus, once he was let loose in the theatre, could behave like a clown. So too could Shakespeare. One thinks of that absurd magician in *The Tempest;* the preposterous Caliban; the air-borne Ariel; the ridiculous "reconciliation" at the end. Or, in *Macbeth*, one thinks of the witches and their singularly repellent soup, of the ghost at the banquet—in a white tie?—of the hoary legend of a man supposed to be invulnerable, of the fantasy of a forest on the march. Yet—or so I understand—there are students of Shakespeare who, once they have surmounted their natural disdain for this kind of pantomime, profess to find good sense in each of the plays—and do not do it by assuming before they begin that they know what the play is about. It may be that disdain does not always engender comprehension.

Lloyd-Jones' treatment of the play is indeed less cheerful but is quite summary; yet, if we pay Aeschylus the high compliment of our attention, we should at least give him enough of it. Nineteenth-century scholars, we are told, because of their insistence on Progress, wrote things about Aeschylus which "had no relation to what is in the text"; now that we are emancipated from the idea of Progress, no doubt the text will at last receive proper scrutiny. We shall see.

"One of the advantages to be got by ceasing to demand from Aeschylus a sophisticated and advanced theology is that of being free to recognise the naïve dramaturgy of the *Eumenides* for what it is" (p. 64); and one of the advantages to be got from recognising the naïveté of the dramaturgy is that of being free from the obligation of looking at it at all closely. The comment continues: "The issue lies between the law of Zeus, who as champion of Dike, demands through his προφήτης Apollo that the doer shall suffer, and the ancient τιμή (function) of the Erinyes, who pursue the slayers of their own kin."

One would have thought that Aeschylus, however naïve and incompetent, had made reasonably clear the following ideas: that in the *Agamemnon* Zeus is indeed the champion of the law that the doer shall suffer—and, incidentally, that here there is no hint of any dissension between Zeus, or Apollo, and the Erinyes; that the working of the law in this instance has resulted in the impossible dilemma that Orestes both must and must not avenge his father; that some Erinyes will pursue him if he does, and others if he does not; that in the *Eumenides* Zeus is *not* the champion of this law, and, in fact, is now insisting, through Apollo, that this doer, namely Orestes, shall not suffer—and that this is what all the row is about, between the Olympians and the Erinyes. Now it is the Erinyes that champion the law, and Aeschylus writes for them a long and passionate ode in which they insist precisely on this, that they are defending Dike, and the Olympians infringing and abolishing it. This may not be Hesiodic; I hardly think it is: it is however what Aeschylus keeps on saying, with emphasis.

We turn to the other half of the statement: "The Erinyes, who pursue the slayers of their own kin". Lloyd-Jones is of course by no means the first who has sought to interpret the play, and the whole trilogy, in these terms. We all know something about chthonian cults; we know that this is what the Erinyes were for, to pursue slayers of their own kin. Nor are we mistaken, of course; nevertheless, being now free really to read our text, thanks to the collapse of Progress, we will read it, just in case. The text is our sole authority here, not what other writers have said about kinship, matriarchal society, chthonian religion, and the rest.

These Erinyes, here, are certainly pursuing one who slew his mother, but are we entitled to set aside, as a passing delusion, Orestes' information (*Choephori* 925) that if he did not kill his mother, his father's Erinyes would pursue him—for *not* slaying his mother? Continuing to read the text, undisturbed either by learning or by imagination, we find at *Eumenides* 335 that they say themselves: Our function is to pursue *τοῖσιν αὐτουργίαι ξυμπέσωσιν μάταιοι*, of which a reasonable translation seems to be: "those who plunge into wanton deeds of violence". At v. 421 they drive from their homes *βροτοκτονοῦντας*, which means "man-killers", with no reference to kinship. At vv. 354–356 they avenge "the overturnings of houses"—kin-slaying, by all means; but at vv. 545–548 they keep watch not only on respect towards parents but also on "the comings and goings of guests", which has nothing to do with the slaying of kindred, but may well remind us that they played some part, in the *Agamemnon*, in the pursuit of Paris. Finally—and what Greek scholar will dare contradict Athena?—the goddess herself says, at v. 930: *πάντα γὰρ αὖται τὰ κατ' ἀνθρώπους ἔλαχον διέπειν*, "the function they were given was to manage all human affairs". In short, the function of the Erinyes in this trilogy includes of course the avenging of kindred blood, but is much wider than this; and if, investigating Aeschylus' theology, we misrepresent his conception of these goddesses, preferring something that we have learned from other sources, then our pronouncements are bound to be wrong. Only when we have noted what he says can we begin to think to any purpose about what he means; and then we see that he is concerned not so much with a specific type of crime but with a specific method of punishment. If we persevere, we may even begin to suspect that his dramaturgy is not so very naïve after all. But if we so far defy the text as to assert that Zeus, here, is championing the law that the doer must suffer, when the whole point is that he is defying that law, then what we say next will be wrong.

This has its direct bearing on the dictum that a change of character in Zeus is impossible. Let it be granted that the phrase, since it can be misunderstood, is not the best; yet how can we deny that within the trilogy *something* has happened to Zeus? He *was* the champion of that law; now, in this case, he is insisting that it be suspended. If to this we add that in the Hymn he was a purely Hesiodic Zeus, but at the end relies on persuasion and not on thunderbolts, then, if "change of character" is an objectionable phrase, let us find another that means much the same thing. The fact that Greek literature affords no other parallel except the *Prometheia* is interesting and invites our consideration, but it cannot prove that Aeschylus did not say what he clearly does say. And we should not contradict the text in order to sustain a theory.

Further to this part of the text, Lloyd-Jones maintains, with the warm approval of Ignotus, that the Erinyes and Athena, like Zeus and Prometheus, simply do a deal: "only in the face of a direct threat of Zeus' thunder do they at length accept Athena's tempting offer". Modestly, I propose here what seems to be a palmary emendation: for "direct" read "indirect"—though even that would be too strong. There is Athena's remote allusion to the thunderbolts at vv. 826–829; thereafter Aeschylus throws all the weight upon the idea of persuasion. Ignotus, who is very keen on poetry, might have been expected to see how beautifully imaginative and constructive is this passage about the locked-up thunderbolts—a distant, muffled allusion to the triumphant, all-quelling might of Zeus in the Hymn; something like the allusion in the last movement of Beethoven's *Pastoral Symphony* to the storm theme. But what is Aeschylus' point? The question will not worry Ignotus, with his new theory that the poetic validity remains the same, whether what is going on inside it is something profound and imaginative, or only a kind of divine horse-trading. (I call it a new theory, perhaps wrongly, but if it is not new then it does not possess even the attractiveness of novelty.) Why does Aeschylus do it? Clearly, we are being reminded, through Athena, that Zeus is still all-powerful; he has not gone soft. The thunderbolts are there, a last, not now the first, resort;

but, as Athena says, "What need of them?"—and Athena is right, for now Zeus prevails by other methods. She continues to speak to the Erinyes with forbearance, dignity, high courtesy; she relies not on sheer force but on persuasion and intelligence. What she offers is honour and reverence from the citizens; what she asks is that the land of Attica may enjoy the blessings of peace and righteousness, that the Erinyes, or Eumenides, may protect the pure in heart and implacably punish the wicked. She, like the Erinyes themselves, has already said that if the fear of retribution were removed, a city would be delivered over either to tyranny or to anarchy. How Ignotus can believe that what is going on here is only vulgar blackmail but that the "poetic validity" is unaffected, that must remain his own private mystery. If the high seriousness of the poetry, Athena's ascription of this last victory not to any primitive Hesiodic Zeus but to Zeus Agoraios, and the solemnity of the final procession (which is perhaps not easy to recapture in university class-rooms) are only a cover for threats and blackmail, then Athena is a smooth operator indeed, and Aeschylus' fine poetry bogus.

We have been doing what Ignotus commended: taking a (comparatively) objective look at the foundations, those on which the important new discovery rests. It is founded, necessarily, on certain assumptions, conscious or unconscious. Among those which we have found time to distinguish are the following: that anything said in a play represents, immediately and directly, what Aeschylus believed and meant, regardless of what personage is saying it, when, why, to whom, or in response to what—regardless too of what may just have happened or is about to happen; that other things said in the text we are at liberty to disregard if they strike us as naïve or foolish, or if we happen not to have noticed them; that Aeschylus never *composed*, never exercised any intelligent or sustained control over what he was doing—he never thought of a play as a unity, a *continuum*, only as a series of remarks, nor ever intended that there should be any connection between what he was thinking and what he was putting on the stage for the audience to look at and listen to (confident, apparently, that the audience would know as by instinct what to pick out and what to throw away); that the imagery, verbal and sometimes visual too, which is prominent and eloquent in the *Oresteia* at least, may be entirely left out, as being, like the action, no reflection of his real thought; finally, that during these dismal decades no approach to metaphor, personification, figurative language, was known (not at least in Attica—for things may have been different in Boeotia, where Pindar was brought up), so that we are to take everything as literally as possible, stopping short only at real hilarity.

If these assumptions are valid, if we may pick and choose like this, what defences exist against the temptation—Peitho, cruel offspring of Ruin—to make a play mean just what suits us? What assurance is there that in another fifty years this new Aeschylus will not seem as dated as does to us now the Aeschylus popular fifty years ago? For what has happened is quite simple; Greek Tragedy is still at its old game, playing the chameleon. Two generations ago the belief in Progress, in sweetness and light, was dominant; scholars fathered these *idées reçues* upon Aeschylus and tried to find in him an elevated Zeus-religion. Today, we can see clearly enough that this was a local aberration, sustained only by neglecting the evidence that did not suit. The time in which we are living now has no faith in continuous progress, but is fascinated by the primitive, the dark, the irrational. Punctually Greek Tragedy takes on the corresponding colour. One set of *idées reçues* takes the place of the other; that is all. The pendulum was bound to swing, no doubt; but need we stand directly in its path and get knocked flat? The new *idées reçues* can easily be fathered on Aeschylus if we can accept the assumptions just listed; they take away all our controls. If we can persuade ourselves that in no way was Aeschylus an intelligent artist, it is easy to conclude that he was not an intelligent thinker either.

Our argument has been, so far, that the new primitive Zeus of Aeschylus rests upon nothing more solid than the refusal to read poetry as poetry and drama as drama. If we read railway timetables in a spirit of lyrical ecstasy we are not likely to catch our trains, nor to understand how Aeschylus was thinking if we read him as if he composed like a railway official. But there is another simple confusion that underlies much of the writing about Aeschylus.

We have the natural desire to investigate the course of what we call Greek religious thought. We collect what evidence we can find; we discover a fairly steady development from Homer to Plato and Aristotle. We then construct a kind of curve that runs from the very earliest times through Homer to the exalted theology of Plato, and we try to give Aeschylus and Sophocles their proper station on the curve. While the circumambient atmosphere was strongly impregnated with the idea of Progress, it was taken for granted that Aeschylus, who in any case appeared to be a grave and thoughtful poet, must come fairly close to Plato. (About Sophocles one was not so sure; he seemed to be more of an artist than a serious person.) Therefore, Aeschylus was set down on the curve, perhaps No. 2, next to Plato, perhaps No. 3, after Euripides, in virtue of his efforts to create an elevated Zeus-religion. Times change; belief in Progress evaporates. It becomes natural to evaluate Aeschylus again—with the results that we have seen: he is pushed back on the curve from second or third to seventeenth or thereabouts, next to Hesiod—and the more incompetent an artist we suppose him to be, the simpler this achievement becomes.

In either case difficulties arise. There was Nilsson's puzzle, that the elevated Zeus-religion seems to have had no effect on posterity. There was Farnell's dilemma, mentioned above. There is the new doctrine so impressive to Ignotus: Aeschylus was backward, in comparison with Xenophanes and Heracleitus. There is the difficulty that Lloyd-Jones finds in the *Heliades* fragment, that the darkened Aeschylus suddenly begins to discuss Zeus as if he positively had a mind.

All this is quite unnecessary; we have made a simple mistake, deceived, probably, by our modern words "religion", "god", "theology", and so on. What in fact is the Greek for "religion"? The surprising but surely correct answer is that there is no Greek word for "religion"; there is only a periphrasis like τὰ περὶ τοὺς θεούς, "what pertains to the *theoi*". Then we ask, "What is the meaning of *theos?*" In answering this question we must be cautious, but so much is known to everybody, that a substantial part of the answer is "a Power"; one of those Powers who control the general course of things, whether for good or ill. Then we may ask, "What is the Greek for 'theology'?"—and it is here that things become interesting. If we say that "theology" is enquiry or speculation in respect of *theoi*, then it becomes evident that there are two distinct kinds of "theological" interest, both of which fall within that area of thought for which the Greeks had no word, only a periphrasis. The one kind I will call the metaphysical enquiry about the *theoi*. It takes the nature of the *theoi* or *theos* as the direct object of speculation; it seeks to answer this question: "It being agreed or assumed or known that God (gods) exist, what is His (their) nature?" The other kind (merely to be irritating) I will call the Hesiodic enquiry—for everybody recognises that Hesiod, in many parts of the *Theogony*, was not speculating or being poetic about the nature of the gods, but about the nature of the universe, how it came into existence, how it is constituted, how it works. From your observation or intuition about the way in which it works, you deduce the identity and nature of the Powers responsible for that working. In the metaphysical enquiry the nature of the *theos* is the sole object of thought; in the other, the real enquiry is into something else, normally some important part of human experience, and the *theoi* are resultants. Therefore it is sheer confusion to proclaim that Plato comes out Head of the River, with Xenophanes and Heracleitus second and third, and poor Aeschylus nowhere; it proves only our failure to notice that they have been rowing on quite different rivers.

The tragic poets, to speak generally, are much more interested in human experience than in abstract "theological" thought, but they will occasionally cross the line into the metaphysical enquiry. This, naturally, is extremely confusing; but then, as Haemon says to his father, the gods' best gift to man is common sense—and sometimes it does come in handy. The two different modes of thought are clearly illustrated by Euripides. In the *Hippolytus* for instance he represents Artemis and Aphrodite as *theoi* who, on this occasion at least, are jealous and cruel. He makes the Huntsman pray, to Aphrodite: "Lady, forgive him; he is young. *Theoi* should be wiser than men." The goddess does not forgive, and of course cannot, being a *theos*—no more than Cholera can forgive the country that does not know the laws of sanitation. To complain that the poet was giving an unworthy picture of the Divine Nature would give a very poor picture of one's own intelligence: Euripides, here, is not pursuing the metaphysical path. Similarly, in the *Heracles* he can put before us his vindictive Hera, and yet, later in the play (v. 1345) can write: "The god, if he is truly god, can be in need of nothing"—not, therefore, of vengeance, like this Hera or like Artemis at the end of the *Hippolytus*. We do not accuse him of being confused in mind, or of playing leapfrog with Xenophanes, now more backward, now even more advanced. All we can complain of, if we think it worth while, is a certain abruptness in passing from the one kind of "theology" to the other.

If we actually *read* Aeschylus, in the persuasion that the same man both wrote the poetry and designed the plays—and we certainly have no evidence to the contrary—we find something similar. That the same god, Zeus, should first lay down the law that the Doer Must Pay, and then, in the same trilogy, ordain that a particular Doer shall not pay; that he should first be presented as a god of sheer power, might, and violence, and then as one who relies on persuasion and intelligence—these and other such contradictions, considered as parts of a metaphysical theology, would be absurd—but the absurdity is of our own invention. Aeschylus' theology is truly Hesiodic in this, that he will use the *theoi* as an explanation, or a picture, of the way in which this or that came into existence. In spite of which he, like Euripides, will have his metaphysical moments, as when he declares in the *Agamemnon* (1485 ff.) that nothing comes to pass among mortals apart from Zeus, and in the *Heliades* fragment that Zeus is the Sky, the Earth, all that exists, and more than that. There is no need to be embarrassed by it; all we need is a certain mistrust of English equivalents and our own certainties.

But the word "religion" can make things just as difficult for us. We call Aeschylus a "religious poet" and speak of "the almost Hebraic intensity of his religious thought"—and there is nothing wrong with that. But then we confuse ourselves by bringing in our associated ideas of personal piety, devotionalism, dogmatics, liturgiology, and stained-glass windows. For example, Agamemnon comes home victorious and gives thanks to the θεοὺς μεταιτίους, "the gods my partners". This was regularly interpreted as arrogance and blasphemy in him, until Fraenkel firmly put his foot on the idea and showed that it was perfectly normal—as of course it is. Farnell could not understand why Aeschylus was not furiously prosecuted for portraying Zeus as he did in the *Prometheus;* what he had not taken into account is that the word "religion" covers a much wider area in Greek than in modern languages, and that many of its modern connotations may be, on occasion, quite irrelevant to a Greek context. Again, it was this simple fact that made Sophocles' *Electra* so puzzling to Jebb.

We touch here on what may be a real difficulty for the modern mind, which has inherited an age-long distinction between the "religious" and the "secular". Awe and reverence for the Divine we can understand, or hope we can, and this the normal Greek could feel too, strongly. What we find difficult is that this should have been combined, quite naturally, with hard thinking about political or social problems which, to us, have little to do with being "religious", with worship, with seeking holiness. The problem of Justice, of crime and punishment, which is at the heart of the *Oresteia*, may seem to us to be the concern of moral or political philosophy, and these are weekday occupations. What we overlook is that the Greeks had invented neither sociology nor Sunday; "religion" was coterminous with life itself. They went to the theatre neither as passionate theologians nor as ardent worshippers, but as serious people ready to contemplate serious matters, and accepting that with all truly serious matters, good or bad, the *theoi* are intertwined.

Here was the source of Farnell's dilemma, of Nilsson's puzzle, and of certain other mistakes, which comprise that of supposing that Greek religious thought can be reduced to a doxography. For why did "Aeschylus' Zeus-religion" have no discernible influence on posterity? The answer is quite simple: it was never a Zeus-religion at all, whether "advanced" or otherwise; Aeschylus, in an age of poetry, was grappling with certain realities —realities of life here and now—which very soon fell within the province of the philosophers when serious poetry died the death; as it did, when intuitive thinking gave place to intellectual analysis, when "religious" myth, as a means of conveying thought, was superseded by prose. It was the same idea of "Zeus-religion" that led Farnell to his impossible dilemma. The High God, he assumed, must have been the object of great adoration not only in Cult, which is likely enough, but everywhere else too, as in the theatre; to His apostle Aeschylus He must have been the object of intense theological striving: how impossible, then, that His apostle should have said about him what he says in the *Prometheus*, and should have said it with impunity. Incredible indeed, if Aeschylus had really been an apostle trying to peer through the veil of mortality to some otherworldly reality, to some Divine Essence, and if his audience had been composed of nineteenth-century believers. But neither he nor they were anything of the kind. Aeschylus was contemplating our world as it is, with its problems and apparent contradictions, sometimes finding their solution, sometimes not, but always in the faith that there is an ultimate unity which (as he says) we might as well call Zeus.

He says this in the *Agamemnon*, in the passage which we traditionally sterilise into nothing in particular by explaining that it is borrowed from religious cult:

> *Ζεύς, ὅστις ποτ' ἐστίν, εἰ τόδ' αὐ-*
> *τῷ φίλον κεκλημένῳ,*
> *τοῦτό νιν προσεννέπω*

(Zeus, whoever He is, if that name is acceptable to Him, by that name I address Him. Though I weigh all things, I can form no image except of Zeus, if a man is truly to cast from his heart the vain burden of thought.)

We explain that Aeschylus is employing a traditional formula, designed to safeguard the worshipper against any error of nomenclature he might fall into in calling upon the god. The great advantage of this is that, in turn, it relieves *us* of the burden of thought: the poet is not really *saying* anything; we need pay no more attention than we do to a clergyman who, at the end of a commonplace sermon, intones: "And now unto God the Father . . ." A pious formula; no more.

As it happens, Euripides uses exactly the same formula, at *Troades* 844 ff.:

> Thou that holdest up the Earth, that hast thy seat upon the Earth, whoever Thou art, beyond man's power to know, Zeus: whether Thou art the Law in Nature or the Mind that moves in man: to Thee I pray, for Thou dost guide all mortal things.

But this is quite different. In the first place, we are quite sure that Euripides was no clergyman, and in the second place the context makes it clear that he was positively thinking, not merely intoning. He is postulating an Ultimate, unknowable; it may be Natural Law, it may be Mind, but whatever it is, men call it Zeus—and that is good enough for the poet.

But by what right do we say that Euripides is really thinking, and that Aeschylus, using the same words, is merely repeating a formula? Certainly Euripides goes on to speak metaphysically about his Zeus, and Aeschylus does not—yet Aeschylus does go on to talk sense, and it is sense that we miss, so long as we take refuge in the idea that he is only being ecclesiastical. Life presents us with many grave problems, some of them unanswerable (as we will illustrate in a moment from the Danaid trilogy). Here is "the vain burden of thought". We can lay it aside only by believing that Zeus has come, in triumph, not to be cast down again, like his predecessors—Zeus, "whoever he is"; not that his identity among gods is doubtful, but that no name, no personality, can be vast enough for one who is Earth and Sky and more. To acclaim the triumph of Zeus, this is wisdom. It is a prudent recognition of the limitations of the human mind; it is also the expression of a faith that things do ultimately make sense and unity. It is the same line of thought that we find later in the play (vv. 1485 ff.): "What happens in the lives of men apart from Zeus?"; we find it also in the last verse of the *Trachiniae: οὐδὲν τούτων ὅ,τι μὴ Ζεύς*, "Nothing is present here but Zeus." And if it is wisdom to acclaim Zeus, what is the corresponding folly? So much is clear: the man of folly must continue to bear the weight of unanswerable questions. The punishment of the unbeliever, one might suggest, is not to go to Hell but to go mad.

From this point of view, let us for a moment return to the Danaid trilogy. Believers in the pious Aeschylus explain that in the first play our eminently religious poet was proclaiming his firm faith in Zeus who protects the oppressed. A comforting religion! But what are the facts? First we meet the Danaids, victims of moral violence and oppression; they appeal to Zeus, and all our sympathy goes out to them. But also to the King and his subjects, whom the arrival of the pitiful Suppliants have placed in so fearful a dilemma. Zeus has his chance of bringing everything to a satisfactory conclusion, and justifying his advertised function of Protector of the Oppressed, by drowning the wicked Egyptians at sea. He does not take it; that is *not* the comfortable way in which things work. From this point we have to resort to conjecture, but we may be fairly sure that disaster of some kind befell the innocent Argives, or their king at least, and that the Danaids escaped the Egyptians not by grace of Zeus Hikesios, but by murder; also, that for this they had to make some kind of expiation. Zeus, unquestionably, presides over the whole action: what, then, do we make of Zeus? As we do not possess the last two plays, we must move warily, but we do know that Zeus' daughter Aphrodite played an important role toward the end, announcing that she is the universal power of love, marriage and fruitfulness, and if she has this province, presumably it was Zeus that gave it to her. Zeus is apparently a little more, to Aeschylus, than the Protector of the Oppressed. Evidently, the Danaids have to submit, somehow, to this universal power; and that may prompt the question what they should have done in the first instance: should they have married their detested Egyptian cousins? That sounds monstrous. Yet by resisting they brought (it seems) death to Argos, and even so had to marry their cousins in the end. Where is the sense in this? But—talking of sense—the Serving Maids ask (vv. 1057–1058): "How am I to scan that abyss, the mind of Zeus?" If the mind of Zeus is unfathomable, we may expect to find, now and then, situations that do not neatly clear themselves up. Zeus has his laws, and they certainly will operate, not always as we would wish. Zeus did not save the Danaids from their oppressors, but he did, apparently, see to it that they married *somebody* in the end.

It looks as if Aeschylus was not simply trying to create an elevated Zeus-religion, and unless somehow we can destroy the authority of the texts—as for example by assuming that a fair proportion of what he composed never passed through his mind at all—we are driven to the conclusion that he was rather a thoughtful man. Whether his thoughts were "advanced" does not seem to matter very much; whether they were "monotheistic" seems, in the circumstances, an odd question to ask but an easy one to answer: projecting his thoughts toward the Ultimate, he certainly does not suggest that he found it to be a

Divine Committee, whether orderly or disorderly; whether they were "profound" is perhaps another matter, since we may have different ideas of what constitutes profundity. But evidently we must be a little careful of words like "theology", "religion", "gods"; and it will do us no harm to remember that he and Plato (or Xenophanes) were, like Shakespeare and Bacon, not trying to do the same thing at all.

2. How Intelligent Were the Athenians?

Not very. In 472 B.C. Aeschylus produced for them a dramatised version of the second Persian War, of 480–479. The great majority of the audience must themselves have played a part in the events, whether as combatants or as refugees from the city; the Acropolis, just behind them as they sat in the theatre, was still littered with the buildings that the Persians had destroyed. The historical event was as immediate and familiar as well can be; yet Aeschylus gives what is, in important respects, a very unhistorical account of what happened. To be quite brief about it: of the four messenger speeches the third (so we are often told) seriously exaggerates the importance of the minor action of Psyttaleia; the fourth, beginning with an entirely false account of a disorderly Persian flight to the north, ends with an impossible disaster on the Strymon; further, the pretence is made that Darius, the wise predecessor of the reckless Xerxes, had never left the bounds of Asia, when in fact his Scythian campaign had carried him dangerously far behind the Danube; finally, the play represents that Xerxes arrived alone in Susa, a ragged fugitive, when in fact his defeat in the bay of Salamis had been no more than a serious check making a second campaign necessary, so that the King prudently handed over the command to Mardonius, and himself returned to Susa, where he had important committee meetings to attend. We cannot indeed assert that the Athenian audience, regaled with such inaccuracy, cheered like mad, but they did give the first prize to the trilogy of which *The Persians* formed part, which makes it likely that the play was not received with dissent and with cries of: "Hey, Mister! It didn't happen like *that.*"

Literary criticism can be surprisingly simple: one shrewd look, a confident diagnosis, and there you are. Thus Page (*Agamemnon*, p. xvii, note):

> The astonishing distortion of historical truth in this play is well exposed by Richmond Lattimore; according to Aeschylus, "the battle of Psyttaleia was a major engagement", the battle of Plataea was "an insignificant mopping-up operation"; in this and other respects the desire to glorify Athens suppresses or distorts the well-known facts.

So too Ignotus:

> Take away the poetry from *The Persians* . . . and what is left? Anti-historical rhodomontade, propaganda, ill-directed emotionalism.

Ignotus is paraphrasing, in rather more furious language, part of what Professor Lattimore has written about the play in his *Poetry of Greek Tragedy;* he is saying, again, that material that is intellectually shoddy can be transmuted by poesy into fine gold, or silver at least. (Lattimore would apparently settle for silver.) Those who think this to be nonsense may reflect that there is the possibility of examining the evidence—for there is some—to see if the play really is based on anti-historical rhodomontade and propaganda, diversified by ill-directed emotionalism. If it is, then we cannot think very highly of the general level of intelligence that prevailed among the Athenians of the time, that they were deluded by fine poetry into accepting so empty a glorification of themselves and giving the prize to propaganda that would certainly not impose itself on anybody outside Athens; if it is not, then we cannot rate very highly the critical methods of those who have asserted it—and they have been fairly numerous. Cornford once defined propaganda, in his *Microcosmographia Academica*, as "the art of nearly deceiving your friends without quite deceiving the enemy". Judged by this standard—perhaps an austere one—our play, as propaganda, fails miserably; it is impossible to see who would be taken in by it, unless perhaps the distant and stupid Triballi, who notoriously could not read the Greek newspapers.

"Take away the poetry, and what is left?" If we could put the question to Aristotle, his reply would be: "What is left would be the σύστασις τῶν πραγμάτων, the putting-together of the material." It is possible to examine what material Aeschylus used for his play and how he disposed and handled it. Perhaps it is worth doing: it might tell us something about his intention, also, perhaps, about the relationship of poetry with *poiesis*.

Doing this, we will first dispose of the notion of propaganda, or the glorifying of Athens, or the celebration of the triumph, which is always cropping up to obscure the sense of the play. It need not take us long.

Among the evidence that would be cited in its favour comes first, I imagine, the fifteen verses of dialogue exchanged by the Queen and the chorus-leader (vv. 231–245). For the reader's convenience I give a summary, which does not pretend to be a translation:

—Where is Athens?
—Far away to the west.
—What desire took my son there?
—All Greece would fall to him.
—Is it so strong a city?
—Strong enough to have done us much harm already.
—What else? Has it wealth?
—Yes, a treasure of silver in its soil.
—Do they use the bow and arrow?
—No, the spear and shield.
—And who is their lord and master?
—They are servants and subjects to no one.
—How then can they withstand an enemy?
—Well enough to have defeated Darius' powerful army.
—There is little comfort here for the parents of our soldiers!

It takes no great subtlety to notice that the passage is introduced abruptly, even clumsily; from which we can infer either that Aeschylus was not quite so clever as we should have been had we been writing the play, or that there was something more important, to him, than smooth dialogue, namely that these points should be clearly made, and made *now*, before the Messenger's entrance—for there would have been little difficulty in making them smoothly enough later on, at various points in the play.

Now, we shall probably agree with Ignotus and Lattimore that poetry in poetic drama makes a big difference, and that many critics of Greek Tragedy might as well have been criticising plays that were written in prose—but how poetic is the above passage? More so, of course, than my bald summary indicates, yet it seems fair to say that it comes as near to prose as the Greek tragic convention allowed. Shakespeare, when he was being patriotic, did very much better than this:

> Come the three corners of the world in arms,
> And we shall shock them.

Or,

> This precious stone set in the silver sea . . .

So too, for that matter, did Euripides. However, we must concede to the Propagandists or Glorifiers that one or two of the fifteen verses may well have caused a glow of pride in the Athenian audience: the two references to Marathon, and the suggestion that had Athens fallen, so too would have the rest of Greece. But Athens was not unique among Greek cities in relying on the spear and shield, not on the bow and arrow, nor in being the slave of no despot; and the discovery of the rich vein of silver at Laureion was indeed cause for thankfulness but scarcely for pride. That is, taking into consideration both style and content, we can hardly suppose that Aeschylus expected the passage to bring the audience to its feet, cheering. Herodotus, in what he has to say about it all (VII, 139), pays a much warmer tribute to Athens.

How far does the theory of propaganda explain what follows?

The Messenger, in his dialogue with the chorus, "groans when he thinks of Athens" (v. 285), and the chorus speaks of "hateful Athens" (v. 286)—some compensation, perhaps, for the way in which the Athenian poet describes the battle; everyone knew that the Athenians had been invited to capitulate, like the Thebans and many others before them, and that they had refused, preferring to abandon their city: our propagandist does not mention the fact. Everyone knew that of the confederate fleet, nearly two-thirds were Athenian ships: Aeschylus gives no hint of it, but steadily ascribes the victory to "the sons of Hellas". He may have exaggerated the importance of Psyttaleia (a point that we will consider later), but it is Herodotus, not Aeschylus, who tells us that the hoplites that did the damage were Athenians; Aeschylus calls them Greeks (v. 452). The Messenger's most serious departure from historical verity is the story of the disastrous retreat: this, as invented by Aeschylus, confers credit neither upon Athenians nor even on Greeks, but exclusively on the unwelcoming and unsustaining nature of the Greek land: the Persians were destroyed by hunger, thirst, and exhaustion.

In my survey there is one passage that I take leave not to mention, the ode in which the chorus laments the defeat, and sings like this:

> O Athens, Athens! city powerful beyond our expectation, brave and daring beyond our conception, resolute and clear-sighted beyond belief! With thy multitude of ships and the valour of thy citizens, how has thou brought us low in deadly disaster and bloodshed—though indeed with inconsiderable and reluctant aid from the Peloponnesians.

I pass over this passage only because Aeschylus did not write it, but wrote instead:

> O Zeus the King! Thou hast destroyed our proud and mighty host; the cities of Susa and Ecbatana thou hast hidden under a dark veil of mourning.

Finally, if Aeschylus thought he was glorifying Athens, he was nowhere more inept than in his account of Plataea. In sober fact, the Athenian hoplites rendered no small service to the Greek cause in this battle by defeating the formidable Theban infantry on the other side, after stubborn fighting: our propagandist, having ascribed the victory at sea to the "sons of Hellas", ascribes the victory by land to "the Dorian spear", and does not mention that Athenians were even present at the battle.

Since this interpretation falls to pieces wherever one touches it, and "has no relation to what is in the text", it is natural to ask why it ever came into existence—which of course it did long before the enlightened 1950's. We find one clue in the terrible charge of "anti-historicism" and "astonishing distortions of historical truth".

The word *distortion* was well chosen, though perhaps by accident. Distortion, the deliberate alteration of optical or photographic truth, is common, and acceptable, in the arts of painting and drawing; we are to believe, apparently, that in a play that represents historical events a similar distortion, or departure from literal truth, is reprehensible, or perhaps to be allowed only if we do not much notice it; if it is "astonishing", then it is well to have it "exposed". A similar stern ethic is implied by the charge of being "anti-historical"—a vice, it seems, that brings us to the verge of the unmentionable. We all know that with reference to events past there is only one standard of Truth, and that it is entrusted for safe keeping to our Institutes of Historical Research; what we can forget, it seems, is that in certain earlier and less responsible epochs this was not understood. Shakespeare for example was not overburdened with historicism, and when he distorts what he found in his chronicles—as most notably in *Macbeth*—we are content to say that he is being "unhistorical", recognising that he could hardly have set himself in opposition to a historicism that did not yet exist. We will not plead that those for whom he wrote *Macbeth* knew and cared much less about early Scottish history than did the audience of Aeschylus about the facts of the Persian war; this would mean that the dramatist may be allowed to contradict history if he thinks that he will not be found out—an immoral excuse for sin.

Going a little further back we find that Medieval dramatists would quite unaffectedly bring together upon the stage Biblical characters and contemporary figures like knights or friars. Critics of the last century tended to be a little condescending about this: it illustrated the quaint lack of historical sense in the Middle Ages. Recent scholarship, with more understanding, draws attention to the positive, not the negative: what was achieved by the anachronisms was a certain dramatic and moral immediacy; historical reality was neglected, but another kind of reality achieved, for the intrusion of contemporary figures made the significance of the drama timeless; the events were not safely tucked away in a distant epoch, and in a distant country too, but had much to say to the present audience. Indeed, it would not be difficult to invent a phrase that would make this dramatic technique sound intellectually respectable, even *avant garde;* something like "the significant juxtaposition of temporal planes" might serve. The nineteenth-century criticism now sounds stuffy and, as it were, provincial.

Some dramatists, then, and presumably their audiences too, have been happy to modify or neglect historical truth in favour of moral or some other kind of truth. Our own acute historicism now makes that impossible—but this is of fairly recent growth, a matter of two or three centuries only; and of course anyone who is not deluded by the idea of Progress will at once admit the possibility that the growth in us of this sense has been balanced by the enfeeblement of some other. Certainly the practice of Elizabethan and Medieval dramatists can prove nothing about Aeschylus and Athens; it does however suggest that when we express grave astonishment at his neglect of historical accuracy we may be doing no more than show that we have not really thought about it, but are instinctively taking with us into a different age ideas that belong only to our own. It may be only another instance of diffraction. If a play or film produced today in Moscow, London, or New York altered recent history as freely as does the *Persae* we should immediately and no doubt correctly assume that the motive was propaganda or glorification; when Aeschylus does it, we at once assume the same. We may be right, but there is the chance that we may be wildly wrong. Inspection of the text shows that we are wildly wrong, since we cannot attribute the motive to him without having to admit that in such an attempt he was inconceivably unsuccessful. It will show too that having guessed at one motive we have disabled ourselves from really looking at the evidence, which points to an altogether different one; but there is another point to discuss before we deal with that.

It will be remembered that one of the facts that make the 1950's look like a watershed is the belated recognition that the plays were written as poetry, not as prose, and that this makes a difference. Lattimore's treatment of the play shows clearly what has been gained, but it shows no less clearly, as I venture to think, that this new weapon alone will not deliver us from chaos. What we shall have to consider is the difference between "poetry" and *poiesis*.

To illustrate the gains first. Lattimore writes like this (*Poetry of Greek Tragedy*, p. 35) on "the great catalogues of proper names":

> Hecatean stuff of genealogy, map-making and history is turned into poetry—poetry rather than science; for the names of the Persians, if not fictitious, are assembled without regard to fact, but with regard to colour and association and, as much as anything, sound, which makes resonant and realistic and saves from abstraction the *idea* of the bulk, wealth and population of the Persian Empire. The catalogues open splendours to ear and eye, while the laments of Persia, not always a separate element but combining with the name-lists, work on the mood.

This is the complete answer to the kind of irrelevant criticism which complains that Aeschylus did not take the trouble to consult the Persian *Army List.* Accurate lists would have done just as well—provided that the names would scan and not sound monstrous on Greek lips—but no better. What the dramatist had to do, as Lattimore says, was to make the lists fulfil their proper function within the play, not outside it; he was not recording, but constructing something. He had to consult historical accuracy to this extent (and doubtless did), that any well-known name, one that the audience would expect, must be on the list—not as a matter of accuracy, but because its absence would be vaguely distracting.

It is well to have it recognised, as it is here, that the responsive imagination also is part of the human mind, that the poetry in poetic drama is one of the channels through which the dramatist approaches us, and that if we choke it, whether because we do not respond to poetry or because we regard it as only an agreeable addition to something already complete, then we frustrate both the dramatist and ourselves. But if we rely on poetic analysis to do everything for us, we shall be disappointed. It has its limits, and we should recognise them.

Lattimore does not speak of "propaganda"; he says only, as many others have said, that Aeschylus set out to "celebrate the Greek triumph". His analysis of the play goes like this: Aeschylus, having the intention of celebrating the Greek triumph, had somehow to cast into dramatic form material which was really a theme for epic. His answer to the problem was to concentrate —to throw all the weight upon Salamis, with its addendum Psyttaleia, and this he "magnifies into a major battle, with cavalry by thousands." It is Salamis that dominates the first part of the play, and lamentation for the destruction of the ships that dominates the close; Plataea, sandwiched in between, is reduced to "an insignificant mopping-up operation" (*Classical Studies*, p. 95; a view slightly but not materially modified in *The Poetry of Greek Tragedy*, p. 31, note). To continue: The third part of the play could not be made very impressive. "As for Xerxes, who cares for Xerxes? Is there anything dramatic about a man getting so precisely what he deserves? (I merely ask.) He is in danger of becoming a moral proposition instead of a man. Aeschylus can rescue him only by turning him into sheer emotion." Further: "Aeschylus' plan entailed another weakness in the play: While we rejoice in the victory of Greece and freedom, these Greeks are far away and lost from the mind after the Salamis episode. Herodotus, idealising them less, and enabled, as Aeschylus was not, to write from a Greek point of view, brought home their triumph with more force." The general conclusion is that Aeschylus' choice of a contemporary theme was not very successful; he "works a strong magic, but it is magic; there is little real feeling (one can only be personal) . . . The incantation of names is spell-binding, and goes soft on analysis."

Perhaps one is almost persuaded, as one is completely persuaded by what the same critic says about the poetry; yet there are difficulties. Plataea, in the play, a mere mopping-up operation? We can appeal from Lattimore the critic to Lattimore the splendid translator:

> And there the crowning height of sorrow waits for them,
> punishment for their sacrilege and godless minds.
> They came to the land of Hellas, and they took no shame
> to spoil the statues of the gods, to burn their temples.
> And now the altars of divinities are gone, their houses
> torn up, pitched over from their bases, beaten to rubble.
> Behold, they have wrought evilly, and not less shall be
> the evil that they suffer, now and still to come; the springs
> of evil have not yet run dry, they still gush over.
> Their life blood shall be sacrificial, the clotted gift
> to earth at Plataea underneath the Dorian spear.
> Into the third generation the piled dunes of the dead
> voiceless shall indicate before the eyes of men
> that one who is mortal should not think too high.
> For lawless violence comes to flower and bears a crop
> of ruin, and the reaping of it is full of tears.

An "insignificant mopping-up operation"? It hardly sounds like it. How can we say it?

Again, it is obvious that after the Salamis episode "the Greeks are far away and lost from the mind", but why must we think straightway that this is a fault or inconvenience in the play, without even considering the possibility that it may be exactly what Aeschylus intended? The answer to each of the two questions is the same: we begin with the assumption that we know what Aeschylus' purpose was: to celebrate the triumph; then we consider what his dramatic problems must have been—and the rest follows, including the statement, which we will examine later, that he concentrates on Salamis and turns a minor incident into a major land battle. It all stands to reason—but it hardly stands up to an examination of the text. If instead we adopt the method commended by Ignotus, namely, scrape away modern accretions and look objectively at the foundations, we shall find that it is only some of those obstructive *idées reçues* that cause some of our work to "have no relation to what is in the text". We shall find that Aeschylus was not trying to make propaganda, was not celebrating a triumph, has not concentrated on Salamis, has not exaggerated the military importance of Psyttaleia, has not sandwiched Plataea, and has not indulged in rhodomontade or emotionalism, ill-directed or otherwise. We shall find also that a major element in the structure of the play is one which these and other such interpretations, being of the *a priori* kind, are doomed not to notice. Let us begin our scrutiny of the foundations.

The *parodos* is no inconspicuous one: it occupies about one-eighth of the whole play. It is firmly laid out in three sections, distinct in rhythm, and therefore in the music and dance too. The first of the three contains practically nothing but a list of the kings, princes, and other notables who, from all parts of the empire, have marched forth with Xerxes. As Lattimore well says, it creates in our minds a deep impression of the extent and power of Xerxes' dominions. It is not uncommon for a dramatist to begin at the opposite pole to the one where he will end; we may recall the first presentation of the kingly Oedipus, or the "Brave Macbeth—well he deserves that name".

So too does this play begin with a picture of the apparently invincible might which, at the end, is shattered.

At vv. 61–64 there is a hint of anxiety: parents and wives are anxiously counting the days, for they have already become so many; but there is no anxiety in the middle part of the ode. Under the command of their *θούριος ἄρχων*, "vehement leader" (v. 73), *ἰσόθεος φώς*, "a man equal to a *theos*" (v. 80), the great host has gone forth by sea and land, a flood of men that surely none can resist (vv. 87–92), because the *theoi* (or *theos*) gave it to Persia to prevail on land, in sieges and with massed cavalry, and she has learned to look upon the rough sea, trusting to the fine-spun cables and her bridge of boats. (I take it that *δέ* in v. 109, cannot be adversative: "and", not "but"; also that the reference is to the bridge, not to ships in general. I also follow most recent editors in transposing vv. 93–100, so that the stanza follows v. 114.)

At this point the confidence of the chorus gives way. The reason is not the lack of news, still less the coming of bad news; it is the thought that the *theos* is *δολόμητις*, "guileful", and that Ate smiles and leads a man to his ruin. We ourselves, if we are deceived by the guileful fallacy of the Single Curve (p. 66 above), shall have to say that Aeschylus richly deserved all that Plato said about him, and the other poets, for daring to suggest that God can deceive; but it may be wiser to deduce Aeschylus' theological notions from Aeschylus himself rather than from Plato.

At all events, it is on this thought that the chorus goes on to say, with a second abrupt change in the visual and aural pattern: "Therefore my heart is filled with black fear. 'Alas for the Persian host!': is *that* the news we shall hear? Persia has been emptied of her men, and their women are torn with anxiety."—So does Aeschylus begin what is to be his celebration of the national triumph.

It would not be surprising, nor undramatic, nor unhistorical (if we may believe Herodotus), had Aeschylus now produced a First Messenger announcing jubilantly that Xerxes was in possession of Athens. Such a scene, with no great difficulty—with a little of that dramatic irony, of which he knew something—might well have furthered his obvious purpose by recalling to the minds of his audience their heroic resolution to abandon all rather than submit to the Persian. For whatever reason, he did not think of it; instead, he produces the Queen, with her ominous vision. It is an interesting fact that some dramatists, Aeschylus, Sophocles, and Shakespeare among them, are addicted to dreams, prophecies, and the like, while others, like Euripides, Ben Jonson, Ibsen, Shaw, are not. What such foreshadowings do is plain enough: they suggest that there is something in the nature of things that is at work in the event. The import of Atossa's vision is clear—unless we know enough of modern psychology to explain it away as an ordinary anxiety dream. However, we will simply note the fact: Aeschylus did not use a First Messenger, and did invent the dream.

"Beseech the *theoi* with sacrifice", says the chorus, "that they will avert anything untoward in the vision and fulfil what is good; further, call to our aid the spirit of Darius." Certainly, this chorus had not been able to learn from the chorus of a later play, the *Agamemnon*, that neither by libation nor by sacrifice can we bend the inflexible will of the *theoi*—with which, on the whole, modern thought agrees: if you have done something wrong or foolish, you have to take the consequences. The Greek *theoi* do not forgive (though men may); they do not act as benevolent magicians, suspending the operation of their own laws.

So far the play shows no sign of celebration, propaganda, or anything else of the kind; but now, when the Queen is on the point of going home to perform her sacrifice, Aeschylus abruptly introduces the fifteen verses which we summarised above. We have seen already that if he did it expecting from his audience what one scholar has called "a fervent response", he did remarkably little to deserve it. Now we can do what the audience had perforce to do—take the passage in its full context. The poet has caused us to reflect upon the extent and power of the

Empire, the irresistible flood of men, aided by "Ares the Bow-master" (v. 85), who, as the Messenger is going to tell us, let them down (v. 278); upon the destiny allotted to Persia, to rule in Asia, and upon the fact that the Persians have learned also to look unafraid at the sea. Then came the sudden chilling thought that the *theos* is guileful; next, the Queen's vision and the hope of propitiating the gods. So far, the play has been directed along a straight course; now, awkwardly, comes the dialogue in which Marathon is mentioned twice.

We will imagine someone in the audience whose mind, so far, has been wool-gathering. At this moment the name Marathon penetrates his ears, and he says to himself: "Ah yes! Marathon! A glorious victory that was", and he spends the next five minutes glorying. But we must not hold Aeschylus responsible for what comes into the head of a spectator who has not been listening, and such a spectator is no model for a critic to copy. There is no need to deny the obvious, that the audience must have felt a glow of pride; still less need to deny what is even more obvious, in the text—the reason why Marathon is mentioned: the first time, to establish that Xerxes has led forth the husbands and sons of anxious wives and mothers against no puny foe; the second time, that free citizens can fight better than the slaves of a despot; and here we may recall (or anticipate) that in his account of Salamis Aeschylus records or invents the threat by which Xerxes encouraged his captains: any one who flinched would have his head cut off. They ordered things better in Greece.

That is what the poet is saying about Marathon; the only question is whether we shall respond to what he says or to what we ourselves imagine. He says too that the enemy has ample financial resources and better weapons, as well as a better political system. Does it not look as if he was inviting his audience not to cheer but to think? At least, almost like a historian, he reminds us of three facts that help to explain the Persian defeat: one economic, one military, and one political. Now we can understand why the style of the passage is so unemotional, so entirely devoid of rhodomontade; also why the Queen ends it as she does: "Small comfort here for the parents of our soldiers!" Perhaps also we can see purpose, not mere clumsiness, in its timing: it comes between the vain hope of averting consequences and the dire news that the natural consequences have already happened.

There is however a difficulty, though a familiar one. We are only recording facts if we say that up to the beginning of the passage the thought is predominantly "religious", then becomes matter-of-fact, and then becomes religious again; at least, it continues on such lines as these.—The Messenger arrives; what had been only a general apprehension, based on thoughts about the *theos*, and then had become real fear, prompted by the dream, suddenly crystallises into terrible fact, and we are made to see again and again that the *theos* or *theoi* or *daimon* (for it makes no difference to Aeschylus) has been at work. "Alas for our great army that left Asia for Greece!" "Yes indeed", says the Messenger; "their ships destroyed us and our bows and arrows did us no good. How I groan when I think of Athens!"—"Athens, hateful to her foes, has widowed Persian wives."—"Well, what the *theoi* send we must accept. Listen to the names of Persian lords now dead and mangled . . ." Then the Queen says: "What a disaster, what shame and grief for Persia! But how many ships did the Greeks have, that they ventured to join battle with us?"—"Three hundred and ten against one thousand two hundred and seven. But some *daimon* turned the balance in their favour; it is the *theoi* that preserved Athens."—"What, Athens is still unravaged?"—"A city stands while its citizens live."—"Who began it? The Greeks, or my son, exulting in the number of his ships?"—"What began it was an evil *daimon* or alastor. A man came from the Athenian camp . . . Xerxes perceived neither his guile nor the resentment (*φθόνος*) of the *theoi* . . ." Later, as if to confirm all this, we are told that the *theos* himself inflicted a final disaster on the Strymon, and it is entirely logical that the succeeding ode begins by ascribing the ruin of Persia to the *theos* who here is called Zeus.

But is not this a one-sided representation of what goes on during this part of the play? Certainly, but it is one of two sides, and the one which the Propagandists take no account of—which is a mistake. We will now look at the other.

As so many have said, Aeschylus describes the battle itself vividly, like an eye-witness; also without any apparent religious preoccupations, once he has finished with the *daimon* or alastor—surely the most interesting of all *daimones*, being the only one of whom we know the name and address: Themistocles of Phreatto, or his slave Sicinnus. For supernatural trimmings of the battle itself we must turn to Herodotus. This transparent *daimon* assured Xerxes that the Greeks were on the point of flight; in fact, when they had got him in the right place, for them, they fell upon him like so many lions, fighting valorously and with perfect discipline for all they had: νῦν ὑπὲρ πάντων ἀγών. We read the long speech; there is no question but that the victory was gained by the superior intelligence, courage, and skill of the Hellenes themselves. In spite of which, Aeschylus can say (*i*) that it was achieved by the Hellenes, (*ii*) that it was given them by the *theoi;* not understanding which, some of us prefer to substitute for both (*iii*) by the Athenians—as indeed we may, if we add that it has no relation to what is in the text, but is what we know he must have meant. There is no sign here that the Athenian poet is being patriotic; indeed, a civilised poet would in no case celebrate a victory by dwelling, as Aeschylus does here, on the numbers and high rank of the slain, or by telling how their bodies cover sea and shore (vv. 273 f., 421), battered by waves and devoured by fish (vv. 576–578).

Such is the other side of the picture. If we are at a loss, perhaps the rest of the Messenger's report, unhistorical though it is, will put us on the right track.

To his third speech, a not uncommon response is to say that in it Aeschylus greatly, even absurdly, exaggerates the military importance of what was quite a minor action, and then to guess why he did it. Was he perhaps covertly paying honour to

Aristeides, the political rival of Themistocles?—for Aristeides was in command on Psyttaleia. This has been suggested. Or, having paid tribute in the second speech to those Athenians who fought afloat, who would be mainly of the poorer class, is he now paying tribute to the hoplites of the richer class, and thereby suggesting that the glory belonged to all the citizens, irrespective of class? But which are we to do, in reading a play: keep both eyes on the text, or squint, with one eye on the play and the other on Athenian politics? Aeschylus does not even mention that those who fought on the island were Athenians; Herodotus does, but not Aeschylus. Therefore Athenian politics have nothing to do with it. It is true that Aeschylus gives it almost as much room as he does Salamis: in a historian, that would imply that it was deemed to be of almost equal importance; in a dramatist, it means that it is being made of almost equal dramatic significance.

Lattimore, I think, runs into unnecessary trouble through not keeping both eyes on the play. He writes as follows (*Poetry*, p. 33, note): "His account of the action on Psyttaleia magnifies it into a major battle, with cavalry by thousands; there is some difference between a poet using his imagination and a rampant liar". Therefore, he argues, since Aeschylus was not a rampant liar but did describe the action so inaccurately, he could not have witnessed it himself; during the fighting he must have been posted at some place, perhaps on Salamis, from which Psyttaleia was out of sight.—But in order to make the assumption work, we must make another, and a hazardous one: that between 480 B.C. and 472, when he produced the play, he had never met anyone in Athens who could tell him that the action was in truth not terribly important. Eight years are a long time in which not to pick up such information: did veterans in Athens never meet and talk? Nor is this all. Every member of the audience must have been familiar with Psyttaleia; it was in no remote part of the Mediterranean, but in full view of anyone who took a boat out of Piraeus or strolled along the shore. Everyone would have known that a major battle there was a preposterous idea. And not only that: Aeschylus begins his account by describing the island, or islet, as "small and scarcely affording an anchorage"—not therefore an easy place on which to disembark a large army, to say nothing of thousands of horses. If he has really exaggerated like this, the imputation against which he needs protection is that of being not just a rampant liar but a maniac. Yet when we remind ourselves where we are supposed to be, in a theatre looking at a stage, not in a lecture-room listening to an eccentric historian, we see at once that Aeschylus is not thinking of it at all as a major military action; it is we who add that notion to the text, because we have missed the point. As for the thousands of cavalry that operated on the inconspicuous and rocky island, not a word in the text mentions or remotely suggests any horse at all.

Few of us indeed are immune from such deceptive tricks of memory—but there it is. Aeschylus, *ex hypothesi*, was concentrating all upon Salamis; in furtherance of this design he increases the importance of this day's work by transforming into a major operation what was in fact a mere evening's addendum —and the cavalry slip in while we are not looking.

But if we keep both eyes on the text and remember that it is the text of a play, not a historical treatise, the speech becomes surprisingly sensible. What we are looking at and listening to, in the theatre, is the Messenger giving the incredible news to the stage-audience: the Queen and the Royal Council. When he has done with the sea-fight he says: "But my tale is not yet half-told". Our immediate response will no doubt be what the Queen puts into words for us: "But what can be worse than this?" Two speeches are still to come; they may be anti-historical, but we might as well see exactly what they contain.

First: "Those Persians who were the strongest, bravest, of highest birth, those on whom the King most relied, have been most shamefully and ignominiously slain." If Herodotus had said this—which he does not do; he says only "many Persians" —we might reasonably ask what was his authority for saying that this detachment was composed of the very *élite*, the Royal

Guard as it were. Since it is a dramatist, not a historian, that says it, we should ask, if we wish to ask the reasonable question, whether there is an intelligible dramatic reason for the statement. Those who can in no case tolerate any departure in a play from historical accuracy deserve our sympathy indeed, but not necessarily our attention.

When we put the right questions to Aeschylus we do not always get foolish answers. We ask him why he turned it into the Royal Guard: the answer is obvious. The Messenger is giving dire news to the stage-audience. He has told them of the destruction of the fleet; now he will tell them of a disaster that strikes nearer home: of the shameful and humiliating butchery (Aeschylus' word, not mine), on land, of the flower of the Persian nobility. Aeschylus makes of it a catastrophe that ranks with Salamis not in military importance, which is a modern accretion best scraped away, but in bitterness and shame. We have been told that the *theos* was not uninterested in what was happening on this September day: it is as if he gave the Persians two reeling blows, one with the right and then one with the left. Guesses about Aristeides are, to say the least, unnecessary.

The Messenger concludes the speech by saying that Xerxes, overwhelmed by the double disaster, uttered a loud cry of despair and instantly took to flight. Therefore we may expect to be told that the speech does after all grossly exaggerate the military importance of the battle, since the flight is made to be its immediate consequence. The argument would be convincing if we had, in effect, removed from the play something important which Aeschylus put there, that Xerxes is in conflict not only with the Greeks but also with the *theoi*—as indeed the Queen now says: "Hateful *daimon!* How hast thou frustrated, ἔψευσας, the Persian intention". Xerxes has made a catastrophic error (in the play): the *daimon* "deceives" him. Perhaps it is not the fault of Aeschylus if our minds do not go back to "the guileful *theos*".

Second: There is the tone of the Messenger's last speech. It gives a picture of the entire Persian host, those not slain already, streaming northward in disorderly flight, through Boeotia, Phocis, Doris, past the Malian Gulf, across the Spercheius, through Achaea, into Thessaly. They have been suffering from hunger, thirst, exhaustion; in Thessaly many perish. The rest go on, into Magnesia, to the Axius, Lake Bolbe, Mount Pangaeus, and the country of the Edonians. Thanks to the catalogue of proper names, we receive the impression of an almost endless flight. Quite unhistorical of course—though Herodotus records that a similar disaster, with dysentery added, befell that part of the army that marched with Xerxes across Thrace. No Greeks pursue or harass them; new agents of destruction are now at work: hunger, thirst, exhaustion. The Greeks are indeed "far away and lost from the mind"; we shall find this a fault and a surprise only if we knew, before even coming into the theatre, what Aeschylus intended, and knew that it could not have been this.

The Greeks are lost from the mind, but the Persians go on, dropping by the wayside; one would say that the Devil himself was on their tail, if only the Greeks had known about the Devil. If we do not understand what is going on here, the Ghost of Darius will come to our rescue a bit later. He says to the chorus: "No! Never invade Greece again, not even with a bigger army. The very soil fights on their side: *αὐτὴ γὰρ ἡ γῆ ξύμμαχος κείνοις πέλει.*" "How so?"—"By destroying swollen armies with famine." The Greeks themselves played their glorious part, and have finished, so far as this part of the story is concerned; now the physical nature of Greece herself takes over and deals the next blow. Finally, on the Strymon, the *theos* himself completes the ruin. Finding the river frozen, "out of season", the Persians thank the gods (says Aeschylus), even the infidels among them, for giving them an easy passage; but the *theos*, deceptive to the last, melts the ice, "and those were luckiest who died the soonest". The chorus, in the exordium to its next ode, declares it was "Zeus the King" who has filled the cities of Persia with mourning. We may think that this is no more than a pious and nearly meaningless formula, for we are well used to the sanctimonious; yet it is so evidently the logical culmination of the whole presentation, so far, that we run grave risks if we do not take it quite seriously. Aeschylus does not say, before his audience, "We Greeks triumphed over the invaders"; he does say: "It is Zeus the King who filled Persia with mourning". On the whole, perhaps we shall side with Grote, who found in the play "the stamp of a poet and a religious man"—but of what nature was the religion?

It may sound odd but is nevertheless true, that a small matter of dramatic structure can make its inconspicuous contribution to the study of theology. The miracle at the Strymon gives us the opportunity of reflecting that the "disposition of the material", which the audience cannot ignore, not being able to witness a play backwards or inside out, is not safely to be ignored by the critic either. The timing may reveal much.

If our imagination is equal to the strain, let us suppose that Aeschylus, who was not unduly inhibited by what had actually happened, had contrived such a miracle earlier in his story—at Sardis, or during the crossing of the Hellespont; the *theos*, we will suppose, brings upon the army some disaster such that only a part of it reaches Greece. The *theos*, in such a case, would be no less signifying his displeasure at the Persian attempt, and even more clearly would he be giving the victory to the Greeks —but he would be an entirely different *theos;* we could now say, indeed we should have to say, that he is an omnipotent deity who, for his own purpose, *proprio motu*, intervenes in human affairs, setting them on a course which otherwise they would not have taken. (The *Tyrannus* is not being forgotten.) Aeschylus could never have arranged his material like this, because this is not the way in which he thought. What he does is to produce his miracle only when the Persian army is already at its last gasp: many have died at Salamis, on Psyttaleia, on the long retreat, before Aeschylus brings the *theos* out of the background into the foreground to act alone.

Since he was not going to pass over without mention what still remained to the surviving Persians of their march—Thrace, which they traversed "in much distress"—and since he could so easily have invoked new agents like snow, ice, and disease to work more destruction there, we can say that from a mere play-making point of view the miracle was unnecessary as well as belated. Therefore, since he could have done without it, there may be some temptation to regard the miracle as no more than a vague display of supernaturalism: "Aeschylus was a religious poet". But for that, the structure of the play is too well-designed. We recall how the earlier scenes were laid out. We found it possible to suggest that the fifteen matter-of-fact verses, directing our attention to certain natural causes of the Persian disaster, were an interruption of the religious interpretation of the event which had prevailed up to that point. But we see now that the "religious" and the "natural" or matter-of-fact interpretations have continued side-by-side. Though "the gods gave the victory to the Greeks" there was nothing supernatural in the way in which the Greeks achieved it, and what the Persians have suffered on the retreat has been ascribed to "natural" causes in the strictest sense of the word. That is, we have seen what we may call the natural agencies working against the Persians in their full natural energy before we see the *theos* acting alone. In our imagined alternative we should inevitably have felt that the *theos* was the real agent, the others only subordinate, doing his will and acting as he made them act. The "disposition of the material" is indeed important. Those who invented or borrowed the phrase "puppets in the hands of the gods" can never have studied the way in which the plays are designed.

One point remains here: the flight and dissolution of the host is not only unhistorical; it is also inconsistent with what happens later in the play, for whence comes the army that is to perish a second time at Plataea? The sensible answer is given by H. D. Broadhead (p. liv of his edition): "If nothing is said about the picked forces left behind with Mardonius, that is because for the moment they are *dramatically* irrelevant."

Before we move on the evocation of Darius and the middle

part of the play there are some features in the landscape that we should not fail to notice. The chorus, in its despair, exclaims (vv. 515–516):

> ὦ δυσπόνητε δαῖμον, ὡς ἄγαν βαρὺς
> ποδοῖν ἐνήλου παντὶ Περσικῷ γένει
>
> (Calamitous *daimon!* how heavily hast thou jumped upon the whole Persian people!)

It is using language very like that of Creon at the end of the *Antigone* (vv. 1344–1346):

> τὰ δ' ἐπὶ κρατί μοι
> πότμος δυσκόμιστος εἰσήλατο
>
> (A crushing fate has jumped upon me.)

Yet Creon, repeatedly, says that it was all his own fault. It may be that the chorus of our play, similarly, does not think Persia to be the victim of an inexplicable and arbitrary doom.

The Queen now confirms, by implication, a suggestion made above, that it is futile to try to appease the gods: "You", she says to the chorus, "read my dream badly". Nevertheless, she will offer the intended sacrifice: too late, she knows, except that things may yet take a better turn. She will also call upon the spirit of Darius. When she returns, after the ode, it is not in royal pomp, as before, but more humbly, on foot (vv. 607 f.): Aeschylus, being a man of the theatre, knows how eloquent a purely visual effect can be.

The evocation of Darius was an intelligent idea: it enabled Aeschylus to extend our field of vision forwards, backwards, and sideways: forwards, to bring in Plataea; backwards, to give a picture, historical or not but certainly dramatic, of a prosperous empire now suddenly ruined; sideways, to let us see something, at last, of Xerxes himself, prime cause of that ruin. We have heard little of him hitherto; only that he is a θούριος ἄρχων, "impetuous commander", who has led his great army out of Asia ἐπὶ πᾶσαν χθόνα, "against every land" (vv. 73–75); is ἰσόθεος φώς, "a mortal with the power of a *theos*" (v. 80); was intending to avenge Marathon, until a *daimon* deceived him into fighting the battle in the wrong place. Now we learn more. The Ghost is appalled when he learns that Xerxes has dared to yoke the Hellespont and close up the Bosphorus. "But so it is", says the Queen; "some *daimon*, it seems, worked on his mind" (v. 724). The Ghost replies: "A mighty *daimon* that took away his judgment".

It is no doubt a startling idea, that two verses in a play can upset an anthropological finding, but so it is; and since our subject is *poiesis*, perhaps we may pause for a moment and consider what it can have to say to anthropology. Once more (I fear) the point at issue concerns *daimones*, and it is as follows.

Those who have read Professor E. R. Dodds' interesting and important book *The Greeks and the Irrational* will remember that its first two chapters establish a clear difference between the religious and moral ideas of the Homeric Age and the succeeding Archaic and Early Classical Ages—"Archaic" for short: the former was a Shame Culture, the latter a Guilt Culture. It goes without saying that the proposition is documented carefully and fully; we are concerned with it here only insofar as one branch of the argument overhangs the ground of literary criticism. When it does that, literary criticism is entitled to speak up. The position reached in the second chapter is that the Archaic Age was burdened with a sense of guilt not felt in the Heroic Age: "This haunted, oppressive atmosphere in which Aeschylus' characters move seems to us infinitely older than the clear air breathed by the men and gods of the Iliad." Everyone will agree that some such difference is apparent, whether or not it seems "older". Men were now weighed down, as they were not before (so far as we can tell), by a consciousness of dangers like the *φθόνος* (jealousy, resentment) of the gods, by Ate, the idea of inherited guilt, and the like. The evidence is abundant. In due course Aeschylus comes on the scene. To Glotz, he is "ce revenant de Mycènes" who (remarkably) was nevertheless a man of his own time. Deichgraber asserted that he "revived the world of the demons, and especially of the evil demons". Dodds, who quotes these judgments, has of course actually read Aeschylus, as distinct from using him as raw material; he therefore knows that this kind of thing is nonsense, and that Aeschylus was a man of reason. His argument is: Aeschylus did not have to "revive" the world of demons, for that was the world into which he was born; his purpose was to lead his fellow-countrymen out of it by showing, as at the end of the *Oresteia*, that it was capable of a higher interpretation.

Most of us will agree with Dodds, and with the evidence, that Aeschylus was not lost in darkness, and that the end of the *Oresteia* is one of the things that prove it. But what about his fellow-countrymen? *Ex hypothesi* they were in the dark, and the poet set himself to lead them into the light. How did he set about it?

> That such evil spirits were really feared in the Archaic Age is also attested by the words of the Messenger in the *Persae* . . . Xerxes was tempted by an "alastor or evil daemon". But Aeschylus himself knows better; as Darius' Ghost explains later, the temptation was the punishment of *hubris;* what to the partial vision of the living appears as the act of a fiend, is perceived by the wider vision of the dead to be an aspect of cosmic justice. (p. 39)

So it is also in the *Agamemnon:* "Where the poet, speaking through his Chorus, is able to detect the overmastering will of Zeus ('worker of all, cause of all') working itself out through an inexorable moral law, his characters see only a daemonic world, haunted by malignant forces". Cassandra sees the Erinyes as a band of daemons drunken with human blood, and to Clytemnestra's excited imagination they are personal fiends.

In effect, Anthropology has called upon Criticism to testify that this is what the poet is manifestly doing in his plays: creating characters who live in a mental world other than his own, and making an opportunity, here and there, of indicating to his audience that the one world is not real, and must be drastically reinterpreted. Criticism will not so testify. The student of poetic drama and the theatre will need a lot of convincing that anyone capable of writing a play at all, and wishing to say something like this, would choose, or could hope, to say it in such a way as this; or that any audience, however dedicated to theology and indifferent to poetry and action, could witness a play like the *Agamemnon*, vividly and solidly compacted of men, gods, and *daimones*, and then, in four verses, distinguish the voice of the poet himself, speaking through a chorus which hitherto has been as firmly in "the daimonic world" as everyone else in the play. No audience could possibly take the point. Similarly, it would not be reasonable procedure in a playwright to spend so much imaginative energy on inventing Cassandra's visions, on so gripping the audience that it almost sees what she is seeing, if his purpose was to persuade them, in the middle of it all, that she is seeing nothing but the unrealities of superstition.

But there is no need to argue very hard about this, because the appeal to the *Persae* fails on all counts. In the first place, the audience has no reason at all to suppose that the Ghost is going to speak with "the wider insight of the dead". Of course, it would readily accept the idea, given the hint, but Aeschylus has done the wrong thing: he has given them to understand that Darius is being evoked in the hope that he will be able to offer practical advice, some κακῶν ἄκος, "remedy for disaster" (v. 631). What is put to the audience is not some aspect of eschatology, but the very dramatic movement whereby the Ghost, instead of giving a remedy, can only prophesy even worse disaster. In the second place, what the Ghost does explain later (vv. 808 and 821) is not that the Messenger had got it all wrong, being Archaic in his thought; he is talking solely about Plataea and the punishment for hybris that will descend on the remaining Persian army. There is nothing whatever to send the minds of the audience back to Salamis and the *daimon* who was also Themistocles. What the Ghost now says is of course tantamount to an assertion that a cosmic justice will be operating, but what was said by the Messenger, and apparently understood by the Queen and the chorus (which very soon begins to sing about Zeus), is left untouched and uncorrected. Thirdly, and worst of all, if the wider vision of the Ghost is to correct the partial vision of the living Queen, it was not intelligent of Aeschylus, near the beginning of the scene, to show that the two of them are in perfect accord about *daimones;* as we have noted, the Queen says: "Some *daimon*, it seems, worked on Xerxes' mind", and the Ghost corroborates: "A mighty *daimon* that took away his judgment". Sometimes, in fact, a play will hit back.

Therefore Poiesis has to inform Anthropology that something has gone wrong. The facts of the play are not what the hypothesis predicted; they do not confirm, but disprove, that the enlightened poet was trying to wean his audience from their darkness. What has gone wrong is a question that we had better postpone until we have finished looking at the play.

We return then to the Queen and Darius. The audience has heard them agree that it was a *daimon* that impelled Xerxes to invade Europe. It next hears that a prophecy has been fulfilled: that the Empire was destined to fall, sometime. (Pericles, though unprompted by divination, said the same about another Empire: "It won't last, you know; nothing does.") Darius had been sure that it would not fall for a long time yet, but the recklessness of a young man (v. 744, *νέῳ θράσει*) has brought it about; and when a man is bent on ruin, the *theos* helps him downhill—as the career of Hitler might suggest. It was obviously to reinforce this point that Aeschylus gave Darius, presently, his historical speech. Broadhead well says (p. xxxi of his edition) that if the speech is historically inaccurate, the inaccuracy is dramatically unimportant; the point to be made is that Xerxes' predecessors, on the whole, had wisdom and brought peace and prosperity to Persia, but that he, neglecting wise counsels, has ruined everything (p. 190). The slow decay of an empire was a theme that suited Gibbon; on the stage, things have to move rather more quickly and decisively. Aeschylus did indeed have his own great interest in history and geography, but he did not write this speech merely because he liked history and did not mind being inaccurate—and those who assume that he distorted history in order to glorify Athens may be invited to explain how Athens was glorified by one considerable distortion here: for Aeschylus implicitly denies the known facts that Darius himself had sent Datis against Eretria and Athens, and at the time of his death was planning a second attack. (This matter is silently put right in the final ode.)

What dismays Darius is that his son dared to lay a yoke upon the sea: to shut in the great Bosphorus (v. 723), to control the elemental (ἱερόν) Hellespont with fetters, like a slave, to control the Bosphorus "where a *theos* flows" and to interfere with its course (vv. 745 f.). "My son is a man, but in his folly he thought to control the *theoi*, all of them, even Poseidon." By the time Herodotus wrote, Xerxes had been turned into the story-book Oriental tyrant: when a storm broke his first bridge he had the sea lashed with whips and the engineers executed. Aeschylus, even if he had heard such tales, would not have used them, having no desire to make Xerxes only a foolish monster. Nor does he mention Xerxes' other engineering exploit, the canal dug through the isthmus of Athos—out of mere ostentation, Herodotus opines, and the desire to leave a lasting memorial of himself. But it is natural to ask: if, for Aeschylus, interfering with the sea was wicked, why not interfering with the land?

Ignotus has assured us that it is now respectable to conceive that the Greek poets thought like poets; let us then do it. Aeschylus is using the Sea as a symbol of natural limits that exist and may not be defied, except at peril. Destiny, we were told earlier, had given it to Persia to be supreme on land; she has learned to venture on the sea—and Destiny seems not to have approved. We apprehend that the attempt of the Asiatic to cross the barrier of the sea and dominate Europe was against the nature of things. Hence the constant refrain, "Ships!" Aeschylus was no simple-minded enemy of all major civil engineering; the Bridge of Boats was poetically useful to him, and the Canal was not.

Now the Queen explains to Darius why "vehement Xerxes" did resolve to attack Greece: evil advisers taunted and tempted him that he, who had inherited so much wealth from his forbears, was sitting at home in cowardly fashion and doing nothing to increase it.

Aeschylus always thinks two explanations better than one. Strange, until we understand. The Queen and Darius have already agreed on a "supernatural" explanation; now the Queen gives a perfectly "natural" one—and the Ghost shows no surprise. It is exactly what we have had before: the victory of Salamis was won by the Greeks without any supernatural aid (unless Themistocles was supernaturally clever), and yet it was given them by the *theoi*. Xerxes is like Paris in the other play. We are told of him that he is one of those who are corrupted by wealth; he was not strong enough to resist temptation; like bad bronze he could not stand up to a hammering—and if Helen was as beautiful as everybody says, there was certainly nothing supernatural in the temptation. Yet the *daimon* Peitho, daughter of Ate, must needs be brought in as a second cause.

We have already seen the point of what the Ghost says next: "Never invade Greece again". The reason he gives confers no glory on Hellenes or Athenians; we understand once again that the Persians were challenging something in the nature of things. Finally, there is the climax of the whole scene: the last overthrow that Darius so thunderously prophesies and Lattimore so thunderously translates—and the prophecy is the more dramatic that the stage-audience has been given the impression that its cup of misery is already full. As an artificer of plays, Aeschylus is not always as naïve as one might think.

About the Plataea speech, let us make an interesting mistake: let us say that Aeschylus here commits the technical error of dividing our interest, just before the climax, between his central character and someone else, namely the Persian army. In the speech the army is to be destroyed by the Dorian spear, also by Zeus for its own hybris and sacrilege. For the time being, Xerxes is "lost from the mind". Of course we can come to Aeschylus' rescue by reminding ourselves that but for Xerxes the army would not have been in Greece at all; we could even surmise—if only the play were not going on meanwhile—that it was under Xerxes' orders that it had overthrown the temples. The fact remains that Aeschylus himself has not said this, and it is a little hard on an audience if it has to amend the text while the play is in progress: it might miss something that was being said. What Aeschylus ought to have done (we will say) is to represent the doomed army as yet another victim of Xerxes' ambition, cast away into destruction by *his* hybris, not its own.

Something of the kind seems to have been in the mind of an intelligent young critic (myself) who wrote, thirty years ago: "Xerxes is the sinner on whom the vengeance of Heaven falls . . . The play is the tragedy of Xerxes' sin." The statement, true or not, had a corollary, for I also wrote: "The weakness of the play is . . . the lack of a clear focal point in the action . . . There is neither a strong central character whose will or mind dominates the whole, nor is there a predominating character whose existence serves as a constant point of reference—like Hecuba, for example." I felt like Lattimore: "Who cares for Xerxes?"

It now seems that not even Aeschylus cared for him as much as we might expect; he seems to have cared more for the *theoi*—for if there is one thing that is never lost from the mind during the play it is certainly the *theos* or *theoi* and sundry attendant *daimones*. We shall certainly think the *Septem* superior to the *Persae* inasmuch as it does have its impressive central character; the point is however that our aesthetic judgment should come after, not before, our understanding of Aeschylus' *poiesis* here. We saw that Xerxes was denounced by Darius because in his bridge-building he had defied certain elemental powers, certain natural limits; he thought he could do anything. The Plataea speech does not mention Xerxes or cause us to think of him in particular, but it does represent the army as doing the same kind of thing: it thought too that it could do anything, that there are no limits. It found that it was wrong. That is to say, Aeschylus has not made the mistake of dividing our interest just before the climax; it is we who do that, by trying to be interested in the wrong thing.

For modern readers, the rest of the play is dull: that does not absolve us from looking at it with care. There are three points to consider: the strange concern shown both by the departing Ghost and by the Queen for the reception and the re-robing of the tattered King; the last choral ode; the *commos* that ends the play.

The first of these has much exercised commentators, and indeed it does seem an odd business. Some have asked if Aeschylus contrived it as a way of getting the Queen off the stage. Surely not; if we look at the way in which he gets rid of the Messenger in this play, or the Messenger in the *Septem* (v. 820), or the Herald in the *Agamemnon*, we see that he was content to let a character simply walk off.

The audience of course, not being brought up to our naturalistic theatre, will assume, unless otherwise directed, that when Xerxes arrives from Europe he will arrive into the theatre; the acting area represents Susa—not the Council House or the royal graveyard or the city gates but Susa. The only topographical indication we are given is that the royal palace is somewhere off-stage, but the Queen never says: "If my son comes first to the palace I will bring him to you"; the audience could never imagine that he might first go home for a bath and change of clothes and then come to meet his Counsellors. Therefore the scene which is vaguely suggested here is that the Queen may first return to the stage, with robes, and there meet and comfort the incoming King. Broadhead, who writes with level judgment about all this part of the play, rightly comments (p. xxi): "In spite of disaster she must at least restore appearances: her son must still be recognised as the monarch of a great empire".

We have heard something like this before: "My son, if he succeeds, will become splendid in the sight of all; if he fails—Persia cannot call him to account, *οὐχ ὑπεύθυνος πόλει* (v. 213). If he lives, he will still be her king." Now Darius tells her—his last instruction—to prepare for Xerxes *κόσμος εὐπρεπής*, "seemly raiment". As it happens, he has only a moment before said that "Zeus chastises pride; he is a stern accounter, *εὔθυνος βαρύς*". The Queen says that none of these disasters grieves her more than the dishonour of his torn dress; she will bring the raiment and comfort him. "Aeschylus", we say, "is portraying Atossa as the loyal and loving mother". But he is not making her say these things to show that she is the mother; rather does he make her the loving mother in order that she may say these things. (We are always ready to say that Greek Tragedy is religious drama, and then think of it as being entirely secular.) Broadhead remarks, in passing: "Of course, regal trappings meant little to a Greek". True; but in Aeschylus' plays there is evidence enough that his audiences could respond naturally enough to the significance of robes and the like. In short, the audience here is being led to expect, or half-expect, the spectacular rehabilitation of Xerxes in both the metaphorical and the literal sense.

It does not happen. We cannot tell how far Aeschylus went in realism, but he certainly arrives in what represented rags; for him, there are no royal robes and no words of comfort; only reproaches and his own confession of guilt and shame. As Broadhead says, in the final scene the harvest which hybris reached (v. 822) is made visible in the person of Xerxes. Perhaps the connection between the end of the Darius scene and the *commos* is not so loose as some scholars have found it. Certainly Aeschylus was not racking his brains wondering how on earth to get Atossa off the stage.

Finally, what does one have to say about the intervening ode? It is largely a catalogue of names. Prompted by Lattimore, we can see that it corresponds to the earlier one which "makes resonant and realistic and saves from abstraction the *idea* of the bulk, wealth, and population of the Persian Empire", for it is a long list of Greek islands or cities that were won by Darius, the prudent king, and have now been lost. We may be sure that the names would be heard with deep emotion by any Greeks who had been on the right side in the war, but the emotion is very far from "undirected": it is directed, firmly, by the contrast we have recently had before our eyes and ears: the contrast between a prudent king, successor to a race of prudent kings, and a reckless one who could not rest content with what he had and with his father's instruction to seek no more (v. 783). But if then our minds were taken up with the poet's historical inaccuracies, naturally we shall not now understand what he is saying now. What the last two verses of the ode say is not very clear, but is something like: "But now we are enduring the complete reversal of this at the hands of the *theos*, smitten as we are by great blows inflicted on the sea". Since this is the way in which Aeschylus was thinking, it is no wonder that he carefully avoided mentioning that most of the Greek ships were in fact Athenian.

At last we have finished our scrutiny of the *poiesis;* we have taken what is, I hope, an objective look not only at the foundations but also at the structure. Now we can ask our question again: how intelligent were the Athenians?

The interpretation confidently put forward by Ignotus and others we find to be impossible: Aeschylus was not laying before his audience patriotic and emotional stuff redeemed by fine poetry. We can, theoretically, strip away the poetry and leave only the skeleton; the skeleton alone firmly says No to this. What then can we deduce? We must be careful not to deduce too much. For example, we cannot say that the Athenian audience would in no case have relished a play on its recent war which indulged in propaganda, rhodomontade, and emotionalism. A crowd, after all, is a crowd. We may have our opinions about this; we might reflect on what more than one archaeologist has said, that really vulgar objects are rarely found in Attica, or indeed in Greece. All we have proved is that Aeschylus did take this popular subject (as we may call it), and did present it to the crowd in this way, with no concessions to passions or stupidity; and we are justified in assuming that the crowd, on the whole, was capable of responding—for if Aeschylus did not know his audience by this time, he was never likely to. Although we can never prove that it might not have responded also to something inferior, we can at least be fairly certain that it could respond to this.

So much for its spirit; now for its intelligence—and here we come back to the conflict of evidence between Anthropology and her cousin Poiesis.

In the earlier part of this chapter we saw that the doctrine of a backward and confused Aeschylus, improbable from the start, proves to be impossible when brought to the test. Since then we have encountered the more promising idea that Aeschylus himself was a man of reason, and was trying to lead his audience out of its unreason. That theory appealed to the text of this play, and we saw that the appeal was rejected. The remaining possibility is clear, and we will briefly argue that there is no cause for dismay.

Let us first take this point. Those many critics who have never been deluded by the idea that Aeschylus was being patriotic have said that he was presenting a moral truth: the gods resent and punish human presumption. He obviously was; the text, to say nothing of the *poiesis*, makes that clear. If now the complaint is made that the doctrine contains nothing new but is as old as the hills, the answer is obvious: men still find refreshment in looking at hills. Therefore we can say at once that Aeschylus was paying his audience no small compliment—Greek meeting Greek—in taking for his subject the agonising, tumultuous, and eventually glorious experience from which they had just emerged triumphant, in lifting it above the dust and heat of battle and of politics, especially of Greek international politics, inviting them to consider it as an embodiment of an eternal truth.

Yet this moral interpretation, which accords so closely with our ideas of religion, does not accompany the dramatic facts all the way. The play sets forth not only what the gods do, not only the moral lesson; it also, without any fuss, sets forth the way in which they do it. What we call, separately, "natural" and "divine" causes are interwoven throughout; they range from the most matter-of-fact to the purely religious—or impurely religious, as Plato might have said, objecting rightly, from his point of view, to a god who deceives, but wrongly from that of Aeschylus. Nowhere is the interweaving more clear than in the treatment of Themistocles' stratagem: only by inventing sophisticated arguments and by treating the text, here and there, according to our own convenience, can we escape the conclusion that it must have made immediate sense to the audience. May we ourselves be mildly poetic about it, and suggest: "Xerxes' gullibility was the Nemesis of his overweening self-confidence"?

In this there is nothing un-Athenian. I have already cited the end of the *Antigone*, where Sophocles informs us that the angry gods and their Erinyes are going to do things which, on his own evidence, happen in the natural course. His *Electra* we may regard either as fine naturalistic drama wrapped up in piety, though a piety for which we have to find excuses (for gods ought not to smile upon matricide), or as a unity, in which we see not only that Dike the daughter of Zeus works, but also how she works. If it is objected that these plays were written later, when the Athenians had nearly come to their senses, I reply that no evidence has been adduced from the plays to show that Sophocles was so much more intelligent than Aeschylus, or conversely that he too was trying to draw his audiences gently towards the light; and if that does not work, we will go back to the *Choephori*, and remark again that there too what Apollo commands is, on the evidence of Orestes himself, exactly what he would have had to do in any case.

All the evidence points to this, that Aeschylus was talking a language, using religious imagery, which his audience would understand. Not of course that his mixed audience of farmers, gentlemen, artisans, and men of boats were in such matters on his mental level. A man does not become one of the two or three great dramatists of the world without being exceptional. The point is that he and his audiences were on common ground, although the poet could dig there more deeply than most and much more deeply than some. It is what we should expect; it is the normal relationship subsisting between artist and audience in an age when the arts are of common interest and not the pleasure of a few. On this point an interesting observation is made by Professor B. A. Wright in his recent book *Milton's Paradise Lost* (p. 44). Milton's famous heterodoxies, Wright says, are confined to his treatise *De Doctrina Christiana*. The theology of the poem is "entirely catholic doctrine, using 'catholic' in its proper sense". In the poem "there is nothing that need offend the orthodox Christian; as a poet Milton had the sense to be judicious in this respect". It is certainly what we should expect of a poet who conceived himself to be addressing the generality of men; similarly, when the evidence is that the popular Athenian dramatist presumed on being understood without exposition, mouthpiece, or ventriloquism, it is what we should expect.

We have had to point out, once or twice, that what we sometimes call the "supernatural" is, in the plays, regularly natural. It does not follow from this that Greeks, or Athenians, of the Early Classical Age were free of sheer superstition: unusual people if they were. (Still less does it follow that they were not aware of, and subject to, experiences which are properly called Irrational, since they are beyond the reach and control of reason. This is an entirely different matter.) Poiesis had to tell Anthropology that something had gone wrong somewhere. One possible source of error is the assumption that the presence, in a given period, of some unreason proves the absence of all reason. In ordinary life we rarely meet such absolutes. Another possible source, especially when some of the evidence comes from poetry or another of the arts, is that we may take literally what was felt imaginatively.

We have been concerned a little with Themistocles in his capacity of *daimon* or *alastor;* let us then continue our argument by considering him for a moment in his other capacity of theologian.

Those who know Herodotus will recall the charming story that he tells, in VIII 111, of Themistocles' dealings with Andros. Soon after the battle of Salamis the allied Greeks were raising contributions for continuing the war. The Andrians refused, and Themistocles blockaded the island. He told them that the Athenians had brought with them two very powerful *theoi*, Peitho (Persuasion, this time) and Ananke (Compulsion). The Andrians replied: No wonder the Athenians were rich and powerful, having at their disposal such convenient *theoi;* they themselves however were badly off in their wretched island, and had two *theoi* who liked it so well that they had taken up permanent residence: Penia (Poverty) and Amechania (Incapacity). Being under the control of these *theoi* they were not going to pay, since the power of the Athenians was at no time superior to their own powerlessness. Perhaps we should assume that Herodotus was not quoting the authentic text of the diplomatic exchange, but the wit who invented it—presumably not long after the event—would have been puzzled at the dictum: "We must be on our guard against the temptation to believe that (Aeschylus') gods and demons are represented as being laws or forces of a spiritual kind". These four *theoi* are perhaps not spiritual, but they are not Demons—except perhaps Poverty (who, as we now know, is daughter of Income Tax). It is indeed strange that these four should be among the *theoi*, like Sappho's Immortal Aphrodite on her richly-worked throne, but so it is; and according to Aeschylus even Aphrodite makes the crops grow. Professor W. K. C. Guthrie does well to warn us, in his *Greek Philosophers* (p. 3) that in spite of what we owe to Greek culture "the Greeks remain in many respects a remarkably *foreign* people". The Iconoclast emperors of a thousand years later, coming from the Taurus Mountains, found them foreign, and nearly smashed the empire in trying to smash the Greek images, which they confused with sheer superstition; a fact which may remind us that England too had her Iconoclasts under the Commonwealth, high-minded Men of the Book, whom we now think of as fanatics, imaginatively underprivileged. The line that separates reason from unreason does not always coincide with that which separates prose from poetry. The "haunted, oppressive atmosphere" may not have been as bewildered as we suppose. If it was not, we can more easily understand why the gay and charming late-sixth-century Maidens in the Acropolis Museum, or the intelligent-looking Ephebi, should appear to be so unconscious of being haunted; for it never did seem a likely hypothesis that the dark cloud brooded only over the Theatre of Dionysus at the foot of the Acropolis, leaving the summit in sunshine.

Pursuing this line of argument a little further, we might briefly consider, side-by-side, the Athenian poets and the Ionian philosophers, for here is another hypothesis which does not nimbly and sweetly recommend itself unto our gentle senses, namely that the one city in Greece which at the time was making the most spectacular progress in several directions was mentally retarded, in comparison with Ionia. Is it not possible that something has gone wrong here too?

Fifty years ago, when test-tubes and evolution were all the rage, it was natural that the young student of Greek should be given a somewhat theatrical picture of what happened in Ionia. After some centuries of legend and poetry, played in a diffused light and with music, a brilliant spotlight was suddenly thrown upon Miletus: one saw Thales predicting eclipses and Anaximander and Anaximenes being brilliant and profound (as of course they were); the Atomic Theory itself was only just round the corner. At one stride the Greeks had reached manhood; Greek Thought had begun. It was very exciting, but not quite true. For one thing, Greek thought, in one form or another, had been going on for quite a long time. For another, the Milesians, as one discovered later, had not fully emancipated themselves from "the divine"; they had not fully realised that the gods belong to religion and that Natural Philosophy deals with a godless and material universe. According to Aristotle, Thales declared that "Everything is full of gods", and his immediate successors called their postulated primary substance *theion*, presumably because it was eternal and alive—which, as Guthrie observes (p. 33), made it unnecessary to enquire what makes it move.

At this point it may be interesting to notice a slight difficulty into which Burnet fell. In his *Early Greek Philosophy* he called this "the non-religious use of the word *god*" (p. 14); and then (p. 80) sought to confine it to Ionia: "The spirit of the Ionians in Asia was, as we have seen, thoroughly secular; and so far as we can judge the Milesians wholly ignored traditional beliefs". But such a distinction between the religious and the secular is surely an anachronism. Burnet has to argue that Ionia was "secular" because the migration had cut loose the Ionian Greeks from their religious traditions, and that the Aegean islands were, in contrast, thoroughly religious because there the traditions had not been interrupted. But did the Greeks of Ionia not have their "religious" observances, and was the mainlander Hesiod being typically Ionian (because his father had come from Cyme in Aeolis) when, as Burnet says (p. 14) he speaks of "*theoi* who were never worshipped by anyone" and "are mere personifications of natural phenomena, or even of human passions"? The *daimon* who took away Xerxes' judgment, the *theos* who flows in the Bosphorus, appears to have had respectably ancient and not insane ancestry.

Certainly, philosophers are different from ordinary folk, but these early philosophers, having no technical vocabulary, must have derived their language from current speech; and in any case they presumably wished to be understood, except perhaps Heracleitus the Obscure; so that when we find them using the words *theos* and *theion* as they did, we can be fairly sure that it was at most only a natural and intelligible expansion of ordinary language. Our word "religious" has indeed a lot to answer for.

So far, then, the Milesians and the Athenian poets are on common ground: for each, the universe is *theion*, full of *theoi*. As we have seen, Aeschylus draws no line between the "divine" and the "natural" causes of the Persian catastrophe, or between the "divine" and the "natural" temptations that overcame Xerxes and Paris; nor did he feel the need to explain any of this to his audiences. And when an ancient *theos* the Erinys made Achilles' horse stop talking, was the phenomenon religious or non-religious?

The decisive difference between the innovating Milesians and the Athenian poets, who also could think, is that the Milesians gave their undivided attention to that aspect of the "divine" cosmos which is of no immediate concern to us as human beings, while the Athenians pondered its human, moral, political aspects. The Milesians were, as we say, disinterested; it was the basis of their whole achievement. They were disinterested as is the pure scientist today. We need not rehearse the geographical and other reasons which help to explain why this should have happened in Ionia and not on the Greek mainland, but we may note that the Ionian poets too did something similar; for while Aeschylus, Pindar, and their like were contemplating the conditions of human life, man and the *theoi*, the Ionian poets were concerned rather each with the world of which he himself was the centre; they were individualists, not communal poets. We may note another fact. Not long after the time of Aeschylus another Greek of undeniable intelligence and seriousness, having given much attention to what the Ionians were doing, said in effect: "But this kind of thing, you know, is not really *important*", and this man, Socrates, was also an Athenian. It is true that Socrates was not satisfied with the Athenian poets either (according to Plato), but that is another matter, and we need not discuss it here. The point that now concerns us is that Athens, for whatever reason, continued to think about Man, leaving it to Ionia and to Ionian émigrés in Italy to explore other reaches of the universe—as indeed later she was content to leave it to Alexandria.

This, in itself, is not a sign of unintelligence, though a highly scientific age may think so, until it thinks twice. There is a corollary.

The Milesians threw overboard the traditional anthropomorphism of the Greeks: we often take this as a sign of their higher intelligence. We delude ourselves. All it means is that they were doing things for which the necessary medium was prose. In parallel fashion, mathematicians today have almost stopped using prose and write instead in mathematical symbols. This indeed reflects an advance in mathematical thinking; it does not mean that those of us who still use prose are backward. It would indeed simplify life if it were true that all prose is more intelligent than all poetry, and that poetry rich in imagery is less intelligent than poetry that approximates to prose. Since this is not true, if we wish to compare a given prose-writer with a given poet, we are put to the necessity of evaluating what each is saying, in his own medium. The medium alone tells us nothing. The Milesians and the Athenian poets were addressing themselves to very different problems. They were also addressing very different audiences: the former, any individuals who chose to be interested; the latter, their fellow-citizens assembled in one place on a solemn occasion. This entirely accounts for the fact that the former did not, and the latter did, use anthropomorphic terms: *now* we can start to think about them. The short cut that we are inclined to make is seductive but illogical, and it only leads to bewilderment when we find Aeschylus saying things—as about Zeus in the *Heliades* and about Aphrodite in the *Danaides*—which an anthropomorphist has no business to think, much less to say. But the Ionians and the Athenians did not inhabit different worlds, divided from each other by a chasm like the one which only Satan, of all the Devils, could traverse in *Paradise Lost*. In these two passages, Aeschylus is not very far from Ionia, and when Heracleitus imagines the Erinys to be keeping an eye on the Sun's orbit, he is not far from Athens and Aeschylus. Guessing about "influences" is a waste of time; they were all intelligent Greeks.

Therefore there is certainly no extraneous reason for trying to escape from the evidence given us in such abundance by the *Persae* (and the other plays), and for asserting either that the Athenian poets were incapable of coherent thought or that their audiences were incapable of following it—even though the generality of people then, as so often, might also be capable of superstition. All we have to do is to believe what we ourselves say when we call Aeschylus a great dramatist, and to conceive it likely that at a time and place where the other artists were notably intelligent, serious, and competent, the dramatists were not unintelligent and incompetent. Examination of their work will show if they composed coherently or not—if we are willing to examine their work on its own terms, and to keep our own certainties and expectations in abeyance. They thought they were poets and dramatists; the Athenians thought the same: it is only as such that they will be properly understood by us. If the process of understanding has not always, apparently, been an easy one, a possible explanation has recently been put in plain language by the scholar who wrote:

> Since the academic mind most frequently works, by training no less than temperament, according to the principles of a purely prosaic logic, it tends to assume a similar mental process in ancient poets.

I would myself have hesitated to be so blunt. The scholar from whom I quote is Ignotus.

III

The *Odyssey*

It would be reasonable to go straight from Aeschylus to Sophocles, but some writers are not entirely reasonable. If first we go backwards, to Homer and the *Odyssey*, we shall, for one thing, have a change of scenery, which may be some relief, and for another thing we shall see that poiesis is by no means a matter of dramatic composition only—a point that was very clear to my distinguished predecessor in this field, the Stagirite.

There are two Homeric questions. There is the one first asked by Lachmann and eagerly debated ever since: one Homer, or two, or a multitude? The other is: What are the poems about? How did Homer think? We can consider the poems either as historic monuments (which they are), or as poems (which they are). I admit that the two questions are not entirely separable. It is indeed possible to examine some purely archaeological, philological, or historical aspects of the poems without considering their poetic qualities at all, but, ideally, one cannot do the converse. If this chapter takes very little notice of the more famous Homeric Question, the reason is that it is concerned with the *Odyssey*, as a poem, from a particular point of view: we shall be using it as a means of testing Aristotle's assertion that structure, "the disposition of the material", is all-important. We will test it by performing a kind of experiment. I choose the *Odyssey* rather than the *Iliad* because its structure is more taut, and it is more taut because the *Iliad*—notably in the Catalogue of the Ships—incorporates much more quasi-historical material. If the same poet wrote both poems, on which question I need express no opinion here, he was much more conscious in the *Iliad* of having a function additional to that of being a profoundly tragic epic poet.

For the purposes of this chapter I shall assume what is in any case obvious, that some major poet gave to the *Odyssey* what is substantially its present shape. Book XI may be a later addition; I can afford to express no opinion, because the present argument would not be affected; still less would minor interpolations affect it. Other suspected passages will be considered as they turn up.

It is traditional to say that the structure of the poem is one of the surest signs of the poet's genius. The raw material of which it is composed is abundant and diverse, far flung both in time and space, yet it is organised by Homer into a plot of the utmost clarity and simplicity, so that the action occupies only thirty-seven days. Is this not a masterstroke? Certainly—but let us not suppose that when we say this we are saying anything of great importance. The plot is an example of poiesis on the grand scale, and poiesis has to do with more than literary skill: it has something to do with mind and thought. To illustrate the point I have composed and here present the plot of a new *Odyssey*. It uses the same material as Homer's (or as nearly as makes no difference), but disposes it in an entirely different way. The reader is asked to imagine my plot to be realised in a poem by a poet not inferior to Homer: by a poet, I mean, with all of Homer's humanity, vividness, power, with all of Homer's delight in everything that he sees or imagines in the world about him, whether wicked pirates, faithful servants, enterprising traders, or wine-dark seas in fair weather or tempest, or gentlefolk enjoying their games, or a beggar scrounging at a rich man's gate; whether impossible marvels like Circe, the horrible Laestrygonians, the lawless

Cyclops, or nearly possible ones like Nausicaa and her god-fearing relatives. If the reader will do this, then two questions will follow. The first: if the great Homer had used my plot, should we not now be saying about it exactly what we say about his, that it shows literary genius? The second: what happens now to the innocent idea that the Greek dramatists merely dramatised Saga, since we shall have here precisely the same saga-material set forth in utterly different ways, and meaning (as we shall see) utterly different things in con sequence?

For yet another reason I have undertaken this enterprise. By different men at different times grave faults have been found in the *Odyssey*, and variously explained: from my alternative poem it will become clear, I hope, that the faults should be imputed not to Homer but to the critics, for they have assumed without question that Homer was trying to do one thing, and in some respects doing it not very well (unless an interpolator can be blamed), when in fact he was trying to do something rather different, something that lay outside their personal experience of literature; and that instead of trying to enlarge their own experience by studying Homer's poiesis and drawing the obvious inferences from it, they found it more natural, and certainly easier, to blame the poet.

Let us first review some of these criticisms, beginning, as is right and proper, with that excellent early-modern critic Longinus—for Longinus, after all, was separated from Homer by about a thousand years, and in social structure and habits of thought the Roman Empire was as alien from the Homeric age as our own is. In his impressive comparison of the *Odyssey* with the *Iliad* Longinus writes like this:

> The *Odyssey* shows that when a great genius is in decline, a special mark of old age is the love of telling stories. The *Odyssey* is Homer's later poem, an epilogue to the *Iliad*. The *Iliad*, written when Homer's inspiration was at its height, is full of action and conflict; the *Odyssey* for the most part consists of narrative, the characteristic of old age. It is the sunset of Homer: the grandeur remains, but not the intensity.

You seem to see the ebb and flow of greatness, a fancy that roams through the fabulous and the incredible; it is as if the Ocean were withdrawing into itself, leaving its bed here and there high and dry. I have not forgotten the tempests of the *Odyssey*, the story of the Cyclops, and the like; if I speak of old age, it is nevertheless the old age of Homer. Yet throughout the poem as a whole, the fabulous prevails over the real. Genius, when it has passed its prime, can sink into absurdity—for example, the incident of the wine-skin, of a hero on a wreck for ten days without food, of the incredible slaying of the Suitors. Another sign of old age is fondness for the delineation of manners; for such are the details that Homer gives, with an eye for description, of life in the house of Odysseus; they form, as it were, a Comedy of Manners (κωμῳδία ἠθολογουμένη).

Longinus, then, found that the *Odyssey* lacks the grandeur and intensity of the *Iliad*—and few will quarrel with him for that—but his criticism fails; it illuminates Longinus, but not Homer. It fails because he comes to the poem with a specific demand, namely that it should display epic sublimity, and when he finds that it does not do this, instead of asking whether it meets different demands he finds a less laborious explanation: Homer, when he came to write the *Odyssey*, was quite an old gentleman, past his best, a bit garrulous, φιλόμυθος, interested now in quiet things like the delineation of character and manners. It is of course an impressive passage, but the criticism is of that unconstructive kind that is content with negatives: "Aeschylus was not so clever as Sophocles in constructing plots"; "Thucydides had no idea of the importance of economic affairs"; "the slaying of the Suitors is incredible".

From this springboard I jump to a modern critic of the poem—a scientist, once a colleague of my own, therefore an intelligent and civilised man. He read the *Odyssey*, in E. V. Rieu's translation, and told me how much he had enjoyed it: so vivid and entrancing a story. But he, like Longinus, boggled at the slaying of the Suitors, though not for the same reason. What was merely incredible—the wine-skin and suchlike, he, being a scientist, could take in his stride; what worried him was the gods, especially Athena, popping up from time to time to make things easier for Odysseus, particularly in the fight with the Suitors, stealing the hero's thunder, "making him look half a fool".

This critic, like Longinus, was looking at the poem, naturally, from his own point of view, and that was something like this: "In the poem I find things familiar to me. There is a hero in distress. He has one ambition, to get home. He meets difficulties of all kinds, but being bold, resourceful, and courageous he surmounts them. Some of the incidents are marvellous, but *that* does not upset me. He does get back home, is confronted with a final test, passes it triumphantly, and all is well. It is that familiar thing, an adventure story, and it is supremely well told. Incidents like those of Circe or the Cyclops confirm my diagnosis. But in a tale of this kind, gods are a nuisance—at least, gods who pull the strings for the hero at a crisis."

And what do we say in reply? Useless to talk to a scientist about "the epic tradition of divine machinery". He would be quick to point out that this only says again, in different words, that Homer used gods even when they are a nuisance to his story; and he might well ask if the Greeks were such that the greatest of their poets lacked the courage or the originality to throw overboard a tradition when it was cramping and cumbrous.

Then there is Telemachus' journey to Sparta. It is an attractive episode, and, as Aristotle wisely said, the epic form is hospitable to such—but does it *do* anything for us, and for the poem, other than decorate it, at rather undue length? Because when at last Telemachus does return, the little news that he has been able to pick up is already out of date, since Homer contrives that Odysseus should get home first. Naturally, it has been suggested that this part of the *Odyssey* was originally a separate lay, having Telemachus for its hero. Very well; but whose idea was it to bring it into the *Odyssey?* It may indeed be a law of nature that an interpolator is a fool as well as a nuisance, but if the interpolation is so obviously useless, why ever did it remain in the poem? In fact, as Delabecque has shown, in his *Télémaque et la structure de l'Odyssée*, the episode is so carefully worked into the main fabric, with so many deft links, that if Homer did not himself compose it (which he may well have done), he at least adopted it, quite deliberately, and therefore with some idea in mind. What was it?

One part of the episode is even more challenging, namely the long description in Book II of the Assembly held in Ithaca, for it accomplishes practically nothing. Telemachus calls the meeting, makes a protest against the Suitors, and receives very little support; then he demands a ship, gets consent of a kind—and immediately acquires a ship by other means: through the agency of Athena. What is the point of it all? It is easy to make it sound inept; what is not so easy is to make such a degree of ineptitude sound plausible, even by invoking an interpolator.

One might also ask, about the whole theme of the Suitors, if it is not a little bourgeois. That young gallants should riot in the house of an absent man, waste his substance and persecute his wife (or widow), is deplorable conduct indeed, but is it of epic dignity, worthy of being set alongside the tragic theme of Achilles' wrath? Longinus evidently thought not; to him it was only Comedy of Manners.

Then, naturally, there is the ending of the poem. (I say "naturally" because the Greeks were notoriously bad at endings: the *Iliad*, *Odyssey*, *Antigone*, *Ajax*, *Trachiniae*, *Medea:* an impressive list.) There is some consensus of opinion that Homer ended his poem at XXIII 296, where Odysseus and Penelope are reunited and Athena prolongs the night for their comfort and joy. The poem we have goes past this point to what Myres called "a poor, drivelling, misbegotten end": the friends of the slain Suitors (as Myres put it) prepare to take vengeance on Odysseus and his party; these in turn arm themselves with zest, so that old Laertes cries out in delight: "Dear gods! What a day is this to warm my heart! My son and grandson are competing in valour". But Athena intervenes with a great cry to make them all drop their weapons and conclude a peace—and Myres, himself the gallant commander of a gunboat in the First World War, is bitterly disappointed, and refuses to debit an ending like this to Homer.

Here, then, are some features of the poem which, from time to time, have been found weak, puzzling, or spurious. We will put them into cold storage for a short time while we contemplate Homer's *σύστασις τῶν πραγμάτων*; then we will take them out for a second look.

The immense variety and amplitude of Homer's raw material need not be expounded in detail. There are, to begin with, the many and various echoes of the Trojan War: the Wooden Horse; the calamitous return of Agamemnon; Menelaus' wanderings, and his return, with Helen; Helen herself, living in royal splendour at Sparta; Nestor, Achilles, Ajax, and other heroes among the shades (if Book XI is genuine). Then there are the many fabulous marvels with which the imagination of the Greeks and others had filled the unknown reaches of the sea—some of them immemorial folk-tales. There are the many vivid sketches taken from contemporary life—pirates, beggars, and the rest. It is God's plenty, and all is set down with the greatest possible enthusiasm and solidity. If in other respects the poem were a complete mess, with all this material loosely stuffed into sacks, it would still give inexhaustible pleasure.

But upon all this profusion Homer has imposed a form which is clarity itself. The masterstroke, as Horace pointed out, was the decision to begin *in medias res*—in fact, near the end, with Odysseus, already for seven years a prisoner, now on the point of being set free. This, the starting-point, is made clear with great brevity; very cunningly Homer keeps back the story of Odysseus' wanderings, those past and those to come, so that we may have them in unbroken sequence. For the tale of the past wanderings he contrives the perfect setting: it is told by the suffering hero himself, and to an audience that has dined well, has been enormously impressed by the stranger's prowess at games, and is prepared to listen, if need be, all night. This half of the material is enfolded within the other half—all that concerns Ithaca and Telemachus: after his brief proem, Homer begins where he is going to end, in Ithaca. The poem is made to circle round itself, like a snake; or, since there are those who do not much care for snakes, let us say rather that Homer designed his poem in what musicians call ternary form, A—B—A: Ithaca, with the son seeking news of his father—the whole story of Odysseus' wanderings—Ithaca, and the triumph of father and son. (Current attempts to explain Homer's form as a reflection of the sculptured pediment, or of geometric art, exercise the fancy rather than nourish the understanding. A poem exists in time, the visual arts in space. I cannot see what point there can be in saying that a Town Hall is in the form of a sonnet, or a limerick in the form of a petrol station. I know that Erik Satie composed *Trois Morceaux en forme d'une poire*, but that was intended to be amusing. What there is in common between the sense of form of Homer and of his contemporary painters and designers must be sought at a deeper level than this.)

We say that one sign of Homer's literary skill is that on such varied material he was able to impose a form so simple—but we need to be careful. Both Plato and Aristotle, as it happens, compare a work of art to a *ζῷον*, a living creature, complete and purposeful in every detail. It may be that their metaphor commends itself; but our talk of "imposing" a form suggests the carpenter rather than the creator. I think that it could be argued (though I would not care to undertake it) that this ternary form of Homer's already implies something, vague though it may be, about his mind and habit of thought; I do not believe that he selected this out of several possible forms merely by the exercise of literary judgment. The form itself implies too much. Perhaps the point will be made clear from my alternative *Odyssey*, which I now submit to the reader's admiration.

My poem begins at Troy. The war has just ended. Odysseus

and his men load rich booty into their little fleet, and they set sail, after so many years, for Ithaca. Odysseus, in one mood, rejoices at the prospect of seeing wife and son again; in another, he wonders anxiously if he still has a wife and son. Yet they are quite willing to do a little piracy on the way, so that (as in Homer's narrative) they raid the Cicones: they gain some plunder, though some of the men are lost; the others sail on, glad at heart at their escape, but lamenting the loss of their dear companions. The other incidents happen one by one, as in Homer, caused whether by the gods, or by the folly of Odysseus' men. So, little by little, the glory slips away, the bright hopes fade; what was at first eager expectation slowly turns to despair. This downward movement continues implacably until Odysseus alone is left, the sole survivor of the fleet, cast ashore on Calypso's island.

Here is the nadir of his fortunes. He is a prisoner, aching to get home—and it is a capital point that neither Odysseus nor the reader knows if he still has a wife and home to return to. But at last the tide turns; the gods resolve that Calypso must let him go to take his chance. Now the long downward movement is answered by a vigorous upward movement. Odysseus battles hard, but—alas!—again he is shipwrecked. Will he again fall victim to a beautiful but baleful goddess—or even worse? No! This island is inhabited by the kind and god-fearing Phaeacians. They cannot indeed tell Odysseus—or us—anything about Ithaca, Penelope, and Telemachus, but at least they know where Ithaca is. So, after proper entertainment, they send him there, and he is home at last.

It is at this point that the constructive skill of the present poet becomes most evident. We have climbed back, roughly speaking, to the emotional level on which the poem began: Odysseus had left Troy for Ithaca; now he is in Ithaca. Being wily, as well as anxious, and remembering the trusty swineherd, he thinks it prudent to pay him a visit before going near the city. Eumaeus is still there, still trusty.—That is good!—Odysseus learns from him that Penelope and Telemachus are both alive and well.—That is very good!—But now there comes a double check. The first is the fact that Odysseus' house and property are at the mercy of a wild gang of Suitors, and that Penelope, at last, being almost persuaded that Odysseus must be dead, is on the point of choosing another husband. What is worse, Laertes has withdrawn in despair, and nobody in Ithaca shows any disposition to control the violence of these men. When these untoward facts have been properly exploited by the poet, Eumaeus gives the rest of his grave news. It is barely a month since Telemachus—so gallant a young man, so like his father—left Ithaca for Pylos, Sparta, goodness knows where, in search of news about his father; and not only that: the Suitors have laid an ambush for him, to murder him on his way home—if indeed he does find the homeward path from that treacherous sea that Odysseus himself knows so well. It is a bitterly ironical turn of circumstance, that as soon as the wandering hero returns in safety, it becomes a question whether his son can ever return.

When our second Homer has had the time to make the most of this unlucky situation, he may bring back Telemachus in safety—by all means with the help of Athena, provided that Athena has not spoiled the story by declaring in advance that this is what she is going to do. Father and son are now reunited, and at last the dramatic rhythm of the whole poem gathers all its force for a final upward thrust that will carry us, with barely a check, to the triumphant conclusion. The two men will gather around them a few faithful retainers; by cunning and courage they will give the Suitors what they deserve—though of course not until we have been shown how fully they deserve it—and at last the long-tried husband and wife are at peace in their own home. Here the poem ends.

Certainly I am no impartial judge, but I fail to see how this plot is intrinsically inferior to Homer's. Obviously it lacks some of the specific virtues of Homer's; for one thing, the action is not so concise. On the other hand, it has countervailing virtues: its control of dramatic rhythm strikes me as being particularly fine, especially in the double check, which—just at the right moment—infuses new and vigorous life into the plot. But if this is true, then we have not said the last word, but only the first, when we have said that Homer's ordering of the material shows literary genius. Of course it does, but something more than craftsmanship is involved in poiesis; there is more than one way of being an excellent craftsman.

As for my plot, the reader may well feel like echoing what Bentley said to Pope: "A very pretty poem, Mr Kitto, but it is not Homer." Of course we are postulating in our own poet a full command of surge and thunder, but that will not be enough; my poem will never be Homeric. What is more interesting is that my plot, from the bottom upwards, is entirely unhellenic; conceivably Hellenistic, but certainly not Hellenic. If this is true, we must ask why.

Comparing my plot with Homer's, we see at once that mine has rejected Homer's ternary form in favour of one which swings along with vigour, up or down, but always forwards. This difference, evidently, is connected with the major difference, which is emotional and mental: my poem relies throughout on suspense and surprise; Homer's does not, except in a subordinate way. When my poem begins, we lean back comfortably in our seats to hear what is going to happen to the hero. It may be almost anything, and I say *almost* anything because there is one thing that must not happen to him, namely ultimate disaster. With increasing apprehension we shall follow him on his downward path; with increasing hope on his upward path. Like him, we shall be suddenly cast down when we discover, after the excitement of his arrival in Ithaca, how desperate the situation there is; we shall ask ourselves anxiously if Odysseus has survived all these perils only for his son to be overwhelmed by worse. Then, relieved on this score, with growing excitement we shall follow their daring adventures to the final triumph. Yet all the time, deep down, we shall have felt the assurance, though sometimes a little tremulously, that surely all will come right in the end. Why? Because it always does, in romantic adventure stories—and that is precisely what I have made, out of Homer's own material: the plot of a romance, with the typical shape and movement of a romance. The reason why a disastrous ending is impossible is that it would blow this delightful world to pieces.

My plot depends on suspense, on keeping the listener in ignorance. Homer will have nothing to do with this; he is as careful to forestall surprise as I have been to create it. Naturally, in Homer's plot also Odysseus never knows what is going to happen next, nor for that matter do we, the readers; but *we* do know what is going to happen last, because Homer tells us at the beginning of Book I, and again at the beginning of Book V; and throughout the poem, but especially in the second half, the destruction of the Suitors is foreshadowed repeatedly. My poem carefully keeps back from the reader what has been happening all these years in Ithaca; it is with this that Homer begins. By way of proem he invents the scene on Olympus, with the philosophic speech from Zeus: "Men are born to trouble in any case, but they make things far worse for themselves by their own wickedness—and then blame us gods. Take Aegisthus for instance . . ." "Then what about Odysseus?", says Athena, with the result that she is given permission to see that he gets home. "We will deliberate", says Zeus, "how it shall be done." Therefore the return of Odysseus is no tremulous hope; it is a certainty.

From Olympus we go in Athena's company straight to Ithaca, and spend some long time there, enough to see with our own eyes what is going on. Odysseus of course knows nothing, but *we* do; it is not being kept back from us, as in my poem.

After going to Pylos and Sparta with Athena and Telemachus, and much enjoying the trip, for Homer is a lively poet, we return to Olympus, at the beginning of Book V. It is an old complaint, that the second Council of the Gods is only a duplication of the first. In fact, it is not. At the first council, the subject to which Zeus was addressing his unfathomable mind was Aegisthus; the case of Odysseus was raised from the floor of the house by Athena, and only an interim decision was taken; a second meeting, to deal more particularly with Odysseus, was implied, and here it is. Besides, this time Athena is more outspoken, and this time she has more to be outspoken about. At the first Council the misdeeds of the Suitors were mentioned only incidentally (I 91 f.); this time, when we have seen something of it for ourselves, Athena says more: that no one in Ithaca is giving a single thought to the excellent king who once ruled them like a wise and kind father; and, what is worse, the Suitors are now actually plotting to murder his son. "What king need practise kindness, generosity, justice, if tyranny and lawlessness go unpunished?"

A second opportunity for dramatic surprise has been thrown away. It was a powerful turn in my plot that Odysseus reaches Ithaca only to learn that Telemachus has just left it and is in peril of being murdered on his way home. Homer will have none of this: he makes Zeus instruct Athena to take care of Telemachus; therefore we know that he will be safe. My plot revels in the appeal to certain emotions—anxiety, in this case—in which Homer has little interest. Then (vv. 29 ff.) Zeus is made to announce his plan for Odysseus: he shall be set free, shall make a boat, reach Scheria, and be conveyed to Ithaca—a plan which is much better placed here than it would have been at the beginning of Book I. The second Council is no interpolation; one sometimes wonders if some of the most disruptive of Homer's critics have themselves ever read a book.

Surprise then, major surprise, is in general excluded: we already know roughly what is going to happen to Odysseus. So too is it excluded in respect of the Battle in the Hall: there is no lack of excitement in the details, but since we have been told explicitly that Athena and Zeus are helping Odysseus, the result of the fight is certain.

But is there not something familiar in this forestalling of surprise? Indeed there is: it is normal in the Greek tragic poets. Not only do they, like most tragic poets, and like Homer, use myths which in general outline were already known; they also regularly foreshadow the important event of the play. We may be taken aback by the manner or the extent of the disaster, but not by the disaster itself. In the *Agamemnon*, who is surprised by the murder of the King—who, I mean, other than the King himself? The chorus is surprised that he should be killed now, and by his wife, but retribution of some kind they distinctly feared; and as for the audience, the killing of Agamemnon, Cassandra, Clytemnestra, Aegisthus, is carefully prepared. So too is the liberation of Prometheus, the self-blinding of Oedipus, the defeat of the Persians, the downfall of Creon (in the *Antigone*), the destruction of Phaedra and Hippolytus, of the children in the *Medea*.

What are we to say about this? That the Athenians, being timid people, disliked surprises; or, being dull people, could not follow a play unless they were told the plot in advance? For at least two reasons this kind of thing will not do. One is that among the extant plays there are some that rely on surprise from beginning to end: the *Iphigeneia in Tauris* for example, the *Ion*, and *Helen*. Agathon's *Antheus* was probably of this type, since here, as Aristotle tells us, the dramatist took the trouble to invent both the plot and the characters. In the *Ion* indeed, in order to accentuate the surprise, Euripides wrote a prologue in which Hermes foreshadows a conclusion at which the play fails to arrive, evidently to increase the piquancy. The second of the two reasons is that Shakespeare too (as we shall see in a later chapter) foreshadows in much the same way, and that both Shakespeare and the Athenian dramatists foreshadow when they are composing tragedy, and avoid it when writing a less profound kind of drama.

But does this help us at all, seeing that the *Odyssey*, for all its forestalling of surprise, is not a tragedy? It may help a lot, if we will look a little further.

The reason why the tragic poets, Greek or English, discount surprise is that they are concerned with that serious aspect of human existence in which law prevails, in which offence will incur disaster, in which the very nature of things will have the last word. Thus, in the matter of the Persian War, to Aeschylus the Athenian citizen the outcome was no doubt astonishing, but to Aeschylus the tragic poet it was natural, and to indicate that it was natural he involves gods in the action (which accordingly some of us interpret to mean that it was unnatural or supernatural). This is what Homer does too; and he was thoughtful enough to assist my present argument by being quite explicit about it, in the two Councils of the Gods. In rearranging Homer's material I saw an opportunity of constructing a romantic story, one which should obey the principle implicit in plays like the *Iphigeneia:* keep the cat in the bag as long as possible; then, when the audience is quite sure that the bag is empty, produce another cat. Much has been said about the romantic colouring of the *Odyssey:* there is no need whatever to object, so long as we are clear that it is a matter of colouring only, not of structure and substance. Homer, in constructing his plot, worked from what we must surprisingly call a religious point of view. It is true that his "religion" is neither Platonic nor Strict Presbyterian (for these do have something in common: a strict theology, Elders, and No Music, only hymn-tunes); it is true that Homer allows Athena to do charming conjuring tricks, like turning herself into a swallow, and that he obviously relishes the scandalous tale of Ares and Aphrodite, neither of which would have gone down well in Geneva. But his Mediterranean mind could easily combine such things with the serious idea that the gods, collectively, prefigure something that we could call a world order, and it is within such a framework, or against such a background, that he constructs his plot. This, ultimately, is the reason why it feels so different from mine: mine implies no such background.

This does not in the least mean that Homer was preaching a doctrine or being theological, still less trying to "advance thought"; the mere fact that such a divine governance is so completely taken for granted throughout the poem shows that it was part of what Cornford called the "circumambient atmosphere", shared by poet and listeners alike. It is in fact implicit in the ternary structure: the undeserved misfortunes of Odysseus, the disorder in Ithaca, and the concern of the gods thereat, are all put fairly and squarely before us in the first few books because these are ultimately what the poem is about. Homer's is not a world in which *anything* can happen; it is one in which certain things *will* happen, even if we have to wait for a long time: of course the gods are not indifferent to lawlessness and disorder. We are bound to assume that Homer's audiences not only agreed with this but also accepted it as a natural basis for a serious poem; otherwise we should have to assume something else which is surely unlikely, that they were as much puzzled or disappointed with some aspects of the poem as some of its later readers have been.

Having considered Homer's *σύστασις τῶν πραγμάτων*, his plot, assisted, I hope, by the consideration of a very different arrangement of the same facts, we will open the refrigerator in which we left certain doubts or difficulties.

To my scientific friend, as to many others, including perhaps Longinus, the help given by Athena to Odysseus and Telemachus in the fight was matter for regret: Odysseus is the hero, and he would have been more of a hero without the divine aid that caused the Suitors' weapons to fly askew. From an unhellenic point of view, yes; from Homer's, no. From his, an Odysseus who should conquer without divine aid would be nearly meaningless; he would lack a certain seriousness, a certain public stature. What is at stake, for Homer, is rather more than the heroic triumph of his Odysseus; behind this, or rather *in* this, there is the triumph of Order over Disorder. That is something to which the gods are not indifferent; something that concerns any member of human society—which is the reason why I have just spoken of the "public" stature of the hero. Athena's help is essential to the poem. But if so, why is the heroism of Odysseus necessary? Why *both?* Briefly, because the maxim *Do it yourself* never commended itself to Olympus. "The god" did not stop Xerxes with a thunderbolt; in Aeschylus' recreation of the war, the Persians are already ruined by the courage and intelligence of the Greeks, and by certain natural causes before the god openly declares his interest by freezing the Strymon. Orestes, in the *Choephori*, is not only directly commanded by Apollo; he also has his own commanding private reasons. It is the standard conception. We should not fail to notice that at XIII 375 f., although Athena promises her help to Odysseus, she leaves it to him to devise the means. The world of these poets is not really a world of magic, even though Athena can become a bird, or appear to Telemachus as Mentes or Mentor: indeed, when she does choose to appear as one of these wise and intelligent men, it is noticeable that oftener than not what she says is no more than what he might have said; but the fact that it is Athena, not Mentes or Mentor, who says it gives to the advice a certain resonance: it matters nothing to the mechanics of the plot, but it does make the incident somewhat more than a detail in a purely personal story. Athena may have her "special means of transport", namely golden and imperishable sandals, and a "special weapon", accurately described: a great, heavy spear with a blade of sharp bronze, but not on this account does she cease to embody a perfectly clear moral idea. In the *Iliad* a god will show his, or her, power through a Diomedes or Hector—but these had power to start with; a god never magically transforms and uses a nonentity. A god could "help" such a man as Thersites only by making him, as we too might say, supernaturally ugly and vulgar. It is a poetic and vividly imagined world, but not an irrational one. The really irrational world, in which men cowered in bewilderment before discordant demons, did not arrive (as we have seen) until the fifth century—and in Athens. In Homer, men and gods are in a real sense partners, μεταίτιοι, as Aeschylus remarked, in a forgetful moment. Odysseus' victory without Athena would have been romantic and unhellenic because not significant of anything in particular, but no more unhellenic than would be Athena's without Odysseus.

We will move on to Longinus' Comedy of Manners, and to the idea that the whole theme of the Suitors falls below epic standards of dignity.

To be fair to Homer, we might first remind ourselves of a subsidiary point. In a rich country, the United States for instance, food and drink do not have the same status as in a poor country like Greece, where the gods are more grudging. Wastefulness was moral obliquity, not an economic virtue. But apart from this, in his handling of the Suitors Homer works two ideas for all he is worth, and Longinus appears to have taken neither into account. One is their moral violence, on which Homer insists more and more as the poem goes on: they are ill-mannered, wasteful, plunderers of another man's wealth, loose-living, and finally plotters of murder, and, in the case of Antinous, of usurpation. All this is brought to a climax that is by no means undramatic when Athena, taking the form of Mentor, comes to Odysseus' help in the fight. Agelaus threatens him (her): "Mentor, keep out of the way. We are going to kill these two men, the father and the son. Then we shall kill you as well; we shall confiscate your estate too, and reduce your family to beggary and shame". The fool does not know, of course, that he is talking to a goddess; even so, it is hardly Comedy of Manners.

The second idea is one that would not perhaps naturally impose itself on a critic living under the Roman Empire. As we have seen, Homer's plot, unlike mine, has a political reference, provided that we use the word "political" in its wide Greek sense. Homer of course does not make much fuss about this; as he was a Greek, composing for Greeks, there was no reason why he should; but there are several passages that do not make the degree of sense that we expect of a great poet until we realise that the political framework is present to Homer's mind, whether consciously or quite unconsciously. It does something, perhaps quite a lot, to explain his structure.

First of all, it goes without saying that Odysseus is always the good, wise, and just king, and this is more than a simple characterising of the hero. A picture of such a king is given (as it happens) by Odysseus himself, in a speech that he makes to Penelope (XIX 106 ff.), in which he represents her as the queenly counterpart. He says, in E. V. Rieu's translation:

> Your fame has reached to Heaven itself, like that of some perfect king, who rules over a populous and mighty state with the fear of the gods in his heart, and he upholds the right. Therefore the dark soil yields its wheat and barley, and the trees are laden with ripe fruit, the sheep never fail to bring forth their lambs nor the sea to provide its fish, all because of his wise government; and his people prosper under him.

We notice the same assumption—unless indeed we should say, the same imagery—as in Aeschylus: Dike, Order, is indivisible; the moral, physical and (here) economic worlds are one. So in the *Eumenides* (930 f.) Athena says of the Erinyes, as the ministers of Dike, that it is their function to order everything for mortals: *πάντα γὰρ αὗται τὰ κατ' ἀνθρώπους ἔλαχον διέπειν.* Accordingly they invoke upon Attica fruitfulness and wealth, the implied condition being (vv. 1018 ff.) that the Athenians revere the Erinyes, the defenders of Dike. The same feeling underlies the long prayer in the *Supplices* (625 ff.): because Argos has chosen to reverence Zeus Hikesios the chorus prays that the city may be free of war and pestilence, that its crops may be abundant and its cattle fertile. It pervades too Homer's description of Scheria: the people are just, generous, and god-fearing, and (or therefore?) everything is orderly and beautiful; the fruit trees bear at every time of the year. Under the government of a just king "the sheep never fail to bring forth their lambs nor the sea to provide its fish"; and such a king was Odysseus. *'Αδικία*, lawlessness, is not a moral phenomenon only.

But in Ithaca, order and government are in abeyance: this is implied throughout. For nineteen years the king has been absent; his son, at the beginning of the poem, is a mere lad, quite helpless; Laertes has given up and gone to his vineyard on the hillside (I 188 ff.); even Penelope laments that her troubles have caused her to neglect her duties toward guests, beggars, and messengers who have come on public business (XIX 133 ff.). The royal line is in danger of extinction. Antinous admits (I 386 f.) that Telemachus is the natural successor, though Eurymachus at once hints that another might be chosen; but in any case the Suitors are planning to murder him. In the end, when Eurymachus turns king's evidence, hoping to save his own life, he asserts what we can well believe, that Antinous was the ringleader, anxious not so much to marry Penelope as to make himself king (XXII 48 ff.). All this intelligibly connects itself with several notable features of the poem, and they in turn with each other.

We saw that much of the first four books can be accused of having little organic connexion with the rest of the poem, however delightful it may be in itself. But, as many have pointed out, the episode of Telemachus' journey, instigated by Athena, had an ulterior purpose, and one that Athena declares more than once, namely that Telemachus should win renown. It is the poet's way of making the helpless lad grow up; so that at the end of the poem, although it is only thirty-seven days distant counting by the calendar, he is a mere lad no longer, but a young hero, one who can stand valiantly by his father's side, his destined and worthy successor. The real point, of course, is not what happens to Telemachus as if he were a real person, but what happens to our conception of Telemachus as the poem goes on. At his first meeting with Athena, when she is Mentes, he is simply a charming, well-mannered boy. Mentes-Athena tells him that his own qualities and parentage are such that surely his house will continue to be glorious; he can say in answer only that his father is dead, his property being wasted, and he himself likely to be killed. It is Athena-Mentes who urges him to *do* something: to call an Assembly, and to undertake the journey.

During the journey, two things happen to Telemachus—that is, to our conception of Telemachus: he gains in poise, and he gains in stature. At III 21 ff., he contemplates with alarm the prospect of accosting the great Nestor, but Athena, who is now Mentor, reassures him: he has his native wit, and if that fails, the gods will inspire him. From that moment he speaks to the great with confidence and dignity. Equally important is that the great accept him instantly, both as the son of the renowned Odysseus, and on his own obvious merits. Even before the journey, but after his talk with Athena-Mentes, he spoke to Penelope with a new authority that took her aback (I 356 ff.); then he firmly told the Suitors, to their surprise, that he intended to be master in his own house, and would be willing to succeed Odysseus as king. Towards the end of IV, Penelope laments that he, a mere boy, should have gone into such danger; when we see him home again, he is much more than a boy: at XX 266 ff. and 304 ff. he speaks with great authority to the Suitors, and at XVII 45 very firmly to his mother. On each occasion, Homer tells us, his behaviour caused astonishment. We moderns know that a young gentleman should not speak like this to his mother, but how did Homer's audiences respond? With the reflection, I suspect, that under Athena's guidance Telemachus is becoming quite kingly. It is perhaps no accident that in this part of the poem Homer twice makes him improve on a course of action proposed, the one by Eumaeus and the other by Odysseus himself (XVI 146 ff. and 308 ff.).

The whole episode then, leisurely and delightful though it is, has its close relationship with the rest of the poem; but what about the abortive meeting of the Assembly? It is easy to say that it does nothing to advance the action; one can say the same of the Herald scene in the *Agamemnon*, if one has not understood the play; but in each case the episode does a great deal for the composition and the idea that is shaping it.

Anyone who is disposed to regard this part of II as an interpolation should consider two facts. It is already foreshadowed by Athena at I 272 ff., so that the two passages stand or fall together; and there is a significant repetition of the same theme at XVI 376 ff., when Antinous has just returned from his unsuccessful ambush. He is now taking Telemachus very seriously indeed, and openly warns the others that the time has come to dispose of him. He is dangerous, says Antinous; he may summon an Assembly and denounce us; we may find ourselves banished, for the people now are regarding us with disfavour—a fact for which we must, and easily can, take the speaker's own word. Here, the point is clear enough: what happens to the Suitors is so much more decisive than what Antinous feared: they are not banished, but put to death; and not by order of any Assembly, but by Odysseus himself. If Homer found some use in one passage for the idea of an Assembly, he may have found it in two. Perhaps the first is worth looking at in detail.

It is on Athena's prompting that Telemachus summons the meeting. Old Aegyptius opens the discussion: "This is the first time that we have been called together since Odysseus left for Troy. What is the reason? Is the army returning? Is an enemy approaching? Is it something that concerns the public welfare?" Such indeed it is, as we soon learn, even though at first it may seem to be only a private matter.

In response to Aegyptius Telemachus comes forward: in the names of Zeus and Themis (Right) he challenges Ithaca to protect his house from unlawful spoliation. Antinous, in answer, makes an impossible demand. Again Telemachus invokes Zeus—and at once two eagles appear in the sky and hover above the meeting. Haliserthes can read the omen: unless the Suitors give way at once, vengeance will come upon them. The next speaker, contemptuous and defiant, is Eurymachus. He does not believe in birds, nor in justice or moderation either. Finally, Telemachus demands that a ship be given him at least, in order that he may find out, if he can, whether his father is alive or dead; if dead, he will give his mother to a new husband.

Then Mentor rises; he makes a speech that may explain to us why it was his form that Athena chose to assume. He denounces, not so much the Suitors, who are indulging their wickedness (he says) at the risk of their own lives, as the rest of Ithaca, which is doing nothing to stop them. The last speaker, Leiocritus, is another of the Suitors. He defies Mentor, the rest of Ithaca, and Odysseus himself, should he return. He does however suggest that Telemachus should have a ship, though with the sneer that it will be a long time before he sails from Ithaca.

So the Assembly breaks up; and since in the event it is Athena who provides the ship, despite the Suitors, it is understandable if one or two literally-minded critics have found the whole episode a waste of their time. But we should remember that all this was written in Greek, for Greeks. There was a period in English literature too when the connexion between religion, morality, and politics was both close and obvious; it did not long survive Shakespeare, and when we today meet it in Shakespeare, as often as not we fail to see it. The fact that this Assembly accomplishes nothing is the whole point. In the first book we saw the lawless behaviour of the Suitors within the palace, with Telemachus unable to check it. What Book II does for the poem is to bring the lawlessness out of the seclusion of the palace and put it upon the public stage: it is not a Greek idea that ἀδικία, lawlessness, is a matter only of private conduct and consequence. Telemachus challenges the *polis* to deal with it, and the *polis* either cannot or will not. Aegyptius asked: "Or is it something that concerns the public welfare?" But of course it is: what was the *polis* for, if not to see justice done between man and man? But in the absence of Odysseus the King, public order has broken down; the Assembly has not even met. Zeus sends two warning eagles to signify his displeasure.

It all coheres intelligibly. In Homer's *Odyssey*, in contrast with mine, more is at stake than the return and triumph of the hero. There is the question, expressly raised by Athena, if the gods are content that disorder should prevail unchecked; there is the constant picture of Odysseus as the good king, and for that matter of Penelope as the virtuous queen, contrasted so often with Clytemnestra; there is the moral disorder in the palace; there is its counterpart, the breakdown of public justice in Ithaca, both crying out for the return of the King and the reassertion of authority. It was this wide frame of reference that made the ternary form inevitable: at the outset Homer needed to show us what is at stake.

All this, as it seems to me, makes quite impossible the idea, accepted by several scholars, that Homer's poem ended at XXIII 296, with the reunion of Odysseus and Penelope. The reason why this is impossible is that it would be the perfect ending for my *Odyssey*, and if it is right for mine, it must be wrong for Homer's. Certainly, before we can feel sure that the whole of Book XXIV is Homer's work there is much philological and other evidence to consider, but if Homer did not compose it as it stands, the composer was surely working on Homer's own foundations. It is not merely that the idea of counter-vengeance has been raised twice already, once by Odysseus to Athena (XX 36 f.) and once by Odysseus to Telemachus (XXIII 117 ff.): obviously, an interpolator of XXIV could be clever enough to interpolate these passages too, by way of preparation. One could indeed maintain, rightly, that a counter-vengeance, or something like it, is implied in what Antinous said in his remark (quoted above) about a possible meeting of the Assembly; but the major point is that the existence and the well-being of the body politic is implied throughout the poem—implied rather than insisted on, for why should Homer insist upon something that any Greek audience would take for granted? As Telemachus brought his private wrongs upon the public stage, to be recognised by Mentor, not to mention Zeus, as a grave public matter, so it is natural, even inevitable, that Odysseus' personal reassertion of justice, within his own house, should have its public counterpart. The palace may have been purified by sulphur, but Ithaca too needs something of a purification—at least, a reassertion of authority and order. In any case, no Greek audience could think that the tale had reached its conclusion in a bedroom, when over a hundred young men of Ithaca were lying dead just outside the house. The old Laertes is, surely, using words that Homer wrote for him, when he cries: "Dear gods! What a day to warm my heart! My son and grandson are competing in valour." The King, so long absent, has had his just vengeance, and is ready, with his son, to quell counter-vengeance. But the end is to be conciliation and peace, and it will be strange if Athena is not there to bring it about.

But it may be said: "This is all very well, but among these philosophic generalities where does Nausicaa come in, and the horrible Laestrygonians, Argus the faithful hound, and all the rest? What do they contribute to a supposed theme of order prevailing over disorder?"

So far as I can see, nothing at all—but the question is misconceived. It is understandable if a modern reader should resist, almost instinctively, the attribution of serious thought about the universe to Homer, even to the tragic poets, except perhaps Euripides. These men, we think (rightly) were poets; they were essentially imaginative, creative; we must enjoy them, quite simply, for what they were, not look into their work for what is not there. Hence my own question: But what about Nausicaa? However, the facts are, as it seems to me, decisive; if we feel a difficulty, the explanation is straightforward: we are unconsciously transferring to a different age assumptions based on our own. We ourselves have had no direct experience of a culture that is intelligent enough to produce great poetry but has not developed prose as a medium of communication, except on the everyday level. It may to us seem axiomatic: if no prose, then no sustained thinking; brilliant imaginative insights, yes, but the serious use of the mind as an intellectual instrument did not begin until the time of Thales.

The conclusion is not valid; the existence of conscious mental activity in relation to (say) the nature of the universe, or of human society, may not be simply equated with the existence of prose; it may be the case—and I think evidently is—that intelligent reflection, what I have just called the serious use of the mind, was always there, though in a simple form; that what called for the use of prose was the desire not merely to state the results of thought (for which poetry is a perfectly satisfactory medium) but to question and demonstrate them, and to carry thought still further. In fact, is it not the great difference between Homer's *Odyssey* and mine, poems presumed to be alike in many respects, that Homer's is intelligent, serious, responsible, while mine is not? Mine, surely, would strike a Homeric audience as second-rate, rather empty, in comparison with Homer's. Each (we will presume) has its direct and passionate observation of persons and things, each gives delight and excitement—mine, indeed, rather more excitement than Homer's—but mine restricts itself to a small corner of human experience; it silently assumes, as Homer's does not, that major things like the governance of the universe and the well-being of human society may be neglected. A stranger to our culture might conclude from my poem that ours is a superficial and irresponsible society; he would of course be wrong, not realising that what is serious in our culture does not find expression in our romantic tales but elsewhere—in philosophy, religion, science. Homeric culture had no "elsewhere", so that it is the opposite error to which we are exposed: that of being incredulous when, in what we take to be a work of pure imagination, we are confronted with a serious and consistent concern with certain important moral and political matters. We have forgotten that poetry was the one medium of public communication: no prose, no Church, only poetry; or, if we do not forget it, we fail to work out the implications.

Moreover, we speak, reasonably, of "progress" in thought and culture, and then deceive ourselves by our own metaphor, thinking of progress as a linear movement, from the primitive to the advanced. So do we fall into the absurdity of saying either that Aeschylus was nearly as "advanced" as Plato, or "backward" in comparison with Xenophanes—Homer of course being very much in the rear. We should think of the progress as being radial rather than linear; advances are made in various directions from a common centre. This enables us to give a reasonable explanation of the fact that the great tragic poets—Aeschylus, Sophocles, Shakespeare, the poet of the *Iliad*—obstinately deal with the same obstinate material, and in much the same way. They are at the centre, where *backwards* and *forwards* are words without meaning. Progress in this connexion—the discovery of more powerful mental techniques, the acquisition of more and more knowledge—is a matter of increasing specialisation, of advancing from the centre in one direction or in another. Herodotus' *Historia* is an interesting illustration. In reading Herodotus we have sometimes to remind ourselves what the word "historia" meant to him: "enquiries", "researches". In his work history, geography, and anthropology have just separated out from Epic (though without completely cutting the umbilical cord), but have not yet become distinct from each other, and they have not said goodbye to the religious and moral interpretation of things. In our day the radial movement has gone so far that a modern work of sociology will be full of statistics and graphs and no doubt of wisdom, but may well be hardly within shouting distance of theology or ethics, while if it contained a lively sketch of two men in a pub discussing the 3.30 we should feel a certain incongruity. Yet what could be more "social" than that?

In Homeric society, mental activity had hardly begun this radial movement towards remote and far separated points—which is not the same as saying that mental activity did not exist. The circle was still very small; therefore what it contained was all in close and natural contact. We will notice presently that Homer brings Athena, no less, into a Homeric equivalent of a public-house brawl, and we must assume that his audiences were neither shocked nor bewildered. That which was destined, in the long course of time, to become scientific and abstract was still very close to the concrete. Therefore the world of Homer's poem is more complete, more solid, than the world of my *Odyssey:* my poem, by implication, leaves out so much, but Homer's, instinctively, keeps in touch with the whole of his world. The world of my poem extends from the Laestrygonians at one end to Nausicaa at the other, and there it stops, abruptly; Homer's goes on, for it includes a concern for Justice and for the foundations of human society—just as real and natural to him as pirates and a faithful hound—and it includes the gods; and the gods do not inhabit some Platonic other-world, but a world that makes a continuum with ours.

Here too there is need for caution, lest we suppose that the presence of the primitive excludes the possibility, not of the advanced, but of what was destined to become the advanced.

The gods, we might say, live just over the brow of the hill from us: how much further their region extends, who can say? Yet it too seems to have, on the far side, its boundary: Necessity, or Moira (Apportionment), for the gods too inhabit a world that they did not create but inherited. Although their region has in it terror, faery, and a streak of comedy too, it is to a large extent an extrapolation of our region: what happens here, whether a single event of an unusual kind, like an earthquake, or a general tendency, has its direct or its ultimate explanation in something that happens over the brow of the hill. Many things befall us which are inexplicable or cruel; therefore the gods are, or can be, cruel or capricious. The loyal Philoetius, when he meets Odysseus in the guise of a beggar, cries: "Father Zeus! how cruel you are! You caused us to be born, yet you deal out to us misery and suffering." The cruelty of the gods emerges as an explanation of something that happens with fair regularity. So too Eurycleia, full of her great news, runs upstairs to tell Penelope that Odysseus has not only returned but has also killed the Suitors; and Penelope says: "It cannot be true. Odysseus is dead. The Suitors must have been killed by one of the gods, unable to bear their wickedness any longer." As we know, she is half wrong, half right. *Quod ubique, quod semper*, shows the hand of a god; their presence, throughout classical Greek poetry, serves as a philosophic enlargement of the human world. The poets, from Homer to Sophocles, were really saying, "This is how the world works"—with the unspoken rider: "So that we had better take care." The theology of the philosophers, as we argued above, really was a "theology"; they were not extrapolating.

In the amalgam that we know as Homeric Religion there are of course many primitive elements that had no future, but these in no way preclude the presence of other elements that had a very distinguished future indeed: natural philosophy, obviously, is rooted in this idea of generality, and this idea is as consciously present in Homer's poem as it is absent from mine. Homer, just like the tragic poets, though less consistently, interweaves divine action with the human because, or when, he is seeing the human action in its general or universal aspect; what we see as a law or a general principle, he will represent as the act of a god. Early religion was more than primitivism, more than piety, though it comprised both; it contained also that element which was to grow into philosophy and science. In illustration, we will notice the way in which Homer describes an impromptu boxing-match; this will bring us back at last to our question about Nausicaa.

The story begins with what is clearly a traditional joke—like the one several times repeated in the poem: "How did you reach Ithaca? Not on foot, I suppose?" The beggar's real name was Arnaeus, but they called him Irus, because he was always running messages for people. Irus, an insolent bully, picks a quarrel with Odysseus, himself in the guise of a beggar, and challenges him to a fight. This quarrel by the door catches the attention of the young gentlemen; Antinous is enchanted at the idea of a fight between a couple of beggars, and proposes that they should make a regular match of it: the winner shall take his pick of the black puddings that are roasting, and shall sit down to dinner with the company, like a real gentleman. All agree; Odysseus is helpfully cunning, and Telemachus intervenes to assure the beggar of a fair fight. When he strips for action all are astonished at his physique. Irus is panic-stricken, and only the direst threats of Antinous persuade him not to turn tail. Odysseus looks at his man wondering whether or not to kill him, but thinks it wiser to let him off lightly; therefore he merely smashes in the side of his face, to the intense delight of the Suitors. Then he drags Irus out by one leg, props him up against a wall, gives him his stick, and tells him to squat there and keep the dogs and pigs out. The laughing Suitors warmly congratulate the winner; Antinous gives him a large pudding; Amphinomus gives him two loaves and with all courtesy drinks to his health and future success.—It is a brilliant piece of descriptive writing, amusing, sharp and clear, with no fuzzy edges, and with no philosophic nonsense in it.

But I have cheated. I have narrated the story as it would appear in my *Odyssey*, and in one particular Homer tells it differently: even in a story of this kind he must needs make Athena interfere, to increase Odysseus' stature for the fight. Could anything be more unnecessary, even on Homer's own showing? We need no assurance that the great Odysseus, victor in many a stern fight before Troy, is well able even in his present guise to stand up to a beggar, but Homer actually introduces Irus with the remark that he had great bulk but little strength or endurance, and when Odysseus throws off his rags, his physique already impresses the Suitors, before Athena magnifies it. Perhaps we murmur to ourselves: "Traditional divine machinery", which, being interpreted, means: "Take no notice of it; think it away, and enjoy the story for its own sake". Treat the whole story, in fact, as it will be treated in my poem, where it will be only a brilliant bit of naturalism. But it is Homer's audience that we must think of. How will they have taken it? Are we to suppose that they were so anaesthetised by tradition that they would take no special notice of Athena's intervention in such a scene?

Our question is answered by the sequel. Homer continues by

reporting some observations made privately by Odysseus to the courteous Amphinomus: "Man is a helpless creature! He has to take what the gods send. Look at me, for instance. I was born in a good position, yet I must needs take to the lawless life—and this is the result. Now, look at these Suitors, just as lawless. The man they are robbing and insulting is very soon coming back . . . I drink to your health, Sir, and I hope that when he comes back you will be safely at home, for there will certainly be bloodshed." Amphinomus took the gold cup from Odysseus' hand and went back to his seat, much perturbed. But this did not save him, for Athena had marked him down to be killed by a spear thrown by Telemachus.—We feel sorry for Amphinomus, as Homer clearly did, but he had touched pitch, and God is no respecter of persons.

But Homer has not yet finished with his vivid and amusing story of the boxing-match. A little later in Book XVIII Penelope chides Telemachus that he had allowed the Suitors to insult one who, though a beggar, was their guest. He replies, in T. E. Lawrence's translation:

> I cannot order all things according to reason, for those men's wicked imaginings pull me hither and thither, and I get help from none. Still, this brawl between Irus and our guest did not end in the least as the Suitors wished, for the stranger proved the doughtier. O Zeus and Apollo! would that these Suitors in our palace might every one lie vanquished in house or court with hanging head asprawl, as Irus now squats by the precinct gates, not able to stand upright or make off home (wherever home may be) because his limbs are all abroad.

Perhaps this shows that it was not thoughtlessly, from mere force of habit, in a traditionally epic spasm, that Homer caused Athena to intervene in order to increase, unnecessarily, the strength of Odysseus for a fight with a flabby braggart. She intervenes of course in a similar way on many other occasions, to make him look mean or royal, as may suit the occasion, just as she takes Telemachus in her special care: this one instance is instructive partly because the reason for it is so clear, partly because, for us, it is so obtrusive, yet obviously so natural for

Homer and his audiences. The story of the fight, though it begins with a jest and continues with such gaiety, reveals itself, if we become solemnly analytical about it, as a paradigmatic myth. Irus is insolent, as are the Suitors too; Odysseus quells his insolence, as he will quell theirs; Athena helps him against Irus as she will help him against them; and the prayer of Telemachus to Father Zeus and Apollo—one of the many instances of foreshadowing in this part of the poem—makes it clear how, and why, we must be continually aware of the divine involvement in the story: the gods, over the brow of the hill, may do all sorts of different things, but one thing they certainly do is to hate and punish, in the long run, human lawlessness, this being a deduction from human experience—aided perhaps by hope.

It may be that we shall come yet a little closer to the mind of both Homer and his audiences if we notice that he does not do what a maladroit writer or speaker might do today: he does not first tell his racy story of the fight, and then, to everybody's embarrassment and slight resentment, go all solemn and point the moral, during which time we respectfully lay down our pipes or cigarettes and leave our wine untasted. Homer, in his religious exercises, is quite unembarrassed; he brings Athena into this casual brawl as if it were the most natural thing in the world—as, to him, it evidently was. It is we that have divided the week into Sundays and ordinary days.

Now, a short while ago, after a passage of moral earnestness, I posed the apparently awkward question about Nausicaa and the rest, and said in reply that the question was misconceived. Now we can see the reason. We today, having considerably extended our mental activity from the centre in many directions, feel that there is a wide gap between what is, to us, abstract thought and what are, to us, the immediate and vivid realities of life—boxing-matches, black puddings, pirates, and the rest. For Homer and his contemporaries the gap did not exist. Homer composes with a continuous awareness of a world which to him is one: its beauty, perils, wonders, its common things whether lovely or hateful, are no more real to him, and no less real, than its divine inhabitants, who give us what we enjoy and what we suffer, often capriciously but on the whole maintaining certain regular courses. That the Sun rises and sets with such regularity shows that a *theos* is there; that insolence and lawnessness usually come to a nasty end shows the same thing. The gods were not a pious, or an intellectual, hypothesis; they were one of the obvious facts of life.

If our redrafting of the *Odyssey* has achieved its purpose, it has vindicated Aristotle's dictum that the most important element in *poiesis* is the arrangement of the material; and by this is meant not simply giving a more or a less elegant shape to something which in either case remains virtually the same thing, but that the arrangement is itself, in the hands of a good poet, a way of saying what he means, a ground plan, as it were, which underlies and articulates the whole significance of the work. My *Odyssey* "says" one thing; Homer's, something quite different.

We have said that Homer could never have invented my plot; why not? We find a clue in the passage already quoted from Cornford (p. xx). He was speaking of history, but it seems true of any serious composition: that it is "cast in a mould of conception, whether artistic or philosophical [I myself would add 'or both at once'], which, long before the work was even contemplated, was already inwrought into the very structure of the poet's mind"; and this, he says, is no personal matter, for "the mind of every individual . . . is not an insulated compartment, but more like a pool in a continuous medium", since every age has "its scheme of unchallenged and unsuspected presuppositions".

My romantic plot would have been impossible for Homer because it is based on an entirely different set of suppositions, natural enough to ourselves but remote from those of Homer's time. Here we have the reason why to Longinus, my own scientific colleague, and certain other critics, some parts of Homer's structure are weak or puzzling; the structure does not fit the new set of assumptions. Much of it will still make sense and give pleasure, but not all of it. Cornford says finally that this element of thought is always difficult to detect and analyse; but we have seen, I hope, that the responsive study of the *poiesis* of a great poem can sometimes make a little clearer to us some of the fundamental assumptions of its age, even though they may have been half unconscious and unspoken.

This is true because Homer's audiences—or those of Aeschylus or Sophocles or Shakespeare—will naturally have shared the poet's own "scheme of unchallenged and unsuspected presuppositions", since these are poets who expected to be understood by the general. The point may be obvious, but it is important for this reason: one is sometimes told that if the intended significance of a poem or play is to be revealed only by a long and patient analysis, then what is so revealed must be wrong, since the poet must have expected to be understood, or substantially understood, at once, and the original audience could not possibly have so analysed what it was listening to. The objection would be valid if ideas never changed from one age to another. I have myself been told, as critic: "This interpretation does not accord with one's experience of reading the play". The answer is: "Whose experience? Of a reader in 1960, 1760, 260, or 460 B.C.?"

Unless a poem is eccentric, as these two epics are not, it is central—central to the spirit and ideas of its own time; but having said that, we should not commit the folly of thinking that the poems were composed not by Homer, or by two Homers, but by the Homeric Age. We have said that the plot of the *Odyssey* is more than a sign of literary genius—but it certainly *is* a sign of genius, and we have good evidence that it was not devised by the Homeric Age. As it happens, Aristotle helps us to imagine what the poem might have been like, written by a second-rate poet. He knew epics written by inferior poets, and makes two criticisms of them. Homer, he says, stands alone among poets making each poem a real unity; the others imagined that they could do this if they chose a single hero, like Theseus or Heracles, and narrated what happened to him. The comment implies—what is obviously true of both the *Iliad* and the *Odyssey*—that Homer had a real subject and the others not; that Homer took command of his material, selecting and arranging it for his own clear purpose, while the others allowed their material to command them; it did not really pass through their minds, to be sifted, organised, and made significant, so that what unity their poems had was only external and mechanical.

Aristotle's other criticism, which also sets Homer in a class by himself, is that Homer is the only epic poet who knew how much a *poietes* should say in his own voice, namely as little as possible: "for he writes a short proem and then introduces characters who say or do everything, while the other poets are continually taking a hand themselves, αὐτοὶ δι' ὅλου ἀγωνίζονται. But when a poet speaks in his own person, he is not being a *mimetes*". Homer, having his subject, and acting as master of his material, was able to convey what he meant in and through his medium, like the sculptors of whom we spoke earlier; so to speak, he did his thinking at the drawing board. Weaker poets could not do this; they had to talk, moralise, explain the point. But to do this, Aristotle says, is to fail as an artist; it is to cross the line that divides the *mimetes* from an Empedocles.

But this affects the other partner, the audience or reader, in a way that we might well consider. The difference between Homer and an inferior poet, in this regard, is clear. Let the composer of a *Heracleid* or a *Theseid* be a reasonably good poet, capable of delightful or exciting effects; nevertheless, the response that he creates in his audience will be less taut, less alive and imaginative, than the response created by Homer; we might say that it will be less constructive. We might take the Irus episode as an illustration. As epic narrative it can reasonably be compared with one of Theocritus' *epyllia:* the great difference, of course, is that while each is entirely delightful in itself, the Theocritean piece is no more than that, and was never intended to be, but Homer's (once we have understood the implications of his *poiesis*) reaches out beyond itself, as it were, and carries meaning; the listener who is attuned to Homer's art—as the original audiences would be—will find himself thinking about insolence, and the way that the gods have with the insolent. In Theocritus' day the gods were not very effective, and in any case this kind of theme was now assigned to the province of the philosophers, not of the poets. We may also compare Homer's treatment of the episode with the way in which, presumably, it would be handled by one of the more talkative and less mimetic poets. Unlike Homer, he will not have so ordered his material from the start as to involve Athena so closely and intelligibly with the fortunes of Odysseus; he will have begun with the birth of Odysseus, his being wounded on Parnassus, his pretending to be mad, and all the rest of it. He, so we will presume, would tell the story of Irus, perhaps quite as well as Homer, and then, *αὐτὸς λέγων*, would draw the moral, doing this in his own voice because he lacked Homer's constructive ability to make the point without talking. For the listener, the difference is that Homer's art raises him to a higher level of awareness; his imagination will coöperate with Homer's as it cannot do with the other poet's; and from this it seems to follow that Homer's method, the purely mimetic and artistic, not the didactic, is even didactically much more effective. What it conveys is so much more memorable.

Since we recently mentioned Empedocles, and Aristotle's distinction between him and Homer, we might bring him into the present discussion too. From the listener's point of view, what is the difference between Homer, who is a *mimetes*, and Empedocles, who is not? That they have much in common is obvious—"poetry" for example, but Aristotle's distinction is perfectly valid. No one will imagine that Empedocles' poem invited easy listening or reading; quite the contrary. But it is not a matter of the energy of response that is called for, but of its nature. Both poets make demands on our intelligence, but Homer on the imaginative and constructive side, Empedocles on the intellectual and analytical. Reading Homer, we have to apprehend the significance of a *mimesis*, as if in pictures; reading Empedocles we would have to comprehend an exposition.

IV
Sophocles

The foregoing chapter was intended to show that there is indeed a connexion between the way in which a poet thinks and the way in which he chooses and arranges his material. It happens that Sophocles is a poet about whose mind there is a strange diversity of opinion. The view that he had none worth speaking of, but was just an artist, seems to have died away, which is no bad thing; yet if anyone has a taste for the macabre, he can indulge it, mildly, by reading the judicious and thorough review of recent work on Sophocles which is presented by Dr H. F. Johansen in *Lustrum*, 1962:

> The two main problems [says Johansen] which cannot be solved independently of each other, may be summarised as follows: (*a*) Are the Sophoclean gods concerned with mankind, and if so, how are they concerned? (*b*) What is the moral and religious position of the Sophoclean hero? Answers range from the most pious justification of the ways of God to a radically anti-religious hero-worship. (p. 152)

Sophocles, apparently, failed to make himself clear—a strange fault in so classical a poet. Johansen remarks later (p. 162): "One of the great dangers of all writers on religious and moral ideas, particularly those of a poet, is excessive generalization; we may hope that when the storms have died down there will be time to find out how far generalization is valid in these delicate matters". Another great danger is that of taking no particular notice of the facts, and when I say "facts" I mean what the poet actually does, says, and implies in his plays.

1. The *Trachiniae*

One reason for choosing the *Trachiniae* as an example of Sophoclean *poiesis* is that it poses the question of interpretation in an acute form. Not only is there the matter of the Sophoclean gods and of the Sophoclean hero, but there is also the unending debate about the central character: is it Deianeira or is it Heracles? Or is it both, but Deianeira rather than Heracles, or Heracles rather than Deianeira? Closely connected with this, naturally, is our judgment on the quality of the play. Some time ago it was considered not ridiculous to dismiss it as only a bad shot on Sophocles' part; it was "broken-backed", "double-yolked". No longer, I think, do we talk like this, but Johansen himself calls it "puzzling". Yet if a mature work of an admittedly great artist is puzzling, it is at least a possible explanation that we have overlooked something, something obvious enough to Sophocles' own audience—for it is not very likely that he puzzled them as much as he does the twentieth century. Perhaps therefore it will not be a waste of time to examine fairly closely what Sophocles put into his play, what he did not, and how he arranged it all.

We will take this point for a start. There is an impressive array of scholars who argue to this effect: Sophocles was deeply religious, that is to say pious; his gods are just; they inflict suffering on a man to purge him of his pride; so in the end the sufferer makes his peace with the gods; now at last he can understand and accept. Very well. Heracles is certainly a hero; certainly he shows self-will if not also pride, and certainly he is brought very low. Sophocles has been contemplating the story of Heracles, Deianeira, and the robe; he reshapes it to suit his purpose. He therefore takes his play to the point where

Heracles is brought in, suffering agonies, very close to death, and denouncing Deianeira as his murderess. What Sophocles does next is as natural as can be, his religious ideas being those that we have just learned: Hyllus tells Heracles the truth, and to confirm his words a sad little procession comes out from the house bearing Deianeira's dead body. The scales fall from the hero's eyes; at last he sees all. In remorse he makes what peace he can with his dead wife—for obviously we must all make peace with our wives before making peace with the gods. So does he go to his mysterious end. A solemn messenger-speech, describing what happened on the summit of Mount Oeta, assures us that he did indeed go in peace. It is a most impressive ending, and it proves the theory up to the hilt. The only inconvenience is that Sophocles designed something totally different.

Or we may consider the long debate: Deianeira, or Heracles? Let us put the question differently: did Sophocles expect his audience to leave the theatre thinking chiefly of her tragic end, or of his? There is no denying that during the last quarter of the play the audience has had to contemplate the agony of destruction that has come upon Heracles. The suggestion has been made that the scene is an "afterpiece"; alternatively, that throughout it we feel the presence of the unseen Deianeira. Desperate remedies, surely? How clumsy a playwright would Sophocles have to be in order to present, as a mere addendum, the irretrievable ruin of one who was perhaps the greatest of Greek heroes, and to present it not in words only, but visually as well? And if we are to feel Deianeira's presence, what prevented him from letting us *see* her too? Besides, from the very beginning the play has been concerned with the return of Heracles: will he come home again or not? He does indeed return home—and like this! The awful irony of it is enough to show that this is what Sophocles had in mind from the start.

Then the play is really about Heracles, not Deianeira? But how can we say that? Where, even in the work of Sophocles, shall we find a more moving tragedy than of this desolate wife who, at what is for her the supreme crisis, tries to win back her husband's love, but destroys him instead? Even if our common humanity does not rise in protest against any attempt to minimise her tragedy, our common sense ought to: the story of her two suitors is given a prominence that is unintelligible if the play is really about Heracles. She herself, in her opening speech, tells the story of her wooing in great detail and with much feeling. It is told a second time by the chorus (vv. 497 ff.), and we may notice how the ode finishes: it has described the struggle between the River God and Heracles, with the young girl sitting at a distance watching it, awaiting the decision, unable to influence it; then it says that she followed Heracles, "taken afar from her mother, like a lonely heifer-calf".

The manner of her wooing and the joylessness of her married life are impressed on us far too much if Sophocles intended her part in the tragedy to be in any way subordinate.

But if a question admits of no obvious answer—and in such a case a clever answer is no good—it is possible that the question itself is wrong. It implies that either Deianeira or Heracles must have been intended, by Sophocles, to be the focal point of our attention and sympathy; but if this is not the way in which he thought, it is not surprising that we find no satisfying answer to our question.

Aristotle happens to remark that "tragedy is a representation not of people but of a *praxis*, of life, of prosperity or ruin" (*Poetics*, 1450A 15). He may be wrong, of course; still, there are not a few extant plays of which this is manifestly true. We do not, in fact, debate anxiously whether the "hero" of the *Agamemnon* is Agamemnon or Clytemnestra or possibly Cassandra; we see at once that this play is about "something" rather than "somebody", just as we see at once that the *Eumenides* is not about Orestes. It is the whole course of the action that claims, and receives, our attention. We can pretend, if we like, that the *Trojan Women* and *Hecuba* are about Hecuba, but it would only obscure our understanding of the plays. The *Hippolytus:* is it about Hippolytus, or Phaedra, or the two together—or is it about Artemis and Aphrodite? If we understand *praxis* to mean something like "a course of significant action", then, obviously the play is about a *praxis*, and our questions about the priority of the persons no longer have meaning. So far as the *Trachiniae* is concerned there is a third possible candidate for the position of chief character whose name I do not find canvassed in the debate. It is at least true that Zeus is mentioned about twenty-five times in the play; that Hyllus (at v. 1022) cries: "This is what Zeus does to us!" and says later (vv. 1266 ff.) that the gods have behaved cruelly and shamefully; and that the last verse of the play, spoken whether by Hyllus or by the chorus, declares: "Nothing is present here but Zeus". If all this is no more than what Werner Jaeger called "the unshakeable but placid piety of Sophocles", then we shall take no particular notice of it: Sophocles is only being pious. But perhaps there is a chance that Sophocles meant precisely what he says; and since in any case we are a bit puzzled by the play it may be well to look at the facts rather closely. If we do, we shall find that we do not get an unequivocal answer even if we ask the apparently simple question: "Who killed Heracles?"

Let us begin our study of the *poiesis* by inventing an actress who is playing Deianeira and finds herself in some difficulties. She is bothered by three passages. One occurs in Lichas' long speech (vv. 248 ff.), the others in Hyllus' long account of the sacrifice. She takes her difficulties to the producer. "Look here: during that speech of Lichas' I am supposed to be the wife who has been anxious for so long, and is now overjoyed that her husband has come back safe and sound; but I have to stand there and listen to a long account—thirty verses of it—of how he came to be enslaved to what's-her-name in Lydia. What on earth am I to *do* while all that is going on? Hyllus' speech is even worse. I can cope with the description of the sacrifice, the putting-on of the robe, and the rest; but then there are ten verses about the death of Lichas, and another ten about

Heracles telling Hyllus to take him up and carry him away. I am a wife who is being accused by her son of murdering her husband: how can I stand there, acting like mad, while all this irrelevant description is going on? What am I supposed to *do?*"

It seems a fair question; what is the answer? Let us imagine that the producer has been conscientiously reading books about Greek drama. Let him explain to the actress: "You must understand that in the Greek theatre the actors wore masks. Also, the long narrative speech was an established convention: the Greeks had their long tradition of epic recitals, and this carried over into their drama. They expected a narrative speech, and if some details in it were a bit irrelevant, they didn't mind. The speeches are really vivid stories, delivered straight at the audience. So that you must stop trying to do Stanislavsky, trying to 'be' Deianeira all the time. Just imagine that you are wearing a mask, and you'll have no more trouble."

I have invented this little scene as a parable, to illustrate the seductions and dangers of explaining something in a play, something difficult, by reference to something outside it—in this case, an assumed convention of the Greek theatre. The explanation (I hope) sounds plausible; it is likely enough that Athenian playwrights of not quite the first rank wrote messenger-speeches of this kind. Indeed, we find such in the extant plays: there are good examples in the *Ion* and *Helen*—though we must not cite these without remembering that the plays in which they occur are scarcely stern tragedies, but of a kind that lends itself readily to decoration. But our actress found the three passages boring, not decorative; and we should look at least twice at an explanation which in effect says: "The poet did not really *mean* that; it is there for an extraneous reason".

Let us look at the speech containing the first of the passages that bothered our actress. Lichas is answering Deianeira's question: "Has my husband been spending all this time attacking this one city?" He replies: "No; for one year he was in Lydia, a slave. Do not be indignant, for Zeus brought it upon him; but because of this, Heracles vowed that he would avenge himself on the man whom he held responsible, Eurytus: he would enslave him, and his family too. Eurytus, you know, had grossly insulted him; then, later, Heracles caught Iphitus his son and flung him to his death from a high place when he was not looking. It was for this that Zeus had him sold into bondage. Had he killed Iphitus openly, Zeus might have pardoned him, for the gods too have no love of hybris. But now, those who had insulted him are all dead, and their city has been subdued; these women have lost all they had, and are now slaves. Heracles has sent them here to you; he will follow, when he has completed his holy sacrifice to Zeus in thanksgiving for his capture of the city."

Such is the account given by Lichas. The actress complained that about a quarter of it has nothing to do with her. We can add to that the fact that another quarter is not even true: Sophocles has so arranged his material that he needs two messengers, one to give a false explanation of the attack on Oechalia, the other to give the true one. It seems reasonable to wonder why he did it.

We cannot explain it by saying: Lichas was a liar, therefore a second messenger was wanted, to tell Deianeira the truth. We may not say this, because Lichas was anything that Sophocles chose to make him. He might have been frank, even brutal, concealing neither the reason why Heracles attacked the city nor, later, the identity of Iole. The same is true of the other point: why so much about the killing of Iphitus; for the Messenger is going to tell us that Iphitus and Omphale had nothing to do with it. Clearly, since Lichas, for some reason, is going to be made deny all knowledge about Iole, for the same reason he will not give the true explanation here: "his passion for this girl", *ὁ τῆσδ' ἔρως*, as the Messenger bluntly puts it (v. 433). But in order that Lichas should say nothing here about Iole, it was not necessary for him to say so much about the killing of Iphitus; let him say something like this, for example: "Dear lady, I will explain his long absence. In anger, wrongfully, Heracles had killed an innocent man. [Details can be invented.] For this, Zeus punished him with a year of bondage. When this was over, he satisfied his wrath against Eurytus, for Eurytus had grossly insulted him . . . Therefore he collected an army . . . Now he has taken his vengeance . . ." Iphitus was unnecessary.

Why so much about him? One point may be worth noticing, if we can suppose that Sophocles gave some thought to the disposing of his material. Another of the three passages recounts the killing of Lichas himself. He too is flung to his death by Heracles from a high place—and Sophocles does not spare us the horror of it. Twice in one play is rather a lot; it seems that flinging innocent men to their death was almost a habit with Heracles. "But both incidents were in the legend and could not be left out." Do we then suppose that these poets condemned themselves to represent everything that was in their legends? An important part of this one was the apotheosis of Heracles on Oeta, and Sophocles found no difficulty in leaving that out. The repetition may be accidental; let us leave it and return to our first question: why was Lichas' speech constructed like this?

Presumably to make a certain impression on the mind and feelings of the audience, and at this particular moment of the play. Now, the play has been going on for some little time; certain expectations have already been created in the mind of the audience; certain ideas and feelings have already been aroused. We are more likely to understand why Sophocles does these things now, if we have understood what he has done already; therefore we will enquire what he has done. He may have linked one thing with another.

About the *prologos*, the first act as it were, it will be enough to say here (*i*) that it describes the wooing of Deianeira as a strange, even desperate, affair; (*ii*) that her marriage with Heracles has brought her little joy, much anxiety; (*iii*) that never has her anxiety been more acute than at this moment: she learns that Heracles is attacking Oechalia, and she knows from prophecy that the critical hour has come, for this exploit is to end either in his death or in lasting peace.

Many have said, about the *prologos*, that it clearly shows the influence of Euripides; Kamerbeek rightly points out (p. 10 of his edition) that it shows nothing of the sort; in particular, that the opening monologue is quite unlike the formal monologue so often used by Euripides: "New readers begin here". The description of the two suitors and their struggle, like that of Deianeira's joyless married life, are there not simply to explain the past; they are part of the present situation. As we have seen, there is a second description of the struggle in the second ode (vv. 496 ff.): the savage, inhuman combat, with Aphrodite presiding, and the young girl watching from afar, helpless, pitiful, and beautiful; following the victor at last. For the rest, we are given a feeling of long emptiness, and learn that it must end almost at once, either in final disaster or in the fullness of peace and joy.

Such is the situation into which the chorus enters. It is one that in Euripides is almost normal; interesting, therefore, to see how utterly un-Euripidean their first song is.

The heroine is in distress; there enters, to make sympathetic enquiries, a group of friendly young women. In Euripides—in the *Medea*, *Hippolytus*, *Alcestis*, *Andromache*, *Orestes*, *Electra*—they address or apostrophise her, commonly singing, it seems, in small groups, perhaps individually; as a rule they are perceptibly feminine: in the *Hippolytus* they have come from doing washing at the spring; they are warmly sympathetic, eager for news. The *parodos* of Sophocles' own *Electra* is not essentially different, either in form or in spirit. It is true that in the *Trachiniae* also they have come out of sympathy—but here it is Deianeira herself who must let us know this (vv. 141 f.), for Sophocles makes the chorus open up at once, in unison and in full voice, with a large and Sophoclean theme:

Sparkling Night as she dies gives birth to the blazing Sun, then lays him down in sleep. I call upon the Sun to bring Deianeira news of her husband, for she is in torment for his long absence. He has been buffeted as if by one rolling wave after another, yet always without fail some god preserves him from death. She ought not to abandon herself to grief. It is no painless lot that Zeus gives to mortals: sorrow and joy come in turn to all, just as the Bear circles for ever round the Pole. Sparkling Night does not endure, nor tribulation nor wealth nor joy nor grief. Remember this; for who has ever seen Zeus unmindful of his children?

One scholar reminds us that this doctrine of "the wheel of things" is Orphic and Pythagorean. True; but there are occasions when we must not allow our learning to obscure our understanding: the important fact is not the origin of the doctrine, but that it is proclaimed here, at this moment, when the *prologos* has ended and before the main action begins. It is indeed not without importance that the idea is old and familiar: if it were a new one, the audience—those who were not too dull to take in a new idea—would be saying to itself: "By Zeus! this is interesting!" or, "Fancy Sophocles doing something to advance thought!" As it is not new, they will experience no intellectual distractions, and will therefore be able the more easily to respond to it as part of the play. Or we may remember the comparable passage of the *Ajax*, on Day and Night, Summer and Winter, and the other passage in the *Coloneus* (vv. 607 ff.); Sophocles, we will say, is always exhibiting the sudden vicissitudes of human life, but at the centre of his thought is a point of stillness, like the Pole star; it is the secret of the serenity of his art. True, and pertinent; but we could say as much if this were a detached poem. It is not; it is said here and now, and we have not discovered what we might about Sophocles' thought unless we have taken full account of that fact. The "timing", once again, may be important.

It clearly is. We see Hyllus leave, hoping to find news of his father; the next thing that happens to us, in the theatre, is the cosmic imagery of Night and Day, the Bear, the corresponding alternation of joy and sorrow in human affairs. That is: the action set in motion by the *prologos*, the personal history of the wife of Heracles, is placed against a new and vaster background; not, now, merely the house in which she is living, but Night, Day, the Bear. Again, the chorus puts it to Deianeira, and to us: in the past some god has always preserved Heracles from death; further, Zeus does not disregard his offspring. Is this only optimistic piety on the part of the simple village maidens of Trachis, and the Bear only a passing astronomical embellishment? Perhaps, though we have not been told yet that they are simple village maidens; and what they sing has, as it were, the backing of full orchestra. It might be wiser to suppose that Sophocles intended rather more than decoration. At all events, what he chooses to put into our minds at this moment is this, that in the regular course of things it may be expected that Deianeira's long years of anxiety will give place to years of peace.

The audience, even if it does not know already the outline of the story, will have surmised that it is not going to happen. Perhaps we may go further. When Deianeira said, in her first verses: "Call no one fortunate or unfortunate until he is dead . . . I know, even before the day of my death . . .", the audience may have guessed that she herself may not be far from that last event. Certainly, being so impressively reminded that alternation is the eternal rhythm, it will be disposed to ask itself, as the action unrolls, why in this case the rhythm is broken.

There is also Zeus. The last verse of the ode is: "Who has ever seen Zeus unmindful of his children?" Jebb's note is interesting: "Racine has an unconscious echo of this verse: *Athalie*, II, 7: 'Dieu laissa-t-il jamais ses enfants à besoin?' " Certainly Racine knew his Sophocles intimately: in him it may well be an unconscious echo; for us, it may be an interesting contrast. In *Athalie* God indeed does not abandon in their distress His children who remained faithful and are in peril from the worshippers of Baal, but causes them to triumph over their foes; will it be only fanciful in us, or on the contrary just what Sophocles intended, if we ask ourselves once or twice during the play if Zeus is being unmindful of his son Heracles?

After the ode there is another speech from Deianeira, sad, like the monologue. It does nothing to advance the action; it does deepen our sympathy with her, and by telling us more about the prophecies it makes us feel even more strongly that the crisis is near. It comes at once; the preparation has been a long one, but now things happen swiftly. The Messenger comes with his great news: "He is back, he has triumphed; he will soon be here with the first-fruits of his victory!" Therefore all is well; for Heracles it will be lasting peace, for Deianeira peace and joy. She gives thanks to Zeus and calls for a hymn of gladness—in which, we notice, the house is called *μελλόνυμφος*, and that may mean "awaiting a bridegroom" or "awaiting a bride".

Our purpose was to set Lichas' speech in its full context. We have now done it, but for two details. As the hymn ends, Lichas arrives and confirms the good news: Heracles will soon be here, but has something to do first. He must fulfil a vow that he made when he was beginning his attack on the city: to make thankoffering to Zeus, if successful; therefore he is occupied with this, and is consecrating altars on the summit of Cenaeum. That is one detail; the other is rather more obtrusive: Lichas is followed by a company of women, presumably under guard. "In Heaven's name, who are these? and whose are they? They are in pitiable state, unless I am deceived." Lichas explains to Deianeira that they are the captives from the city whom Heracles picked out for himself and for the service of the gods. They remain in the orchestra during the scene. Should we see in this too the influence of Euripides? For he also, from time to time, fills his orchestra with enslaved women, and when he does it, we know what we are expected to feel.

We have no idea yet why Heracles attacked Oechalia. Lichas now tells us, and we have seen that he conceals the truth. Even so, what he says is not very reassuring: Eurytus' outrage, the revenge that Heracles takes upon Iphitus, the punishment inflicted by Zeus, Heracles' oath that he will requite this by enslaving Eurytus and his family too—and finally what he has done: the men dead, the women taken into slavery, the city destroyed; and "You may expect to see him when he had performed to Zeus his holy sacrifice of thanksgiving".

How did Sophocles expect his audience to respond to this? Perhaps we are tempted to suppose that Greek audiences responded, in the theatre, as we do, in our studies. Thus Bowra, in his *Sophoclean Tragedy* (pp. 132 f.), remembers that Heracles, like Achilles and Odysseus, had been a renowned "sacker of cities", and supposes that Heracles, as a son of Zeus and half-divine, was entitled to exercise the destructive anger of revenge, so grave a sin for the ordinary man. The Heracles legend dates from the heroic past; Sophocles creates what he imagines such a hero to be. Heracles, being a Hero, cannot be judged by ordinary rules. If he chooses to sack Oechalia, we common men may not pass judgment, only look on in awe. (Perhaps too we may thank our lucky stars that we do not live in the Age of Heroes.)

It is natural that we should think like this. Our background, in these matters, is one of legend, the epic poets, and cults. Jebb thought like this about the poet and his audience: Sophocles, in composing the *Electra*, took his willing audience back to the epic conception of Orestes' vengeance as a heroic deed that raised no moral problems, so that it would not have occurred to the audience to ask awkward questions; similarly, for Jebb, the Heracles of this play was a portrait of the great hero of ancient legend—in which fact lay the explanation of the comparative failure of the play. It is natural that many scholars should have explained the shape of the *Ajax* by remembering an important fact which Sophocles apparently forgot, that Ajax was a great Attic Hero worshipped in rites performed around his tomb. But *was* the Athenian audience so intent on matters that fill our horizons? In this particular instance, can we be certain that they would contemplate Heracles with awe, and not presume to judge? Can we be certain indeed that Sophocles was merely drawing a picture of what he imagined Heracles would have been like? As we cannot be certain, we had better go on with the text.

Lichas ends his tale. The chorus bids Deianeira rejoice. She says:

> I do indeed rejoice, with all my heart.
> To learn of this good fortune of my husband
> Calls forth in me a joy that runs to meet it.—
> And yet, the cautious cannot help but fear
> At great success, lest it be overthrown;
> For I am moved with pity, as I look
> On these unhappy women, driven from home
> To foreign soil, their fathers killed; once free,
> Condemned henceforth to live the life of slaves.

Evidently, she is very uneasy, and what makes her uneasy is the plight of these wretched women. Therefore we may infer something about the response that Sophocles expected from his audience: guided by Deianeira's uneasiness, having just been told in a passage otherwise unnecessary that Zeus has already punished Heracles for one act of violence, it may well be asking itself: "In what spirit will Zeus receive Heracles' thankoffering for his total destruction of a city?" It is not exactly a question of how they, or we, should judge the acts of a demigod, but of how Zeus will judge him; in other words, of what will be the natural outcome of his conduct. It sounded a bit wild, perhaps, when (according to Lichas) Heracles had vowed to enslave Eurytus and his whole family in return for what in fact was a punishment inflicted by Zeus; the destruction of a whole city goes much further.

But the situation is worse, much worse, than we yet know; Sophocles contrived two messengers. When Lichas is off-stage, the first Messenger, honest fellow, comes to life again, denounces Lichas for a liar, and tells Deianeira the truth: Heracles destroyed the city for no other reason than to get Iole; "Eros, alone of the *theoi*, bewitched him into doing it" (v. 354).

These gods are a nuisance. Jebb, in his note on v. 447, takes it for granted that "Iole's relation to Heracles was excused by the omnipotence of Eros". But the important question is not whether this "excuses" Heracles; the most complete excuse will not cancel the consequences. Even so, this Messenger is not a very reliable witness; he is deplorably weak on capital letters; for later (vv. 451 ff.) we hear him saying to Lichas: "I heard you say that Heracles wrecked the city through his longing for this girl; that the Lydian woman and Iphitus had nothing to do with it, only his passion (eros) for this girl." Put that way, it sounds a little different. And he says more. He says that Heracles, wanting the girl, demanded that her father Eurytus should give her to him as his concubine, *κρύφιον ὡς ἔχοι λέχος*. Not many fathers would do such a thing; Eurytus would not. That was the reason why a whole population is either dead or enslaved. He says even more, for he tells Deianeira not to imagine that Iole has been sent here merely as a slave; no, is it likely? As he says to Lichas (vv. 427 f.): "Did you not declare on oath that Heracles was bringing her here as his wife, *δάμαρτα*?" Does the omnipotence of Eros "excuse" this? Even if it does, who is going to pay the bill?

We hear more about Eros or Aphrodite in this part of the play. Deianeira speaks of Eros when she is beseeching Lichas to tell her the truth. What she says in this speech is entirely consonant with all that we have seen of her. For Iole, she has nothing but pity, now as before: Iole intended her no harm, but has been brought to ruin by her own beauty, and through no fault of her own she has brought ruin on her country too (vv. 464–467). She understands the power of Love; Heracles has had many women, and of not one of them has she made an enemy; she would be mad if she took offence at Heracles because he has fallen victim to this "malady". Lichas can, and must, tell her the truth without reserve.

In passing, we should note that Lichas comes out of it well. Some critics have been hard on him, suggesting even that there is a kind of rough justice in what Heracles is going to do to him. Perhaps these have never found themselves in Lichas' embarrassing situation: having to explain to the respected wife of their employer that the beautiful young girl whom they have just brought to the house is going from now on to occupy the front bedroom. In reply to her appeal he says: "Dear mistress, since I find you so understanding, so reasonable, I will tell you everything. It is just as this man says. Heracles—to be fair to him—did not deny it or tell me to conceal it. I acted wrongly, if you do think it wrong, because I feared that the truth might hurt you." In the circumstances, it was no unreasonable fear—and may it not also reasonably prompt the reflection that Lichas showed more consideration for Deianeira than her husband is doing?

Then comes the third ode, which begins with a stanza on the omnipotence of Aphrodite. To our surprise, perhaps, it makes no reference to the immediate situation, but goes back to the fierce conflict already described to us by Deianeira. Her first suitor, the River God, seemed very incongruous in the setting of this play. He assumed three forms, of which the most attractive was barely human, since he still spouted water from his beard. The ode, beginning with Aphrodite and her power, continues by describing the fight in barely human terms, and concludes with the picture of Deianeira, led away like a calf from its mother. She said herself (v. 25) that when the River God sought her she was terrified lest her beauty should be her ruin; it is just what she has said about Iole. It must be that the power and violence of Love is near the heart of the play, yet we should remember: it is not love in the form of mere infidelities that Deianeira resents; she says it, and we have no right to disbelieve her. What makes her bitter is the ingratitude of it—

> Such are the thanks he gives me,
> My great and loyal husband, as they call him,
> For my long watching over his house and home . . .
>
> (vv. 540–542)

and what she finds unbearable, when she has had time to digest the news, is that she will be thrust into a corner, in her own house. Therefore the convenient god Eros must be made to excuse rather a lot: Heracles' dishonouring demand to Eurytus, the destruction of a city, and this unconscionable treatment of a loyal, understanding, and indeed greatly forbearing wife. It is too much, even for Eros. However, we are beginning to understand, it may be, why the natural rhythm of Day following Night, Joy following Sorrow, does not fulfil itself here.

We are in danger of overrunning ourselves. We began with three passages that troubled our actress. The first one, the killing of Iphitus, appears natural enough now that we have placed it in its context. Is Zeus unmindful of his offspring? The answer seems to be No; he takes notice of what they do. About the second, the killing of Lichas, we have already made a tentative suggestion. Let us look at the third.

This is the passage in which Hyllus describes how Heracles called to him, in his agony. There is nothing remarkable in it, except that our actress did not expect to be treated to so much barely relevant narrative during an accusation of murder. Why did Sophocles put it in? Not, this time, because he found it in his sources and did not have the courage, or sense, to leave it out; we can be fairly sure that he invented it. Why should he invent it? We can discover the reason by experiment, the simple experiment of rewriting it. We will make this part of Hyllus' speech run after this fashion:

> My father saw me running out of the crowd to his help, but he cried out: "Stand back, my son, stand back, lest the burning venom seize you too, and you share my death!" Nevertheless we took him up and placed him on a litter; men are bearing him home, that he may die here, not among the multitude, on that accursed mountain.

This meets every demand of the story (which indeed does not demand it), and is no less interesting, as narrative, than the original. The difference is clear: my version makes Heracles a normally considerate father; the original does the opposite: "Take me up, my son, even if you must die with me".

We are dealing with the play in disorderly fashion, but it is too late to alter that now; therefore we will turn at once to the other scene in which father and son are together.

When Heracles knows that his end is near, he commands Hyllus to marry Iole. Why? That is to say, why does Sophocles make him do it? One writer explains that Sophocles is introducing an unexpected trait of tenderness and justice in Heracles: he now sees that Iole should receive some recompense, and does his best for her. Another sees in it a sign of Heracles' almost god-like stature: the demand, however strange or terrible from a human point of view, has in it a quality of inevitability and of ultimate rightness. Jebb explained, in his note on v. 1224, that "it was rendered indispensable by the plot, if the poet was to avoid a contradiction which must otherwise have perplexed the spectators". Although Bowra has already pointed out (*Sophoclean Tragedy*, p. 142) that this is no explanation at all, it seems to be still worth discussing, in view of the settled delusion that these dramatists often did not what they would have chosen but what the myth made them do.

Jebb reminds us that Spartan kings, and the tribe of Hylleis, were descended from Hyllus and Iole; it was, so to speak, a fact of ancient history; also that the story of Heracles' love for Iole was ancient. It had been the subject of an epic poem, *The Capture of Oechalia*, by Cresphontes of Samos. Whether Deianeira figured in this poem is not known. Pherecydes (sixth century) had tidied up the myth by making Heracles demand Iole not for himself but for Hyllus. This however was of no use to Sophocles; he, for his own evident purpose, has made the conduct of Heracles deplorable: he makes Heracles demand Iole for himself. This put him in the awkward position of having to square his plot with known history: Hyllus did marry Iole. "It was necessary, then," says Jebb, "that the marriage should be imposed on him by his dying father's inexorable command."

That is the reason why Sophocles contrived the scene: he had to do it, and it has no further significance.

But the hypothesis does not explain the facts. I myself am not much of a dramatist, especially in comparison with Sophocles, but if I had got myself into such a fix, I hope I should have got out of it more sensibly. Hyllus has to marry Iole, in order that the plot may not contradict history: the sensible thing is to do it as quietly as possible, for why call attention to it? Let Heracles say, among other testamentary remarks: "One thing more, my son. I have ventured much for Iole, and she has suffered much; therefore I would have you take her to wife when I am gone"—a remark which would, incidentally, make the desired "tenderness and justice" a little clearer than it is in our text. Hyllus will reply: "A dying father's request is a sacred command. I will marry her, and cherish her." This could be made to sound reasonable, unobtrusive, and even edifying, and it reconciles the plot with the myth.

Sophocles does something very different. His Heracles makes Hyllus swear in advance to do two things for him. The first is to bear him to the summit of Oeta, place him, yet living, on a pyre and burn him; the other is a mere detail, "a slight favour, after the great one" (v. 1217): he shall marry Iole.—And why? Is he thinking of her well-being? If he is, he refrains from saying it; his declared reason is that no other man but his son may take her who has lain at his side—just that, and nothing more. Now, if we are to look at the facts, the facts are that each request horrifies Hyllus beyond measure; the first will make him the murderer of his father, while as for the second, he cries: "But who could do this? She, who alone shares the blame for my mother's death and for your present plight? Who could do this, unless avenging spirits were driving him to it? Better for me to die than live with my bitterest foe!" (vv. 1233 ff.). That is to say, instead of being quiet about the marriage, Sophocles is as noisy as he knows how: "It is bad, to be angry with a sick man, but how can one endure such folly?" (vv. 1230 f.). Sophocles no doubt had some reason for inventing this; clearly, it was not the necessity of satisfying the demand of the myth. About the funeral pyre, Heracles is willing to give way somewhat; about the marriage he remains adamant, though Hyllus continues to protest:

> —Am I really to be taught to behave abominably (δυσσεβεῖν)?
>
> —There is no abomination, if you are going to give me pleasure (τέρψεις).

So, despite his revulsion, and under threats of his father's curse, Hyllus gives way—and the myth is satisfied. But obviously, Jebb argued the wrong way round because his attention was fixed not on the play but on something outside it, the myth: Sophocles did not invent the "inexorable command" in order to bring about the marriage; he invented Hyllus' passionate resistance in order to make Heracles inexorable. The mere mechanical necessity existed, of course. But Sophocles does not merely obey it, for he would have done that quietly; he uses it and makes it significant. Significant of what? At least we can see that Heracles is behaving toward Hyllus now just as he had on the summit of Cenaeum, and toward Deianeira when without a thought he sent home Iole to supplant her, and toward Oechalia, when he destroyed so many in order to win a girl, and toward Iphitus and Lichas. There is consistency in the *poiesis*, and if we still ask why the normal rhythm broke down, and why Heracles' homecoming was not so triumphant as once was hoped, we have now at least part of the answer.

Who did kill Heracles? We asked the question earlier; perhaps it sounded foolish, since the answer is so evidently "Deianeira"; but we will ask it again.

We followed the action to the point where she is brought face to face with what for her is disaster. If we talk in lordly fashion of female jealousy, we shall not have been reading the play properly; the monologue at the beginning and Deianeira's first speech to the chorus were not written merely to fill up time.

She never has had much joy of her marriage, and now she never will; she is confronted with the ruin of her life, unless she can win back the love of the husband in whom she can forgive so much.

As for what she now does, it is natural for us to think of it as an Aristotelian *hamartia:* Sophocles has given her many virtues, but not shrewdness; it is her simple-mindedness that now brings her to ruin; one error destroys her. True; but this may not be the way in which Sophocles thought of it: we miss something if we concentrate too hard on her personal tragedy—though we shall certainly miss much if we think of it too little. I fancy however that it is not strictly according to Aristotle that her error destroys not only herself but Heracles too, and that his destruction should become the consummation of the play.

Let us notice, to begin with, that she does not use the supposed love-charm until she has consulted the chorus. If the chorus had been one of Solicitors, not of Trachinian maidens, she would have received better advice; as it is, what she gets is almost pathetic: "If you have reason to trust it, I think you are right . . . There is only one way of finding out—to try it." There is no point in amassing evidence from other sources to show that current Greek opinion was against the use of magic. Of course it was; but what we, in the theatre, are being told is that Deianeira's use of it seems reasonable to those whom she can consult. Already, the consultation, to some slight extent, makes her mistake typical rather than sharply individual. Then, we may fairly note that since Lichas is about to return, she must act quickly, if at all.

But there is more. When she has reason to suspect the truth she is terrified that "a fair hope of mine may have worked deadly mischief"; she observes that one should never "act hastily in a matter that is obscure"; "I read my lesson now, when it is too late to help" (vv. 666 f., 669 f., 710 f.). Nothing remarkable in this, perhaps? No; but now Sophocles goes on to illustrate precisely the same *hamartia* in Hyllus, and twice in one play is rather a lot. He enters, denounces his mother for deliberately murdering his father, sees her retire without saying a word, and comments vindictively: "There, let her go, and may I never see her again! Let her go, and enjoy it! May she experience the same delight (τέρψις) that she has given to my father!" But of course he too is mistaken; and the Nurse tells us what he said when he discovered the fact (vv. 932 ff.):

When he saw her dead he uttered a great cry. He saw now, poor boy, that he had driven her to it, for one of the servants had told him, too late, that she had done it innocently; and now he is passionately mourning her, and lamenting his own reckless accusation.

So that it happens twice: Deianeira and Hyllus both act too hastily and in ignorance, and have caused great mischief—though in fact Hyllus has not, since as we know Deianeira would have killed herself in any case (vv. 719–722), a fact which makes the repetition even more interesting. The suggestion has been made that when Sophocles wrote this play, and the *Tyrannus*, he was preoccupied with the thought that ὀψιμαθία, learning the truth too late, is a fertile source of disaster; but it seems hardly likely that so plain a fact would have come to his mind, with the force of a revelation, when he was now elderly. Rather this: that our human universe at best is a precarious and brittle thing; on the whole, it has a recognisable pattern, the alternation of sorrow and joy; but if someone throws a great spanner into its delicate works, as Heracles has done into this Trachinian microcosm, a smash may be expected. We must inevitably act in ignorance very often, and hasty action is a possibility always to be reckoned with. Heracles has no true cause of complaint if the fact works against him here. For who started it?

Deianeira then, intending something very different, destroyed Heracles. Yet how can we respond to certain implications of the drama without feeling that another agent was at work, Zeus? Let us recapitulate, and then continue.

A little while ago, contemplating what Heracles has done to

Oechalia, remembering how Zeus had already punished him for the killing of Iphitus, and not forgetting the last verse of the first ode, we found ourselves wondering what Zeus might be thinking of this wanton destruction of a whole city. Does Sophocles not tell us? Twice (vv. 237–241, 287 f.) we were told that Heracles was about to offer holy sacrifice to Zeus in return for his triumph. When Deianeira heard the news, and saw the wretched train of captives, she did not say: "What a glorious victory!" but something rather different. Hyllus begins his narrative by saying that Heracles came to the place of sacrifice "after sacking the city of Eurytus, bringing with him the trophies and first-fruits of his victory". The scene is set. Now, it may or may not be true that Sophocles had heard of only one kind of magic venom, a kind that needs heat to make it effective: in either case it is the fact that it was the heat from the sacrificial fire that caused the venom to begin working on Heracles' flesh. Must this not be the god's reply to Heracles' offering, for an audience that presumably believed in Zeus (whatever the phrase may mean)? If not, then Sophocles created a terribly imaginative piece of drama—by accident.

But if it is unsafe, and therefore illegitimate, to trust to the imagination in reading ancient drama, it is nevertheless highly respectable to read the text.

As Lichas promised (vv. 287 f.), Heracles does return home after offering his sacrifice, though he hardly returns in triumph, or to Deianeira. The burden of his long speech (vv. 1046–1111) is that he who has destroyed so many monsters is now himself destroyed—and by a woman, a female, his wife; that he who bore so many a stern conflict without flinching, without a groan, is now blubbering like a child. He is like Oedipus, for as Oedipus is struck down, as if by a malignant fate, at the point where he was apparently supreme, namely his intelligence, so is Heracles struck down in what was his great glory—his physical strength and endurance: "Look now at my hands, my back, my chest, my poor arms!" Those who want to find a "hero-worshipper" in Sophocles must do it without much support from Sophocles, for in these two cases at least it is the comparative littleness, not the greatness, of the hero that we are shown; and those who wish to find his heroes purged by their sufferings will not find it in the way in which the suffering hero speaks about his dead wife, or to his son; only perhaps in the final scene of apotheosis, which Sophocles forgot to include in the play.

But we were going to report not on these matters, but on what is said about Zeus and the thankoffering made on the summit of Cenaeum. Did Zeus play any part in it? Heracles appears to think so, whichever reading we adopt in v. 995: "O Cenaeum where I built my altar! What a cruel return, O Zeus, have you made me for my rich offerings!"

Next, we find him calling the robe that is destroying him "a robe woven by the Erinyes". Inevitably, the phrase recalls to us, and perhaps did to the Athenian audience too, the words used by Aegisthus when he saw the body of Agamemnon, killed by Clytemnestra (*Agam.* 1580): "Glad day of retribution, when I see this man lying here in a robe woven by the Erinyes!" There, the net thrown by Zeus around Troy (*Agam.* 355 ff.), though by the hand of the sacker of Troy, had become the net thrown around Agamemnon by the Erinyes, though by the hand of Clytemnestra. Heracles of course is denouncing "the treacherous daughter of Oeneus" who is destroying him, but his mention of the Erinyes tells us more than he means: as the destruction of Agamemnon was a direct consequence of what he had done, so is the destruction of Heracles. Later, it is true, Heracles declares that it is "blind Ruin" that has destroyed him, but we know better; the Erinys is concerned, and we know what she is.

But the mention of the Erinys may send our minds less far afield than to the *Agamemnon;* she has been mentioned already in this very play (vv. 895 ff.). When the Nurse has given to the chorus the bare news that Deianeira has killed herself, it says:

ἔτεκ' ἔτεκεν μεγάλαν ἁ
νέορτος ἅδε νύμφα
δόμοισι τοῖσδ' Ἐρινύν

(The new bride has indeed borne her child, a great Erinys for the house.)

The Erinys is the minister of Dike; the death of Deianeira is a natural consequence of what Heracles has done.

Then there is Hyllus, a tragic figure rather like Theseus in the *Hippolytus*, one to whom everything has happened at once; his father is dying, his mother is dead. He cries (v. 1022): "This is what Zeus does to us!"—a thought that he expands in the bitterness of his last speech:

Look upon the cruelty of the gods! they beget men, are called their fathers, and look unmoved on sufferings like these! No man can see what is to come, but what is present here is pitiful for us, discreditable for them, hardest of all for him who is enduring this blow.

Finally, there are the last four verses of the play, spoken presumably by the chorus-leader:

You have seen violent death, strange and terrible suffering; and nothing is present here but Zeus.

Which final words Jebb paraphrases, correctly of course: "Zeus is manifested in each and all of these events".

It is indeed reassuring to discover that purely dramatic implications can be trusted—sometimes at least. They made us feel that what happened on Cenaeum was the work of Zeus, not of Deianeira only; that Zeus was punishing Heracles for a second time, and in a more terrible way, for a more terrible act of wanton violence. Now we find, as it were, documentary evidence that this is just what Sophocles meant. Zeus is in each and all of these events; it is the *theoi* that have brought about the sufferings which make Hyllus so understandably bitter; the first-born of the new bride is Death, an Erinys, and it was an Erinys that wove the robe.

It is plain enough, surely, that the long debate on the unity of the play is nothing but a mistake generated by our own ingrained "cult of personality". The *parodos* gives us the scale on which we must think, a scale natural enough to the original audience, unnatural or at least unfamiliar to us. Once we see what the scale is, that question of unity ceases to exist. The *parodos* set before us a natural rhythm which justified hopes of peace and joy; also the confident belief that Zeus will not be unmindful of his son—as indeed he is not. What follows falls into place. At the end, the audience of course will inevitably have in mind that Heracles was taken from his funeral pyre to Olympus, to become a god. That however is not the end of this *praxis*. This one ends where it does, with the destruction of Deianeira and Heracles, and the misery of Hyllus their son.

But this gives rise to a different problem of unity, difficult for us only, because for some three centuries we have been doing our thinking in mainly scientific terms, not religious. For us, "religion" has shrunk into an "unshakeable but placid piety"; for us it is not natural to express in "religious" terms our conception of how the universe works. We asked: "Who killed Heracles?" and have found two answers: Deianeira, and Zeus. Where then is any unity in the action? The question is not new to us, and there is no need to spend much time on it; for who routed the Persians, in Aeschylus' play: the Greeks, seconded by the soil of Greece, or the *theos?* As there, so here: Sophocles does what he can, or what he judges to be enough, to show that in the given circumstances what Deianeira does is what a Deianeira would do; she is desperate, she does a desperate thing, and its results are frightful. If she had been wiser, if she had suspected the truth, she would not have done it. But then, we are not always wise, and often we cannot know the truth, and sometimes we do act too hastily: look at Hyllus for example. She does what she *would* do. What she, so innocently, does to Heracles becomes also the punishment visited upon him by the *theos*. There is nothing new in this, nothing to puzzle anyone who has understood the *Persae*, or the fact that Cassandra is done to death by Clytemnestra and Apollo at once, and for different reasons, except that in each case it is the satisfaction of anger. So too in the *Antigone*, ruin descends on Creon because the *theoi* are affronted by what he has done, and their Erinyes lie in wait for him, but also because Antigone, Haemon, and Eurydice do what they would naturally do, in their circumstances. Either we grasp the sense of this consistent mode of thought, or we reduce to artistic and mental nullity one play after another—for there is nullity, if they are full of rhetorically pious gestures which, on examination, mean nothing.

But there are other structural features in the play that we must look at if we are to examine it properly. There are the enfolding prophecies, and—even more striking—there is the fact that Heracles is destroyed not only by Deianeira and by Zeus, but also by Nessus the centaur: the venom that was the Hydra's blood and was the death of Nessus, becomes the death of Heracles too. Sophocles meant this so seriously that he invented an oracle to emphasise it, that none should cause the death of Heracles but one already dead. Yet he is far from suggesting that there is any "justice" in it. The Hydra is indeed left outside the frame, but clearly we are not to see anything wrong, when Heracles rid the world of a noxious monster. Nessus is within the frame, and about his death Sophocles is explicit: Heracles shot him from the river-bank because he was laying a lewd hand on Deianeira. There seems to be no reason in justice why Heracles should suffer vengeance for that, yet he does, and Sophocles is emphatic about it. What was he thinking of?

To this question, as we saw earlier (p. 37) some modern scholars return a confident answer at once: he was not thinking at all. The affair of the venom, like "the superstitious handling of Hector's sword", is an upsurge of "the dark substrate of Sophoclean tragedy", as Lattimore puts it (*Poetry*, p. 77), an "atmosphere of unreason, barbarism, primitive passion, where logic cannot reach". F. J. H. Letters was of the same opinion:

the play "is riddled with primitive magic", utterly unlike the other six plays in its "primitive and daemonic myth". Yet, as we have seen, the play is in important ways strangely like the *Tyrannus*, and we should say odd things about one or two Shakespearian plays if we took this short cut from the poet's myth to his real thought. We do not infer from *The Tempest* that Shakespeare had relapsed into a belief in magic, and why it should be quite different with Sophocles does not seem clear—unless Ignotus put his finger on the spot in making the gloomy diagnosis which I ventured to quote earlier.

The half-primitive Sophocles was indeed confidently endorsed by Ignotus, but it may be that since then we have found some reason to mistrust confidence. On this matter of unreason, it happens that Sophocles has bequeathed us an unusual amount of evidence. I propose now to examine it.

The dead centaur destroys the living Heracles: trying to be cautious, we note that in no fewer than five of the seven plays Sophocles uses the idea of the dead reaching out to destroy the living. (I have discussed this elsewhere: *Form and Meaning*, pp. 193 ff; I hope that the repetition is pardonable.) Therefore, not being very sure of ourselves, except that temporary certainties can deceive any of us, we will take bearings from the other instances, beginning with "the superstitious handling of Hector's sword".

Sophocles was deliberate about this. We may surely presume that everyone in his audience would recall the great scene in the *Iliad* in which Hector and Ajax fight their duel until the coming of night parts them, whereupon they exchange their gifts. In three particulars, not unimportant ones, Sophocles alters the story: he invents the bitter hatred that Ajax bears toward Hector; he causes Hector to have been tied still living to Achilles' chariot and dragged along to his death; he invents the detail that he was tied to it by the belt that he had received from Ajax. In passing, we may glance at Jebb's comment on v. 1031 of the play: "It is not known whence Sophocles derived this version, which strangely mars the very climax of the *Iliad;*

possibly from one of the two cyclic poets." We note the implication: a respectable tragic poet would never have interfered with the story, but must be following an existing "version". On this occasion it looks as if Sophocles was the malefactor, perhaps not knowing the rules.

The first time the sword-and-belt theme is announced is Ajax' famous ironical speech (vv. 646 ff.). We will place it where Sophocles did—in its context:

This hateful sword I will bury; let Night and Hades keep it evermore. I had it from Hector, my bitterest enemy. The proverb is true: the gifts of enemies never bring good. Therefore I shall know for the future that I must yield to the gods and revere the Atreidae. Winter has to make room for Summer, and Night get out of the way of Day. Why should I too not learn modesty?

The deep irony of the speech is that Ajax learns the truth about this all-commanding rhythm, and learns it the hard way, only when by his own act he has put it out of his power to accommodate himself to it, even if such pliancy were in him. All he can do now, as he sees it, is to do what Winter and Night do: ἐκχωρεῖν, "make room", ἐξίστασθαι, "get out of the way". As Lattimore truly says, "Ajax has seen that his death is necessary by sheer logic". But we must remark that Sophocles brings together the sword, the truth of the old proverb, and the rhythm of Nature. It is odd, but there it is.

The second appearance of the theme (vv. 817–822) does no more than emphasise the personal hatred that Ajax had for Hector, but the third (vv. 1028–1039) goes much further. Teucer says:

Look! Even in death Hector was to destroy you! Think on what has befallen these two men: Hector was dragged to his death by the belt Ajax gave him, and now Ajax has died upon Hector's sword. Was it not an Erinys that forged the sword, and Death (Hades) that made the belt? I declare, though another man may demur, that it is the *theoi* who have brought this to pass, like all else.

In fact, "Nothing is here but Zeus"; and from the last sentence that Sophocles wrote above we may perhaps infer that he was consciously saying something new, or something old but in a new way. At all events he does, formally and explicitly, connect what is for us a mere double coincidence with the Erinys and the *theoi*. Primitive superstition? The main structure of the play is as reasonable as can be—or shall we say, as reasonable as the imaginings of a poet can be. Ajax, never able to "think mortal thoughts" (vv. 761, 777), so acts that suicide is the only way out. So far as the logic of the play goes, the instrument of death might be anything—a dagger, for example. But Sophocles makes it Hector's sword, and he makes it abundantly clear that Ajax does not kill himself merely because he has that sword; there is no magic in it.

Not quite understanding this, let us take another case. In the *Electra*, when Clytemnestra has screamed for the third and last time, the chorus sings (vv. 1417 ff.):

> τελοῦσ' ἀραί · ζῶσιν οἱ
> γᾶς ὑπαὶ κείμενοι.
> παλίρρυτον γὰρ αἷμ' ὑπεξαιροῦσι τῶν
> κτανόντων οἱ πάλαι θανόντες.

> The dead are stirring;
> Those who were killed of old now
> Drink in return the blood of those that killed them.

If we had no context, or thought that we could make better sense by neglecting it, we could build on this passage an impressive argument for supernaturalism or irrationalism: the angry dead live on in their graves, rumbling with indignation, until at last their ghostly and grisly arms reach out and kill their slayers; the dead drink their blood. We do not say this because the whole play shows that it would be nonsense; its every detail shows that the old crime is recoiling upon its authors in the most natural way possible: those who are suffering from the murder and the usurpation are doing what they can, what this Orestes and Electra (though not this

Chrysothemis) *would* do, to reverse the situation. The tide is turning, παλίρρυτον, "refluent". The play further insists that Apollo and Zeus and Dike and Ares and the Erinyes (vv. 1384 ff.) are active in what Orestes and Electra are doing. Therefore we know where we are: when the murdered Agamemnon reaches out to kill his killers and drink their blood we are in the presence not of superstition but of reason itself; not "where logic cannot reach" but where dramatic imagery takes over. Further, the picture of the vengeful dead cannot prove that the Athenians of the time believed in vengeful dead; what it does prove is that the imagery would be understood. Prospero's magic in *The Tempest* does not prove that Shakespeare's audience believed in magic, only that they had heard of it and could take it as a dramatic device.

The remaining instances are more transient. Antigone says in her long *commos* (vv. 869 ff.):

> O my brother! through an evil marriage you were slain, and I
> Live; but your dead hand destroys me.

Here indeed there is nothing nightmarish, but the essential idea is the same. "The evil that men do lives after them" would be a reasonable gloss.

What we find in the *Tyrannus* (1451 ff.) is perhaps more interesting. Oedipus is begging Creon to send him away from Thebes. Where? We should not be surprised if he went on to say: "Anywhere will do, if it is far enough from Thebes". What he does say is:

> My home must be the mountains, on Cithaeron,
> Which while they lived my parents chose to be
> My tomb: they wished to slay me; now they shall.

Why should Sophocles have written this? It is so transient a detail that one would hardly notice it, except that the idea is habitual with him. If we do listen to it, do we not receive some such impression as this, that there would be a certain "rightness" in it, if Oedipus were to die where his parents had designed? When I say "rightness" I mean not a moral rightness, but something more like the rightness that we attribute to a right-angle. An action begun but frustrated would at last be fulfilled; a pattern would be completing itself.

Such are the other Sophoclean passages that use the idea of the dead killing the living and may guide our understanding of the Centaur's revenge. The suicide of Ajax is the closest parallel, and in connection with that it may be helpful to look at a Shakespearian suicide, that of Cassius in *Julius Caesar;* for when he kills himself it is with the same sword with which he had helped to kill Caesar, and Shakespeare too makes some little fuss about it. He makes Cassius say to Pindarus (V 3):

> with this good sword
> That ran through Caesar's bowels, search this bosom;

and

> Caesar, thou art reveng'd
> Even with the sword that killed thee.

So also Brutus, a little later:

> O Julius Caesar, thou art mighty yet:
> Thy spirit walks abroad and turns our swords
> Into our proper entrails.

Shakespeare at least is using the sword significantly; it becomes a manifest symbol of Dike, however we translate the word in a Shakespearian context: what Cassius had done recoils upon him. This is clear; what we cannot see, in the *Ajax*, is any logical or moral connection between the duel and exchange of gifts, and the suicide. What makes it the more puzzling is that in the main fabric of the play we have a complete explanation of the tragedy, as we have seen, so that the sword-and-belt looks like something irrational superfluously added to something rational—as when the man explained that the heavy picture on his wall was kept in place partly by magic, partly by four long screws. Superstition, I take it, is something put in the place of reason; what Sophocles gives is something added to reason. What is more, we are told that the sword was forged by the Erinys, and the connection between the Erinys and Dike is normally a close one.

What we are considering is apparently a matter of some substance, for we find exactly the same ideas and difficulties in the *Trachiniae.* Here too is a complete and logical explanation of the catastrophe, on two levels as usual: it is Heracles' own moral violence that leads to his destruction, through Deianeira and by Zeus. Hector's sword has its parallel in the Hydra's venom: neither seems to have any real connection with the main argument of the play. It is true that there is some link of a moral kind between the killing of the Centaur and the destruction of Heracles: we can point out that it was a conspicuous fault in Heracles which caused the venom to be used against him, for had he remained loyal to his wife, she would never have given it a thought. This is indeed in the play, but what is made much more prominent is that the Centaur, though dead, achieves a revenge to which nothing in justice entitled him. Therefore this too is an apparently unnecessary addition to an argument already complete. Yet, as the Erinys forged the sword, so has the Erinys woven the robe; and in each case all that happens falls within the circle of divine action, both what is moral and understandable, and what is not.

How interesting will it be, if we discover that Shakespeare does something comparable, with Cassius? For just before the speech quoted above Shakespeare makes him say:

> This day I breathèd first; time is come round,
> And where I did begin, there shall I end;
> My life has run its compass.

A spectator who had only at this moment come into the theatre might find this a distressing irrelevance; he might even wonder if Shakespeare, being unduly superstitious, believed it to be particularly unlucky for a man to commit suicide on his birthday. But of course the point is that this play too has already established its firm structure of reason; coming out of that, the passage derives overtones from it. We cannot explain it logically, not because it is bogged down in unreason, but because it is conceived imaginatively. Lattimore rightly says of Ajax that he "has seen that his death is necessary by sheer logic"; the same is true of Cassius. But in each case, the poet looks beyond. What Cassius further sees, Shakespeare does not put into words, and I would rather not try, but he does see, by a flash of illumination rather than by logic, that his death is part of, or in harmony with, something much vaster, some cosmic order. A *praxis* has completed itself, has come full circle, and the completeness is expressed in poetic (or dramatic) logic: he turns the same sword upon himself; and then, the action is set also against the background of Time itself: "Where I did begin, there shall I end". It is no shapeless, random, meaningless universe. The Birthday is not logic, but rather an extension of logic.

Therefore, we find Shakespeare doing something comparable to what is done by Sophocles, though by no means so conspicuously, or at least, not here: Cassius is killing himself with that same sword—and lo! it is his birthday; Ajax' suicide is a natural culmination of his whole way of life—and lo! the sword he has in his hand had been Hector's; Heracles' conduct recoils on him, but the instrument is the venom of the Hydra and Nessus, both of whom he had killed, with every justification. In these two plays, Sophocles, as we might put it, works out the main action in the clear daylight of reason, and then adds to it a substantial fringe that exists in a sort of logical penumbra where *we* can see only coincidence, or at the best only a sketchy logic; and this he does deliberately, inasmuch as a ready dagger would have served as well for Ajax, and with very little trouble we could invent for Deianeira's love-charm a source that would not involve Nessus; and we cannot ride away on the vague idea that he does it for "dramatic effect", because each time he says, with emphasis, that the same Erinyes and gods are at work here as in the main section, which stands in the full light of reason.

Surely the inference is clear: he is seeing our universe as one which is orderly throughout, both where we can see and where we cannot; or let us say, since we are apt to confuse order with comfort and "natural justice", a universe which has its own steady mode of working and is the reverse of chaotic. Where we can see clearly, as in the main action of the play, we can see (that is, the poet represents to us) a completely logical process; when the action is extended into the penumbra, we cannot see it; our eyesight is not good enough. If it were, he suggests, if we were omniscient, like the gods, we should see how every event is linked, however remotely, with every other, as in an infinite web.

Here is the source of that feeling for "pattern" that haunts his work, and comes to the surface momentarily even in that passage of the *Tyrannus* where in fact the pattern is not going to be completed. The idea of the dead killing the living is but a sharply dramatic way of focussing it. An event in the past suddenly leaps across dark space like an electric spark, and makes contact with something in the present. It does not explain, or justify, or control; that is not its function. The justification or explanation is given in the main part of the play, in the daylight. "Ajax has seen that his death is necessary by sheer logic"; what is more important is that *we* have seen the logic whereby he has brought himself to such a pass. The sword looks like a casual coincidence; it certainly does not help to explain why he is killing himself. It is no cause, but there is a link: the poet embeds it in the same context as Night and Day, and he says that the Erinys made it. Such sudden flashes —like Cassius' remark that "today is my birthday"—are an imaginative statement of faith: what is out there in the dark is not random.

This method of composition may well remind us of what Plato does in some of his dialogues, the *Gorgias* for example: he will take the argument as far as logic can go, and when it can go no further he will continue in a myth, expressing what he believes but cannot prove. The myth, in Plato, is not a sudden relapse into unreason, nor is the analogous feature in Sophocles' work. It is true that Hector's sword, the recurring idea of the dead killing the living, take us into a region "where logic cannot reach", but when we examine not the poesy of the plays but the *poiesis* too, we discover that this region is not below logic, but is on the far side of it.

Heracles then is destroyed by Deianeira, by Zeus, and by the dead Centaur, and the final declaration: "Nothing is here but Zeus" amounts to a declaration of unity: our universe has its regular way of working, both in what we can see and understand, and in what we cannot. One important aspect of the play remains, and it is one which is evidently bound up with this: the oracles. Oracles must seriously concern us when we turn to the *Tyrannus*, a play that can be so enigmatic for us; therefore it might be useful to consider here what we can know about the dramatic function of oracles, before we attack that play.

To the modern reader it may seem evident, especially if he is not quite sure when Stoicism and astrology came into the Greek world, that divine prophecy implies divine control: "so-and-so *shall* happen". Indeed, there is a prophecy of this kind in the *Philoctetes:* for no discoverable reason the gods have determined that Troy shall be captured in the following summer, and by two named persons: Philoctetes and Neoptolemus. So there it is: the gods have decided, and men can do nothing but go through their prescribed motions. But it would be simple-minded to assume, as one or two writers have done, that divine prophecy always means this; that the characters of these plays are "fate-driven men" and therefore of little interest to us today. There is other evidence, and as for the divine decree of the *Philoctetes*, it is very plain, if one looks, that it is quite peripheral, no more than a useful datum.

We might take a precautionary glance at those two classic works the *Antigone* and the *Nautical Almanac*. The latter is full of precise prophecies, but those who make them are not under the delusion that they exercise control over the celestial bodies about whose future movements they are so certain. The astronomer can prophesy because he is in possession of all the relevant facts, and if one of the prophecies failed, there would indeed be perturbations in astronomical circles. Teiresias' prophecy in the other work we have mentioned before: he tells Creon: "So-and-so is going to happen to you, because the gods are angry with what you have done". So-and-so does happen to him, just because the people concerned behave as we might have expected; of divine intervention there is no sign whatever. It was from studying the behaviour of birds and of sacrificial meat on a fire that Teiresias foresaw what was to come: if we allow for the difference between the imagination of a poet and the mathematical procedures of an astronomer, we can see that these two great works have something in common: in each case the prophecy is of the type: "this is going to happen", not "this shall happen", and in each case the basic assumption is that the events dealt with are such as obey certain natural laws—the one, of the physical universe, the other of the human universe, admittedly a less predictable one because more complex.

In the *Trachiniae* there are the two separate oracles; how does Sophocles use them? The first concerns the period of Heracles' absence, the critical attack on Oechalia, and its ambiguous outcome: death, or lasting peace. It is given to us at the outset, to an effect that we have noted already. The fact that Deianeira knows that the decisive hour has come cuts out a lot of dramatic lumber; the action jumps at once to a point near its climax. A similar tightening of the tragic interest is achieved by the second part of this oracle, that it will be death, or peace. About this, enough has been said already.

What of the second oracle, that no living creature, but one already in Hades, will cause the death of Heracles? This one is not divulged to us until nearly the end of the play, and the fact is important. Perhaps we say, too readily, reading the play analytically rather than imaginatively: "When Heracles learns from Hyllus that the venom came from Nessus, he knows indeed that his end is near"—just as some commentators tell us that the purpose of Teiresias' prophecy in the *Antigone* is to break Creon's obstinacy. It does that, of course, but is that all? If so, the elaborate description of the birds and the sacrifice was only padding; and if the audience needed to be assured that Heracles' death is indeed near, it would readily take his own word for it: let him say: "O my son, I see the grim figure of Death advancing upon me. My time has come; it is the end . . ." Clearly, the oracle about Nessus, mentioned now for the first time, does much more than this; it suddenly reveals to us that the strange, tortuous history of the venom is not, as perhaps we had thought, a succession of coincidences; it was foreseen, therefore not random.

But foreseen, or predetermined? Sophocles employs oracles much more than Aeschylus or Euripides, and it is important that we should not misunderstand his use of them, if we can avoid it. As we have seen, he is willing to use the idea of determinism in the *Philoctetes*, though incidentally. The climax of the main action there comes when Neoptolemus redeems his promise and his honour by making ready to take Philoctetes not to Troy but home to Greece, and is assured by Philoctetes that because of his bow, the villainous Atreidae will be powerless to stop him. The thought is simply not in our minds at this moment that Neoptolemus cannot take him home because the gods, for no assignable reason, have made certain arrangements for the capture of Troy. This prophecy certainly remains on the fringe of the action. That made by Teiresias in the *Antigone* does not imply determinism, but has the specific and intelligible dramatic function that we noted in it. What of those in the *Trachiniae?* What we say must take full account of the fact that in the main structure of the play all the weight is thrown upon certain voluntary actions of Heracles', all of the same kind, and on what others do in consequence, notably Deianeira but also the minor characters; and upon the idea of a rhythm that prevails in human affairs but breaks down in this instance. What these other characters do, in the circumstances, is perfectly natural, and they are characterised so far, and no further, that what they do shall seem natural. Earlier in the discussion we used the metaphor of an infinite web of events, extending up to the present: does it extend also into the future? Our evidence is that the answer is certainly No, if we mean that the agents can only fulfil something already laid down for them; rather, they are on the front edge of the web and continue the weaving, by what they freely do. The conception of prophecy that best fits the evidence is that implied in Aristotle's one remark about the gods, ἅπαντα γὰρ ἀποδίδομεν τοῖς θεοῖς ὁρᾶν (1454B 5): "By convention, the gods can see everything" —what given persons will do in given circumstances, what "unforeseeable" chances will arise to influence them, what the outcome will necessarily be—everything; and what is implied by the word "necessarily" is precisely what is implied by the conception of Dike and the Erinys, used whether by Sophocles or by Heracleitus: the universe has and obeys its own principles. Prophecy, in a play, is a kind of dramatic shorthand.

Such is the real unity of the *Trachiniae:* the prophecies, the "pattern", the half-seen actions of Zeus, the vividly presented actions of all the human characters, are all well-considered parts of a solid structure. The barbarous and primitive disappear; a poetic declaration of faith takes its place. The division of interest between Deianeira and Heracles arises only when we substitute a romantic focus for the one which Sophocles was using.

As an interlude in this chapter, and as a modest experiment in Comparative Literature, it may be of interest to look for a few moments at a fairly close Shakespearian parallel to the apparently mocking oracles of the *Trachiniae*. In *2 King Henry IV*, as Act IV ends, the King is at the point of death, and he says:

> It hath been prophesied to me many years
> I should not die but in Jerusalem,
> Which vainly I suppos'd the Holy Land.

Now he sees what the prophecies really meant: a room in Westminster Abbey called the Jerusalem Chamber. Why did the gods play this cruel trick on him? What was Shakespeare thinking of—if he was thinking? He was assuredly thinking, but to answer the question "About what?" we have to go some way back, since Shakespeare too had his command of long-range *poiesis*. I trust that the excursion will not prove a waste of time, and, if we find that great tragic poets have certain things in common, that this will not appear incredible.

We shall have to start out from what is virtually the first play of a trilogy, *King Richard II*. In this "trilogy" prophecies abound, no less than in the *Trachiniae*.

We recall the opening of the play: Richard has exiled Mowbray and Henry Bolingbroke, Earl of Hereford. For the solemn verdict of Trial by Combat he has, at the last moment, substituted his own decree, which Shakespeare makes to sound rather arbitrary: perpetual banishment for Mowbray, ten years for Bolingbroke, at once reduced to six, as a favour to his father Gaunt. His reason for stopping the combat arouses in us the suspicion that Sophocles was not the only master of tragic irony; it is:

> For that our kingdom's earth should not be soil'd
> With that dear blood that it hath fostered.

At the end of the play it is Richard's own blood that soils the earth of his kingdom, and in the two plays that follow blood flows in streams all over England.

Next, the scene in which the Duchess of Gloucester implores Gaunt to avenge on Richard the death of her husband, Gaunt's brother. We hear Gaunt's remarkable answer, the Socratic answer, that it is better to suffer than to do wrong. The tragic dilemma is posed, fairly and squarely: the King is "God's substitute, His deputy anointed in His sight"; if the King has done wrong, as he has and will do again,

> Let Heaven revenge; for I may never lift
> An angry arm against His minister.

But this is exactly what his son Bolingbroke is going to do; for upon Gaunt's death Richard plunders his estate, now lawfully Bolingbroke's, and he comes back from exile, lawlessly, to claim the lawful dues that the King has taken from him. It is what Aeschylus called the *πρώταρχος ἄτη*, the crime that began crimes—unless we can more fairly impute that to Richard. Henry Bolingbroke demands of Richard merely his estates and honours, no more—and we must believe him; but he is supported by many who can endure Richard no longer, and he backs his demand with the threat of force. So, little by little, the deposition comes about.

York had warned Richard in terms that Aeschylus or Sophocles would have recognised:

> Take Hereford's rights away, and take from Time
> His charters and his customary rights;
> Let not tomorrow then ensue today;
> Be not thyself; for how art thou a king
> But by fair sequence and succession?

Richard is affronting Dike—whatever the Shakespearian English for Dike is—and Dike, as we know, has the habit of reasserting herself, and not always gently.

Richard returns from his Irish war to find himself and his cause in very poor state, and here comes the first of the prophecies that we will notice—an interesting one, because although it is made, or implied rather, by a bishop, it is not fulfilled (III 2, 27 f.):

> Fear not, my lord: that Power that made you king
> Hath power to keep you king, in spite of all.

So too Richard, in his reply to Carlisle:

> The breath of worldly men cannot depose
> The deputy elected by the Lord.
> For every man that Bolingbroke hath press'd
> To lift shrewd steel against our golden crown,

God for his Richard hath in heavenly pay
A glorious angel: then, if angels fight,
Weak men must fall, for Heaven still guards the right.

Richard may be a good poet, but he is a bad king, a bad prophet, and a bad theologian: a bad prophet because the expected angels do not appear; a bad theologian, because he should have known that worldly men can depose a deputy elected by the Lord; they can, and they did. Heaven will not stop them any more than the gods stopped Creon from killing Antigone. What Heaven does is to make them pay the inevitable penalty. What that is we learn from a later and more successful prophecy made by the Bishop of Carlisle (IV 1,134 ff.):

My lord of Hereford here, whom you call king,
Is a foul traitor to proud Hereford's king;
And if you crown him, let me prophesy,
The blood of English shall manure the ground . . .
And in this seat of peace, tumultuous wars
Shall kin with kin and kind with kind confound;
Disorder, horror, fear, and mutiny
Shall here inhabit, and this land be call'd
The field of Golgotha and dead men's skulls.

It all comes to pass, in the next two plays, and Shakespeare makes plain why it came to pass; there is no mystery. The deposition has shaken loyalty and trust and introduced violence instead. The Northumberland party itself, having helped Henry to become king, resents being treated by him as a king must treat disobedient subjects.

For this prophetic service the Bishop is arrested by Northumberland, and soon Henry is saying:

On Wednesday next we solemnly set down
Our coronation.

Richard is sent to the Tower.

But before Wednesday next arrives, in fact at the close of this very scene, Shakespeare inserts a short passage in which the Abbot of Westminster hints to the Bishop and to Aumerle that a plot should be devised against the new King. Regarding this, I take leave to discuss briefly what is, to my mind, an interesting mistake made by A. W. Gomme in his Sather Lectures (*The Greek Attitude*, pp. 36 f.). Gomme, in his stimulating way, is comparing Homer and Shakespeare in their use of their "historical" material. The argument—a perfectly sound one—is that each poet used it as he could make it significant, but that each found in his "chronicles" material that he could not assimilate yet did not feel able to leave out. A Shakespearian example is this plot:

> When he wrote *King Richard II*—the vain, weak, lovable man so unfit to be a king, thrust aside by the ruthless Bolingbroke, the man so obviously born to success in this world—there he found, *in his chronicles*, a story which he could make into a play by transforming the story of what happened into one of "what would happen" without deserting historical truth, or rather (such was Shakespeare's way) partly transforming it, leaving a good deal of incongruous historical residue.

But much more than the Abbot's plot is inorganic or at best only peripheral, if we read the play as one about persons: the tragedy of the weak but lovable man thrust aside by one who is neither. If the thought we carry away with us is: "Still, Richard was the finer man of the two", just that, then, to go no further, the speech of Gaunt is detachable, not functional. It is the problem of the *Trachiniae* over again; the *praxis* must take precedence over the persons—and then the structure becomes intelligible and the play more pleasurable. The plot is far from "incongruous residue". Law has been overthrown, violence now reigns; a plot laid against the new King, even before his coronation, speaks eloquently, with Aeschylean eloquence, of the insecurity brought about by the deposition. It is a dramatic prelude to the streams of blood that manure the soil of England in the next two plays; for men who might have respected the Deputy appointed by the Lord are not necessarily going to respect the deputy appointed by Lord Northumberland—least of all, Northumberland himself. From the crime that began crime, the tragedy grows and spreads, almost as if Shakespeare had taken Aeschylus for his model. Henry is big enough to pardon Aumerle, but he cries: "Have I no friend will rid me of this living fear?"; Exton posts north, has Richard murdered, and receives from Henry no thanks, but the curse: "With Cain go wander through the shades of night." The play began with Henry Bolingbroke, Earl of Hereford, chivalrous, loyal, "lusty, young, and cheerly drawing breath", willing to stake his life against one whom he thinks a traitor to his King; it ends with Henry mournfully following the coffin of that same King, and saying:

> I'll make a voyage to the Holy Land
> To wash this blood from off my guilty hand.

It is the first announcement of the Jerusalem theme. Had Henry read Aeschylus he would have known that blood spilt on the ground remains, calling for more blood.

When the next play opens, a period of rebellion and bloodshed seems to have closed, and Henry is saying:

> No more the thirsty entrance of this soil
> Shall daub her lips with her own children's blood . . .
> The edge of war, like an ill-sheathèd knife
> No more shall cut his master. Therefore, friends,
> As far as to the sepulchre of Christ . . .

Henry hopes

> To chase these pagans in those holy fields
> Over whose acres walked those blessed feet . . .

but at once comes news of insurrection in the West, and soon the North is in rebellion. Worcester "broke his staff" rather than serve Richard any longer; it was his brother Northumberland who was Bolingbroke's chief supporter: now the two of them regret "that sweet and lovely rose" and revile "this thorn, this canker, Bolingbroke". They will support Mortimer, the lawful heir, against him, and so clear the name of England "from the detested blot of murderous subornation". The battle of Shrewsbury is fought, and the incomparable Hotspur killed, because Worcester could not trust "the kind and liberal offer of the King" and conceals it from Hotspur, "for treason is but trusted as the fox".

The sorry tale continues: mistrust, bad faith, rebellion. Henry, in the middle of the next play (III 1,76–79), recalls the prophecy made by Richard to Northumberland:

> "The time will come that foul sin, gath'ring head,
> Shall break into corruption"—so went on,
> Foretelling this same time's condition
> And the division of our amity.

At the end of the scene Henry says:

> And were these inward wars once out of hand
> We would, dear Lords, unto the Holy Land.

At once there follows the double treachery at Gaultree Forest. Soon (IV 4) the Jerusalem theme recurs. Henry is in Council:

> Now, lords, if God doth give successful end
> To this debate that bleedeth at our doors,
> We will our youth lead on to higher fields
> And draw no swords but what are sanctified.

Now at last good news come from all quarters: "There is not now a rebel's sword unsheath'd". So that all is well, and at once Henry is taken sick and swoons. Later, lying at the point of death, he asks:

> Doth any name particular belong
> Unto the lodging where I first did swoon?

Warwick tells him that it is called Jerusalem. Then Henry, like Heracles, knows all:

> Laud be to God! even there my life must end.
> It hath been prophesied to me many years
> I should not die but in Jerusalem,

> Which vainly I suppos'd the Holy Land.
> But bear me to that chamber; there I'll lie;
> In that Jerusalem shall Harry die.

And perhaps we should hear an echo of it in the last speech of the play, when Prince John lays odds that under the new king

> ere this year expire
> We bear our civil swords and native fire
> As far as France.

Not indeed "as far as to the sepulchre of Christ", but foreign wars are at least more glorious than civil wars.

Perhaps it has been no small feat to write even so much about these plays without once mentioning Falstaff and Prince Hal. They do exist, and are important, but the continual prophecies also exist and are important; and they are surely close enough to those of the *Trachiniae* to deserve our attention. In the English plays, they contribute nothing at all to the mere plot. In the Greek play, as we have seen, the prophecy about the fifteen months is used as a dramatic convenience; its promise, or half-promise, of peace sheds what we know to be a delusive light over the play, just as does Henry's desire to drive the infidel off those holy fields, and thereby to wash the blood from off his guilty hand. The second prophecy in the *Trachiniae* is exactly like the one about Jerusalem inasmuch as we do not hear of it until it has been fulfilled, but in an unexpected way. None of them controls or even influences what the actors do—being indeed in this respect unlike the Witches' prophecies in *Macbeth* and those of Apollo in the *Tyrannus;* they serve rather direct our minds to certain immutable principles which underlie the events, as to the eye of a geologist the rock-formation underneath a landscape explains the scenery. The ironical fulfillment of the prophecies given to Heracles and Henry certainly does not imply a God or gods who deceive; rather, it emphasises, by its sharp point, the way in which we deceive ourselves. So too with Macbeth: he was to be invulnerable except to a man not born of woman, and until "Great Birnam wood to high Dunsinane hill shall come against him"; but the security that this seemed to promise the criminal proved to be an illusion. Such ironies are like the sudden tearing away of a veil.

To a Hellenist, the most interesting of Shakespeare's prophecies may well be that made in the Temple Garden by Warwick, in *2 King Henry VI* (II 4)—interesting, because it might almost be Shakespeare's version of the first five verses of the *Iliad*. A fierce quarrel between Richard of York and young Somerset of the house of Lancaster had been submitted by them to adjudication by rose-buds; the verdict of those present—one of them a Lawyer—has gone decisively for Richard. Somerset says he will appeal—to his sword. Toward the end of the scene Warwick says:

> And here I prophesy: this brawl today,
> Grown to this faction, in the Temple garden,
> Shall send between the red rose and the white
> A thousand souls to death and deadly night.

This trilogy is not very highly esteemed; as historical drama, a picture of "what did happen", it can be tedious: Gomme found the plays "hardly come to life before II 5 of the Third Part," also that the first two parts "show very clearly the lack of tragic interest in characters which are just bad" (p. 66). But Warwick's prophecy (and of course other details in the structure) were intended to turn "what did happen" into "what would happen"; our present-day sharp interest in particular persons and events obscures this from us—as it notably does in the *Trachiniae*. Once again, when we see the structure in its designed perspective, it begins to make more sense. There may be no tragic interest in characters who are just bad, but in neither trilogy is Shakespeare expecting us to look at his characters severally. Neither is Sophocles in the *Trachiniae*. These plays are bigger than we sometimes think.

2. The *Tyrannus*

There is no question, this time, of fumbling composition, nor of the direct and powerful impact which the play makes, whether in performance or in a reading. Yet perhaps in the cold light of the morning after, one asks what it all amounts to, and perhaps is not very sure of the answer. Certainly the answers that are given by critics offer the usual variety, and one can meet classical scholars who, long familiar with the play, think of it only with a cold respect: the perpetual ironies are overdone, the coincidences are too much to take, the play is no more than a *tour de force*. A *tour de force* in the theatre is indeed not to be sneezed at, but if the *Tyrannus* is a play that addresses itself to the nerves and emotions but not seriously to the mind, then we must not include it among the world's great works of art. We have ourselves just met another problem. We have reached the conclusion that the normal function of prophecy and of "divine" participation in Greek plays is to link the particular action with some steady principle or law: we should be hard put to it to argue the same here. In this important matter the *Tyrannus* seems unlike the *Trachiniae* or indeed any other serious Greek play: it is by direct intervention that the gods operate here: the whole action is started by one such divine intervention, and is given a decisive turn by another. An oracle comes to Laius like a bolt from the blue, and another one, later, to Oedipus; without the first, nothing would have happened, and without the second, nothing of special note. Nor can we say, if we confine ourselves to the text, that Sophocles does anything to explain why the gods should have so acted; and if we do not confine ourselves to the text, then we may go wrong. If it is a sound argument, that we make our best contact with a poet's mind by first looking with care at what he has "made", then there is reason enough for looking carefully at the structure of the *Tyrannus*.

For a special reason we will follow, this time, a special procedure. It is a commonplace of criticism that the play is exceptional in this respect also, that everything bar the discovery has already happened. Therefore it might be wise, as it is certainly not difficult, to establish clearly what has happened. For another reason too: the Oedipus Myth, perhaps more than others, has the deceptive trick of acquiring in our minds a quite unreal solidity: we think it has an objective existence; but as we said earlier, a Greek myth never "is" but is always "becoming". Anthropologists and psychologists analyse and discuss "the myth"; that is their affair, and no doubt they know exactly what they are doing. Our affair is with the play; our *mythos* is what Sophocles lays before us between the moment when we enter his theatre and the moment when we leave it; recollection of other men's plays about Oedipus may help our later reflections, but will only distract our immediate attention.

Sophocles' story, as distinct from his play, begins with Iocasta's account of Oedipus' birth (vv. 711 ff.). I give it in Jebb's careful translation:

> An oracle came to Laius—I will not say from Phoebus himself, but from his ministers—that the doom should overtake him to die by the hand of his child who should spring from him and me. As for Laius, foreign brigands killed him at a branching road; as for the child, he was not three days old when Laius clamped his feet together and had him cast over a precipice.

This is the only reference in the play to Oedipus' birth. I venture to suggest: an equally valid translation of the relative clause would be "a (some) son who will be born to him and me"; also, since our word "should" is ambiguous (because it may imply a measure of compulsion), we could equally well translate: "the doom was going to overtake him".

As to this passage, it has been suggested that Laius was guilty of hybris in trying to frustrate the will of the gods by destroying the child. Two comments only: (*i*) The suggestion is never made by Sophocles, and it is not for us to add something to his text. (*ii*) What opposite fault should we now be imputing to Laius if in the face of so dire a threat he had done nothing, but had allowed events to take their course? We shall have to return to this matter of hybris; meanwhile, let us note that Sophocles shows no interest in any guilt on the part of Laius, either when he begat the child or when he destroyed it (as he thought). The text indeed is consistent with the assumption—which of course it would be foolish to make—that the fatal child had been conceived already.

Sophocles' *mythos* continues with the two shepherds who, between them, saved the child, so that it was reared by Polybus and Merope. Then comes the incident of the man who got tipsy and opened his mouth too wide—"Remarkable indeed", says Oedipus, "though hardly worth the attention I gave it" (vv. 777 f.). He asks his parents about it, has their reply, and then, because the rumour spread, and annoyed him, he decides to go to Delphi. Now comes the second bolt from the blue. Like the one that descended upon Laius, this one comes quite stark, with no hint of cause or purpose. Next, the affair at the Three Ways, so shaped by Sophocles as to absolve Oedipus from serious guilt. The truculent charioteer and the old man tried to hustle Oedipus off the road; he angrily struck at the charioteer; the man in the chariot aimed a murderous blow at his head, and if Oedipus had not been quick on the draw, the prophecy would have been fulfilled upside-down; father would have killed son. As the story is given us, it makes us see that there was fault on each side, inasmuch as Oedipus might have merely expostulated without striking, but if we are to speak of hybris, then the hybris was exclusively in the charioteer and Laius. Was Oedipus gravely wrong to go on and kill the whole party, as he thought? Here we must beware of the documentary fallacy. If it were a real event, yes, no doubt—if only we knew the circumstances. Did the others violently set upon Oedipus, and get killed while he was only defending himself? Did he pursue them and kill them wantonly? Such questions do not exist; they take us outside the frame of the picture. The dramatic purpose is clear: there were no surviving witnesses, "but for one frightened man who escaped and could give no clear account, except that they encountered a whole band of brigands" (vv. 118–123). There was violence; that is made clear. But even if we go outside the play and insist that Oedipus was wrong in killing the rest of the party, this would have nothing to do with the fulfillment of the oracle.

Finally, the Sphinx. By his own intelligence, aided only by the *theos* (vv. 35–39), Oedipus saved Thebes and accepted in return the vacant throne that was gratefully offered him; we are left to understand that with the vacant throne went the vacant Queen.

Here ends the past story, embedded in the present action. It justifies two general assertions. One is that Sophocles has made no attempt to moralise it. He has not made the begetting of Oedipus an act of wickedness or folly. It will do us no harm to notice that this is a different state of affairs from that presented by both Aeschylus and Euripides. The chorus of the *Septem* (742 ff.) recalls "the ancient sin": three times was Laius warned by Apollo that only by remaining childless could he assure the safety of Thebes, but the desire for offspring overcame him, and he begat his own death. We do not know if Aeschylus went back to the curse laid on Laius by Pelops: Laius had stolen Pelops' son Chrysippus, and so used him that the boy killed himself in shame. Whether Aeschylus included this or not, he made the begetting of Oedipus a deliberate and wanton defiance of the god. Such also it is in the *Phoenissae* of Euripides (17–22), where Laius, desiring children, consulted Apollo and was told not to beget children "in despite of the gods", but he did, "being in his cups and giving way to pleasure". In Sophocles' play there is none of this, and Sophocles must have expected his audience to listen to what he was saying, and not to confuse themselves by trying to graft on, as they listened, recollections of perhaps half a dozen other Oedipus plays that they might have heard. Sophocles has not made the begetting of Oedipus a crime or culpable folly; he has not made the slaying of Laius a wanton act; he imputed no blame to Oedipus for accepting the throne and the Queen.

The second point is that he has made no attempt at all to make us feel the presence of some controlling Power in the background: twice the god speaks, and having spoken, withdraws and leaves the event to be shaped by those concerned in it. Why did things fall out as they did? We are told: what happens, barring the oracles, is presented as being entirely within the competence of those who become involved. Laius might have destroyed the child; in fact, he thought he had. For reasons that may be obvious, but are not suggested by Sophocles, he did something that was just as good—except that it wasn't. Why did the shepherds save it? The motive of the Corinthian is fairly clear: willingness to bring himself to the favourable notice of his king; the Theban shepherd's motive is expressly stated, and at a moment when the audience would be disposed to listen. It comes at the end of the critical scene of discovery. Oedipus has at last established the facts beyond any doubt whatever (v. 1176): "What oracles?"—"That it would kill its parents." If on the stage the next five lines were cut, nobody would feel the loss unless he knew the play well.—"Why did you give the child to this man here?"—The question is unnecessary, except for the sake of the answer:

> I pitied it, my lord; I thought to send
> The child abroad, where this man lived. And he
> Saved it, for utter doom. For if you are
> The man he says, then you were born for ruin.

That was his motive: pity. Then, a man gets drunk—unhappily, a common occurrence. Polybus and Merope might have told Oedipus the truth: "Well, my son, you are old enough now . . ."; they did not. We are not told why; no reason why we should be. But we are told (v. 787) that they got no second chance: Oedipus went straight to Delphi. Father and son met at the Three Ways; there was boorishness and violence; men were killed. About the marriage, nothing is said at all: the widow of the late king became the wife of the new king.

It may seem an odd thing to say, but the whole story, oracles apart, is so true to life. Not of course in any naïve and naturalistic sense; I do not mean that the play might have been called "Oedipus Tyrannus, or A Typical Day in Thebes"; I mean that every single detail, the oracles apart, rings true. We know that a man can bet on a certainty and lose, as Laius did; that virtuous intentions, like the shepherd's pity, can produce disaster; that people do shrink from admitting an awkward truth, as did Polybus and Merope; that coincidences do occur, like the meeting of Oedipus and Laius; that some men are boorish and others irascible, and that a fracas can suddenly blow up out of next to nothing. "But," they say, "it is fantastic that all these things should happen together, to one man!" And are we to suppose that Sophocles was unaware of this? He insists that no other man but Oedipus had ever suffered the like; he also knew the difference between drama and reporting; that drama must sharpen its point in order to penetrate more deeply. The story is so untrue to life, in the literal sense, that our conclusion should be not that Sophocles was being rather silly, but that we ourselves are probably on the wrong track if this spoils the play for us. If we can see that the play gives no balanced picture of life, then we should be clever enough to see a little more, that the Greek tragic form was never designed to do this. Elizabethan drama, with its much ampler form, can do something of the kind, and so can the novel; but the notable differences in length, texture, and style between these and the Greek tragic form should tell us that the Greeks had more modest ambitions. It is a form that is hardly capable of giving a wide picture; it is however remarkably well adapted to the stating of one general truth about life.

To come back to our preliminary survey.—Punishment for wrong-doing is not in the picture at all, nor is there the slightest suggestion of a divine purpose. If Sophocles is saying "This is what life is like", we can only deny it; if he is saying "This is what life *can* be like", then we are compelled to agree, though we shall add that it is an extreme case. Nothing in it is impossible, barring the oracles. Every point, taken separately, may well be within our own experience; Sophocles brings them together, making them all bear upon one piercingly sharp point—and we would like to know why. We nourish the hope that a steady look at his *poiesis* may tell us something.

"Barring the oracles": we are always having to say that. If we can be sceptical enough to suspend our conviction (if we have it) that the prophecies, or the prophesying deities, *compel*—an idea which the other plays contradict—so that the people concerned here are only puppets dancing at the end of a divine piece of string, then the facts of the play seems to make this a tenable hypothesis: the god, twice, issues a dire warning, once to Laius, once to Oedipus. Having warned, he withdraws and leaves them to handle the situation. Each is an intelligent and resolute man; each does what he thinks to be the intelligent thing, in the circumstances; and each fails. The hypothesis may or may not be confirmed; yet we may notice that the play contains not two prophecies but three: Teiresias tells Oedipus that he is going to finish as a blind man—and he does. When he has blinded himself he says, explicitly (vv. 1329 ff.): "It was Apollo, my friends, Apollo, that brought to pass these evil sufferings of mine". Apollo, then, is evidently an external Power who does with Oedipus what he will? Not quite; for not only does Oedipus at once add: "But the hand that struck was mine alone", but also, a little later, he explains at length why he *had* to do it: both in this world and the next the possession of his eyesight would have been intolerable to him. "It was Apollo", but it was also what we might call, in our untheological language, a psychological necessity. But this is normal; it is what we find in the *Choephori*, for instance. Apollo straitly commands Orestes to kill the murderers—so that the god, an external Power, directs and controls the man? Not quite, because Orestes goes on to give the reasons why he would have to do it in any case. We certainly should not jump to the conclusion that the two major prophecies in the *Tyrannus* must mean that the gods are imposing an arbitrary doom for a purpose at which the playwright never hints.

We have been examining, by way of precaution, what the myth became when Sophocles had shaped it to his requirements. Now we will consider the structure that he made out of these raw materials. For convenience only, we will divide the play into four main parts: (*i*) from the beginning to the end of the first ode; (*ii*) the scenes with Teiresias and Creon; (*iii*) from Iocasta's entry to the discovery and the self-blinding; (*iv*) all that follows. We shall see that the second and the fourth both end in a way that the raw material, the "story", neither requires nor suggests, and that the third contains much that does not arise inevitably from the myth, and is itself rather surprising.

The first portrays Oedipus in the sharpest possible contrast to what he will be at the end. Nothing to wonder at in this. He is the great and devoted king, almost god-like in his eminence, intelligence, wisdom; he is as remote as can be from the public calamity, except that he is king of the afflicted city. Next, the plague is described—twice; once by the Priest, once by the chorus.

The plague: can we use it to help us determine the approximate date of the play, for which there is no external evidence? Internal evidence would suggest, as probable limits, 435 and 420 B.C. Athens had her two visitations of plague in 430 and 429. Did the real plague suggest the fictive one? Many scholars have thought so, and therefore propose a date round about 427. No one will doubt that Sophocles could have described a plague out of his imagination; nevertheless, the assumption that the description of the Theban plague is based on experience of the Athenian plague is a natural one to make; but if we make it, there are implications to face vastly more important than the question of date. In the Athenian plague, it is computed, something like one-quarter of the inhabitants died; Thucydides reports that there were houses in which nobody survived. Therefore a dramatist was doing no light thing who, within a few years, represented a comparable plague to an audience of Athenians: he was deliberately renewing memories of an immeasurable disaster. Sophocles gives a picture of Thebans dying day by day and night by night; that is exactly what had happened in Athens, within recent memory—on our assumption. From the play we receive the same impression as from Thucydides: a whole people suddenly confronted with catastrophe, inexplicable and unendurable. If the play was produced at any time in the 420's, it is impossible that the audience should not have vividly remembered their awful experience, or that the playwright should not have intended it.

The Theban plague, of course, has the dramatic function of forcing the issue, and if we read the play as in an ivory tower, that will be enough; but is it enough when we think of the (assumed) time and place of its production? Sophocles was no resourceless dramatist; it is not hard to think of other ways in which he might have "forced the issue"—for example, a solemn command from the god, reinforced by dire menaces. It is reasonable to suppose that he chose plague deliberately. Could he have done it? Why should he have done it? These may not be questions that we can answer, but they should certainly be asked.

Next, when we consider the way in which the plague is described, twice, we can hardly fail to see how the nature of the plague is proportioned to its cause. We know what Oedipus has done to his parents, the source of his own life: the consequence, emphasised in the descriptions, is sterility: the fields, the animals, the human kind, are all barren. If we demand Justice from life, or from the gods, we shall be indignant at this: Oedipus had done these things in complete ignorance and innocence, and in any case, why should Thebans die like flies for what another man had done? Yet we know that events do not always accommodate themselves to our ideas of justice. If a man is momentarily careless with a match, he may cause a fire in which people die—and he himself will often be safely off the premises. What happens here, to Oedipus and the Thebans, is not Justice, but it is Dike; it is an example of the way, the often cruel way, in which things work. After the discovery the chorus apostrophises Oedipus and says (vv. 1213 ff.):

> Time sees all, and Time, in your despite,
> Disclosed and punished your unnatural marriage—
> A child, and then a husband!

"Punished", δικάζει; Dike is at work.

If we are rightly inferring Sophocles' thought here from the construction that he has made, part of it is that the plague, the Theban one, is a direct and natural outcome of what Oedipus had done. Ignorance and innocence have nothing to say in the matter. Grave offences were committed against the natural order; they were left unpurged, because unknown. At last Nature herself (as we should say) rises in revolt—and such revolts are apt to be indiscriminate. The Greek gods too are no respecters of persons.

There is another point of structure that we should notice: having made the plague so prominent in these early scenes, Sophocles allows it to fade away. The chorus, even though it represents the citizens of the afflicted city, never alludes to it again: Oedipus or Creon mention it (at vv. 270–272, 327, 333, 515 f.); so too does Iocasta, at her first entry (vv. 635 f.). Thereafter it is totally fogotten. One interpretation of the play that has been propounded is that the citizen-poet is laying before his citizen-audience a picture of the ideal King who will properly and nobly do his duty by doing his utmost to deliver the city from peril, even at the cost of his own life—an interpretation which may proceed smoothly from some general theory about Greek political thought, but founders on the simple fact that it never occurred to Sophocles to mention that the city in fact was delivered. Naturally, we could infer it, but if we are really attending to the play, we shall not even think of it. We must not put constructions of our own in the place of what the poet has constructed.

Such are the plain facts of structure which bring themselves to our notice when we look at the first of our four sections of the play. When we turn to the second, we say, correctly, that it begins—or, more strictly, continues—the long and stealthy process of discovery, and does it with consummate skill: vague hints are dropped, which the quick mind of Oedipus combines into a certainty. It is here too that the theme of Blindness is first announced—a theme that dominates the play much more than the plague does. All this is clear, but a simple question suggests itself and demands an answer: why should Sophocles have designed the whole passage in such a way that it leads to an unmistakable climax that does nothing to help the plot? For it ends in the violent scene in which Oedipus, virtually, commits a stupid and unpardonable crime in decreeing for Creon either death or banishment. It is such a jangling climax that it takes a long passage of music and lyric poetry to calm things down to the point where the detective work, so harshly interrupted, can be resumed; and we should notice that when at last Oedipus does give way it is not in the least because he is persuaded that he may be wrong, but simply as a reluctant favour granted to Iocasta and the chorus. It is, and is described as, an outburst of sheer tyranny: why is it there?

We can say: "Sophocles is showing us how irascible and violent Oedipus could be". Of course he is; but since the character of Oedipus was not an unalterable fact in history but was the invention of the poet, we still want to know why he invented an Oedipus who could suddenly go to the verge of judicial murder. It does not help to explain the past, unless we were quite wrong in saying that the past story has not been moralised by Sophocles. Oedipus did indeed show hot temper in hitting out at the charioteer, but that is very different from this. To resent an insult, even hotly, is one thing; to condemn an innocent man to death is quite another. In any case, Oedipus' hot temper (as we saw) was only one of many strands that led to the fulfillment of the oracle.

But if the present outburst does nothing to illuminate the past, neither does it do anything to affect the future. That is already settled and only awaits discovery. Why then is it there?

One fact we must not overlook, namely the general resemblance between the few verses that end the present passage and the more elaborate altercation in the *Antigone* between Haemon and his father (vv. 727–739): in each case the implication is that the King is behaving in a way that would destroy the rights of a citizen and make the *polis* a thing of naught. Looking back to the beginning of our play, we see that he who then was the wise monarch is now a tyrant. Are we not bound to ask ourselves what this has to do with the fulfillment of the oracles? The connection seems remote.

In our third part of the play also there is much that does not seem inevitable. When Creon has been allowed to go not exactly in peace, but with a declaration of Oedipus' undying hatred for him, we move into the scene in which Iocasta reassures Oedipus, and in doing it, so terribly frightens him. Then Sophocles writes, as a kind of centre-piece for the whole play, a very impressive ode. It has given rise to unending debate; for the reader's convenience I offer a summary:

May I ever observe purity and reverence in word and deed, for the eternal and unwritten laws enjoin it. Hybris it is that breeds the tyrant. Hybris, when allied with wealth and power, begets a mounting pride which is always overthrown; though may the god never end that contention which is for the city's good. But the arrogance that does not fear Dike nor reverence the holy shrines—may it perish! If such acts be held in reverence, why should I join in the sacred dance? No more will I go to the seats of prophecy, if these oracles are not manifestly fulfilled. Great Zeus, overlook it not: Apollo and his prophecies are losing honour; religion is failing.

Such is the substance of the ode. Why did Sophocles write it, and write it for this particular moment of the play?

It is indeed a surprise. Why, in the first place, should Sophocles make his chorus, at this point, sing about purity and reverence and the observance of the unwritten laws? We naturally ask: how would these virtues have saved Oedipus from fulfilling the prophecy? To that question there is no reasonable answer. It might be said, at a pinch, that a reverent and pure man would have stood in the ditch beside the road, not even swearing, and let the chariot pass by; but about the marriage we could not say anything even as hopeless as that: Sophocles has said nothing at all about the marriage except that it happened; on this score he has given a handle neither to moralists nor to psychoanalysts. Our only legitimate reflection can be that an exceedingly cautious man, in his circumstances, might have reflected that there was perhaps one chance in ten thousand that the widowed queen, being of such an age, might be his mother.

In the second place, whose is the hybris? Some have said, of Iocasta; some, of Oedipus; some, of both. One scholar has made the spectacular suggestion that all through the ode we are to think of Laius: grotesque enough, but at least it shows that a difficulty is felt.

Here we may remind ourselves what the nature of our question is. We are not enquiring into the mind and behaviour of a historical figure, like Alexander or Tiberius: did he suffer from hybris? In a matter of that kind it is natural that interpretations should differ, but our concern is with something in a play. The first assumption to make is that the dramatist expected his audience to see his point: the meaning, the reference, ought to be apparent. To us, it is not in the least apparent, as the long debate proves. Of this fact there are alternative explanations. One is that, for whatever reason, the poet never did make his meaning plain; that instead of producing clarity he produced only fog, being in something of a muddle himself. In that case we are not likely to resolve the muddle that he did not resolve, and had better say: "Sophocles did not manage to make his intentions clear". The other possible explanation is that he did make himself clear. In that case it is we who are in a fog; an obstinate something will have got between ourselves and the play, and we have seen already that this is by no means impossible. When we have finished our scrutiny we will return to this and our other surprises, hoping that between them they will make sense.

But the ode raises one more question—in fact, two. In the previous ode, as indeed in the next one, the chorus is wholly loyal to Oedipus, just as it was at the beginning; why then does Sophocles now make it pray that the oracles be manifestly, χειρόδεικτα, fulfilled? They cannot be fulfilled unless the King kills his father and marries his mother. The question does not seem an easy one to answer. Another is allied to it: what size of mind did Sophocles have, that he should equate the literal verity of oracles with the validity of religion itself? Was he, so to speak, a Fundamentalist from the Bible Belt? And if he was, how did he manage to write so many intelligent plays?—The ode does indeed give us something to think about. Can we really believe that in the middle of a play like this, which certainly does not make it evident that Sophocles' gods are strictly concerned with virtue and wickedness, the poet suddenly puts on his surplice, ascends into his pulpit, and bids us pray for purity and reverence, follow the Unwritten Laws, avoid hybris, fear Dike, and above all believe in oracles? Excellent advice, no doubt—but what has it to do with the rest of the play?

We continue our scrutiny.—What follows is a scene which, like the condemnation of Creon, we could not have predicted from what we know of the myth. It is not "myth" but pure invention. What makes it the more interesting, and revealing (for us), is that the sequence that we find here is exactly the same as what we find in the (presumably later) *Electra*—with one challenging difference. In the other play Clytemnestra, terrified by her ominous dream, comes out and offers prayer and sacrifice to Apollo that he will save her from what seems to threaten. At once there enters the old man with good news: Orestes is dead, killed accidentally, at Delphi. She is triumphant—but not for long: the message was a false one, designed to throw her off her guard; the guile that she has used against her husband is now being used against her by her son, and soon she is dead. In the *Tyrannus* the Queen, badly frightened, comes out and offers prayer and sacrifice to Apollo that he shall deliver them both from what threatens. At once the man from Corinth enters with good news: Oedipus' father has just died, peacefully. Iocasta is triumphant—but not for long; before the scene closes she has gone in to hang herself. So does Apollo answer the prayers of these two queens.

The parallel is very close, except that it seems to break down at a critical point. For Clytemnestra's prayer is in the highest degree blasphemous; Iocasta's is innocent; she is no criminal but a woman suddenly smitten with fear. Clytemnestra deserved what she got, but what punishment has Iocasta earned? We must be very stony-hearted to think that she has earned any whatever. How then could Sophocles equate the two women in this way? Or is he (as I once suggested) only being theatrical? It certainly is no casual moment in the play, and yet it does not seem easy to understand.

The final scenes too, our fourth part, contain much, perhaps even more, that is unexpected. Oedipus, now blind and ruined, gropes his way out of the palace: to what consummation is Sophocles going to guide his play? What could seem more obvious? The god's clear instruction, Oedipus' own decree, Teiresias' prophecy that the great King will become blind, a beggar, wandering in exile, all point to the inevitable and dramatic ending: Oedipus will now depart from Thebes for ever. But the inevitable ending proves not to have been in the least inevitable, for Sophocles.

The last section may seem to lack impetus and tautness. If it does, we can fall back on the old incantation, that the Greek dramatists preferred to end quietly, though if we do cherish the notion we had better not read the *Electra*. Similarly—for this too would only be a way of avoiding thought—it might be said that Sophocles avoided exiling Oedipus for the sake of the *Coloneus*, written some fifteen or twenty years later, for in that play Oedipus, now an old man, has only recently been driven out of Thebes.—A plausible guess, if the ending of the *Tyrannus* is in fact tentative, a kind of half-close. But is it? We must look at the dramatic facts of the case, and if it appears that the scenes before us are a logical and convincing ending to the *Tyrannus*, then we need not invoke the *Coloneus*.

We note, in the first place, that Sophocles is not in the least self-conscious in his avoidance of the obvious ending: no fewer than six times does Oedipus demand his exile. The Messenger (vv. 1290 f.) reports that Oedipus is going to cast himself out of Thebes, to fulfil his own curse; twice (vv. 1340, 1410) Oedipus beseeches the chorus to drive him out; three times (vv. 1436 f., 1449 ff., 1518) he begs it of Creon, and Creon refuses. This is one dramatic fact. Another is the surprising way in which the relationship of Oedipus and Creon is handled. We remember well enough what the situation was when last we saw the two men together; now Creon has been vindicated with an awful completeness, and Oedipus has been proved to have done things far worse than he had falsely imputed to Creon. It is a *peripeteia* such as an ordinary dramatist might dream of, yet Sophocles appears to be hardly interested in it. Further, although he was so subtle in the drawing of character, he has so far given us a picture of Creon which is a little vague; here then is the opportunity to make it much sharper—to show Creon as vindictively triumphant (which Méautis does indeed say Sophocles has done), or nobly forgiving, or at least *something* interesting. But this master of the dramatic art, having contrived so splendid a reversal of situation, so good an opportunity of developing the character of Creon, throws it away with both hands. He makes Creon say (vv. 1422 f.):

> No exultation, Oedipus, and no reproach
> For injuries inflicted brings me here—

and when he has said this, he has said all that Sophocles allows him to say about it. He continues: "But do not affront Thebes and pollute the sunlight by standing here, in the sight of men"; but this is no personal harshness on the part of Creon, for it merely repeats what Oedipus has already said about himself

(vv. 1410–1413). Oedipus answers: "Since against my expectation you are so generous, grant me one request . . ." We see at once that Creon can forgive and forget, but the point is made with all despatch, almost as if it were only a necessary nuisance.

Sophocles then does not end his play "dramatically": he makes little of the complete reversal of situation, and the pathetic climax of the blind and broken king groping his way into exile he was content to leave for Euripides to exploit in his *Phoenissae*. What else have we to notice, positive or negative, in this last part of the play?

One point that we would like to understand we have noticed already: Oedipus blinds himself, and would like to separate himself totally from contact with men, if that were possible; the blinding, predicted by Teiresias, is both the act of Apollo and what he himself has willed. Leaving this for the moment where it is, we find other things to engage our attention.

Creon, sympathetic towards Oedipus, has made sign to one of his men that he should bring the two girls to their father. Why this? They are brought out, Oedipus makes his very moving speech to them, and at the end they are taken back again. It is natural, but not inevitable; we should not think it odd if the play had ended without our seeing the children. We look at the scene; we say at once, and reasonably, that the tenderness and love which Oedipus bears them brings out an aspect of his character which hitherto we have not been shown. That is true, and if the play were a tragedy of character, it would be enough; but Sophocles is not intent, first and foremost, to show us what Oedipus was like: the *praxis* takes precedence over the persons:

> But my unhappy daughters, my two girls,
> Whose chairs were always placed beside my own
> At table, they who shared in every dish
> That was prepared for me—oh Creon, these
> Do I commend to you . . .

It is a picture of a domestic happiness now shattered beyond recall; more than that, for it was a domestic happiness that concealed a domestic horror. Further: the main burden of the speech is that the future of these two girls is blasted irretrievably—and for no fault of their own. When we reflect that this point, though perfectly natural, was no inevitable part of the play, we see what Sophocles is doing: he is enlarging the area of disaster.

May we look back to a moment in the play which can easily escape our notice on the printed page? The scene of Oedipus and the two shepherds comes to its fearful climax: Oedipus, with his last despairing cry, rushes into the palace, and the chorus begins its grave song on the littleness of man.—But not yet; we have forgotten something. Out in the orchestra, somewhere, are two actors who must make their exit before the chorus can begin its dance. At a moderate computation, the two shepherds will have to cover forty feet of space before they disappear from our sight, and forty feet, in the theatre, is a long way—and they certainly will not march off briskly. Now, Sophocles has interested us in these men. One of them, as we know, had witnessed the killing of Laius; then, coming back to Thebes, he saw the killer on the throne, and begged Iocasta to send him away into the hills, as far as possible from the city. This we were told, in some detail, by Iocasta (vv. 758–764). Now, suddenly, he has been brought back and closely questioned—not about what he must have feared, the killing, but about something that had happened much earlier and, incredibly, proves to be far worse. There is also the Corinthian. He came into the play with such confidence, such bright hopes; now he has to stumble out of it, all his hopes destroyed. The long and slow exit will give the audience time to spare a thought for these men too. We will not lose our sense of proportion; nevertheless, these men too are suffering—and all because they did not destroy a baby.

> The cease of majesty
> Dies not alone, but like a gulf doth draw
> What's near it with it; 'tis a massy wheel
> Fix'd on the summit of the highest mount,

> To whose huge spokes ten thousand lesser things
> Are mortised and adjoined; which, when it falls,
> Each small annexment, petty consequence,
> Attends the boisterous ruin.

This is Rosencrantz, speaking to Claudius. Shakespeare too had his command of tragic irony: the speaker of these lines was indeed a "small annexment" who went down in the boisterous ruin which engulfed Claudius himself, Gertrude, Polonius, Ophelia, Laertes, and Hamlet—a ruin which, in this play, issues from the rotten state of Denmark. There is no rottenness in Thebes: our tragedy has a different basis. Nevertheless, the *Tyrannus* has a similar amplitude, and it is one which our modern preoccupation with the central character tempts us to overlook. As we underestimate the size of *Hamlet* unless we see that Laertes and Ophelia, even Rosencrantz and Guildenstern, in their several degrees, are Hamlet's colleagues in disaster, so do we underestimate the scope of the *Tyrannus*, and to some extent its import too, unless to Oedipus himself we add, as tragic victims, not only Laius and Iocasta, who are dead, but also the two children, whose future is ruined, and the two shepherds—and why should we forget the Thebans who were dying of plague? Some are at or near the centre of the disaster, some on the outskirts, but all are affected. The play is not concerned merely with what the gods did to the man Oedipus; beyond that, it explores what human experience, in one of its aspects, can be like.

One more question about the children.—Having brought them on to the stage, for these reasons, why does Sophocles take them off again in the way he does? If at the end they went out in the train of either Oedipus or Creon, with nothing said, nobody would be surprised or even interested; yet the very last bit of action in the play is that Creon detaches them from their father's embrace. It is not an impressive or spectacular action; nevertheless, it is the fact that Sophocles concludes his play not with the departure of Oedipus from Thebes, not with a moving speech delivered by the great Oedipus, now fallen, but with this. Why?

The end is a little disappointing. What we expect is a powerfully dramatic close, yet after so splendid a course the play arrives at a terminus which is not very impressive. We think perhaps that as Oedipus sinks in the scale, so Creon should rise, to dominate the scene at the end as Oedipus did at the beginning: we can hardly say that he does. Can we then write like this: "Oedipus does not display his full glory until, paradoxically, he is to all outward appearance crushed and abased"? It would be nice if we could; it does not seem possible, with the text we have. Can we say that he has been purged of his faults and now is truly the Hero? Of course we can—but Sophocles does not. Can we say even that it is the remote and terrible power of Apollo that presides over the close? But we have seen what the last bit of action is: Creon takes the children from Oedipus and says: "Do not try to have control in all things. Where you did have control, it did not remain with you." These are the last genuine verses of the play: it would not be surprising if the idea of control, *κρατεῖν*, proved to be crucial.

We have finished our broad examination of the structure, in the four parts into which we have divided it. Is it coherent? We will look again, in more detail, beginning with the last of the four.

We noticed, perhaps with surprise, that Oedipus demands of Creon three times to be driven out forthwith, and that each time Creon refuses. Why? As Oedipus keeps on saying, the matter is as clear as daylight: there is Apollo's explicit command, and there is his own solemn imprecation. But Creon keeps on saying (vv. 1435–1443): "Yes, I know. I would have done it, but first I wanted to ask the god what should be done . . . Yes, I know; but in our present pass it is better to ask how we should act." In the end he says: "What you ask is in the gift of the god."—"But the gods hate no one more than me!"—"Then you will soon gain your desire."—"You promise it?"—"Ah no; when I have no knowledge I prefer not to speak at random": ἃ μὴ φρονῶ γὰρ οὐ φιλῶ λέγειν μάτην.

No doubt verbal points can be over-emphasised, though everybody will agree that Sophocles took pains with the verbal part of this play. Therefore it may not be accidental that what Creon says here is an almost exact repetition of something that he has said earlier, also to Oedipus. The sharp question was: "Why did not that clever prophet speak out before, when Laius was killed?" and Creon replies: "I don't know, and when I have no knowledge, I prefer to say nothing": ἐφ' οἷς γὰρ μὴ φρονῶ σιγᾶν φιλῶ (v. 569). In itself it is not much, but for us, being perhaps rather at a loss with the final scenes, it may be a useful hint. At the end, as we have just said, the situation is as clear as daylight; when the two men were together before, it certainly was not—except to Oedipus, and he was wrong. Now, Creon will not act without consulting Delphi again, ἵν' ἕσταμεν χρείας as he says: "seeing to what a pass we have come". We remember how Oedipus acted then. When first we heard of and then saw Creon, Oedipus was treating him with marked courtesy: "I have sent to Delphi Creon, Menoeceus' son, my wife's brother" (vv. 69 f.); "My lord, my kinsman, son of Menoeceus, what news do you bring?" (vv. 85 f.); "For this care taken for the slain man we owe great thanks to Phoebus, and thanks to you also" (vv. 133 f.). But this complete trust in Creon goes for nothing. Sophocles, with his purposeful skill, contrives that one circumstance after another shall be dropped into the quick and penetrating mind of Oedipus, beginning as far back as v. 73:

> Now, as I count the days, it troubles me
> What he is doing; his absence is prolonged
> Beyond the proper time.

Hint follows hint. Oedipus, having in any case the king's inclination to fear conspiracy (vv. 124 f.), being so shrewd, so self-confident, swiftly comes to a conclusion which, as anyone would admit, is very plausible. For Oedipus it is a certainty, but we know that he is wildly wrong.

Against this complete certainty, other considerations are brought into play. That Creon, hitherto, has been above suspicion we have noticed already. The Chorus Leader makes bold to say to Oedipus that swift decisions are not always safe ones (vv. 616 f.). The King sweeps this aside with the remark that when an enemy is quick to plot, you must be quick too in your counter-measures. Creon takes his oath in denial. He argues that on the face of it the charge is absurd—an argument from probability indeed, but such an argument may at least have probability; it cannot disprove, but it may at least deter. But he has a stronger argument than this: "Go to Delphi and ask! Ask what response was given me, and if I have honestly reported it". This would settle the matter—but Oedipus has settled it already, by his unaided intelligence. All this is reinforced later by the chorus (vv. 649 ff.): "He has never been reckless before; he has taken an oath that should be respected. Do not condemn a friend, on an uncertain charge": ἐν ἀφανεῖ λόγῳ. To none of this will Oedipus listen for a moment; he *knows*. Therefore he acts like a tyrant.

In the final scene, the question at issue is not obscure but very clear; nevertheless, Creon insists on consulting Delphi before acting. It is not, surely, that Sophocles is characterising Creon as the timid or over-cautious man who will not do anything, if he can help it, without going to Delphi first. Sophocles is not primarily interested in characterising Creon. The contrast is clear: the one man will do a desperate thing because he is so certain, in spite of counsels of prudence, and in spite of Creon's challenge that he should go to Delphi and ask; the other will not act, in a serious situation, until he has sought the better knowledge that is available to him.

It looks then as if we may have been a little hasty in saying that Sophocles devised a wonderful reversal of situation and did nothing with it. He seems to have done a great deal, though not what we were expecting. What he has dramatised is not the reversal of the situation of each man with respect to the other; he is not interested in exploiting the fact that he who was then top dog is now bottom dog and *vice versa*, and showing how each reacts to the change. The contrast he does make, quite sharply, is one between Oedipus' total confidence in his own judgment, in what is a very deceptive situation, and Creon's more modest attitude, in a situation that would seem to justify complete confidence. The verbal echo seems not to have been accidental.

Perhaps we may think that we are making a little progress. Our fourth and second areas appear to recognise each other. Now we will try the third.

Being moderns, absorbed in the stage-persons, we confidently expect that the chorus will now say something about the immediate situation. As Jebb put it, in his note introductory to the previous ode: "In accordance with the conception of the Chorus as personified reflection, it must comment on all that has been most stirring in the interval". We would not all put it quite so formally, but we do assume that when the chorus talks of hybris, it will be that of Iocasta or of Oedipus, but we cannot agree which. But is the canon Greek, or home-made?

In the third ode of the *Agamemnon*, what we have learned in the interval, from the Herald, is that victory has at last been won, the long sufferings of the troops have ended, and the King will soon reach home: and alas!—the King only, for his ship is the only one of the fleet known to have survived a raging storm which left the Aegean flowering with dead bodies. The chorus, which "must comment" on all this, has not a word to say about the glorious victory, nor about the King, nor even about the appalling destruction of the fleet; it sings instead about Helen's sin, a lion cub, and hybris—and of course we see the point. In the *Hecuba* and *Troades*, one disaster after another falls upon Hecuba, but the chorus, taking no notice of them, sings about its own miseries—and of course we see the point. Therefore, the chorus will sometimes leave the stage-action where it was and invite us to consider something that underlies it.

But is the one only the new-fangled way of Euripides, and the other the old-fangled way of Aeschylus? No: in the second scene of the *Antigone*, the King has announced his broad policy, issued his decree, and learned from the Guard that it has already been defied, but what the chorus proceeds to sing about is not this, but the fact that Man by his own efforts has raised himself from the Stone Age, so to speak, to the pinnacle of civilisation. Again, we see the point, when it ends by saying that the achievement is precarious, that it depends on our observing Law and Dike; especially do we see the point later in the play when we hear Creon admit that it may be wisest to observe "the laws established", τοὺς καθεστῶτας νόμους, as he has not done. Here too the chorus is commenting not on what has just been happening, but on what the play is about. The first ode of the *Trachiniae* is not entirely dissimilar: it has indeed its direct connection with what we have just been concerned with, the immediate anxieties of Deianeira, but if we see only this, we are not seeing all that Sophocles hoped.

With this we may join another point. On our first survey we professed to be taken aback that the chorus, entirely loyal to Oedipus hitherto and hereafter, should in this ode pray for the fulfillment of the oracles. It is true that Sophocles, in particular, makes his chorus "a dramatic character", as we say, but observation certifies that the Greek dramatists, including Sophocles, will allow this dramatic character to lapse, as often as suits them, and that we, as audience, do not mind a bit. It seems very sensible both on their part and on ours. During the ode on Man, in the *Antigone*, we are not conscious that the singers represent the King's advisers, and the recollection would only be a nuisance; the same is true of the Danae ode later in the play. In the early scenes of the *Septem* it is important and dramatic that the chorus represents women of the city terrified for their lives; in the ode they sing after the exit of Eteocles they are pure Chorus, and we think of them as such. Remembering dramatic realities and forgetting theories, we can readily accept the chorus in this ode too as a purely lyrical body, especially as for the moment it has the theatre to itself.

Now, having looked at assumptions and at alternative possibilities, we will look at the facts of the case. We will ask ourselves if a reasonable audience, not being of the nineteenth or twentieth century, would naturally suppose that Sophocles was telling them what to think about Oedipus, or about Iocasta.

When the chorus begins with its solemn prayer for reverence, purity, and observance of the Unwritten Laws, an audience would not naturally suppose that it was being invited to think about the immediate situation. It is not worth saying twice that Oedipus and Iocasta are not being destroyed because they have lacked virtue. Nor indeed is it clear why Sophocles should need his chorus to tell us what to think about what Oedipus and Iocasta have just been doing and saying: we have seen them for ourselves; that should be enough. Aeschylus could trust his audience to see the point of the storm without being told what to think; could not Sophocles trust his audience here, without giving them choral assistance?

However, we will note what in fact is said about hybris, when the chorus has finished its prayer. Hybris breeds the tyrant. Hybris, once surfeited by wealth, tries to scale the summits but is always cast down. If anyone walks in arrogance, not fearing Dike, not revering holy shrines, led on by "luxury" (wanton pride, χλιδή); if he seeks advantage unjustly, does not shrink from impiety, lays reckless hands on sanctities—may destruction attend him.

As for Iocasta, the audience has no reason whatever for imputing pride, injustice, ambition, sacrilege, to her. It is true that at the end of the scene Oedipus is going to accuse her of being proud, "as women will be", but he is again wrong: the poor woman has only gone in to destroy herself. What about her impiety? In the note introductory to this ode, Jebb speaks of her "intellectual arrogance"; but what are the facts, as given? She has been telling Oedipus, from her certain knowledge, that one oracle has failed: her child was to kill its father; she knows that it did not. She knows that it was destroyed at once, and that Laius was killed by brigands. Moreover, she is not irreligious about it: "The oracles came, from the god I do not say, but from his ministers . . ."; and if Sophocles wanted his audience to see impiety in this, it was a little careless of him not to turn back and rewrite the fourth stanza of the previous ode, where the chorus itself says the same: "I do not believe it. The gods of course do not err, but their human ministers can." Knowing what she does, Iocasta could hardly have avoided impiety more scrupulously.

Inevitably, an idea brought into the play by us drives out something put there by the poet. We have no warrant for thinking her proud, arrogant, sceptical, irreligious; these improvements only obscure the essential point: what she naturally accepted as facts were not facts. That is all. In a short time we shall find Sophocles repeating the idea, in more frightening circumstances.

Perhaps we seem to be on firmer ground if we refer the two stanzas on hybris to Oedipus. We have at least seen with our own eyes the ideal monarch of the opening scenes treat Creon like a tyrant, and the phrase "contention for the city's good" may well recall that contention which was for nobody's good. But how much farther can we go? Oedipus is indeed on the summit, and will be cast down, but he did not ambitiously "scale" it: the crown came to him *δωρητόν, οὐκ αἰτητόν* (v. 384), "a gift, unsought". He said what we all know, that wealth attracts envy (*φθόνος*), but if we say that he was "vainly surfeited by wealth" and corrupted by "luxury" we are putting into the play what is not there, and once again obscuring what is there: what led him to act like a tyrant was his excessive reliance on his own quite natural but entirely incorrect inferences. Like Iocasta, he took for granted facts that were not facts—and in his situation most of us would have done the same. What we may censure in him, if we choose to, is a kind of cocksureness. This it was that betrayed him into hybris.

The picture was made sharp and clear: why should Sophocles want to blur it now by adding attributes of the man of hybris, some of which, applied to Oedipus, would be irrelevant, some contradictory? For he is not one who "sought κέρδος" (gain) unjustly, and far from being impious and sacrilegious, he has twice shown his complete faith in the oracle. In the two middle stanzas, what points toward Oedipus is far less than what does not. Therefore our confident expectation was wrong: Sophocles did not write the ode in order to tell us what to think about either Iocasta or Oedipus; for that, he has given us opportunity enough already. He is contrasting hybris in general with reverence and purity. His audience probably saw the point; it should not be impossible for us either.

Richmond Lattimore has put forward, though with hesitation, a reading of the ode which we will examine, lest someone else take it up without hesitation. May not the hybris be lust? May we not have here "the tragedy of incontinence: lust breeds (plants, begets) the tyrant"? The answer is No. We may indeed grant that it is no objection that at this moment Oedipus is still the son of Polybus and Merope, so far as the chorus is concerned: "The chorus say more than they know." That is possible. So we should arrive at "the child who never should have been born, and who, born in defiance, lays hands on secret places and defiles his mother" (*Poetry*, pp. 95 f.). The suggestion is impossible and would be disastrous to the play, however agreeable to present-day ideas.

In the first place, hybris is not "lust", and would not suggest lust to a Greek. Lust might indeed lead to hybris, as in a case of rape, but one might satisfy lust without incurring hybris. In the second place, where in the play do we find reason or excuse for thinking either of "defiance" or of "incontinence"? In the trilogy of Aeschylus, yes; also in the *Phoenissae* of Euripides, where there is going to be both defiance and incontinence, with drunkenness added; what there may have been in other Oedipus plays of which we know nothing, nobody can say—but there is nothing of the kind in this play. Sophocles could easily have put such ideas into the minds of his audience: he did not; and if a spectator allowed his mind to wander to other plays—well, his mind would have been wandering, and that is the end of it.

There is a third point. The "secret places" would be indicated by the word ἄθικτα ("not to be touched") in v. 891. If Sophocles had even suspected that such an interpretation as this were possible, would he have used the same word ἄθικτα in v. 897 of the sanctities of Delphi, and then followed it, in the next verse, with the word ὀμφαλός, of which the literal meaning is "navel"? Probably not. Sophocles used words with care. "Lust" is impossible.

The ode, then, begins and ends with a stanza on the religious way of life; between them are the stanzas that give a generalised picture of its opposite, the way of hybris. We would like to know why Sophocles inserted such a wide-ranging ode here (having seen that none of it refers us to Iocasta, and not much of it to Oedipus); we would like to know too why he speaks so vehemently about oracles. We may reflect that we are only half-way through the play, and that if Sophocles built it thoughtfully, the rest of it may clear things up for us non-Athenians.

What happens next is the dramatic sequence that puzzled us earlier: Iocasta is treated in exactly the same way as Clytemnestra. On the surface, it makes no sense to us; even less, now that we have had to reject the idea that Iocasta is a hardened irreligious sceptic who deserves anything—from an extremely pious author. She comes out, and she prays in her terror that Apollo will somehow avert what Apollo declared was going to happen. Her actual words are that Apollo shall give them both a εὐαγῆ λύσιν, which Jebb accurately renders (in his note) "a solution without defilement". And what is wrong with that? If Sophocles is saying that she *deserves* what is coming to her, then he was an inhuman bigot. About Oedipus, we can at a pinch say that in no circumstances should he have killed a man, or married a woman, twenty years or more older than himself; but why should we not, for a change, think of Iocasta's situation too? No divine warning was given to her that she would marry her own son, and Sophocles' complete silence about the actual marriage leaves us with the vague impression that she married the new King as a matter of course. The most extreme desperation could find no contributory fault in her. She is totally innocent; she doubted prophecy indeed, but only on compelling evidence. What are we to do? One thing that we can do is to listen.

She receives the great news, of course, with enormous relief. She sends for Oedipus, and he comes out, very nervous—the nervousness reflected in the swift rhythm and monosyllables of v. 954:

οὗτος δὲ τίς ποτ' ἐστὶ καὶ τί μοι λέγει;

(Who is this man, and what has he to tell me?)

Now Sophocles makes Iocasta say more than she said before:

—You oracles from Heaven, where are you now?
—Listen to *him*, and see what has become
Of all those solemn oracles from the god.
(vv. 946, 952 f.)

No distinction, this time, between the god and his fallible human interpreters. Now, though not before, we can call her a sceptic, although we may still point out that she has the facts on her side—as she thinks. If this is hybris, it is like the earlier hybris of Oedipus: its origin is not an evil disposition but a false assurance of certitude.

The dialogue continues:

OEDIPUS: Ah me! Why then, Iocasta, should a man
Regard the Pythian house of oracles,
Or screaming birds, on whose authority
I was to slay my father? But he is dead,
The earth has covered him; and here am I,
My sword undrawn—unless perchance *my* loss

Has killed him; so I might be called his slayer.
But for those oracles about my father,
Those he has taken with him to the grave
Wherein he lies, and they are come to nothing.

IOCASTA: Did I not say long since it would be so?
OEDIPUS: You did, but I was led astray by fear.
IOCASTA: So none of this deserves another thought.
OEDIPUS: Yet how can I not fear my mother's bed?
IOCASTA: Why should we fear, seeing that man is ruled
By chance, and there is room for no clear forethought?
No, live at random, live as best one can.
So do not fear this marriage with your mother.
Many a man has suffered this before,
But only in his dreams. Whoever thinks
The least of this, he lives most comfortably.

At this point we must firmly take no notice of the newly painted signpost that directs us to the Oedipus Complex—that is, if it is the play and Sophocles' mind that we are hoping to understand. That road would take us clean outside the play. One understands how Freud, interested in such dreams and wanting a name for his complex, should have fastened on to this passage rather than the one in which Herodotus records that Hippias, just before the battle of Marathon, had such a dream, or the one in which Plutarch records the same of Julius Caesar just before he crossed the Rubicon (reading his dream more successfully than Hippias): the play is a very well-known one, and Oedipus, though he had no such dream, did at least kill an unknown man who he was convinced was *not* his father, and married a woman who he was convinced was *not* his mother. One may indeed speculate about a possible hidden significance in the myth, but our affair is with Sophocles and his play. He might have betrayed some interest (which he does not) in the emotional relations subsisting between Oedipus and Iocasta; he might, somewhere in the play, have described the wedding, writing a verse or two in anticipation of what Shakespeare wrote (more or less) for his Cleopatra:

> Give me my robe, put on my crown; I have
> Immoral longings in me.

Sophocles did nothing of the kind; and we shall not understand him the better by passing over what he did write in favour of what he did not. If we can forget the Complex, we can see why he made Iocasta speak here as she does. What she is saying is that divine prophecy is no more to be relied on than the most random of dreams. From that she draws the logical conclusion that everything happens by chance, so that *πρόνοια*, which means "forethinking" rather than "foresight", is impossible. The only sensible policy is to live at random, by guess, as best you can. Such is the context in which the dream figures.

Lust and the Complex, then, have nothing to do with this play but are intruders from our own age, and like other intruders do nothing but cause confusion. The dream does have its small part in the whole structure: it is an example of what is utterly without significance—like divine prophecy, disposed of by the facts. We have noticed that now, though not before, Iocasta expressly calls the prophecies "divine"; there is to be no question now that the god's ministers may have got it wrong. Yet Sophocles is hardly asking us to turn pale at Iocasta's blasphemy, but at something else. We cannot blame her for believing the new fact, that Oedipus' father has died peacefully, and that yet another oracle has failed; she would have been foolish not to believe it. Therefore, we see her standing, relaxed and happy, only a yard or two from the edge of the abyss into which she is soon to fall headlong, and as she stands there, not able to see it, she declares that there is nothing to be afraid of: prophecy is vain and everything is fortuitous; and because of that, forethinking is a waste of time, and the only sensible guide to life is the intelligent calculation of the moment.

If we should find evidence that it was from contemplating this scene that Aristotle framed his doctrine of Pity and Fear, we could readily believe it, for whom should we pity more than Iocasta, at this moment, and what should make us fear for ourselves—*φόβος περὶ τὸν ὅμοιον*—more than this, that our most certain knowledge may be false, and that we may walk right to the edge of a precipice, and over it, without being able to see it? The only *hamartia* that we can find in Iocasta is one that we all share: she believes what she has been reliably told. (In her marriage, there is to be found no *hamartia* whatsoever.) We have today our "Theatre of the Absurd": what could be more "absurd" than that she should have married the new King as a matter of course, and then discover that he was her own son? But one difference between our Theatre of the Absurd and the *Tyrannus* is that Sophocles' play has a better plot, and the reason for that may be that Sophocles did not stop short at stating the absurdity, but thought there was something more to say.

We noticed that the answer given to Iocasta's prayer is startlingly like that given to Clytemnestra's, though that was a wicked prayer and this one is entirely innocent: have they in common anything important, or was Sophocles only working an effective bit of "theatre"? They have this at least in common: each believes, or hopes, that the universe is what it is not; Clytemnestra, that *adikia*, offences against the natural order—murder, adultery, usurpation, and theft (cf. *Electra* 69–72)—may stand firm; Iocasta, that what omniscience has foreseen may prove false, so that all is fortuitous. Each hope is blasted.

This terrifying scene, so begun, amounts to an emphatic statement that the course of things is not fortuitous. For Sophocles, it was no transient, casual idea, as is shown by the fact that he repeats it at the end of the scene. When Iocasta has gone in to destroy herself, Oedipus—misreading the situation once again—declares that he is the son of Fortune:

> I count myself
> The child of Fortune, giver of all good,
> And I shall not be put to shame, for I
> Am born of Her . . .

The happy theme is taken up by the chorus: "If I have any power of prophecy, and judgment sure [which it soon appears they do not have], Oedipus will find that he is the son of some mountain nymph of Cithaeron, caught in the embrace of Pan or Hermes or Bacchus". Whereupon begins the short scene, the longest seventy-six verses ever written, which proves him to be the son not of Fortune, but of Laius and Iocasta, and he is put to some shame. Now it is his turn to rush into the palace. That is what we witness; that is the dramatic language devised by Sophocles for saying: "No, not Chance, not a random universe", for it was all prophesied.

We have completed our examination of the third part of the play: if now we can hold the whole structure together in our minds, is coherence visible, or not? The first part sets before us the great and wise Oedipus, anxious for his afflicted city; the second, the intelligent Oedipus shrewdly divining the truth and therefore treating Creon as he does; the third, the mounting tension between confidence and terror, the ode which puts side-by-side the religious and the irreligious ways of life, and then the scene we have just been looking at; the fourth and last, the conclusion which is not the conclusion we might have expected: the children, the unexpected way in which the reversal of situation is handled, and the final assertion and visible demonstration, that "you cannot control everything". And it is all erected against the background of the whole story, complex, frightening, and apparently without meaning; foreseen by the *theos* yet hardly directed by him, certainly not designed by him for any purpose that Sophocles cares to suggest; so that if we bravely assert that there was such a purpose, we must do it without any help from him. Nevertheless at the end of the third ode there is that unmistakable assertion of religious faith.

Confronting this, we—to say it once again—are in the position of having to go back to the text and the play itself through layer upon layer of subsequent thought and assumptions—

modern rationalism, Christianity (perhaps in rather debased modern forms), romanticism and individualism, even Platonism. What was clear may have become obscured, and we have seen already that studies in cult-observances or in anthropology can be misleading.

Thus, to some modern readers the *Tyrannus* poses the problem of determinism and free-will, but to Sophocles it evidently did not. Then, it may seem elementary that tragedy, to be significant of anything, should establish relationship between suffering and guilt; this play does not, unless we add something to it. There is no point in making all we can, and a little more, of shortcomings we may find in Oedipus—hot temper for example—for Iocasta too belongs to the play, and her fate, as we have just suggested, is "absurd". Again, nothing is clearer than that Sophocles "believed in the gods", in a divine government of the world. "Therefore", we may conclude, "he believed in a Divine Providence, a divine plan." Yet there is remarkably little evidence for a Divine Providence in Sophocles, or in Aeschylus either, to say nothing of Euripides: divine law, divine power, yes—but a divine Providence? The Zeus of Aeschylus has been represented as a wise and patient god who leads mankind ever onwards and upwards: Lloyd-Jones has made short work of that. We cannot translate "Lead, kindly Light" into plausible Greek. But what is the alternative? This play, as we have just seen, puts forward as the direct opposite the doctrine of a fortuitous world, and of its logical corollary, a world in which forethinking is a waste of time, in which it is wisdom to live without principle, by intelligent guesswork: "Live at random, εἰκῇ; live as best you can". We have seen what Sophocles thought of that. Further, perhaps not all the weight of the play, but much of it, bears on precisely this point, that the most intelligent calculation may be worse than useless when our most solid facts may not be facts at all; and I say "worse than useless" because it was this that led the confident Oedipus to the verge of a crime which, as Creon indicates, would make ordered civic life impossible.

Our problem therefore is whether Sophocles thought there was some middle ground between a Providence in which he did not believe and a fortuitous world which he completely rejects. If we are tempted to fall back on the idea that his religion was only an "unshakeable but placid piety" we shall only fall among thorns: a mere piety would necessarily have attributed some impious behaviour to Laius, Iocasta, and Oedipus, which is just what Sophocles avoided. The solution of the problem, if there is one, should also answer another question: since in the other plays the relation between suffering and guilt is clear, how came the same poet to write this play, not the least assured of his productions, in which that relationship is missing?

If it is true that one part of the complex which we, perforce, call Greek Religious Thought was the contemplation of the way in which the universe works, with the corollary that the Greeks of Attica were separated from the Greeks of Ionia not by the Pacific Ocean but only by the Aegean Sea, then our problem is immediately simplified. We must ask ourselves again: Is it true, or is it not, that we can be deceived by circumstances, as these people were? That the spontaneous and unpredictable actions of others can thwart plans of ours without our being aware of it? That coincidences occur, and may be crucial? That a man, being ignorant of a material fact, can innocently do a disastrous thing that he would never have done had he known? We can only say that such things are true to experience, even if we add that they do not happen all at once, as in this play—which is a reasonable comment, and must be borne in mind. But if it is true that we can be unavoidably ignorant and therefore deceived and therefore suffer, and that this is one part of the way in which the world works, there is no point in protesting that it is unfair, cruel, not reasonable. The "religion" of the tragic poets has in it something that can be compared, however distantly, to modern scientific thinking: A. N. Whitehead understood that when he said that insofar as modern scientific thought has Greek ancestry, those ancestors were the tragic poets rather than the philosophers. The scientist, investigating the ways in which the universe behaves, discovers many things that could be called unfair and cruel, but he would hesitate to call them unreasonable; they could be called that only if they had been devised by man. If he goes on to think as an applied scientist he will ask himself the question—if he uses slang—So what? "Such-and-such being the laws that operate here, is there anything that we can usefully do, whether for production of good or the avoidance of harm?" He, as scientist, does not ask what is the purpose of it all; he postulates no Providence. Sophocles, in this play, recognises that the world contains what is, from our point of view, "absurd", but as it exists, he will not shuffle away from it. For him, as this play makes very clear, either the universe is *theion* or it is random. If it is *theion*, "Nothing is here but Zeus", then the *theoi* must operate throughout, both in what we can understand and approve of, and in what we cannot. Could he hear us protesting that the *theoi* of the *Tyrannus* are unreasonable, he might reply: "Do you, then, inhabit a universe in which nothing happens that is unreasonable to you? Or have you invented gods who are responsible for what you can understand and approve of, but not for the rest?" If the universe will sometimes behave as it does here to Oedipus, Laius, and Iocasta, then we should take note of the fact, and think.

Therefore when the clever schoolboy makes the objection that no observance of the Unwritten Laws would have saved these people, he should be told, in the first place, that Sophocles saw that first; indeed, he invented the facts from which the schoolboy has drawn his conclusion; therefore the clever one has not finished his thinking about the play, but only begun it.

The third ode polarises the two doctrines: the way of religion and morality, and its opposite. The objection that the former would not have saved Oedipus is at bottom sentimental; it is the eighteenth-century demand, that Natural Justice should be shown to prevail. It does, for some part of the way but not throughout, for who can truthfully assert that life punishes only the guilty? Sophocles is "scientist" enough to confront the facts and not lose his faith. The validity of the Unwritten Laws, attested by experience, is not disproved by the obvious fact that they do not explain the whole of experience. On the other hand, disregard of them leads straight to the chaos of hybris.

Sophocles, as a man of religion, is far from being on the defensive in this play; he mounts a powerful counter-attack. He seems to concede the extreme case: no observance of the Unwritten Laws would have saved Oedipus, even less Iocasta. Therefore—what? Throw over the moral guides to conduct and trust to intelligent calculation? But how intelligent may calculation be, when we can be so much in the dark? And where did Oedipus' calculations lead him, when he was ready to condemn Creon?

We have said "counter-attack"; whom or what would he be attacking? There is an answer that seems reasonable in itself and also explains why in important respects the *Tyrannus* is different from the other plays. It has already been put forward by Mr Bernard Knox in the fourth chapter of his book *Oedipus at Thebes*.

We know that the closing decades of the fifth century ushered in the Enlightenment that goes by the name of the Sophistic Movement. Most Enlightenments have their seamy side; this one did, in the brash immoralism represented, for us, by Plato in his portraits of Thrasymachus, Polus, Callicles, and some others, by Thucydides in the talk which he ascribes to the Athenians at Melos. (The full evidence is set forth by Knox.) As Aristotle might have said but did not, Reason is a mean, the two extremes being unreason and intellectual cocksureness. The excess is a kind of immodesty, the delusion that the writ of rationality runs where in fact it does not. Protagoras had said: "Of the gods, we cannot assert either that they exist or do not. The question is obscure, and human life is too short"; also, "Man is the measure of all things". Protagoras himself was a serious thinker, but we know from more recent instances—"The survival of the fittest" is one—how this kind of thing gets about and by base men is turned to base employments. Further, not all rationalists have the patience, perhaps not always the ability, to distinguish between babies and bath water. It was easy and natural to denounce the "immorality" of myths that had never been intended to be moral. Often indeed they must have been used, as by the Nurse in the *Hippolytus*, to excuse immoral behaviour; what was more difficult was to distinguish between this and the serious use of the myths in poetry; easier, and no doubt more exciting, to denounce them wholesale. One result, naturally, was that the crudities of popular religion were replaced by the crudities of bad philosophy—and in the face of the new brilliance, quiet common-sense would be more bashful. While Socrates was testing the traditional morality, trying to purify it where it needed purifying and to set it on firmer foundations, Thrasymachus and his like were gaining credit from the bright discovery that it was only an ancient hoax, a means of cheating the exceptional man out of his natural rights. In short, it was a period of which one mark was a bouncing pseudo-humanism. It might be polite toward the gods, as the Athenians were in Melos, but the essence of it was: "We are the masters now." Sophocles did not believe it.

A little while ago we were discussing Chance: Mr D. W. Lucas puts the matter into a convenient nutshell in his *Greek Tragic Poets* (p. 24):

Chance need not be opposed to divine providence; events may be ascribed to chance merely because they are unforeseeable; but by the end of the fifth century the idea of random chance, the negation of government by gods who care for right and wrong, was winning acceptance, and, like most of the ideas of the time, is to be found in the works of Euripides.

Iocasta's Chance is clearly not "divine chance". Of the latter, Aristotle gives a good example (*Poetics* 1452A 6 ff.):

In chance events those are most arresting which seem to have occurred as it were on purpose, as for instance when the statue of

Mitys in Argos fell upon the author of Mitys' death as he was gazing upon it, and killed him. Such events do not seem to have happened εἰκῇ, at random.

Iocasta's Chance is the purely fortuitous; it denies the existence of any laws except those we obey when the policeman is looking. We can be confident that Sophocles had good reason for taking it so seriously. "Government by gods who care for right and wrong" is a vulnerable doctrine, acceptable indeed to solid piety, but not proof against scepticism. Sophocles takes up the challenge, as it were. As if in defiance, he takes the Oedipus myth, deliberately eliminates all that could help us believe that these people, somehow, had deserved what came to them, emphasises what we have called "the absurd", and declares his faith—for a poet does not argue—that this demonstrates not that the *theoi* do not exist, or do not care for right and wrong, but that human understanding is not quite so big as the immensity that surrounds us. Then, counter-attacking, he exposes the lawlessness and disorder that must flow from the rejection of moral law and its restraints, and the folly of supposing that our intelligent calculations are to be relied on. The clear-sighted Oedipus was blind; the world is such that cock-sureness is a dangerous delusion.

From such a point of view as this, the exceptional use of prophecy in the play becomes understandable and constructive. First Laius, then Oedipus, are expressly told that something horrible is in store for them. They do not vaguely fear; they know, and accept the knowledge. They do what human prudence suggests; neither is lacking in resolution or intelligence. Each fails, and he fails because the complexity of things is too great. As Creon says at the end, "You are not in control."

Sophocles had a very distinguished friend, Pericles, and he also, according to Thucydides, had his ideas about Chance and Reason. By way of appendix, it may be interesting to compare the two, and in doing it to take up a point that we raised earlier and hastily dropped, since the question was a hypothetical one: what are we to say about the *Tyrannus* if we assume as many scholars have done that it was composed and produced soon after the plague in Athens? There is nothing, I think, to make the assumption unlikely, and nothing to promote it from assumption to probability, still less fact, but it may not be unreasonable to contemplate its consequences.

If we do, we should guard against trifling errors by reminding ourselves that the subject of the *Tyrannus* is not the plague in Thebes. The play begins indeed with impressive descriptions of that plague—quite enough to arrest the attention of an Athenian audience who (on our assumption) were the survivors of a similar plague which had consumed about a quarter of the population—but soon it moves, as we saw, into another region, with the plague forgotten. Therefore one thing we must not leave out of account, if we make the assumption, is the audience. Those Athenians who witnessed the *Persae* saw a poet's recreation of a great triumph: those who witnessed the *Tyrannus* will have been reminded, by the poet, of a frightening disaster.

We recall how it was described by Thucydides—not the physical horrors only, but its moral and social effects too. Whole families, he says, died because others were afraid to go near them. Of those who did tend the sick, many caught the plague and themselves died. The decencies of funerals were abandoned. It was the beginning of a lawlessness never known before: everything was sacrificed to pleasures of the moment, since any moment seemed likely to be the last. No respect was paid to laws human or divine, for men felt themselves to be already under sentence of death; and as for the gods, it seemed to make no difference whether one respected them or not.—It is a picture of total demoralisation.

Thucydides also spares a chapter to describing how the event —οἷα εἰκός, "as was natural"—stimulated superstition: oracles were produced and canvassed; some remembered, "those in the know", τοῖς εἰδόσιν, that Apollo had assured the Spartans that if they fought hard he would be on their side—and look: the plague began as soon as the Peloponnesians had invaded Attica, and hardly affected their cities at all! If the play was written within a few years of the event, all this was within the recent experience of Sophocles and his audience, and the Theban plague would certainly bring it back to life.

Thanks also to Thucydides, much as he hated talking, we can see this reflected in the mind of Pericles, and it may prove that he and Sophocles did have something in common. In the speech he made just before the outbreak of the war, Pericles (according to Thucydides) said something that has a familiar ring (Thucydides, I 140): "The course that events take can be as stupid as the plans that men make. For that reason we commonly ascribe to chance (τύχη) what happens contrary to our expectation."—Here I follow Gomme and others in taking ἀμαθῶς in the active sense, not passive, "unforeseeable", agreeing also with Gomme in seeing a tinge of irony in it: *we* call it stupid because we do not see the causes. Now, the course that events did take, during the first year of the war, corresponded closely with what had been foreseen; the sagacity of Pericles and those who had agreed with him was justifying itself. Then came a bolt from the blue, the Plague. It must have seemed to many that it made nonsense of rational calculation: what reliance can be placed on reason, γνώμη, in a world that can suddenly turn upside down like this? What is the use of it? So, after a promising first year of war, Athenians were suddenly in Sparta suing for peace.

Now Thucydides records another speech made by Pericles. Among other things he says this:

> I am not surprised that you are feeling angry with me . . . I have called this meeting to refresh your memories and to make complaint against you, if you are wrong either in being indignant with me or in

giving way to misfortune . . . If, under the stress of our private sufferings, you are relaxing your grip on the public safety, you are condemning me for advising the war and yourselves for taking my advice. And yet, I think I am as good as anyone at seeing what the best policy is and at expounding it . . . I am what I was; I have not been moved. It is you that have changed; it is your weakness that makes you think my policy was wrong . . . Because a great and sudden reversal has fallen upon you, no longer are your minds firm enough to abide by the decision that you took; for a sudden, unforeseen and totally incalculable event breaks a man's resolution.

Pericles then confronts a situation which seemed to mock at reason, but his argument is that we should not allow an apparently irrational event to drive us off the rational course. Thucydides describes the situation as one which created a sheer moral breakdown. If Sophocles had the same situation behind him as he was thinking out his play, what he does with the myth, and the exceptional features of the play, certainly does not become more difficult to understand. For as we have seen, this play, exceptionally, incorporates, and not as a mere datum, two bolts from the blue for which he suggests no reason whatever; and, exceptionally, he excludes the idea that the suffering is traceable to any fault. He presents a picture of what Life can do at its worst; but Sophocles, like Pericles, remains firm; the one a man of affairs and of practical intelligence, the other a poet and a man of religion. Pericles is not shaken by what he calls *τὸ πλείστῳ παραλόγῳ ξυμβαῖνον*, "a totally incalculable event"; he says too (Thucydides, II 64,2): *φέρειν χρὴ τὰ δαιμόνια ἀναγκαίως*, "we must accept what the gods send, since we can do no other". But as he declares that it is wrong, in the face of the unforeseeable and uncontrollable, to abandon reason and courage, so too does Sophocles declare that it is wrong, in the face of the incomprehensible and unmoral, to deny the moral laws and accept chaos. What is right is to recognise facts and not delude ourselves. The universe is a unity; if, sometimes, we can see neither rhyme nor reason in it we should not suppose that it is random. There is so much that we cannot know and cannot control that we should not think and behave as if we do know and can control. The modesty of Creon is a better example than the towering self-confidence of Oedipus.

V

Pindar and Plato

How INTELLIGENT were the Syracusans, during that time which was so dismal in Athens? We have some slight evidence.

The First Olympian is a poem that Pindar composed, in 476 B.C., on what was clearly a most important occasion, for him, namely the first time he received a commission from the most powerful single man in the Greek world, Hieron of Syracuse. Now, Pindar was one who did not take lightly either the dignity or the responsibility of being a poet, and for this ode, one of his most brilliant, he put forth all his power and all his technique. For subject, he chose the double myth of Tantalus and Pelops his son; the ostensible link between the myth and the occasion is that Pelops lies entombed at Olympia, where Hieron had gained the victory that was being celebrated. As Pindar tells the myth—severely modifying its traditional shape, for a reason which he is good enought to explain—Tantalus was one who was signally honoured by the gods, but "was unable to digest his great bliss": he committed great hybris and consequently suffers great punishment. But his son Pelops was a great hero indeed, and god-fearing; therefore he won great glory and for ever receives honour at Olympia. Hieron himself (v. 113) has reached the summit of human greatness.

Could anything speak more eloquently, or more seriously, to

one who was entering upon the dangerous path of kingship? On other occasions, we know, Pindar came forward as counsellor to this high personage, often expressing his thought directly, as in "Seek not to become Zeus"; on this first occasion it might have been tactless in him to say more; certainly it would have been inartistic, because unnecessary. "Look on this picture—and on this." At other times and places, bishops and the like have preached grave sermons to kings about the obligations laid upon them by their station; Pindar did not preach; for one thing, he was a Greek poet, and for another, he was composing an ode, with music, to grace a feast. Yet he said what he meant, unoriginal though it was—and he said it without putting it into words. This evidently implies an audience that could be trusted to see the point; and since the ode is in the old tradition of the paradigmatic myth, there is no difficulty in supposing that they did have the intelligence to see the point, even though it was conveyed silently, in poetry of rare brilliance.

In such significant use of mimesis there is, of course, nothing that is peculiarly Hellenic; what is peculiarly Hellenic is the fact that it was used so consistently. As we shall see later, it is the source of that Hellenic economy and restraint that we justly admire. In Greek literature the skeleton is more important than in other literatures, and accordingly the flesh is less ample. Aeschylus writes for Eteocles that final speech about Polyneices and Dike just before the two brothers kill each other, and he leaves his audience to draw the obvious conclusion, one which Shakespeare might have put into a memorable speech.

We now have to face the horrid fact that even some writers of prose would do this kind of thing, with of course the same consequences: we can gravely misunderstand their meaning if we insist on reading them as prosaically as possible. With Xenophon, for example, we are safe; he was not an exceptionally imaginative writer, and he makes no great demands on the imagination of his readers—but what about Plato? He had imagination; here and there he credits his readers with some. In this connexion we have already mentioned the *Protagoras*

(p. 4), but it deserves more extended consideration, as also does the *Gorgias*. We shall find that even Plato could write in this mimetic tradition—as indeed Aristotle implies, when he includes "the Socratic dialogues" among his few illustrations of mimesis in prose.

If we read through the dialogue in a quite unresponsive way, we receive much the same impression as when we read through certain Greek plays in the same spirit—the *Ajax* or *Trachiniae* or *Troades* or *Hecuba:* it seems to have been put together with an unreasonable lack of care. We have, first, the short proem, which enables Socrates to be the narrator throughout. Then there is the long and vivid scene with young Hippocrates, all aflame to be introduced to the great Protagoras, hoping to become a pupil of his. On the grounds that it is still too early in the day to go paying calls, Socrates detains him in conversation, eliciting from him that he has little idea what Protagoras actually teaches, and whether his teaching will do him good or harm. In the company of these two we make our way to Callias' house, and Plato certainly takes his time over his amusingly satirical description of the great Protagoras, his awe-struck disciples, and Prodicus and Hippias. At last, when all are assembled, Socrates puts his question to Protagoras on Hippocrates' behalf, and "At this point", as one Platonic scholar once said, "the true business of the dialogue begins". This seems to imply that what we have had so far is nothing but a sort of cranking-up, or a big spoonful of jam to cover up the pill that is now to be administered; but even so, what would be "the true business of the dialogue" on this showing? For Plato reveals himself to be as unable to keep himself on a straight course as the writers of the plays just mentioned.

He presents us in succession with a short and over-elaborate speech from Protagoras on his own profession; a long and not unimpressive myth, also from Protagoras, designed to persuade, rather than prove, that ἀρετή, excellence, or virtue, can be taught (a proposition that Socrates has denied); arising out of this, a long dialectical passage on the question whether the virtues are one or several, this ending not in any agreement, but in a display of restiveness on the part of Protagoras. At this point Plato represents that the discussion is on the verge of breaking down, because Protagoras will not, or cannot, answer Socrates' questions briefly, and Socrates is too dull-minded to take in Protagoras' long speeches. Another dramatic interlude ensues. All those present are anxious for the debate to continue. Callias becomes the tactful host, and suggests an impossible compromise; Alcibiades is impetuous, and treats it as if it were a boxing-match; Callias invokes Prodicus and Hippias, each of whom makes a speech—and either of these, if it were necessary, would itself establish Plato's repute as one of the world's great parodists. Hippias, with rare pomposity, suggests that they appoint an umpire, an arbitrator, a moderator as it were—a notion which Socrates at least takes seriously enough to demolish.

However, after a great deal of talk an agreement is made: first Protagoras shall ask questions and Socrates answer them, and then the other way about. On the above conception of "the true business of the dialogue" we would naturally expect the revival of the question if virtue can be taught, or of the other, whether the virtues are several or only one. Reading in this way, like platelayers doggedly plodding along a railway track, we ought to be gravely puzzled, for Plato should be immune from "naïve dramaturgy" even if Aeschylus was not, and unlike Sophocles he was not hampered by an inconvenient myth which he could hardly be expected to get into reasonable shape. Plato at least was in sole charge of what he wrote. But he makes Protagoras bring up an entirely new topic, namely Simonides' poem. It is true that Protagoras makes the pretence that it arises out of what has gone before, but in fact it does not, and it is introduced by the remark that an important part in education is the study of literature, with the object of being able to understand what the poem means, and whether it is well or badly written, and to answer questions about it. Protagoras then delivers an elaborate disquisition on the poem, in which he claims to find a contradiction. The whole company applauds fervently, and yet another dramatic interlude follows. Socrates pretends to have been made quite giddy by the brilliance of the speech, and to have not the least idea what to say in reply; so that, just to gain time, he appeals to Prodicus as an expert in semantics: what did Simonides, being, like Prodicus, a native of Ceos, understand by the word χαλεπόν ("difficult")? The expert witness promptly and confidently says κακόν ("bad")—an opinion which neither Protagoras nor Socrates can take seriously.

By this time Socrates has sufficiently recovered his wits to reply, and the reply takes the form of a long and highly sophistical exposition of the poem, well supplied not only with fallacies in argument but also with incorrect Greek; for we ourselves, as teachers of the language, should have little patience with a pupil who thought that ἀγαθὸν μὲν γενέσθαι χαλεπόν meant the same as γενέσθαι μὲν ἀγαθὸν χαλεπόν. When this astonishing performance is finished all that happens is that Hippias has to be restrained from giving yet a third interpretation of the unlucky poem. Then more conversation about what they shall discuss: Socrates makes plain his own view that discussing poetry is rather a degrading pastime for men of intelligence, and at last we get back to the original topics. Once more, if we are to be quite unimaginative in our reading of the dialogue, difficulties confront us. Socrates uses more than one fallacious argument, one of which Protagoras notices (350c)—and if Protagoras saw it, obviously Plato saw it first; and the doctrine arrived at about the Good and the Pleasant is not only unsatisfactory in itself, but also is completely at variance with what is said on the subject in the *Gorgias*. In this final part of the dialogue Socrates first disposes of Protagoras' thesis that the virtues are separate, then of its modification that they are similar though distinct; next, having proved—with the help of some bluff—that the virtues are one, he arrives, *via* the present doctrine of the Good and the Pleasant, at the conclusion that virtue is knowledge; and he ends by pointing out, with bland surprise, that during the discussion he and Protagoras have changed places: at the beginning Protagoras affirmed, and he himself denied, that virtue can be taught, but now Socrates is affirming it and Protagoras denying it.

Of course, Plato made one obvious error in constructing the dialogue: he forgot Hippocrates—much as Sophocles forgot first Ismene and then Antigone herself. Perhaps he was rushed into publication before he had really finished the work; if we can finish it for him, we may deserve well of posterity. Let us at least make a beginning:

Thereupon I made a sign to Hippocrates. He had been sitting on a stool, listening intently to what had been said. He rose, moved towards the door, and waited there for me. We went out together, and on the way home I said: "Well, Hippocrates, you have been lucky; you have seen and heard not only the great Protagoras but also Prodicus and Hippias. What did you think of them?" At first he was reluctant to answer, but I encouraged him to speak out and not be coy, and at last he did. "I am sure", he said, "that I have missed something, because these are distinguished men. If I have, you will correct me, Socrates. As for Hippias, I confess that he seemed to me nothing but a . . ." He bit his lip, and blushed. "Yes?" I said. He looked confused and did not reply. "Come, Hippocrates", I said, "we are alone, and surely you can trust me not to denounce you. The word you were going to use—was it by any chance 'windbag'?" He burst out laughing and said, "Socrates, are you a diviner, or did some god tell you?" "And Prodicus?" I said. He look a bit puzzled. "Tell me, Socrates," he said, "is it possible for a man to be very learned, and yet in some ways a bit stupid?" "We will talk about that some other time", I said, "because you really went to see Protagoras, and I am anxious to know how he struck you."

We will not continue. In some such way as this a writer who was not a Greek, and not Plato either, might have prolonged the dialogue in order to say things like these: that Protagoras is an estimable and an able man, but one who devotes his abilities to the elegant presentation of what he thinks he knows already, and has no conception of real intellectual discipline and not much patience when something of the kind is set before him; that the philology of Prodicus is, in any large context, nothing but inept pedantry; that none of them has the least idea what the spirit and purpose of a discussion is, but think it a personal competition, or a *concours d'élégance*—anything but a joint effort to reach the truth; that their hangers-on are in fact hanging on to a sham; that the study of literature, one of the great stand-bys in this "liberal" education, is another sham, since you can make a poem mean just what you like (in their conception at least)—"For did you not notice", says Socrates to the dejected boy, in the unwritten part of the dialogue, "how first Protagoras gave an account of Simonides' poem that was designed, not to illuminate the poem, but to show how clever and original Protagoras is, and how then I gave them a quite preposterous account of the same poem, and they all swallowed it whole? Time after time I left the door gaping open for them; I played all kinds of tricks both with logic and with language—and not one of these literary experts took the slightest notice."

But Plato does not, in this or in any other way, explain the purport of the dialogue. He was writing in Greek for Greeks; here, as in the *Gorgias* too, he remains faithful to the Greek conception of *poiesis*, which may be expressed in our homely saying, "Why keep a dog and bark yourself?" Putting it in rather more formal terms, Plato shows us but does not tell us; he relies on his reader to read with that degree of imaginative coöperation that makes direct statement unnecessary and the result more effective. The alternative is to suppose that he never succeeded in getting this dialogue into intelligible shape.

Further, if we were a little dull, we might ask why Plato took the trouble to attack in this way men now safely dead, Protagoras, Prodicus, and Hippias. We are in fact not so dull; we understand at once that Plato is vindicating his own educational ideas against the more fashionable and showy ones used by such as Isocrates. We understand that the dialogue as a whole is concerned not with strictly philosophic questions of the unity or diversity of the virtues, and of the Good and the Pleasant; these are the occasion rather than the substance of the dialectical passages: they are designed in such a way as to lead directly into the grand conclusion which is the basis of the whole: Virtue is Knowledge, and those who are not pursuing knowledge cannot be teaching virtue. The substance is the question of philosophic method. If Plato were arguing here as a professional philosopher, so to speak, the occasional fallacies would be fatal. As it is, they are not, for the point is—and he makes it quite clear—that the proposition he argues can be disproved only by better use of the same method.

Herein lies the point of the ironical ending. Socrates, early on, is made to be sceptical of Protagoras' assertion that ἀρετή, excellence, virtue, can be taught; at the end, Socrates is arguing that it can, and it is Protagoras who is reluctant to agree. "How odd!" says Socrates; "you and I have changed sides". But of course this is only Plato's fun. At the beginning Socrates denied that virtue is teachable because he denied that Protagoras either knew what virtue is, or had command of a method that could find out, or indeed "teach" anything—only persuade. At the end Socrates has proved that virtue is knowledge—or at least put Protagoras in the position of not being able to disprove it—and has exemplified the method by which knowledge is to be attained.

The structure of the *Gorgias* is of the same kind. If we are bewildered by it, on the grounds that instead of pursuing a continuous argument, as do most of the other dialogues, it takes up and then drops a number of topics—and argues some of them in a way which is a little short of convincing—the reason would be, once more, that we have not attuned ourselves to Plato's *poiesis*. We must be ready to allow our minds to reach out.

It seems likely that one ancient reader of the dialogue *was* bewildered—the scribe or editor who added to it the subtitle περὶ Ῥητορικῆς, On Rhetoric; because of the three distinct sections into which it may be thought to subside, the first indeed has to do with rhetoric, though from an unusual point of view; the discussion with Polus certainly begins with rhetoric, though it is mainly concerned with other matters, and if Socrates were really arguing against rhetoric on the basis of the extravagant claim which Plato causes Polus to make—that rhetoric confers absolute power—then the argument would be worth nothing; but the third and longest part, the argument with Callicles, has nothing to do with this ostensible subject—for Callicles despises rhetoric almost as much as Socrates does; while the impressive myth that concludes the work is as remote from rhetoric as anything can be.

Once more, the unity of the dialogue, that is to say Plato's real concern, is to be apprehended by some slight effort of the imagination; it is not in the *lexis*, the text. Ostensibly Plato is discussing at one moment rhetoric, at another the paradox that a tyrant like Archelaus can indeed do anything that he chooses but not what he wishes: ἃ δοκεῖ αὐτῷ but not ἃ βούλεται; at another, Callicles' doctrine of the natural rights of the stronger; at another, Callicles' doctrine that the best life is the life of unrestrained pleasure; at another, the proposition that the Good and the Pleasant are not the same. In most of his dialogues Plato takes up a subject and sticks to it; here, as in the *Protagoras*, he does not.

Needless to say, there is no difficulty in seeing the real unity and subject of the dialogue, once one has understood that Plato does not always write that kind of straightforward, closely reasoned exposition that we expect from a philosopher. His true subject here, as I suppose everyone recognises, might be briefly put in some such form as the following.

The all-important question is πῶς δεῖ ζῆν, How are we to order our lives? The all-important art, or science, is the one which, in respect of the soul, is analogous to medicine in respect of the body: it may be called ἡ πολιτική, the science of living what is truly the best life, of knowing what is good, and not being deceived by shams. Plato's method, here, is something like the method of the sculptor—the carver, not the modeller:

he begins, as it were, with a varied set of current ideas and steadily cuts away the false until we are left with the true.

Therefore, first (and gently) the high claims of education through rhetoric are disposed of, in the *persona* of Gorgias: when Socrates denies that rhetoric is an art, he means, and makes quite clear, that it is not *the* art, the science of Good and Evil. With the "art of rhetoric" in the ordinary acceptance he has no concern at all. A certain continuity is given to the dialogue by the introduction of Polus as the next interlocutor; he also professes rhetoric, but in a different spirit. For him it is the means to power. We are therefore still concerned with rhetoric, nominally, but really with a different answer to the question πῶς δεῖ ζῆν. We are concerned with power, absolute licence. Polus' contention that Archelaus is the most enviable of all men is met with the proposition that he is of all men the most miserable; absolute power, joined with absolute ignorance, is absolute wretchedness.

Then we have Callicles, the man-of-the-world, the realist (as he thinks), with his notions of the natural rights of the stronger, and of undiluted pleasure. Here it is that Socrates argues that pleasure and the good are not identical; that we should pursue only those pleasures that result in good, and pursue them, not for the sake of the pleasure, but of the good. Here too, as in the opposite proposition of the *Protagoras*, some of the arguments are less than convincing, as Plato virtually recognises when he makes Callicles say, more than once, οὐ πείθομαι, "I am not convinced"; but again, Socrates can be refuted only by the use of his own weapon, argument. The theory is different from the one advanced in the *Protagoras*, but the interesting thing is that the outcome is the same; for Callicles, the practical man who is disdainful of philosophy, is forced to see his own ignorance, and to admit that since we have to choose between pleasures we need the τεχνικός, the master of the relevant art, or science, to direct us in our choice; and that such direction can come only from that scientific moral philosophy, the "political art", which throughout the dialogue Plato has been vindicating against rivals and substitutes.

So is one false guide after another cut away until only the truth is left. The conclusion of the dialogue (if a personal judgment may be obtruded) is the most impressive and beautiful passage that Plato ever wrote. Few things in actual Greek drama are more imaginative and more right than the way in which the figures of Gorgias, Polus, and Callicles, with the contentions in which they were concerned, are allowed to fade away, leaving only Socrates before our minds—Socrates and his myth and his moral passion—as, through him, Plato makes an almost apocalyptic declaration of faith which is, at the same time, an *apologia pro vita sua*. The final words *ἔστι γὰρ οὐδενὸς ἄξιος, ὦ Καλλίκλεις*, "it is worth nothing, Callicles", distantly recall the dramatic audience, but no word from Callicles, or from the others, is allowed to break the silence that follows.

In each of these dialogues, then, Plato chose to say what he meant not through direct exposition (even in dialogue form) but in quasi-dramatic structures—a kind of mimesis. Doing this, he must have expected to be understood by his contemporary readers, but he ran some risk of not being fully understood by some few readers in the remote future. The temptation is strong, but must be resisted, of inserting here an Imaginary Conversation between Plato and the nineteenth-century scholar who wrote: "At this point the true business of the dialogue begins". In the Conversation Plato would quote Plato, that a work of art is like a *ζῷον*, an animal complete in all its parts, and with nothing unnecessary, and Plato would ask, in the Socratic manner, if we can ever say, of a horse or dog or goose, "At this point the true structure of the animal begins".

In such a case, we may ask, what is the difference between the response given and the response expected? Perhaps we may put it like this: if we read such dialogues as these in the wrong way, it is because we have instinctively separated two elements which, for Plato and his Greek readers, were not separate—the "dramatic" and the "philosophic". We, it may be, pounce on the argumentative passages like a stoat on a rabbit; here (we think) Plato's mind is really engaged—in expounding or arguing a theory of Pleasure (or whatever the topic happens to be). The rest, we think, is only decoration; the scene with Hippocrates is no part of "the true business of the dialogue"; Plato was, among other things, an artist, and one with a markedly dramatic bent; he liked to relieve the strenuousness of the dialectical passages with the charm that his artistry could invest them with.

But if we think like this, we are wrong. If the foregoing brief analyses of the *Protagoras* and *Gorgias* are somewhere near the mark, it follows that the artistic bits are as much part of the intended total statement as the philosophic bits. Both are designed to contribute to one total impact, and must be understood with reference to that combined meaning. In fact, we may be wandering in the wilderness if we gravely compare the two rather discordant theories of pleasure, and try to estimate how many years it may have taken the perspiring Plato to have climbed up from the lower theory to the higher. Each is being propounded, in its given context, as a step towards the important proposition: knowledge is supreme. It behoves us to be a little careful. It is not the case that Plato's mind is focussed on a succession of different themes in the foreground, but rather on one unifying theme in the background. We have to coöperate, to understand that things can be said without being put into words.

None of this is unfamiliar to us. There are extant plays which unintelligibly lack unity if our focus is not long enough; yet Sophocles could not have expected his audience to be so absorbed in the fortunes of Ajax the tragic hero that when he disappears the audience would lose all sense of unity and meaning, nor could Euripides have expected his audiences to be baffled by the un-Aristotelian succession of the scenes in the *Troades* and *Hecuba*. Familiar too is the art of saying something without saying it: Pindar could remind a king of certain of the moral facts of life by using pictures only, and Aeschylus says a great deal, though not to all his modern readers, by first having Zeus throw a net around Troy, and then Clytemnestra around Agamemnon.

There is no need whatever to assert that the Greeks were either more, or less, intelligent than ourselves; the important point is that their intelligence could work rather differently, that (once more) they still held in fusion what we, on the whole, have separated—the artistic and the intellectual, or the imaginative and the analytical. With Plato, I think, we reach the parting of the ways. His more technical dialogues we must (and do) read differently from those that we have been considering. To speak generally, they are conceived and written intellectually, an exposition or argument explicit and complete. They will be written with grace, and the philosophic thinking will itself be imaginative: this does not come into question. The great difference is that in these dialogues the whole meaning is contained in the λέξις, the actual text; mimesis no longer plays any real part. What is called for is an unremitting and acute intellectual response; what grace of language or presentation there may be is an addition to the real statement of the dialogue—something to be grateful for, but no essential part of the total theme.

In the two dialogues we have been looking at, and in others that may be similar, Plato calls for a response which is no less keen, but is differently constituted, inasmuch as the *lexis* does not contain the total meaning, and if we carefully pay attention to nothing but the *lexis* we reduce both the form and the content of the dialogue to chaos or something not much better, since no small part of the meaning is implied rather than stated, implied in the *poiesis* (just as in Pindar's ode), in the choice and disposition of the material. Whether the work in question is a poem, or a play, or a dialogue of this type, its designed significance reaches out beyond what is actually *said;* no amount of purely intellectual attention to the text will reveal it to us; only that, *plus* a constructive and imaginative awareness.

We ourselves exercise precisely this, without thinking about it, in reading lyric poetry, or a good novel. The difference between our age and the one which ends (I think) with Plato is that our own literature, of say the last three centuries, calls in the main for either the one response or the other, while classical Greek literature normally calls for both. This, incidentally, is one answer to those would-be purists who protest against the very idea of finding coherent and intelligent thinking in Aeschylus or Sophocles—or even in Homer. The Hellenistic poets had renounced serious thought; prose-writers after Plato had renounced the mimetic or poietic instrument: up to the time of Plato we must be prepared to find both; and again, there is the inevitable corollary that their readers or listeners would be prepared to supply both.—Now we are in a position to consider Thucydides.

VI

Thucydides

THIRTY YEARS ago it was possible for a Thucydidean scholar, A. W. Gomme, to write this (*Essays*, 1937, pp. 116 f.):

> All historians of Greece and all editors of Thucydides have commented on his estimate of the importance of the Peloponnesian War, and their comments can be divided, roughly, into two classes. There are kindly persons who say, in a patronising way, that it was natural for Thucydides to magnify the importance of his theme; it is a pardonable error, a common human failing; many writers have been thus guilty. Others, of a franker nature, straightway condemn him for his faulty judgment. All alike agree in thinking that judgment manifestly wrong.

Gomme cites R. Harder, who spoke of Thucydides' *Vergangenheitsblindheit*, his "blindness to the past"; and he quotes Macan: "Thucydides magnifies his own subject at the expense of the wars of Hellene and Barbarian, ludicrously missing the oecumenical significance and wantonly compressing the duration and magnitude of the Herodotean theme". The repulse of Xerxes, Macan said elsewhere, was vastly the greater achievement; he explained Thucydides' absurd mistake by invoking "the anti-imperial, anti-Periclean, anti-democratic or at least anti-nautical strata of Athenian society". (We are rarely at a loss for an explanation, especially if it cannot be found in our texts.)

This has a familiar sound: "Aeschylus' Zeus was a beneficent monarch", "Aeschylus wrote the *Persae* to glorify his city". This judgment, like those, has no relation to what is in the text, for, as Gomme remarked, one has only to read what Thucydides actually wrote here (I 23) to see that what he says is true and exact. He is saying that the Peloponnesian War was much more destructive than the Persian: the one lasted, on and off, for twenty-seven years (or for ten, if we insist that the passage must be "early"), while the other was decided in two battles by land and two by sea. In no sense of the word did he regard the Peloponnesian War as an "achievement", and he was not thinking of "oecumenical importance" at all.

Why should it have been so difficult to read what he wrote? For Thucydides did not write poetry, which notoriously can mean anything to anybody, and those who study history are well trained in the close reading of documents. How could it happen that so many should have read into his text what is not there and in consequence not have understood what is there? The adjectives "ludicrous" and "wanton" recoil upon their author—an accident that any critic would wish to avoid.

I take a more recent and much less important instance, only because it points in the same direction. In the preface to his *Greek Historians* Mr M. I. Finley has a few stimulating pages about Thucydides, but one remark is puzzling: "Of course, it is impossible to guess just what the young Thucydides had in mind when he decided, in 431 B.C., to become the war's historian." The text here needs emendation: for "impossible" read "unnecessary", for Thucydides has told us why he did it. In his first two sentences he tells us that when the war became imminent he realised that he was standing on the verge of the biggest event in known history, and resolved therefore to record precisely what should happen. There is no reason for astonishment or surmise; no reason to ask the question, still less try to answer it, as Mr Finley does, why Thucydides departed so far from the regular path of historiography as to undertake the history of an event that still lay in the future. All we need do is read what he says. Why—now and then—can it be so difficult?

It was in connexion with Thucydides that Cornford wrote the passage, quoted earlier, about circumambient atmospheres. Cornford's own attempt to break out of our own atmosphere, the one he made in his book, did not have much success with students of Thucydides; his diagnosis was better than his treatment. For consider the two points from which we have set out. Why did Harder, Macan, and others fail to read the text effectively and therefore, in one important respect, misjudge their fifth-century author so completely? Because they knew that Thucydides is a historian, and knew from the beginning what a historian tries to do and how he thinks: the phrase "oecumenical significance" will sum it up well enough. How else should a historian think? But sometimes the incredible is true; sometimes, as we have seen above, what we take for granted is in fact not given. Thucydides was not thinking like this. Then how did he think? and if we have lost contact with him on these two occasions, is it not possible that we have done it on others also?

1. His Choice of Material

Our whole argument is that the surest way of discovering how a *poietes* thinks is to watch his *poiesis;* that is, to examine first his choice rather than his disposition of material. But was Thucydides a *poietes?* I claim the distinguished support of Mme de Romilly, who writes (*Thucydide et l'impérialisme athénien*, p. 97): "Il ne se contente pas de reproduire les faits: il choisit, il pense, il construit; c'est une réalité élaborée qu'il nous présente, et, par là même, soumise à son jugement." "Il construit", he constructed, "made", something; he was a *poietes* —unlike Xenophon in his *Hellenica*, who merely recorded, guided not by his own thought but by his material.

I suppose that everybody will admit this; there is nothing new in the suggestion that Thucydides was more than a diligent recorder of facts. Mr Finley, for example, speaks of Thucydides' "many attempts, varied in form and tone, to get beneath and behind the facts, to uncover and bring into clear focus the realities of politics, the psychology of political behaviour, the rights and wrongs of power". If now we proceed to examine his choice, presentation, and disposition of material, it will certainly be at the cost of saying much that is very familiar to students of Thucydides and of Greek history: however, besides being a primary and unrivalled source for the history of the War, his book is one of the glories of Greek Literature, and to study it as such may at the worst have the merit of being quaint. We will begin with some of his disconcerting omissions; something may have been gained if, at the end, we see that these are not blind spots in the historian, to be explained on some hypothesis or other, but sure signs that a powerful and recognisably Hellenic mind is at work.

In considering his *poiesis* we shall enjoy one advantage that we have not indisputably had hitherto. We shall be in the company not of a poet, one whose intelligence can be doubted because he was so good a poet, and whose control over his structure can be denied because he was nearly strangled by his myth. Nor did he compose in a hurry, for next month's dramatic festival, and with one eye on the judges. Moreover, he was of the new generation; he had thrown overboard the unenlightened theology that had hampered the minds of his predecessors in Athenian literature—and it will be interesting to notice what remarkably little difference that makes. He composed, as we have said, slowly. We know, because he tells us, that he began his work in 431 B.C. We know, because he tells us, that after his exile in 424 he had, so to speak, nothing else to do: he could work *καθ'ἡσυχίαν* (V 26), "in peace of mind", as Gomme renders it, adding however "in so far as we can use the words 'peace of mind' of Thucydides", for Gomme understood Thucydides better than some. We can be fairly certain that he died, leaving his book unfinished, at about 400 B.C. That is, he was at work on it for some thirty years. In the

Oxford text it occupies about six hundred pages. We know indeed, because he tells us, that he prosecuted his enquiries with diligence and therefore must have spent much time on his researches: even so, his rate of composition was something less than rapid—twenty pages a year, less than two a month. Further, when we reflect how lively and informative the normal Greek was (and is), how many exciting stories he must have heard, how much information, relevant or not, he must have been given, we are driven to the conclusion that one of his chief preoccupations must have been to leave things out. Deliberate elimination was an essential part of his method; he was a carver, not a modeller. He took his notebooks and carved away at them, to the end that what was left (subject to some later qualification) should have significant shape. Add to this the obvious fact that we are in the presence of a man of commanding intelligence. This time at least we may be confident that our author meant exactly what he says, and said exactly what he meant—although, like Plato, he may not always say it in the way to which we are accustomed. In some ways, the Greeks are a remarkably *foreign* people. How then did he think about his subject?

We understand readily enough that he was not writing a "History of Greece from 432 to 404". He never mentions the new buildings on the Acropolis, the first production of *The Acharnians* or the *Troades*, his interesting contemporary Socrates; there is nothing about the busy intellectual or commercial life of Athens. If someone should explain (and surely someone has done so) that Thucydides had no interest in these things, the peaceable reply would be, "Next time, read the Funeral Speech more intelligently". His subject, as he says himself, is just the War, ὡς ἐπολέμησαν πρὸς ἀλλήλους, ὡς ἐπολεμήθη. But this is where our difficulties begin. His conception of his subject can be made to seem so narrow as to raise doubts concerning his intelligence.

A war, even an ancient war, is something like an iceberg: the actual military operations can be compared to that part which projects above the water; underneath, supporting and explaining these, are the political, economic, financial, diplomatic, social, administrative, logistic aspects of the war; and even if we can persuade ourselves that some of them were less complex and pressing in antiquity than today, we cannot think that they were unimportant, or that our historian is reasonably informative about them.

As Gomme says, in the Introduction to his *Commentary*, Thucydides takes much for granted: the normal conditions of Greek warfare, for instance. This we can understand, but the reasons for the other omissions are not so clear; for some he has been severely criticised, and for others desperate explanations have been offered.

It has often been noticed that Thucydides has very little to say about the economic background of the war, either before it broke out or during its course. "He did not understand the importance of these things", we say; "he had no clear idea of what lay behind the Athenian policy of expansion toward the west." To explain the small degree of attention that Thucydides gives to these matters Cornford endowed Athens with political parties, one of which was dominated by commercialists of the Piraeus; these forced on Pericles a policy of westward expansion, but in so circumspect a way that Thucydides never noticed it.

Now, about Thucydides the man we know two things, and each points decisively in the other direction: he owned gold mines in the region of Thasos, and he was sufficiently prominent in public affairs to have been elected at least once to the high military and administrative office of *Strategos* or General. He seems therefore to have been a man of affairs rather than a bookish character who got most of his ideas from Aeschylus. In fact, his introductory chapters on ancient history are so grounded in economic considerations as to be almost Marxist. He remarks (III 86) that one reason why Leontini requested Athenian help was that they were being prevented from cultivating their fields and from importing and exporting goods by sea; he goes on to tell that the real reason why Athens did help Leontini was to prevent the Peloponnesians from importing Sicilian corn, and to spy out the land to see if they could gain control of Sicily—a mixed economic and political reason. Other such passages could be cited, making it clear that he *was* aware of the importance of economic matters. We still need an explanation of why he mentions them only intermittently.

The same is true of the financial side of the war. The mine-owner who had some part in running it must have known, in a general way at least, how wars are run, and that money and supplies are important. In fact he says so, more than once. He reports Archidamus as saying (I 85,2): "War is not so much a matter of weapons as of the money that makes the weapons effective"; he quotes Pericles' prophecy (I 141) that the Peloponnesians, being *αὐτουργοί*, people who work and live off their own land, will not be able to sustain a long war, since they have no capital, either public or private, which a long war needs; in I 121 the Corinthians warn the inland states that they, no less than those on the coasts, are menaced by Athenian power, that they too will suffer if their imports and exports are cut off. We are not compelled to conceive the inconceivable: Thucydides did understand the importance of these things. But the fact remains that it is only in a kind of parenthesis that he mentions so significant a matter as the *εἰσφορά*, or capital levy, which Athens first imposed on herself in 428; the doubling (or trebling) of the tribute in 425 he does not mention at all, though it must have strained relations between Athens and the Allies, and was certainly an important war-measure.

Here and there he does give precise figures of revenue or expenditure, but, as Gomme says (*Commentary*, I 26) they are almost useless to us, because we cannot relate them to the totals for any one year. With reference to the incomplete figures given for the expenditure on the fleet bound for Sicily, Gomme says, loyal to his great author, ". . . partly because he had no trustworthy figures, and would not guess". I very much doubt, for reasons to be given later, that this was Thucydides' reason, but we may notice that elsewhere he fails to give figures where he could surely have got reliable ones, had he wanted them: for example, it could not have been difficult to find out what sum the Athenians expected to raise by the doubling of the tribute —but even the bare fact he does not mention.

"In the matter of finance", says Gomme, "we can unhesitatingly find fault." One has indeed the liveliest sympathy with the student of Greek history, if he is exasperated beyond endurance when such an authority as Thucydides fails to give him important information which bears so directly on his subject. Our concern however, at the moment, is not Greek history but Thucydides' mind; our question must be: What was Thucydides' conception of his subject, that it seemed reasonable *not* to deal systematically with the financial aspect of the war? Or was it simply a curious blind spot?

He says nothing about what must have been a constant preoccupation in Athens: the assuring of food, war-supplies of all kinds, the whole business of keeping the war going. He says that after the Sicilian disaster the treasury was empty and there were no ships, but with great energy they remedied both deficiencies: how they did it we are not told.

If we turn to internal politics the story is the same: Thucydides is uninformative. As more than one writer has said, he speaks of "the Athenians", "the Corinthians", as if they were so many Greek choruses. Indeed he does—but why? It seems hardly enough to state the fact, perhaps complain, and pass on. It may not make sense to us, but presumably it did to Thucydides. Once more Cornford is helpful. After reconstructing the political conflicts in Athens, not understood by our innocent historian, he continued: "We must look behind the official utterances of Pericles, and attempt an analysis of the majority with which he worked. We must stop speaking of 'the Athenians' as Thucydides does; not every Athenian was a Pericles in miniature"—a fact of which Thucydides may have been aware. Of course there is no reason why we should not analyse Pericles' majority, if we think we can do it, but first we should try to analyse Thucydides, a task for which we have more material. But it is unscientific in method to propound reasons why Thucydides neglected party strife in Athens, without observing that he does the same everywhere else, Mytilene for example: in what he says about the revolt he does not mention the name of a single political leader in the city, nor tell us what kind of government Mytilene had at the time, nor whether the revolt was a popular move or one engineered by oligarchs and imposed on the rest. He does say that the commons, given arms towards the end of the blockade, refused to fight the Athenians, but whether out of enthusiasm for Athens or a desire for food, we do not know. We can of course make certain inferences about the internal politics of Lesbos, but in a matter of such importance why should we have to infer? Again, the revolt arose out of an attempt at the unification (*synoekismos*) of Lesbos: historically a most interesting event—except that Thucydides is *not* interested.

Similarly, at V 36 the international situation is radically changed because in Sparta, as Thucydides baldly remarks, "There were now ephors other than those who had negotiated the peace, and some of them were actually opposed to it." Who were they? What did they represent? Why were they opposed to the peace? Thucydides betrays no interest, even though it immediately concerns the war, and though he himself, as he has just remarked, was now well placed for inquiring into such matters.

Certainly Sparta was secretive, but Argos was not, nor Athens, yet Thucydides is no more informative about these. He writes (V 45): "When this dispute arose between Athens and Sparta, those in Athens who wished to abrogate the peace began to inveigh against it." Who and what were these people? Concerning the most colourful and not the least mischievous of them, Alcibiades, we are told a lot—later on; but the anonymity of what was clearly an important political group is a little disconcerting, or at least a point to consider, in a historian of the war. As regards Argos, there is the remarkable story

(V 59 f.) of the battle that did not take place between the Argive and the Spartan forces because two Argives, Thrasyllus and Alciphron, came to a private arrangement with Agis of Sparta. Each army was furious, thinking it had got the other at its mercy. Spartan rage against Agis Thucydides describes later; he tells us at once that Thrasyllus was nearly stoned to death in Argos; how Alciphron fared we do not know. The great Argive defeat at Mantinaea soon follows, and this, we are told, emboldened the pro-Spartan anti-democratic faction in Argos to come into the open and to overthrow the democracy. Learning this, we wonder if the unexplained action of Thrasyllus and Alciphron had some connection with the pro-Spartan group, especially as Alciphron was (as Thucydides tells us) the *proxenos* of Sparta in Argos. Or was it that these two were the only Argives who could see that the triumph expected by the Argives was more likely to prove a massacre? But in that case, how did they manage to buy off Agis?

Time after time we have the feeling that important things were going on behind the scenes, and that Thucydides has no interest. In IV 50 there is recorded the capture by the Athenians of an envoy on his way from the Persian King Artaxerxes to Sparta: we learn that the Spartans had already sent several delegations to Persia, and that now the Athenians sent one; but it does not occur to Thucydides to tell us what matters had been under discussion, and he is totally silent about later dealings with Darius II. What we have to explain therefore is not why Thucydides unaccountably neglected party politics in Athens, but why, roughly speaking, he takes no notice of internal politics, including diplomacy, anywhere—except when, as in Corcyra, the result is massacre. This surely is the reason why the middle part of Book V is so dull. It is often said that it lacks the author's final revision; for instance, it contains no speeches. It may indeed be relatively unfinished, though the absence of speeches hardly proves it, for surely Thucydides did not insert speeches merely to brighten things up. Yet in fact it is a matter of foundations rather than of final touches. These chapters are concerned, in the main, with four years of jockeying for position in the Peloponnese, with the unsuccessful attempt of Argos to supplant Sparta. It could have been a fascinating story; in fact it is frustrating, because Thucydides will not tell us what was really going on.

Then there are occasions when he will record a military event without telling us enough about it to make it intelligible. Here is an instance (III 19):

> The Athenians needed more money for the siege. Therefore for the first time they imposed on themselves an *εἰσφορά*, and this brought in two hundred talents. They also sent out among the Allies twelve revenue-ships, Lysicles being in command, with four colleagues. He sailed around collecting money from various places; then from Myous in Caria he marched up the plain of the Meander as far as the Scandian Hills; there he was attacked by Carians and Anaeiti and was killed, with many of his troops.

And what good does that do us? Thucydides has taken the trouble to find out where the disaster occurred; what he does not tell us is something which most historians would think at least as important as the fact itself: why did Lysicles march up into Caria? Was it a necessary part of his commission? Was it a casual raid? Had he been charged with a mixed financial and military task, with perhaps insufficient forces? Was it a case where the home government could not control a commander at a distance? Was the government itself at fault, or was there no fault, only bad luck? Thucydides appears not to be interested: he records the fact, and then does nothing to make it significant. All we know is that Athenian bones were left in Asia Minor; we have no idea why they got there.

This brings in another matter. Lysicles, presumably, was the Lysicles who was a prominent statesman in Athens at the time: Thucydides does not mention it. Shall we say that he did not like the man, and for that reason will say nothing more about him? That would only be a guess, and not a very good one; it would explain only one instance of what is a general phenomenon: Thucydides has no interest in biographical or personal details. How easy it would have been, and how natural, to give us in half a sentence some indication of who Diodotus was. Or take the case of Archidamus. He is prominent, naturally, in the early part of the *History:* we learn that he was a personal friend of Pericles; we form a distinct impression of his character; he is last mentioned (III 11) as the commander of the third invasion of Attica, but then he drops out, silently. Did he simply retire from active service? Did he die? Thucydides does not think of telling us; from III 89,1 we infer that he had died, but Thucydides betrays no interest.

There were many prominent politicians after Pericles; Cleon is the only one, during the Archidamian War, that Thucydides mentions; similarly, there were many revolutions, as he tells us, but the Corcyrean is the only one which he records. It is a general phenomenon—and surely, not peculiar to Thucydides; for it may be worth considering that the dramatists behave in a way that is not dissimilar. In the *Antigone*, to the surprise of some of its modern readers, Sophocles first forgets Ismene, to the extent of allowing Antigone to say that she is the last daughter of a royal line (v. 941), and then seems to forget even Antigone. Electra drops out of the *Oresteia*, and Chrysothemis out of Sophocles' *Electra.* It has been objected against Thucydides that he was unfair to Cleon in several ways, one of them being that he does not mention Cleon's undoubted ability in administration and finance. He does not—but neither does he mention the fact that Archidamus died, or that Pericles lived with Aspasia, or that Nicias made his money by exploiting mines. It would similarly be reasonable to say of Plato that he gives a vivid picture of Socrates—but the picture does not include Xanthippe. If a modern historian were silent about the administrative abilities of a modern Cleon, he could properly be accused of unfairness; if he recorded of a modern Lysicles only that he was killed in a distant campaign, we should rightly ask why he had passed over the man's political eminence: we shall not understand Thucydides if we expect from him standards of relevance which we take for granted but were not practised either by him or (I suggest) by other Greek writers of his time. We have here another of his omissions.

The catalogue of these could be made a long one, but we will be content with one more only: what does he tell us about the Empire? The Athenian empire was a theme of major importance to a history of this war, but as Mme de Romilly points out in her penetrating study (pp. 84–87), to some of its most important aspects Thucydides pays no attention at all. Except for one allusion in the speech made by the Athenian delegation at Sparta (I 77) he says nothing about Athenian interference with the juridical autonomy of the allies; nothing about her insistence on democratic *régimes;* nothing about the unpopular Athenian "inspectors" (cf. Aristophanes, *Birds* 1022 ff.); nothing about the way in which Athens "avait brutalement affirmé sa souveraineté par le système de clérouquies"; nothing about her "economic aggressions". Equally, nothing is said about the benefits that Athens conferred on her subjects—policing the seas, keeping the Persians at bay, assuring the peace. "Ce qui est sacrifié, c'est ici tout un aspect de la réalité, et, par là, Thucydide se condamne à ne donner de l'impérialisme qu' une figure tronquée . . . Thucydide, lui, ne s'interesse qu'au choc, qu' à la bataille . . . C'est une contre-épopée qu'il a écrit."

The idea of a "counter-epic" is an interesting one, and we will take it up later. That Thucydides was interested only in "the shock of battle" is open to question; however, there is no denying that, from any modern point of view, his picture of the empire and how it was run is "truncated" to an astonishing degree.

These are considerable omissions. For the student of history they are, naturally, regrettable lacunae; for our purpose they are important evidence: they correspond to what we have been calling, in a different connexion, dramatic facts—negative ones indeed, but facts none the less. If we can believe in our author's intelligence, it follows that his conception of his subject was one that made it natural for him to disregard, either entirely or in part, material which we would think indispensable for the history of a war.

Now we must try to consider, as best we can, the nature of the material that he did decide to use. Roughly speaking, there are the speeches, and there is the strictly objective narrative of the military operations and the like; and I say "objective" because it is not much diversified or illuminated by comment. The speeches we will postpone. On what principles does he select the material for the narrative?

The question is not quite a hopeless one; at least we can eliminate. Everybody recognises a markedly dramatic trend in his writing. Very well: the debate that took place in Athens, just before the outbreak, was a critical event, and Thucydides knew it. Here then is a mildly dramatic bit of writing about it:

> The Athenian people, fully realising how momentous was the decision they would have to take, came to this Assembly in unusually large numbers and in unusually serious mood. Even before the *prytaneis* entered, a deep silence had fallen upon the crowd . . .

This was written not by Thucydides but by me. Perhaps it will serve to remind us how infrequently Thucydides indulges himself and his readers in peripheral description of this kind. He will describe a battle, and do it vividly, though within severe limits. He tells us how the Peloponnesians attacked the walls of Plataea, and how the Plataeans defended them; how Brasidas ran his ship aground at Pylos; he does not tell us how the first blockading fleet sailed from Piraeus in 431, or how Athens received the news of Phormio's victories in the Gulf or of Demosthenes' defeat in Aetolia; nor does he describe how, at some crisis, the Piraeus rang from dawn to dusk with the noise of ship-building; nor how, after the Peace of Nicias, the countryfolk, or some of them, thankfully went back into Attica to rebuild their shattered homes. Indeed, there is so little of free description that one might hope to get some hint about the way in which he thought by considering what kind of thing it was, in his narrative, about which he did tend to be "dramatic". It might be a quite instructive parlour-game, to ask one's guests, assuming that they knew their Thucydides, to write down from memory a list of his vividly descriptive passages. The lists would of course vary; none could be very long. Some passages would occur in every list: at random, the Theban irruption by night into Plataea and the grim fate of those who were caught, with the incident of the woman who gave one of them an axe; how Themistocles took refuge with Admetus; how they brought the good news, or the less bad news, from Athens to Mytilene; the Plague; how the Athenians built their wall at Pylos; the description of the sailing of the fleet from Piraeus to Sicily, of the moonlight battle outside Syracuse, of the battle in the Great Harbour, of the awful scene on the banks of the Assinarus.

For a special reason, my own list would include the story of the Corinthian army which, taunted at home for cowardice, fought a second battle with the Athenians, was defeated, blundered into enclosed ground and was killed to the last man by the encircling Athenians. The special reason is that the story occurs in the *Pentecontaeteia* (I 106). This section of the *History* is written with such concentration that the events of nearly fifty years of strenuous activity are packed into what becomes only sixteen pages of the Teubner text (and without any dates), yet Thucydides could spare half a page for this one afternoon's horrible work, though its effect on the growth of the Empire was small, and in any case is not mentioned.

My list would include the description of what followed Demosthenes' defeat in Aetolia (III 98):

Finally they gave way and took to flight. Some ran into river-beds from which there was no way out, some into other places which they did not know (for Chromon, their Messenian guide, had been killed) and were destroyed. The fast-moving light-armed Aetolians killed many on the battlefield itself in the act of running away. As for the main body of the Athenians, they missed their way and plunged into an impenetrable forest; the Aetolians set fire to it, with the Athenians inside. Flight and destruction in every shape and form fell upon the army.

My list would include, again for a special reason, a passage that occurs a little later (III 113), the special reason this time being that Thucydides departs so far from his normal style as to report a conversation. One Ambraciot army had been heavily defeated; then, on the next day, a second one which had come to reinforce the other. Then came a herald from the first army asking permission to bury the dead, knowing them to be about two hundred. "But", he is told, "there are more than a thousand bodies here."—"Then they can't be ours."—"They certainly are, if you were fighting at Idomene yesterday."—"There was no battle yesterday; it was the day before."—"But, I tell you, we were fighting these men yesterday—a relief army from Ambracia."

When the herald heard this and realised that the relieving army too had been destroyed he was overwhelmed by the extent of the disaster; he cried out aloud and went away at once, entirely forgetting what he had come for, namely permission to bury the dead. No greater disaster than this came upon any single Greek state in so short a time during the whole war. I have not recorded how many were killed; considering the population of the city the number, as stated, is unbelievable.

Everybody's list would include the massacre in Mycalessus, which interrupts the narrative of the Sicilian War (VII 29). In Thucydides' normal narrative style it might have run like this:

At about this time the Athenians, being hard pressed for money, sent home some Thracian mercenaries for whom they no longer had employment, instructing them on the way to do what harm they could to enemies of Athens. Therefore they disembarked here and there and attacked several places, including Mycalessus, where they killed many of the inhabitants. Meanwhile in Sicily . . .

That is what Thucydides might have written; this is what he did write (in Rex Warner's translation):

At daybreak he attacked and captured Mycalessus. It is a small city; he caught it unguarded, for they had no suspicion that anyone would penetrate so far from the coast. The wall was weak, here and there in ruins, nowhere high, and the gates had been left open because there was no fear of attack. The Thracians burst in, began to plunder houses and temples and to slaughter the inhabitants, sparing neither young nor old but killing everyone they met, one after another, women and children too; not only that, but the animals too—everything that had life in it. For the Thracian, like all extreme barbarians, is particularly bloodthirsty when he has no reason to fear. So here: there was immense tumult, and destruction in every shape and form. Among other things they broke into a boys' school, the biggest in the place; as it happened, the boys had just assembled, and the Thracians cut them to pieces. This disaster, falling upon an entire city, was greater and more sudden and more frightful than any. . . . Mycalessus lost a considerable part of its population. It was a small city, but in the disaster just described its people suffered calamities as pitiable as any which took place during the war.

If to the four passages that I have particularly mentioned one adds the description of the plague, of the savage massacres in Corcyra, of what happened on the Assinarus and in the Syracusan quarries, of the destruction of the remaining Plataeans, I think it is fair to say this: of the passages of free description, a remarkable number—very remarkable in "a cold and scientific historian"—have to do with death and destruction. It may be objected that by a dexterous choice of passages one can prove almost anything, and in general that is true. My argument is however that these were chosen, by Thucydides, out of an indefinitely large number of dramatic incidents that the war must have afforded but he does not mention; and unless my selection further distorts Thucydides' own selection, we may begin to suspect, when we contemplate this aspect of his *poiesis*, that he was thinking of the war not as a complex political event having its financial, economic, commercial, and other such facets, but as a great catastrophe. Certainly a remarkable number of his memorable and burning passages have to do with the destruction of human life.

Slender evidence, it may be said, by which to determine how Thucydides thought and felt about the war. Then what about reading what he says himself? He wrote a Preface; at the beginning of it he tells us clearly why he undertook his task, and at the end he tells us what he thought about it when the war was over. He begins, as we have seen, by saying that he foresaw that this war would be a bigger event and more notable than any previous one, for reasons that he gives; then he says: "It did prove to be the biggest upheaval, *κίνησις*, for Greece, for no small part of Barbary, one might say for all mankind". Then follows the *Archaeologia*, the point of which is to show that in no previous epoch had an event of such magnitude been possible. Then he says, at the end of his Preface (I 23):

> The most considerable of previous events was the Persian War, but that was quickly decided in two battles by land and two by sea. But this war went on for a long time and brought upon Greece sufferings, *παθήματα*, such as had never happened before in a period of equal length. Never had so many cities been captured and left desolate (though some of them, being captured, received new settlers); never had so many men been exiled or killed, whether in the war itself or in civil strife. Traditions of past calamities which experience had done little to confirm now became credible: of earthquakes, for these were now widespread and violent; of eclipses of the sun, for these were very frequent in comparison with what was remembered from the past; here and there droughts of long duration occurred, and famines in consequence; and especially ruinous and destructive of life was the plague. All these disasters fell upon Greece together with this war.

I have transcribed this passage because so many Thucydidean scholars, though they have read it, have not believed it, being so certain that Thucydides really meant something quite different. Yet it is no casual reflection; it is not a ruminative addition to the story of one particular catastrophe, but the last chapter of the Preface; it is a deliberate retrospective summary. It has of course been debated if Thucydides wrote it soon after the end of the Archidamian War or after 404. I have not seen an argument which has convinced me that it must be "early", but in any case that is not quite the point: it might have been written in, say, 418, and in, say, 402 Thucydides might have considered it again and said to himself, "Yes, that can stand"—in which case, effectively, it was written in 402. But I lay no stress on this. If we knew that the passage was "late" it would be appropriate, and necessary, to point to this fact: in his retrospect of the war he says not a word about a fallen Empire or a discredited political system. Even if we think we know that the passage is "early", it is still to be remarked that it contains not a word about politics, about the effect of the Archidamian War on the international situation or the solidarity of the Empire, not even about Pericles, whom some have supposed to be the Hero of Thucydides' *History;* only about the destruction of cities, the killing or exiling of men, plague, and famine. This is to be remarked also: not a few writers have called the *History* Thucydides' "Tragedy of Athens"—and with some reason; yet in these two passages he speaks not of Athens but of "Greece, some large part of Barbary, almost of all mankind". Is this the way in which he really thought about the war, or is it only a casual remark? It may seem obvious that to Thucydides the Athenian the long war presented itself as the long agony and the final tragedy (perhaps) of Athens; let us however read what he has said here, keep our eyes open as we read further, and reflect that to many scholars it has seemed equally obvious that when he said the Persian War was not nearly so destructive to Greece as the Peloponnesian War, what he really meant is that its historical significance was not so great. As Claudius did not quite say in *Hamlet:* "His words fly up, our thoughts remain below".

In an earlier chapter we considered Cornford's observation about circumambient atmospheres: it will advance our argument a little if we watch the diffracting effect of our atmosphere in a not very important but yet significant misjudgment made by G. F. Abbott in his sensitive and judicious monograph *Thucydides: A Study in Historical Reality*. Discussing Thucydides' style, Abbott says (pp. 183 f.) that the list of belligerents given by Thucydides in II 9 is "one of the things that clog the narrative . . . Here the writer simply treads the beaten track: Herodotus' muster-roll of the Persians, Homer's of the Greek and Trojan forces, will occur to every reader . . . Thucydides conformed to tradition". Two other passages also "clog the narrative": the list of allies on either side in Sicily (VII 57) and the enumeration of Thracian tribes in II 96–97.

We want and expect Thucydides to do a particular thing: to get on with his narrative of the war—much as certain critics want Aeschylus to get on with his play and not waste our time on that garrulous Herald. When Thucydides does not do this, we cast about for an explanation of the evident blemish, and naturally we find it: he was, we discover, something of a bookish character. At II 9, when his mind ought to have been intent on the siege of Plataea, it wanders to Homer, Herodotus, and the literary tradition. But if we have taken seriously what Thucydides has written in his Preface, II 9 becomes not a literary genuflexion and a waste of time, but an impressive restatement of the real theme of the *History*. For let us look: what is the situation? We have had the Corcyrean affair; we have had Potidaea; now comes the sudden attack on Plataea. At last the war is on; the *κίνησις* has begun. At this point Thucydides writes three paragraphs, each of which powerfully conveys the feeling that we are now on the very edge. He says, first, that the two mighty opposites were making ready—building ships, trying to find more allies, raising money. Then he says: "Nothing in their designs was on a mean scale; they put everything into their effort"—though, characteristically, he does not tell us how they raised money, nor whence came the timber with which they built the ships. "All Greece hung poised on the event, as the chief cities came to grips." Prophecies were bandied about (he says), and there was an earthquake in Delos, the first in living memory. General opinion favoured Sparta and was bitter against Athens. Finally, he gives the list of allies on either side; as he said in I 1, sooner or later the whole Greek world was involved. The evident purpose, and the effect, of the passage is to bring home to us, once more, the sheer size of the event. To say that the list clogs the narrative is to criticise from the wrong point of view: our own, not his.

So it is with the other list also, VI 57. Again we look at the context. The Syracusans have won their first indubitable victory over the Athenian fleet, which by now has been reinforced. "A great victory", says Thucydides,

> especially as it was won at sea. The Athenians were in utter despair and bewilderment; much more bitterly than before did they repent of the expedition. These were the only cities they fought which, like themselves, were democratic, and they were strong both in ships and in cavalry. They themselves had not been able to hold out revolution as an inducement, or to apply overwhelming force. They had had more defeats than victories; even before this latest defeat they had not known where to turn, much less now that the unimaginable had happened.

As for the Syracusans, he goes on, they had won control of the situation; their aim now was not survival but the destruction of the invaders. If now they could defeat Athens on both elements, and that too in the presence of their own allies who included Spartans and Corinthians but with Syracuse taking the lead and holding the post of danger; if they could liberate Greece not only from Athenian domination but also from the fear of it—what glory for Syracuse! "Certainly", he continues, "in the whole war greater numbers had been engaged than in this campaign, but never had troops from so many different places met in conflict before a single city. The forces that were present were as follows . . ."

Once more, it is the sheer size of the event that bears down on the writer's mind. It was, of course, a "political" event, but it is not its strictly political meaning, its "oecumenical importance", that causes him at this moment, when the cataract of ruin is poised for its terrible descent upon the Athenians, to pause, to look round upon the scene, to mark how momentous it was and how many Greek cities had armies engaged in it; and if we think the list ill-placed and explain it by remembering Homer and Herodotus (which is more natural in us than it would have been in Thucydides), to that slight extent—yet perhaps not so very slight—we have failed to make contact with Thucydides' mind. Soon, at the end of Book VII, we are reading the sentences which none can forget:

> The number of prisoners it is difficult to state accurately, but they were more than seven thousand. This was the greatest event in the war, and in my opinion of all Greek history; for the victors, the most brilliant; for those who were destroyed, the most calamitous. They were defeated utterly and at every point; there was practically nothing that they had not suffered: armies, ships, everything was destroyed; it was total ruin. From so great a number few returned home. So ended the Sicilian War.

What Thucydides does not discuss is the effect of this failure on the import of corn from Sicily into the Peloponnesus, on Athenian trade to the west, or on the balance of power.

As for the remaining interruption of the narrative, the description of Sitalces' Thracian kingdom, it is certainly not so eloquently dramatic as the other two: it may well be that Thucydides would have written it as an Appendix, had the ancient world known of this amenity of modern life. It is however not irrelevant. Unlike Herodotus' digressions, it does not concern itself notably with Thracian history and customs, but concentrates on the extent and wealth of the whole region, and it seems only fair to Thucydides to recall one aspect of the war that impressed him: that a great part of Barbary also was involved. It involved even this vast empire in Thrace.

So much, then, for Thucydides' choice of material. We noticed, negatively, what he left out; we have been considering, I hope fairly, such parts of his narrative as seem to stand out from the rest, trying to discover what aspect or aspects of the military side of the war appear most to have engaged his attention. What we have found may not be very strong evidence for the trend of the historian's thought, but it is at least in entire accord with what he says himself in his Preface, that the war was to his mind the most destructive event in known history. If closer scrutiny confirms our provisional result, we shall have gone some way toward establishing Thucydides' own point of view, which then we can substitute for our own. Here, for the moment, we will leave this part of our enquiry in order to consider another, namely the structure that he built out of this material, with of course notable additions of his own.

2. His Disposition of Material

It needs no saying that the form of the *History* is unique. It is easy enough to set down its main features: the general absence of discursive or analytical passages (nowhere for instance does he discuss the importance of sea-power), the strictly chronological framework, the speeches, the "dramatic" tendency, the refusal to cite authorities and sources, the decision to treat at length certain events and to pass over with the barest mention others of the same kind and apparently similar importance: for example, the revolution in Corcyra is described and analysed in detail, but others of the kind are dismissed with the remark that there were many of them, and he says much about the fate of the prisoners of war taken in Mytilene, but dismisses in a dozen words each the enslavement or massacre of those taken in Scione, and of the Aeginetans. These features of his composition we should not regard separately, with a different explanation for each; to Thucydides they were, collectively, his natural or at least his chosen way of composing, different aspects of an organic whole.

One general point first, before we look at his method of composing. Within his chosen limits, he works like a scientific historian of the utmost rigour, and yet, as many a writer has said, he seems to compose more like a tragic poet. This is difficult: a scientist ought not to indulge in drama, and although we know historians who wrote for dramatic, rhetorical or moral effect, they have not usually had Thucydides' passion for strict accuracy. It seems an odd combination.

Out of this difficulty there is one road that we must not take, the one chosen by Cornford. His theory found indeed little support, but it is still worth looking at if only as a warning. It was, in brief, that Thucydides, having no helpful predecessors in prose writing, naturally took the Attic dramatists for his model; further, that he inherited, from Aeschylus in particular, a whole system of morality and psychology: Koros begetting Hybris, Hybris begetting Ate, and the like. Two fallacies are involved, apart from the rash assumption that so strong a writer as Thucydides could not say what he thought and meant without a model: this idea confuses the Early Classical with the Byzantine.

The former fallacy may be put in this form: *C* bears a strong resemblance to *B*; therefore *C* is derived from, or strongly influenced by, *B*. Evidently, the truth may be that both *B* and *C* are derived from, or influenced by, *A*. I hope to show that this is the case here, *A* being the natural, instinctive early-Greek way of composing. This is not only a matter of theory; the fallacy has consequences important to our understanding of Thucydides. If we are persuaded that he took over his form, or important parts of it, from the dramatists, we shall cease to give it constructive attention. We shall be thinking, time after time, "Of course, he *would* write like this, being so much under the influence of the dramatists. Being (unfortunately for him) so early a historian, he knew no better." What we should be thinking—so I shall argue—is: "He had to write like this, dramatists or no dramatists, because this is the way in which he thought"; that for all practical purposes he invented his form for himself; that if others had written like this before, as the dramatists had, the reason is that they had also thought like this. We may recall an intelligent remark of Aristotle's, that if a dramatist should find a plot ready-made, he is none the less its *poietes*, its "maker"; he has made it his own.

The second fallacy is not dissimilar, nor is it extinct: it is that if *Z* repeats a moral formula which was first used by the ancient *M*, and then by most of the intervening alphabet, *Z* is not being original; he is doing nothing to "advance thought" on the subject but is simply inheriting and repeating. Now, as it happens, it has for generations been the tradition in my own family that we take some food and drink soon after rising, but when I do this I am not repeating an ancient formula, but satisfying my immediate desire for breakfast—nor do I count myself unprogressive that I have not found a new word for what is always the same thing. How many people, I wonder, have remarked, in response to an immediate experience, "Pride goes before a fall", using an expression which, for all I know, may be, in English, as old as Lydgate? To repeat a formula does not mean that one is not thinking: our personal reflection on a particular event is thereby set in line with what countless others have also found true of similar events: we indicate that the particular is also a universal. If Thucydides will sometimes talk like Aeschylus it does not follow that he was not thinking for himself.

We have mentioned the possibility that *C* and *B* could be derived, in parallel, from *A*. Following this up, let us note, with surprise, that one or two things which Aristotle says in the *Poetics* about Homer are no less applicable to Thucydides. He says (1460A 5 ff.) that one reason why Homer is so much better than the other epic poets is that he does not *talk* much:

Ὅμηρος δὲ ἄλλα τε πολλὰ ἄξιος ἐπαινεῖσθαι καὶ δὴ καὶ ὅτι μόνος τῶν ποιητῶν οὐκ ἀγνοεῖ ὅ δεῖ ποιεῖν αὐτόν. αὐτὸν γὰρ δεῖ τὸν ποιητὴν ἐλάχιστα λέγειν. οὐ γάρ ἐστι κατὰ ταῦτα μιμητής. οἱ μὲν οὖν ἄλλοι αὐτοὶ μὲν δι' ὅλου ἀγωνίζονται, μιμοῦνται δὲ ὀλίγα καὶ ὀλιγάκις.

(He is the only poet who knows what the *poietes* should write in his own *persona*, namely as little as possible, for while doing this he is no *mimetes*. The other poets are continually taking a hand in their work themselves; but Homer, after a brief proem, at once introduces a man or woman or some other character, all of them having character, none without it.)

None, that is to say, is a mere ventriloquist's dummy, the "mouthpiece of the poet" for whom so many commentators have pined. Aristotle says elsewhere (1448B 35) that Homer not only writes well, but also "dramatically", *μιμήσεις δραματικὰς ἐποίησεν*, which again must mean that he works through characters who do and say things.

We do not enjoy Aristotle's advantage of being able to compare Homer with second-rate Greek epic poets, but his point is clear and important. What Homer wants to say, what effect he wishes to make on his reader, is achieved entirely through his characters, what they are and what they say, and through the action, that is, through his direct narrative. Inferior poets, unable to transmute all their meaning into the speech and action of their characters, have to take a hand themselves, speaking in the first person singular, commenting, explaining things. As we say, they keep a dog and bark themselves. Homer's method is truer to the medium, more economical, therefore more powerful. Aristotle naturally does not say anything comparable of the tragic poets: they cannot "take a hand themselves", though a bad one may come near it if he invents a dummy character, or makes someone speak out of character, in order to convey an idea which he, the dramatist, could not otherwise convey.

Since in no small measure what Aristotle says about Homer is applicable also to Thucydides, why should we not apply it and see what it does for us? He also *αὐτὸς ἐλάχιστα λέγει*: in his own person he writes, not indeed as little as Homer, but astonishingly little for a historian: there are the direct comments on Pericles and his successors (II 65), the analysis of revolutionary frenzy (III 82–84), what he says about himself in the two Prefaces (I 1–23 and V 26), certain other passages, but not many; it is true, roughly speaking, that he, like Homer, gives us either direct narrative, what people are doing, or speeches, what they are saying. The normal historian will interrupt his narrative from time to time in order to give his own analysis of the situation: causes, motives, aims, results, reasons for failure or success. In general, Thucydides does not do this.

We therefore in reading him have to decide: did he say so little because he had little to say, or because he had a different way of saying it? Does he in fact write like Plato in the two dialogues we glanced at? If we now proceed to argue that sometimes he will so deploy his narrative that it speaks for itself, we shall be saying nothing that is new; nor will it be a novel suggestion that speech and narrative are sometimes dovetailed in a way that is designedly significant; that "speech looks across to speech" has been remarked by Professor J. R. Finley. It is however a feature of his composition that we must examine, and the point of our comparison with Homer is to suggest that this feature is by no means unique to Thucydides but is recognisably Hellenic. We are not accustomed to it, in a prose writer; some of us indeed will not credit even the Greek dramatists with it, but expect them to have given us their all ready-served, on a plate, with a knife and fork as well: if they state *two plus two* we must not imagine that they knew, and expected us to realise, that the answer is *four*. But perhaps this is not the way to understand either the dramatists or Thucydides.

His deployment of narrative was discussed by Gomme, in his Sather Lectures. He analysed, with other passages, IV 65–109, a section of the *History* which begins with the statement that the Athenians were so elated by their successes that they thought nothing could go wrong with them, whether the forces they had for a given project were sufficient or not. There follow: the affair with Brasidas at Megara, which did not go too well; then the grandiose Boeotian campaign which went wrong and destroyed an army and a general (partly because "a man called Nicomachus from Phanotis in Phocis told the Spartans, who passed on the information to the Boeotians", partly because either Demosthenes or Hippocrates got the date wrong); and dovetailed with this, Brasidas' bold foray to the north, which suddenly undermined the whole Athenian position there and ended in the loss of Amphipolis. As Gomme points out (*The Greek Attitude*, pp. 134–137), Thucydides does not, as he might have done, narrate the Boeotian campaign straight through and then turn to Brasidas' operations; he passes from one to the other and back again. The effect is that we have the two compaigns in our minds at the same time, and cannot help reflecting that (as Adcock has put it) the Athenians might have crushed Brasidas with half the force that was defeated at Delium. "Thucydides", says Gomme, "lets the events tell their own tale; no need for a summary to explain things . . ."

Gomme gives further instances; I will give different ones. In II 85–92 the fighting in the Gulf is narrated. First we are told how Phormio, with twenty ships, defeats the forty-seven Peloponnesian ships by making rings around them; then we hear of the angry astonishment of the Spartan authorities and of their efforts to strengthen both the fleet and its command. Next, Phormio urgently demands reinforcements. The Athenians, we are told, send him twenty ships, but their commander is instructed first to settle a small matter in Crete: the city of Cydonia is theirs for the taking—or so their good friend Nicias of Gortyn has assured them. But Nicias has deceived them, or himself: the squadron wastes time doing nothing more than ravage Cydonian territory, and then rough weather causes more delay. Now we are taken back to the Gulf. It is mentioned that Phormio still has only twenty ships and is now opposed by seventy-seven. The plans of each side are reported, and two speeches: the Peloponnesian commanders try to reassure their bewildered forces, and Phormio is confronted, among his men, with a despondency that alarms him. (Four to one is long odds indeed.) He makes an able speech, but there is in it a certain sophistry to which, one imagines, Athenian naval commanders had not often been reduced. His plan is, as he tells them, not to sail into the narrows if he can help it. But he cannot help it, for the enemy sail in as if against Naupactus, "which had been left undefended". (Thucydides does not *say* it, but it becomes evident that Phormio has responsibilities too great for him to discharge.) There follows the description of the second battle: a catastrophe for Athens, except that one captain, by a brilliant bit of opportunism, pulls the chestnuts out of the fire. During the night the Peloponnesians withdraw, and Thucydides ends the story by saying: "Not long after their retreat there arrived the twenty Athenian ships from Crete, which ought to have been with Phormio before the battle".

Thucydides keeps his eye on the facts, on the persons and what they did; *αὐτὸς οὐδὲν λέγει*, he makes no comment; he says not a word about the folly of "the Athenians" who imperilled the control of the western waters for the sake of winning a small place in Crete.

This is the question that we must try to answer: does he say nothing because he had nothing to say, whether because he simply did not see that the Athenians had been foolish or alternatively because he thought that this kind of thing was no concern of his, as historian; or does he say nothing because he expected his readers to see the point for themselves, without having it put down in black and white? Is he writing here like a plain chronicler, or is he writing as Aeschylus did when he made Eteocles talk about Dike just before his single combat with his brother; or as Sophocles did when he made Creon explain to Haemon how loyalty preserves family, army, city, just before Creon's insistence on loyalty brings down his own house in ruin? It is a question of the response which Thucydides presumed: how is it to be determined?

One or two instances like the two just given prove nothing: they might be accidental. Proof, in such a case, can never be rigid, but in order to be acceptable it must satisfy certain conditions. Such a method of composition must be shown to be habitual in the author; it should be seen to combine naturally with, and to help explain, other features of his composition; it will also be a recommendation if (to put it bluntly) it makes the author and his work look less incompetent than does the other approach—that is, when the author is a Thucydides, one who is not likely to have been incompetent; finally, it will at least not be amiss if the supposed method of composition is such as may be reasonably postulated, having regard to the time and place of the writer. All these considerations we will try to keep in mind as we look at what Thucydides wrote and how he wrote it.

"What a way to run a war!" It may well be that this reflection arises in our intelligent minds as we read about that ill-judged attack on Cydonia—unless perhaps our attention is concentrated on something else, as for example the cost, to Athens, of her naval operations. In that case we shall be thinking: "Twenty-seven *plus* twenty: forty-seven ships; so many men apiece, each drawing so many obols a day . . ." This would be historical research; it would be using Thucydides as a source. But Thucydides himself has conspicuously not directed his reader's attention to this aspect of the war, and if we would understand his mind, we must follow the lead given by him, not our own preoccupations. He has not directed our attention to the cost of the war, not even to the strategic situation in the west. He has on the other hand reported Pericles as saying: "Do not try to add to your empire during the war", and "What I am afraid of is not so much the enemy as your own mistakes". He is soon recording, though without comment, how Phormio and Naupactus were in extreme peril, and how the reinforcements were delayed by a wild-goose chase to Crete. Our question is—and it is a fundamental one—whether our response "What a way to run a war!" is due not so much to our own sagacity as to Thucydides' method of composition; whether he makes no comment for the reason that his *σύστασις τῶν πραγμάτων*, including his eliminations, made comment unnecessary.

We will take another case. Archidamus is at the Isthmus, on the brink of his first invasion of Attica (II 11). Thucydides records a speech that he makes to his troops: why? We can at least, in our turn, record facts. Archidamus says:

Athens is a powerful city. We must expect them to join battle with us when they see us wasting their land and destroying their property, even if they are not already marching out against us. Everyone is moved to rage when he sees, before his very eyes, an unheard-of injury being inflicted on him. He does not stay to think; he acts in anger. The Athenians more than any are likely to do this: they are accustomed to rule others; to ravage, not be ravaged.

At II 18 we are told that his troops were indignant at his slow tactics but he still delayed, "expecting, it is said, that the Athenians would make some concessions while their territory was still untouched, and would not face the prospect of its being laid waste". He moved into Acharnae (II 20) because this was the most populous deme: he hoped that the Acharnians, being so numerous, would compel the whole army to come out in defence of their property. In II 21 the Athenians, seeing the enemy encamped only seven miles from the city—a thing that had not occurred since the Persian War—found it intolerable and wanted to march out and stop it; and in this, we are told, they were violently supported by the angry Acharnians.

If we allow ourselves to think, we shall realise that so far the expectations of Archidamus have been realised; but Thucydides goes on to record that Pericles, convinced that his strategy was correct, summoned no Assembly or other meeting, "where anger and not judgment might prevail and lead to a wrong decision". Instead, he saw to the defence of the city, kept things as quiet as he could, and sent out cavalry to keep the enemy from nearer approach. Thucydides makes no comment on the steadfastness, or on the ascendency, of Pericles. Perhaps, in the circumstances, he judged it unnecessary. Nor did he write a lively description of the Athenians running round in circles: what he leaves out makes it easier for us to attend to what he leaves in.

Another point. Archidamus hopes that the anger of the Athenians will deliver them into his hands; Pericles was afraid that anger might lead to a fatal mistake; later, we shall hear

Cleon recommending the Assembly to act in anger. Did Thucydides expect us, reading the third passage, to remember the other two and do some thinking on our own account?

We will continue by considering the juxtaposition of the Epitaphios and the Plague, in which many scholars have seen conscious design—rightly, as I think. It might be objected that this is fanciful, it simply happened like that; the plague did follow the Funeral Speech.—That would not be quite true: it did happen like that, but it is Thucydides who made it look like this. For one thing, we know, because Thucydides tells us, that an *epitaphios* was delivered every year during the war: this is the only one that he even mentions; the others were carved away. Then, the speech was delivered, say, in March; the plague broke out in, say, July. What happened in the interval? We may guess: one or two debates in the Assembly, certain dealings with allies or neutrals, some financial or administrative measures—small beer perhaps, but beer nevertheless. A different historian might have diligently recorded all this: the Epitaphios (one out of twenty in his complete work), then a lot of detail, and finally the plague. He would have set down "what happened", but it would look entirely different; it would lack the arresting perspective that we find in Thucydides.

For what does he set before us? He has told us (II 14,17) that as a necessary part of their strategy the Athenians abandoned Attica and concentrated themselves within the walls, as if on an impregnable island (I 143,3–5): they are uncomfortable, but safe; from this base they can wage war with fair prospects. Soon he is recording the Epitaphios, giving us Pericles' aristocratic (Gomme ventured to say "romantic") conception of the ideal Athens. One of the ringing sentences is: "We have created, like no other city, continual refreshment for mind and spirit; because of the magnitude of our city the good things of the whole world flow in for our enjoyment". In a few months, within two or three chapters, the impregnable military base, the confident and ennobled city, has become a tortured and demoralised plague-spot; and the plague "first broke out in the

Piraeus" (II 48,2). If this were the only place in the *History* which gave excuse for suggesting that Thucydides, sometimes, gave a thought to the Vanity of Human Wishes, we would dismiss the notion as mere fancy; but is it? We may at least remind ourselves why he undertook to record the course of the war, and what he thought about it all when it was over.

Leaving this, for the moment, where it is, let us turn to another aspect of his *poiesis*. When we bring them into connexion with each other, they should make sense, if we are on the right track.

We have taken note that Thucydides, though so careful a researcher, does not as a rule cite his authorities—less so, in fact, than Herodotus. What inference are we to draw from that? A modern historian of comparable seriousness is careful to document his narrative, and the reason is plain enough: from his serious readers he is expecting an active response, and cites the authorities in order to meet it. He is expecting questions like: "How do you know this? Why should I believe that? Why do you give this version of the event and not that one?" Therefore, citation and criticism of his authorities is a necessary part of his writing. Now Archidamus held the opinion (I 84,4) that there is not a vast difference between one people and another; if we agree with him, we may be disposed to think that as the modern historian has intelligible reasons for citing his authorities, so perhaps had Thucydides for not citing his. This at least we dare not say, that he was not expecting an energetic response: "I have written", he says, "not a Book of the Month but one to last for ever"—and the remarkable thing is that nobody laughs. He expected his book to be read and reread, as he himself must have written and rewritten it, much of it in a style that must have prevented even his contemporaries from reading him easily. He evidently did expect an energetic response—but where was this energy to be directed? Thucydides, I believe, was not a stupid man; therefore we may infer that he did not expect his readers to be concerned first and foremost with the accuracy of his record: this we are to take on trust; nor with his close analysis of the war as a complex political event: he attempts no such analysis. What then remains? Two things at least are clear: we are to read him with sustained attention, and he himself was hopeful that what he had to say would prove true, more or less, of some later epochs (I 22,4). If his concern had been simply to write an unassailable record of the war, it seems unlikely that he would have been so consistently silent about the evidence on which he was relying.

We turn to another marked feature of his composition: its strictly chronological framework. So far as the military events are concerned, he is explicit: his summer-and-winter schedule, explained in V 20, was a sensible method of dating, Greek calendars being what they were; but it takes no great acumen—no more than was possessed by Dionysius of Halicarnassus, for instance—to see that it has its inconveniences: a campaign that lasted for more than one season could not receive continuous treatment, and conversely, a continuous campaign has to be interrupted by events that happened elsewhere.

We may observe however that he is chronological in a way that he does not advertise, and that this is closely connected with his "dramatic" tendency; but before we do this we may spare a moment for one example only of the inconvenience of his method. It will give another opportunity of mentioning Aristotle.

We have quoted Gomme: "Thucydides lets the events tell their own tale". The objection presents itself: what about such a passage as VI 95? We are in the middle of the Sicilian War, but Thucydides abandons it for a moment in order to record the following:

> In the same spring the Spartans marched against Argos and got as far as Cleonae. Here an earthquake occurred, and they went back again. Thereupon the Argives invaded the border country of Thyrea and took from the Spartans a great deal of plunder, which was sold for no less than twenty-five talents. Not much later in the same summer people in Thespiae tried to overthrow their government, but

failed. Help came from Thebes; some of the insurgents were taken prisoner, and others fled to Athens.

Again we may ask, "And what good does this do us?" Very little; certainly it has nothing to do with what is at the moment our great concern: the war in Sicily. Obviously, there can be no question here of the significant ordering of narrative. But it may after all do us some good, if it helps us to understand a profound remark of Aristotle's, one on which valuable indignation has been wasted: *Poiesis* (by which Aristotle does not mean poetry only) is more serious and philosophical than History. But, we say, what can be more serious and philosophic than the *History* of Thucydides? What indeed? "Therefore", we say, "Aristotle must have forgotten Thucydides; he must have been thinking only of the chroniclers". On the contrary, it may well have been Thucydides in particular that he had in mind. His argument is clear and sensible, and V 95 will serve to illustrate it.

The *poietes* assumes complete control over his material; he so moulds and disposes it as to make it mean what *he* means. What does not help his *poiesis* he will leave out; preëxisting fact, as given for example by myth, he alters at will, within limits determined only by common sense. Thereby, as Aristotle says, the *mimesis* becomes pure; like a *ζῷον*, an animal, it will have no spare parts. But this is what the historian may not do. His insights may be infinitely profound, but he is not the master of his material. He must of course in any case select, from all the heterogeneous material available, but having selected he may not alter, not without ceasing to be a historian. His first loyalty must be not to his own conception of the truth but to the facts—and as Pericles remarked, the facts can be stupid, meaning presumably that as they are certainly not clear in prospect, they are not always clear and intelligible in retrospect either. They can be untidy, and the historian is not at liberty to make them neat, as Aeschylus made the Persian War neat.

This Argive raid, and the attempted revolution in Thespiae, happened at this time, and Thucydides did not feel at liberty to pass them over. The suggestion has been made that Book VI was not finally revised; that Thucydides, on a final revision, might have omitted the chapter or placed it elsewhere. The possibility cannot be denied; what we can say is that Book VI does not read like a provisional draft, that in what is at least an advanced version of the book Thucydides did put the two events here, and that on his own principles this is their natural place. We may continue to talk of his *poiesis;* we must however bear in mind the difference between the "poet" and the historian in this regard; and we may acquit Aristotle of the folly of forgetting Thucydides.

The summer-and-winter schedule has its inconveniences. Thucydides does not quite enslave himself to it: we have seen that he passes from the Boeotian campaign to Brasidas and back again when nothing in the schedule compelled him to do it. But the unadvertised aspect of his chronological system is more interesting, and for us more important.

How often, as commentator on the war, does he allow himself to anticipate the course of events? If we omit the two Prefaces, which are special cases, there is, I think, only one such passage: II 65, in which he compares Pericles with his successors. How often, for that matter, is he retrospective? Only, I think, in I 23: "Never so many cities . . .", unless we add the last few sentences of Book VII. A few examples of this aspect of his chronological method will make our point clear; they will show too the intimate relationship, within his *poiesis*, that exists between the schedule, the use of speeches, the dramatic element, and the famous reticence of Thucydides. They will illustrate also the extent to which he relies on his *poiesis* to do his talking for him.

We may look at his handling of the Corinth–Corcyra affair, early in Book I. He writes eight chapters of strictly factual narrative; then he comes to the debate in Athens. We noticed earlier that he writes not a single word descriptive of the scene; if he is dramatic, it is not in this way. There is another way in which he is not dramatic: he tells us, as baldly as can be, that on the first day opinion favoured Corinth, but on the second veered toward Corcyra. Here was material enough for dramatic writing—and Thucydides himself may well have been present at the debate: what persons, considerations, passions, produced the change? He has no interest in this; he treats it all externally —not because he failed to understand the policy of a group of commercial expansionists, or decided to represent only the "official policy" advocated by, or forced upon, the Pericles whom he does not name here, but because, for whatever reason, his interest is limited to what "the Athenians" did. They came at last to their decision, and Thucydides does no more than indicate briefly what he understood to be the chief reasons for it.

Yet in a different sense of the word, the episode is handled in a purely dramatic way. Another historian, *αὐτὸς λέγων*, would have written his own analysis of the situation:

> At this point Corcyra became thoroughly alarmed: Corinth was organising a formidable alliance against her, and she stood alone. Hitherto her policy had been one of isolation and neutrality. It had been based on the following considerations: (*i*) . . . , (*ii*) . . . , (*iii*) . . . What she had not foreseen was that . . .

In due course he would come to the Athenian decision. He would give his own explanation of it, and his own estimate of its wisdom or folly, exploiting, naturally, the historian's birthright, hindsight. This we will call the expository or ruminative method. What does Thucydides do? In particular, what use does he make of his birthright? Or does he pretend that he has none?

It is indeed dramatic that instead of writing in his own *persona* he presents the opposing considerations through two opposing speeches, as also Homer did, and for that matter Plato; but the main point is that he puts us, as it were, on the spot. He lays before us the arguments and considerations that were laid before the Athenian people by the two delegations. "War is coming, for certain. We Corcyreans are in danger from Corinth; if you help us now you will win our everlasting gratitude; you will also have on your side the second biggest navy in Greece." "War is by no means certain, but it will be, if you help these people. We Corinthians have been helpful to you in the past; your best policy now is to return the favour. A timely act of generosity can have a tremendous effect." Such was the choice put to the Athenians: what was the wise thing to do? Thucydides offers no opinion. He tells us merely what choice the Athenians made, and why they made it. As to its wisdom, he says nothing: we are grown-up people; we can read on, and think for ourselves. Sir Frank Adcock has remarked (*Journal of Hellenic Studies*, 1951, p. 5): "Corcyra proved an ineffective and wavering ally of Athens, and after a time relapsed into neutrality. Her government proved not to be really stable; her foreign policy proved not to be trustworthy." Exactly; a historian who was not Thucydides would have said something like this at the end of his account of the debate; he would to this extent have anticipated the course of events. Thucydides does not; yet when we reread this book, when we read again that Athens would secure the everlasting gratitude of Corcyra, we shall be dull-witted indeed if we do not reflect that "Corcyra proved an ineffective and wavering ally of Athens; her government proved not to be really stable." We may wonder if a timely act of gratitude toward Corinth might not have proved to be the better policy; Thucydides does not speculate about a matter that was not put to the test. We shall certainly reflect, when we know our Thucydides, what a perilous business it is, walking blind into the future, as we must do: he himself makes this reflection, in one form or another, about thirteen times. Here is a more elaborate illustration—the way in which he handles the revolt in Mytilene. In III 2–50, we find a combination of direct narrative and speeches—the Homeric method, as Aristotle says. This is interrupted by narration of events coincident but independent: Lysicles' disaster (c.19), and Plataea (20–24). The speeches are: one made at Olympia by the delegation from Mytilene, a short one made by Teutiaplos to Alcidas, and the Cleon-Diodotus antilogy.

We look first at the narrative, and if we wish to look with fresh eyes, we might do well to set down briefly the sort of thing that might be expected. We are told that even before the war Mytilene had contemplated revolt and had asked, though in vain, for Spartan help (c. 2,1). The present revolt was the outcome of an attempt on the part of Mytilene to unite the whole of Lesbos. The attempt was resisted by one city, Methymna, and by certain dissident citizens of Mytilene herself, who were the Athenian *proxenoi* (that is, citizens who represented in Mytilene the interests of Athenian nationals). It was these, and Methymna, and the unfriendly state of Tenedos, that gave the warning to Athens. Being told so much, we would naturally expect some further information: what were the grievances, what were the objects of the revolt, who were the leaders, what degree of unanimity was there, in Mytilene herself and among the other cities of the island? What we should not expect is Thucydides' total indifference to all this. The narrative is strangely external and impersonal, though that did not prevent him from including two short stories. One of these concerns the unnamed man who learned that Athens was to make a surprise attack, and thereupon left Athens at once, crossed to Euboea, went to Geraestus on foot, found a ship just sailing, arrived in Lesbos on the third day, and was able to give the warning in time. The other concerns Salaethus, sent out by Sparta to give the encouraging news that a Peloponnesian fleet was coming, and to assume control: he made the journey, we are told, in a single trireme, landed at Pyrrha, and made his way up a water-course which enabled him to scramble into the city unobserved. (Salaethus was not a lucky man: at the end of the siege he had to surrender, was taken to Athens, and was executed out of hand.) It was indeed important that the warning came, and Salaethus, but it is legitimate even though it may be idle to wonder why Thucydides, omitting so much of greater importance, thought it worth while to describe the two journeys.

Having secured an armistice, Mytilene sent out two embassies. The one sent to Athens is dealt with very briefly, in plain narrative; the one that went to Sparta and addressed there allies at Olympia is reported at length, and in quasi-dramatic form. Why the difference? It is true that the former accomplished nothing while the latter had important results, but we should not get very far with a theory that Thucydides wrote speeches only when the results were important: Teutiaplos' speech, for example, had no results at all. Even so, why a speech, instead of the historian's analytical account of what was said and done? And if a speech, why such a one as this? Nothing of what it contains need surprise us, but who is going to believe that such a delegation, invited on such an occasion to address a large gathering, did not explicitly rehearse the specific grievances that had driven Mytilene to rebellion? Thucydides might have used the occasion for telling us about the oppressive aspect of Athenian imperialism: he did not.

The whole story is concluded by the account of the two debates that took place in Athens after the surrender. The first is only summarised: we are given a bare report of the decision: to kill all the men among the prisoners and to sell the rest into slavery, assisted only by the statement that the Athenians were enraged both by the revolt and by the fact that a Peloponnesian fleet had dared to sail into the Aegean. The second debate is represented by the speeches of Cleon and Diodotus, and if we look calmly at them (as we will do later) we find that a great deal of what they contain has little to do with the fate of the Mytileneans.

These are among the facts of the case. If we believe that Thucydides was a reasonable man, there should be a point of view from which they make sense, though it may not be the sense that we should have expected; indeed if it were, we should not be so continually surprised by what Thucydides does.

We will begin closer analysis with the Olympia speech, and it will assist my own *poiesis* if we postpone consideration of the first part of it (III 9–12)—the part in which they seek to justify their revolt. Having dealt with this at some length, though in a rather surprising way, they come to their immediate proposals. The argument runs: Sparta now has a first-class opportunity of helping her friends and harming her enemies; Athens is exhausted physically (by the plague) and financially. She has one fleet blockading the Peloponnese and another off Lesbos; it is unlikely that she has any ships in reserve. The Peloponnesians therefore should make a combined attack on Attica by sea and by land; this would compel Athens to raise the one blockade or the other. It is in the Aegean, they argue, that the war will be lost and won. Further, they urge Sparta to come forward boldly as liberators: "If you help us you will the more easily strip Athens of her allies and therefore of her strength; the allies will be the more ready to risk coming over to you, and it is upon you that their hopes are set."

Thucydides himself makes no comment; he merely goes on with his narrative. The Spartans were impressed; they acted with energy: *προθύμως ἔπρασσον* (III 15,2). They instructed their allies to muster in force at the Isthmus, marched there themselves with speed, and set on foot naval preparations. But their allies were slow in mobilising: they were busy with the harvest, and had no enthusiasm for the campaign (c. 15,2). As for the Athenians, they launched yet a third fleet, a large one of a hundred ships, and with this they raided the Peloponnesus at their pleasure, even into the neighbourhood of Sparta itself, with the result that the Spartan forces at the Isthmus went home as fast as they could.

The Spartans, we have seen, were besought to act boldly by sea and land. By sea, they were inspired to appoint Alcidas to the supreme command, a man who proved ludicrous as an admiral, and disastrous as a statesman. Thucydides reports, as if verbatim, the advice given him by Teutiaplos: to attack the Athenians at Mytilene immediately upon their capture of the city, on the grounds that they would be taken by surprise. The general principle that he enunciates may strike us as not being specially original; nor is it, but it was far too original for Alcidas, whose only desire was to get back home as soon as he could (c. 31,2).

Sparta was to disintegrate the Empire by a bold attack and by encouraging the subject-allies of Athens to take the risk of revolting. How bold they were by sea we have noticed; at III 32 we learn what was Alcidas' idea of encouraging secession from Athens: having captured prisoners from sundry islands (who had thought that his fleet must be Athenian) he kept them until he should find a suitable place for slaughtering them, which he began to do, until some Samians pointed out to him that this was no great advertisement for Sparta the Liberator. This was an argument that even Alcidas could understand. He went home—and this event, we are told (c. 33,2), was much to the relief of the unfortified Ionian cities, who were in fear that he would land, plunder, and lay waste.

There is a great deal to be said about all this; much of it has been said by others, but it must be said again if we are to understand Thucydides' methods of composition.

We go back to our remarks about his chronological schedule; also to our question why he dealt in quasi-dramatic style, not discursively, with the proposals made to Sparta by Mytilene. One thing we may notice: here, as nearly everywhere else, he keeps pace with the events, neither going back over the past nor anticipating the future—a remarkable thing in a historian, and one that seems to bespeak a special kind of attention in the reader. We might call it the method of immediacy: the delegation comes; it says, "Here is your great opportunity, if you will do this, and do that". The Spartans say, "We will". Thucydides himself says nothing; he merely tells us what happened next.

He relies on the same method later in Book I, when we are nearer to the brink of the war. He reports on the two Congresses of Sparta, and gives the substance of five speeches. Of what is said in the speeches, some part has reference to the past, and may interest us at a later stage; of what refers to the future, we can say what we have said of the Olympia speech: Thucydides puts us into the presence of the actors in the event, or of some of them; he tells us what was planned and hoped for; then he goes on with his narrative. Always we are kept just behind that moving curtain which divides present from future. We watch and listen to the actors in the story as they peer into the dark trying to assess and to shape what is to happen. *We* know; we, like Thucydides, enjoy hindsight. It is inevitably in the light of our knowledge—that is, in the light of what Thucydides will have told us—that we shall read and ponder on what is being said *now*.

Evidently, the method has something in common with the kind of situation that creates tragic irony. "Thank you very much for the warning", says Agamemnon, as he moves toward the palace; "I will cure anything that needs remedy, perhaps by physic, perhaps by the knife". Since, at the play, we know what is going to happen to Agamemnon, our attention is not taken up with speculation whether he is going to kill Clytemnestra or she him; therefore, pulled up all standing by this remark of his, we contemplate other of its implications. Similarly, on a second reading at least, we know what is going to happen (namely nothing at all) when the Mytileneans say, Do this and all will be well, and the Spartans agree and "act with energy". Is it possible that Thucydides too had some feeling for irony? To answer this question would take us too far from Olympia; we will postpone it therefore, and see what happens here.

After the speech Thucydides might have written, *αὐτὸς λέγων*, a few paragraphs of analysis, to this effect.—Athens in herself, apart from her subject-allies, was much more formidable than the other Greeks had realised. Her unchallenged control of the sea gave her a grip on her empire that could not be shaken except by comparable sea-power. Both economically and politically she was better placed than Sparta: control of her policy was entirely in her own hands, while Sparta led a looser confederacy, the members of which were not necessarily devoted to the interests of Sparta. Again, the revenues of

Athens enabled her to wage continuous war, while on the other side, though Sparta herself had her professional army, her allies could not for long absent themselves from their fields, or they would starve. Further, for various reasons, Sparta was not good at fighting distant wars, especially oversea; and however unpopular the rule of Athens might be, Sparta was no inspiring alternative. Therefore, what might have seemed a good opportunity for bringing the war to an end came to nothing.

Instead of doing this Thucydides goes on with his narrative—and, as we have seen, it is a carefully edited narrative, "edited" only in this sense, that he has omitted all sorts of interesting information that we should be glad to have but that did not bear on his point. The narrative and the speech—the second part of it—were clearly thought out, as a unity. What is engaging Thucydides' mind here is not exactly the interesting situation which had developed in Lesbos and came to a head in 428, but rather the way in which the failure of the revolt illuminates the whole war.

Now perhaps we can say a little more about Salaethus, and the reason why Thucydides said so much about him, though it did not occur to him to mention the names of the leaders of the revolt. If one of Thucydides' ideas, as he shaped this part of his *History*, was that Athens had such a powerful grip on the Aegean, and that the Peloponnesians were in consequence helpless in this theatre, perhaps it was no bad idea to give a certain prominence to the story of the Spartan emissary, sent as the herald of massive help: how he had to cross the sea in a single ship, creep into Mytilene like a burglar, and wait for months for the fleet that never came, and in the end was executed in Athens like a pirate. There was also the story of the other man; we will not forget him.

But not only does the episode as a whole show signs of having been thought out and composed as a unity, with speeches and narrative working together; there is also the obvious fact that the considerations which were put above into the analytical passage that Thucydides did not write were indeed present to his mind, and have been made present to our minds too, though in his way.

"The allies were slow in mobilising; they were busy with the harvest, and had little enthusiasm for campaigning": anyone who read these forty chapters as a fragment, or anyone who refused to read Thucydides on the terms on which he wrote, would think that this important detail had been handled rather stupidly. Why were they slow in mobilising? Had it been a wet summer in the Peloponnese: and had Sparta done something, unmentioned by Thucydides, which irritated her allies? Why should a historian make statements that leave us, like this, with one foot off the ground?

But of course he has not done this: he has already said all that was necessary, though it was a long time back—in I 141, where Pericles was propounding that victory was a reasonable prospect. "We should not overestimate the strength of the Peloponnesians. They are *αὐτουργοί*, an agricultural people; they have no capital, private or public, and therefore have no experience of waging long wars or of fighting oversea. They cannot often send out armies or fleets beyond their frontiers because they may not neglect their fields and cannot pay armies. In a single battle they are indeed formidable, but a long war is another thing. Again, they have no central government; when at long intervals they do meet for deliberation, local interests prevail over any collective policy."

That Pericles indeed said this on that occasion there is no reason to doubt; that Thucydides intended us to draw therefrom certain conclusions about Pericles' insight there is no reason to deny. What we obviously must not do is suppose that this is the end of the matter. Is it not clear that only if we recall to mind I 141 does Thucydides' handling of the present fiasco make sense—that (to put it the other way round) in writing what he does in III 15 he took it for granted that the earlier passage would be on call? A modern historian, if he did not wish to repeat himself, might give a footnote: *See above, I 141.* Thucydides neither repeats himself nor inserts the footnote. Such is the way in which he expected to be read.

This, I trust, is obvious (unless we can think that Thucydides, here, was writing like an incompetent chronicler), but it is also alarming: if he has done it once, what guarantee have we that he has not done it somewhere else, or indeed that he is not continually doing it? The idea that he could say things without saying them will be anathema to those who will not even credit the Greek dramatists with the ability or inclination to do such a thing, but the alternative is too dismal to contemplate: it would be that Thucydides tramped along doggedly from fact to fact, slipping in a speech at intervals, choosing his facts from a very narrow range, and often doing little to make them significant. But if it is true, as surely it is, that when we read how Sparta, at the Isthmus, was let down by her allies, we do not feel frustrated because we do remember I 141, we have admitted that Thucydides will compose in a way which is foreign to us, so far as historical writing goes, and we must do our best to face the consequences. We shall have admitted that a passage here may join hands with a passage there and, marvellously, make sense. But we shall also have found at least one reason why he does not talk much; also, maybe, why his book is so short, and why he, apparently, took so long over the writing of it.

We have argued that Thucydides had a definite reason for choosing to include the Olympia speech: we are on the verge of a military operation which he considered important and significant from several points of view; he tells us what was hoped for, in order that when we see how very different the result was we should take particular notice and do some thinking on our own account, he himself having already provided the material for such thinking. (How intelligent were Thucydides' readers?)

A more portentous moment was the outbreak of the war itself, and just before this he gives us a constellation of six speeches. We will inspect those parts of them that look to the future. Archidamus (I 80–81), "the Corinthians" (I 121), and Pericles, all, according to their knowledge and foresight, assess the prospects in terms of sea-power, financial resources, the chances of disintegrating the empire, of establishing outposts in the enemy territory—that sort of thing. We understand what Thucydides is doing here: he is, probably, reporting in stylised fashion things that were actually said; he is certainly omitting much that was said—the rhetorical and emotional talk that men do indulge in on such occasions; but he is also bringing to our notice, for future reference, some of the controlling facts in the situation: we have just seen how significant I 141 proves to be. Since we are interested in Thucydides' methods, let us take for particular consideration what is said, or reported, here about Athenian sea-power.

Pericles relies on it, and is confident of victory, provided that the Athenians conduct the war with prudence. Archidamus—no bad prophet, as it proves—is daunted by it; the Corinthians are optimistic. They talk like this (c. 121):

> We are likely to win. We are stronger in numbers, in experience of war, in military discipline. A navy—which is their strong point—we can build from our own resources and by borrowing money from Delphi and Olympia, and we can outbid them for sailors: our strength is all our own, but theirs is bought with money. Once they lose a sea-fight they are finished, and if they should hold out, we shall have the more time in which to practise seamanship. When we have raised our skill to their level—why, we certainly have the advantage in courage; what is ours by nature they cannot possibly acquire by training.

They say other things, but let us consider these. Nowhere does Thucydides write: "Little did they realise how superb the seamanship of the Athenians now was, nor what constant training was necessary for such perfection . . . The pitiful behaviour of Alcidas, five years later, was to show . . ." Nowhere does he say that the naval might of Athens did not depend entirely on hirelings: he does however happen to mention that the appalling new fleet of a hundred ships, which sent a Spartan army scuttling home from the Isthmus, was manned entirely by citizens and resident aliens.

In lieu of comment, he gives the speech of Pericles. What Pericles has to say on this topic runs like this: "They might indeed fortify some outpost in Attica, but that would not prevent us from attacking them with our navy, which is our strong point. Our navy gives us more experience of land-fighting than land-fighting has given them of naval operations. As for mastering naval operations, they will not find that very easy; we ourselves have been practising them for nearly fifty years, and have not perfected them yet. How then will inland people, farmers, do anything worth while, especially as we shall give them little chance of practising? Relying on numbers and ignorance (ἀμαθία) they might indeed defeat a small squadron; but they will be blockaded, will remain without skill, and therefore without confidence. Naval fighting, like other things, is a τέχνη (art, professional skill); it cannot be acquired in spare moments; rather does it allow only spare moments for anything else." And then he goes on to dispose of the idea that the enemy could improvise a fleet by borrowingmoney from Delphi and Olympia and hiring sailors.

It sounds almost as if Pericles had been provided with a newspaper report of what the Corinthians had said. We may judge that unlikely. The Corinthians may well have said something like that and Pericles something like this, but the dialectical form of it is Thucydides' own: he is putting before us a matter of supreme importance to the whole conflict, and suggesting that on the Peloponnesian side its importance had not been realised.

When we have carefully read the *History*, and then, beginning again, come to the sentence in which Pericles combines the ideas of sea-power and seizing outposts, our thoughts will naturally turn to Pylos. Conversely, when we read about Pylos, we are likely to remember this sentence: Thucydides has already said something significant about it; the episode perfectly illustrates the commanding position that Athens held in virtue of her control of the seas. It did, we may recall, bring Spartans to Athens, suing for peace.—What use Athens made of the victory is another matter.

But there is something else here that may engage our interest, and may or may not reward investigation, on the assumption that Thucydides wrote his book not in sections but, eventually, as a considered whole. As we stand with him on the brink of the whole war he does, twice, make us think of Athenian naval skill—among other things. Out of curiosity, merely to see what happens, let us set down side-by-side what references there are in the *History* to this topic.

In I 49 Thucydides is describing the sea battle between Corinth and Corcyra. The ships, he says, were crowded with heavy-armed infantry: ship grappled with ship and remained stationary while the soldiers fought it out from the decks. There was no manoevering, no skill, only brute strength; it was the clumsy old style, τῷ παλαιῷ τρόπῳ ἀπειρότερον ἔτι παρεσκευασμένοι; it was land-fighting on water, πεζομαχίᾳ προσφερὴς οὖσα. After this come the two passages we have just discussed, in the speeches of the Corinthians and Pericles. The Corinthians thought that in no long time their side might rival the other in skill: what Phormio soon did to them in the Gulf must have opened their eyes and shown them how far they still had to go. "When our skill equals theirs", they had said, "why, we certainly surpass them in courage. What we have by nature they cannot acquire by training." The innocents! As for skill, there is no need to say more; and if we reflect on the discipline and courage shown by the Athenians in the battle off Corcyra—crews rowing, as Gomme points out, with their backs to the enemy, and in silence, trusting entirely to the judgment of the captain—we realise that if the Peloponnesians by gift of nature possessed greater courage, then they were remarkable men indeed. Perhaps Archidamus was wiser than the Corinthians in this too, that he thought the difference between one people and another not very great.

We hear no more about naval skill until we are in the Great

Harbour of Syracuse. Thucydides, reporting facts as always, describes in VII 36 how the Syracusans altered the build of their ships for battle against the Athenians, whom they were now beginning to fear less: they made them heavier and more solid, more apt for ramming, "which indeed was the method used by the Corinthians in the fighting off Naupactus". He remarks that on this occasion, in the confined space, the Athenians would be unable to use the skilful tactics that had been their mainstay, *ᾧπερ τῆς τέχνης μάλιστα ἐπίστευον*; that their light, swift ships would be helpless against the heavier ones of Syracuse; that sheer weight and strength, "which hitherto had passed for ignorance", *τῇ πρότερον ἀμαθίᾳ τῶν κυβερνητῶν δοκούσῃ εἶναι*, were now to crush training and skill—as they did.

Was the bitter irony of it invisible to Thucydides, being the invention of a modern sophist? Well, at the beginning of his account of the last and most desperate battle, he tells us that the Athenians put every available man on the decks, and he records a speech made by Nicias (VII 62 ff.). In the speech Nicias (according to Thucydides) says, twice: "We are reduced to fighting a land-battle on the water". Then he records a speech made on the other side by Gylippus, to this effect: "The Athenians, having already the greatest Greek empire ever known, came here to subdue Sicily. They will be dismayed that you have defeated them on their own element. They have been reduced to copying our own tactics and are crowding their decks with hoplites. They are in utter disorder; their success has betrayed them. They are our bitterest enemies: have at them, in anger!" *τύχην ἑαυτὴν παραδεδωκυῖαν*, "success which has played itself false": is it permitted, is it natural, to think of Sophocles and his Oedipus?

But it is ridiculous to suggest that the historian was really thinking about naval skill in such a way! Yet this is what he has said about it, and unless I have overlooked something, he has said nothing else. But in fact, the more we attend to what he actually puts into his exiguous text, the more surprising does he become. He is not doing his best to be a proper nineteenth-century historian.

We are concerning ourselves just now not so much with his mind as with his method of composition, though naturally it is not easy to separate the two. Therefore let us go on to consider one passage where everyone (I think) admits a measure of deliberate construction, namely the juxtaposition of the two debates over Mytilene and Plataea; then we will look at another passage which will illustrate one use he makes of his chronological system: the debate in Syracuse between Hermocrates and Athenagoras.

The narrative, in the early part of Book III, has interwoven the revolt in Mytilene and its suppression with the capitulation of Plataea; naturally: they occurred at the same time. It is however permissible to observe that nothing prevented Thucydides from concluding each episode in straightforward narrative, as he does for instance at IV 57: he has recorded that the Athenians captured a remnant of the Aeginetans, and continues, in narrative: "The Athenians resolved to put them to death, because of their long-standing hatred of them"; and he is equally brief about Cleon's proposal to capture Scione and put the inhabitants to death (IV 122,6) and about the execution of the decree (V 32). Certainly it was an unusual occurrence that a second debate was held about Mytilene; we are in no way surprised that Thucydides makes much of it. In the case of Plataea, however, it is not easy to see from what source he should have got reliable information about what was said: Gomme, who argues strongly for the general authenticity of the speeches, allows that Thucydides virtually made up the speech of the Plataeans "because he wanted it for his purposes" (*Commentary*, II 346). Assuredly, the existence of the two antilogies, side by side, is no result of automatic writing.

What has often been said about them is that Thucydides is drawing a contrast between his own city, democratic Athens, and Sparta. Thus Gomme: "Immediately before, we had the debate on Mytilene; now that on Plataea: 'that is what Athens was like; this was Sparta, the liberator'. But he does not make the comment explicitly; it is for the reader to understand." (A brief though no doubt eloquent exposition of the same view can be found in *The Greeks*, H. D. F. Kitto, p. 151.) But the reader must first read, and he should be careful not to assume that Thucydides, being an Athenian, will be saying what he obviously would say, just as we must not assume that Aeschylus, being an Athenian warrior-poet, will be saying what such a poet obviously would about the Persian War.

There are one or two awkward facts. Thucydides does not try to conceal it from us that Mytilene escaped judicial massacre, after two debates, only by a few votes and a few minutes. Further, he will soon be recording how merciless the Athenians were to their Aeginetan prisoners and to Scione—and without a word of comment. It would have been disingenuous of him, and ineffective as well, to praise Athens for clemency toward Mytilene and make no comment on her savage treatment of the others. On his own showing, the difference between Athens and Sparta here was indeed something, but nothing to be very proud of. But the great objection to this view is that it does not explain the text.

We are told (c. 36) that the Assembly resolved to kill all the men and enslave the rest, in anger that Mytilene had revolted though being an independent ally, and especially that a Peloponnesian fleet had dared in their support to sail into Ionian waters. Then comes the remarkable story of the remorse felt by many Athenians, which led to the second debate. For this, Athens should have all credit—though in fact it was Athenians who had said at Sparta (I 78,3) that in war men do things the wrong way about: they act first, and do their thinking later. Yet if we are to contrast what the Athenians did to their prisoners of war with what the Spartans did to theirs, an *advocatus diaboli* could point out that if the Mytileneans, like the Plataeans, had been on the spot and not more than two hundred miles away, there would have been no second debate: they would have been killed that same evening.

But if we look at the text of the Cleon-Diodotus dispute, the text of two speeches out of a dozen or more that must have been made but are not noticed by Thucydides, we notice that although the fate of the prisoners is the occasion for them, what they contain is to a surprising extent concerned with other matters. The first third of Diodotus' speech, III 42–43, being a direct reply to much of what Cleon has said, might fairly be described as a short disquisition on the theme *How Not To Run a City*. It ends in his almost despairing assertion that irresponsible imputations of bribery and corruption have made it impossible in Athens for an honest man to give honest advice in a straightforward manner.

Turning back to Cleon's speech we find much the same. His first remark is—and again one asks if Thucydides was capable of irony—"I have often wondered if a democracy is capable of managing an empire"; then he goes on, at some length, to deplore the way in which the Athenians are running their affairs. —Very soon, in his analysis of civil war, Thucydides is going to say *τὴν εἰωθυῖαν ἀξίωσιν τῶν ὀνομάτων ἐς τὰ ἔργα ἀντήλλαξαν τῇ δικαιώσει*": to suit what they were doing, they twisted words out of their accepted meaning" (III 82,4). Cleon is not innocent of this; like Creon of the *Antigone* he speaks of "the laws" when what is in question is one decree; reconsidering of a single administrative or judicial act he represents as a tampering with legislation. He flatters the crowd and traduces reflectiveness and sobriety in judgment in his intellectually dishonest remark *ἀμαθία μετὰ σωφροσύνης ὠφελιμώτερον ἢ δεξιότης μετὰ ἀκολασίας*: "slow wits backed by honest judgment are more useful than clever irresponsibility" (c. 37,3)—as if stupidity were always honest and intelligence irresponsible. He argues of course in favour of violence and terror, of acting in anger and allowing no time for reflection (c. 38,1). In his accusation that the Athenians come to the Assembly as if to a show, there is no doubt much truth; indeed, the next time Thucydides finds occasion to refer to a meeting of the Assembly, when he is describing how the command at Pylos was thrust upon Cleon, he makes plain his opinion that the Assembly, crowd and "better people" alike, did behave with a deplorable irresponsibility. But the truth which there may be in this accusation of Cleon's he uses for the purpose of disparaging responsible debate of any kind. Not only does he pour scorn upon egg-heads—in this context the word seems appropriate—but worst of all he insinuates that they are crooks as well. It is this in particular that moves Diodotus to his despairing outburst before the name of Mytilene is ever mentioned by him.

What has been summarised so far accounts for a considerable part of the antilogy. What are we to think? If we begin by saying that Thucydides had personal reasons for hating the man who had brought about his own exile, that he gives a distorted picture of him, not letting us know, for example, that Cleon was an able administrator—let us reflect that we may be starting off on the wrong foot. He may have hated him; he may have been prejudiced: it might be true but relatively unimportant, and it might obscure from us what is important.

Cleon is introduced with the phrase *τῷ δήμῳ παρὰ πολὺ ἐν τῷ τότε πιθανώτατος*: "at the time he had by far the greatest influence over the people". By an odd coincidence he uses almost exactly the same words when he introduces the only other popular leader whom he brings before us, Pericles of course excepted: this other being the strangely unimportant figure—unimportant, I mean, to the *History*—of Athenagoras. We promised him admission; let him enter now, and let Cleon wait.

Irony? Surely, few people have ever been disposed of in more devastating fashion. Narrative and speech are combined to some purpose here.

We have been made to follow the great invading fleet as far as Corcyra; there it waits for reinforcements (VI 32). We are transferred to Sicily. It is a point at which a historian might naturally tell us what had been happening there, what the political and military situation was. (Thucydides does indeed tell us about that, but in his own way, as we shall see.) He does nothing of the kind at this moment; like Homer, "he says himself as little as possible", and like Homer and the tragic poets, he brings on characters "doing something", that is, debating. He tells us first that news of the threatened attack has come to Sicily from many quarters. Few Syracusans believe it; most are quite confident that such an attack, were it ever made, would easily be defeated; others are merely amused by the reports. Then we have the speech of Hermocrates. We have met him before: it was his statesmanship that had brought about pacification in Sicily nine years earlier—which had the result that the Athenian commanders went home, since there was no more fishing in troubled waters, and were condemned by the popular courts in Athens on the charge that they had been bribed to return: Thucydides makes no comment, even though he was himself a commander who had been condemned.

Hermocrates takes the reports very seriously indeed, and implores the Assembly to do the same. We may not think highly of his tentative suggestion that the combined Sicilian navies should sail out and engage the Athenians on the high seas; the Athenians would surely have relished the prospect. Moreover, his confidence that the other Sicilians would gladly join Syracuse to repel the invader was not justified by the result. Nevertheless, in what mattered most it was Hermocrates who was right and the carefree crowd that was wrong.

Up gets Athenagoras. He is "the leader of the popular party", "greatly trusted by the people". He ridicules the very idea of such an invasion: the story is ludicrous; the Athenians would not be so mad.—We happen to know that already the fleet is nearly half-way there, and Thucydides has not blurred his transition by putting in what Gomme called "twiddly bits".

Commentators have said that the juxtaposition of confident assertion with harsh fact underlines the boldness, or the foolhardiness, according to taste, of the Athenian enterprise. Certainly it can be read that way, especially if one does not read the whole of what Thucydides makes Athenagoras say, for he went on like this, and Thucydides decided to record it: "The silly story is being put about by the enemies of the People, but it is too unintelligent to deceive a man like me. I can see their wicked designs: they are trying to deceive you, the People, into giving them extra powers, that they may subvert your liberties. But you may trust *me;* I will protect you against their machinations."

It is deadly, but why did Thucydides do it? He never mentions Athenagoras again, and this particular folly of his, fortunately for Syracuse, had no effect at all. We have no reason to suppose that Thucydides has any animus against this demagogue; is he merely putting his foot on a toad and squashing it, just for fun? We look at the whole picture: the fleet is already at Corcyra, the Syracusans have reports of it; they are in the main undisturbed or quite sceptical; yet if the trusted leader had had his way—and Lamachus his, on the other side—Syracuse must soon have fallen; and the longer part of the speech sets before us not the boldness of the invasion but the party rancour which clouds the mind of a popular leader and makes him talk perilous nonsense.

Having done our duty with Athenagoras we will return to Cleon, who also was "most influential with the people". The parallel may suggest that Thucydides had motives other than personal ones. This antilogy, as we have seen, expressly and emphatically raises the question how to run a city. Now, not only has Thucydides given us a picture of the way in which a very different political leader ran the city, but in his comparison of Pericles with his successors (II 65) he has drawn our attention to it. Cleon argues emotionally; what Thucydides most praises in Pericles (and in Themistocles) is sobriety and penetration of judgment. He shows how Cleon flattered the crowd; not only does he both tell us and show us that Pericles did the opposite, but also he shows us, in that last speech of Pericles', which in some ways is his finest, how in a desperate moment he rebuked it with dignity and logic—a logic, incidentally, which the Assembly accepted and acted upon. When he wrote down Cleon's demand: "Avenge yourselves at once; do not put off action until your anger has cooled" (III 38,1), did he perhaps think that his more serious readers might recall what he had written at II 22,1? For there, Pericles refused to summon the Assembly "lest the people should make a decision in anger rather than with judgment, and so make a serious mistake". In the Epitaphios Pericles had made it a peculiarly Athenian quality that "we reflect upon a situation correctly, or at least make the right decision; we do not think that speeches impede action, but that the impediment is rather to engage in the necessary action without seeking previous instruction through debate": Cleon scorns debate—except as a means of encouraging a stampede.

We should not, I think, say, not at least in this connexion, that Thucydides is depicting the way in which Athens had degenerated under stress of war, for the reason that later he turns his grave attention to another democracy which had not been much under the stress of war, to show that there too a fatal error could so easily have been made because party bitterness took precedence, in a popular leader, over level judgment. He does indeed say, of Theramenes' modified democracy, that "it was the best polity that Athens had yet had" (VIII 97,2), but it would be small-minded to say simply: "Thucydides was anti-democratic". He thought and felt about the war exactly as he says he did. On the Athenian side it was run, necessarily, by public meeting, and a public meeting, so he noted, is liable to gusts of emotion, such as despair (after the plague), irrational confidence (as after Pylos), blind hopes (as before the Sicilian expedition), party bitterness (as in Syracuse). It needs firm guidance, such as the Athenian democracy got from Pericles—and men like Pericles are rare.

But Cleon also expounds his ideas on the running of an empire. We are not to blame him for saying that the empire is a tyranny, that the subjects hate it, that Athens dare not give it up; Pericles had said the same. But he makes one assertion that has been answered already, by Thucydides' *poiesis*, and makes others that are answered by Diodotus. Twisting words again, he says, of Mytilene (c. 39,2–3): "It was not a revolt that they made (οὐκ ἀπέστησαν); they laid a plot to attack us, and with the help of our enemies they sought to destroy you, though they themselves were safe and had been treated by you with special distinction. From their predecessors in revolt they could learn nothing; in their folly they preferred might to right." But the Mytileneans made it clear, in that part of their Olympia speech that we have not yet looked at, what the "special distinction" was from their point of view: it was merely to be subjugated last of all; and this much at least they had learned from the fate of their predecessors, that their turn would come too, when it suited the convenience of Athens.

As for the policy that Athens ought to pursue with regard to her empire, Cleon poses a harsh dilemma: "You cannot afford compassion. Your empire is a tyranny; nothing but force will serve you. Pity is all very well, in its place, but you have to choose: you can be an imperial people, or you can go in for humane conduct. You cannot do both."

> My gracious liege, this too much lenity
> And harmful pity must be laid aside.

That was said by the vindictive Young Clifford to Henry, when that unlucky king was trying to find a way out of the savagery of the civil wars (*3 King Henry VI*, II 2,9–10). It is also said by Cleon, and—such can our reading habits be—some have thought that it was also part of Thucydides' own philosophy of politics.

In his reply, Diodotus too disclaims any appeal to pity; the question, he says, should be decided with regard to nothing but the interests of Athens. This, naturally, has attracted unfavourable comment, but we should at least notice the other principle with which Diodotus links it: "We are a deliberative assembly, not a court of justice". We will notice too the contrast with what happens at Plataea. Yet a man can well afford to base his policy on self-interest when he believes, as does Diodotus, that self-interest and humane behavior coincide. His argument is that blind rage and violence are foolish—perhaps a more effective argument, in the circumstances, than that they are wicked.

In this antilogy, then, Thucydides does not appear as the loyal son of Athens, proud that his city behaved better than Sparta; rather, he draws a picture of an imperial people barely able to manage its own affairs in a responsible way; one which, on this occasion, is indeed restrained from wiping out a whole city in a fit of unreflecting rage, though on later occasions it is not. And this at least is true, whether Thucydides saw the point or not: one of Diodotus' arguments was that it is lunacy to stiffen the resistance of a city in revolt by decreeing that all the rebels, guilty or not, shall be put to death; but when Scione rebelled, this is exactly what the Assembly did resolve, "on Cleon's motion" (IV 122,6).

But if Thucydides' purpose in contriving the juxtaposition of the two antilogies was not to contrast Athenian humanity with Spartan inhumanity, what was it? Of course the cynical and inhuman behaviour of the five Spartan commissioners moves our indignation more than the blind rage shown in Athens at the first meeting of the Assembly, even more than the stupid violence of Cleon; and of course we applaud the remorse felt by slightly more than half of the Athenians; and if we feel like this, it is Thucydides who has made us feel it, by writing the speech of (or for) the Plataeans, and by setting the Thebans and Spartans in so hateful a light. He moves our compassion for the victims, our indignation with the vindictive Thebans and the cold Spartans, with a power that is certainly not surpassed in Euripides' war-plays. We feel also, it may be, pity and some shame for Greece herself, that a city so distinguished in Greek history should suddenly cease to exist; that she should not even be destroyed, like Troy, in one great conflagration, but that the stones and woodwork should be systematically removed and used elsewhere for the erection of a hotel, and articles of furniture remade and dedicated to Hera—all of which Thucydides, for some reason, reports in detail.

As we read the Plataeans' bitter protest that they, who had done so much for Greece, can now find not a single friend and helper, we perhaps recall Antigone's final despair, that she is being haled off to death deserted by men and gods alike; and if a Thucydidean scholar should find the comparison absurd, we should rightly infer that he had found some secret method of inoculating himself against Thucydides. Yet it would be no less grave an error to call the passage an emotional outburst: it is emotional, it is not an outburst. Once more, when we look into what he wrote, we find in it things that are a little disconcerting—which is true of Euripides' war-plays too. Thucydides is both feeling intensely and thinking intensely—which of course is what we ought to mean if we call him an artist.

Disconcerting things are said. The Thebans are made intelligible, not monsters. From their point of view, which is presented forcibly, the Plataeans are renegade Boeotians who have always rejected Boeotian traditions and the accepted Theban leadership, and have consistently supported the enemy across the border. What they say about their own unheralded assault on Plataea in time of peace should put us on the track—Thucydides' track. They admit that what they did was somewhat irregular, "but then", they explain, "we had been invited by the right-thinking elements among yourselves to correct the errors of your own policy". (Once more, the distressing jargon comes easily, and seems appropriate.) The transition from Plataea to Corcyra will prove to be no abrupt one.

The Plataeans cry out on the crime of killing prisoners of war who have surrendered and now "hold out their arms in supplication", *χεῖρας προισχομένους* (c. 58,3); the Thebans denounce as criminals the Plataeans who, having accepted the surrender of surviving Thebans in Plataea, put them to death, *χεῖρας προισχομένους* (66,2). If we turn back to the passage in which this event is described, II 5, we find that the Plataeans denied the Theban account of it and asserted that in any case the terms of surrender had not been confirmed by oath. Thucydides however states that the prisoners, a hundred and eighty of them, were put to death after the Thebans had withdrawn without doing any damage, and that when more sensible advice came from Athens, the men were already dead. (One might ask here, parenthetically, what about Diodotus? For if the Plataeans had soberly considered what was to their interest instead of acting in anger and giving their prisoners "what they deserved", Thebes would have been paralysed by having so many citizens held hostage in Plataea, and the men would have lived.)

When the Thebans repeat, from the Plataeans, the words *χεῖρας προισχομένους*, we should not be content with saying that the Theban orator flings the words back into the teeth of the Plataeans. The Theban orator is in fact Thucydides. Aeschylus gave much publicity to the natural law: the Doer must Suffer; where should we find a clearer exemplification? —not that Thucydides got the luminous idea from Aeschylus, for such laws have the habit of bringing themselves forcibly to the notice of those who keep their eyes open and can think. Because of what the Plataeans did then, the Thebans say now (c. 67,2–3,5): "Do not listen to their wailings! We could wail too, for men of ours killed by the hatred and wickedness of these Plataeans."

The Plataeans appeal impressively to the services they have rendered Greece in the past: the Athenians had done the same at the first Congress of Sparta, when they said (I 75): "Surely, just because we have an empire, the enthusiasm, courage, and intelligence that we showed then ought not to be requited now with such excessive hostility". Athenians and Plataeans get the same hard answer: "If they were good then and are bad now, they ought to pay double" (I 86,1; III 67,2). Past benefits are rarely accepted in exchange for present injuries. And so we could continue: the Plataeans invoke the oaths of inviolability sworn after the battle of Plataea; they are told in return that they have themselves abrogated the oaths by joining with the Athenians in their sustained attack on Greek liberties.

Obviously, nothing said by the Thebans in any way lessens

our indignation at what was done to the Plataeans; on the other hand, our indignation at what was done should not tempt us to withhold our serious attention from what Thucydides has written, disconcerting though some of it may be. Surely, what the antilogy does, and was intended to do, is to make us understand something of the tangled passions that made the Plataeans in the past, and the Thebans in the present, so vindictive.

We are invited also to consider the Spartans, by whose verdict two hundred exhausted men were put to death. The Plataeans appeal not only to humanity, generosity, and decency, but also to the self-interest of Sparta; they suggest that Sparta too is on trial: "You would be declaring yourselves to put immediate self-interest above what is right and fair" (c. 56,3); "you would be hazarding your reputation for nobility" (57,1); "you would incur infamy" (58,2). When to this they add: "Remember the instability of human fortunes" (59,1), our thought might turn to the narrow vindictiveness displayed by Menelaus in the *Ajax:* he justifies the proposed outrage on the body of Ajax by saying: "These things go by turns; now it is my turn to be contemptuous" (vv. 1087–1090). The reply comes from Odysseus: "We all have our turn to need forbearance". This much perhaps we can admit: had there been a Diodotus among the five commissioners, able to persuade the others to set aside the passions of the moment and take a wider view of what their real interests were, then Plataea might have survived.—But Thucydides says that the Spartans *did* consider their own interests, and nothing else: they decided that their interest was to gratify an important ally, and therefore killed the Plataeans. Quite so; and Mme de Romilly observes (p. 235) that in fact the memory of Plataea remained one of the great weapons of anti-Spartan propaganda during the fourth century. Perhaps it is not so easy to know what one's self-interest really is.

Therefore, looking into the four speeches, the two antilogies, which do not seem to be balanced like this by accident, we find that Thucydides is not, except incidentally, contrasting the ways of his own city and of Sparta; not (so far as I can see) expounding or even adumbrating any philosophy of politics, unless it is that on a true appreciation of its own interest a city will not behave with barbarity, and that a deliberative assembly does well to remember that it is not a court of justice. He is, in the first place, considering the fortunes of two Greek cities. His story of Mytilene ends: "So close did Mytilene come to ruin" (c. 49,4); of Plataea: "So ended the history of Plataea, in the ninety-third year after she had become the ally of Athens". He passes at once to the paroxysm that broke out in Corcyra, and he concludes that episode (IV 48,5): "So ended this revolution, so far as the period of this war is concerned, because of the one party practically no one was left".—"Never so many cities . . . never so many men . . ." Writing almost as a scientist, almost as a tragic poet, he lays before us the motives that led to such results. At the same time, his quasi-dramatic method of composing gives us a picture of what the Athenian democracy could be like in the absence of a Pericles (with which picture we have associated his later vignette of a moment in the life of another democracy), and of what Sparta was like. When we pass to the third episode in what Gomme justly called "this tremendous section of the *History*", the dramatist gives place entirely to the analyst, when Thucydides, αὐτὸς λέγων for once, writes his chapters on revolutionary frenzy as a destroyer of cities and men. There is no sudden break but a steady continuation of thought from the first antilogy to the second, and from that to Corcyra. The unity of this section does not reside really in the fact that the revolt of Mytilene, the destruction of Plataea, and the outbreak of revolution in Corcyra all happened at about the same time; it resides in what Thucydides thought and (in his own way) said about them. Further, now that we have looked both at text and context, perhaps it becomes easier to understand, and not merely to deplore, that he leaves out so much here: does not record other such revolutions as they occurred, never explains that Plataea occupied a position of strategic importance, fails to do justice to Cleon by saying: "By the way, Cleon was extremely competent in administration".

We have much more to consider, in respect both of Thucydides' *poiesis* and of his habit of thought, but this may be a convenient place for a short retrospect.

Looked at from the historical point of view which has become instinctive in us, the *History*, for all its factual accuracy, suffers from grave and surprising lacunae. About his own point of view, he is explicit (I 23), but our own inhibits us from taking seriously and simply what he says; yet a scrutiny of the passages which, typically, seem to have arrested his particular attention does suggest that he was telling the simple truth: he viewed the war as an immense catastrophe, one that was not unlikely to recur, in somewhat the same form.

His method of writing a History, *omnium consensu*, was unique. He refrains, not always but habitually, from offering explanations, comments, judgments, of his own; he relies on objective narrative (though without thinking it necessary to cite his authorities) and speeches. His method is not unique; it is merely early-Hellenic; we find it in Homer, in the dramatists, in Pindar, and in Plato, sometimes. It bespeaks from the reader a certain kind of response, one we readily give to a poet, even to a novelist, but are not accustomed to give to a historian. Everyone recognises in him a strong dramatic tendency. It shows itself not in vivid presentation—"recreation of the past"—but in his disposition of the material. The obvious dramatic juxtapositions are obvious indeed, but this is not a method used for special effects; it is simply the way in which he thought and wrote, "making the story tell its own tale". He makes the whole book do this; it is the complement, and the explanation, of his notorious reticence.

We have looked at certain bits of narrative—Phormio's battles in the Gulf, the campaign of Hippocrates in Boeotia and of Brasidas in the north; we have looked at certain combinations of narrative and speech—Archidamus' speech at the Isthmus followed by the plain statement of what happened in Athens, the Olympia speech in conjunction with the narrative of the revolt, the Epitaphios and the description of the plague: the suggestion is that it does make excellent sense to assume that Thucydides does exercise this purposeful control. The proof, if there is one, can only be cumulative, and it must make unified sense: it must explain together what he puts into his text, what he leaves out; the notable features of his style; the fact that he wrote so slowly and in so concentrated a way; what he says himself about his subject. We shall not be deterred, perhaps, if at the end we receive the impression of a powerful mind which has worked for the best part of a lifetime on a great subject from a consistent—and an Attic—point of view, and if we do not have to invoke limitations of his own mind and of his own time. Our own time might be imposing limitations on us.

Of what has been said already there is one section which, I fear, may have been received with something less than full and enthusiastic acceptance: is it credible that a historian should have thought about Athenian naval skill in the way that has been suggested? If the reader is sceptical, one reason may be that we have not yet placed that matter in its full context. This we will do forthwith, as we try to come closer to Thucydides' mind. We will do this by first enquiring what *he* thought about Athenian imperialism, beginning not with what a devoted admirer of Pericles must obviously have thought, but with what he admitted into his text.

3. His Thought

About the Empire Thucydides tells us little of what we would like to know; we cited the remark of Mme de Romilly, that he gives "une figure tronquée". We will approach him from the other end: set down, without hopes or expectations, what he does say about it—and find, perhaps not to our surprise, that it is serious and coherent, and from his own point of view complete. We shall find too that in a curiously natural way it will lead to, and help to explain, other notable features of the *History*.

There are, to begin with, the few passages that he writes in his own name. In I 19 he briefly compares the empire with the Peloponnesian confederacy: the Spartans led (ἡγοῦντο) their allies not by making them tributary but by seeing that they should have governments sympathetic toward Sparta; the Athenians had taken over the navies of their allies, except of Chios and Lesbos, and imposed tribute on them all. Next there is the *Pentecontaetia*, I 89–117, which is exactly what it purports to be, a factual record, without dates, of the origin and growth of the empire. Then there is the general remark, at II 8,4, that Greek opinion at the beginning of the war was on the whole decidedly in favour of Sparta; and the other general remark, at VIII 2,1–2, that after the Sicilian disaster the whole of Greece, particularly the subject-allies, turned against Athens with enthusiasm. Among the direct statements are also: that in Amphipolis the majority, at first, were unwilling to admit Brasidas (IV 104,4) and that Acanthus went over to Sparta only with hesitation and under a threat (IV 88); on the other hand, that after the capture of Amphipolis, because of the moderation of Brasidas many cities in Chalcidice were eager for revolt (IV 108,5). We may perhaps include here a remark made by Phrynichus the Athenian (VIII 48,5), that the allies were less interested in what form of government they had than in being free of Athens.

These, I think, are Thucydides' only direct comments. If our present enquiry were a historical one, namely how the allies conducted themselves toward Athens during the war, we might say what indeed has been said, that they remained surprisingly loyal; but then, Thucydides has shown in his account of Mytilene how perilous it was to revolt and how dangerous to rely on Sparta. He does not seem to have reported anything that seriously conflicts with his own statement that the empire was not at all popular.

We turn to what he says in his quasi-dramatic way, by implication, in the speeches that he decided to incorporate. We shall of course not suppose that he himself agrees with everything that he reports; we shall note merely what it is, what are the aspects of Athenian imperialism to which he invites our attention. The speeches in question are: of the Corinthians and the Athenians at the first Congress of Sparta; of Pericles, of the Mytileneans at Olympia; of Cleon; of Alcibiades to the Assembly and some part of the speech he made in Sparta; and of Hermocrates and Euphemus at Camarina.

First then we listen to the Corinthians at Sparta denouncing the empire (I 68–71), and then to the Athenians justifying it (I 75–78). The Corinthians, we notice, are almost as bitter in blaming Sparta as in denouncing Athens: it is Sparta who allowed the Athenians to fortify their city after the Persian War, and since then has persistently failed to help those who were being subjugated by Athens. (The account given in I 90–92 of the rebuilding of the walls goes some way toward meeting the former accusation.) They contrast the restless, ambitious, energetic, daring character of the Athenians with the slowness and passivity of Sparta. In similar vein they conclude their speech at the second Congress by saying (I 124,3): "We should realise that this tyrant-city which has been established in Greece has been established against all alike; some she has subdued already, others she is planning to subdue. We must defend our own liberties, and rescue those who have lost theirs already."

What the Athenians say in their reply deserves close attention. They insist, at some length, on the entirely blameless origin of the empire. With due apology they explain that it was chiefly the heroism, daring, and intelligence of Athens that saved Greece from the barbarian—and we may interpose that this, surely, is a fair reply to the mean-spirited assertion of the Corinthians that the Persians failed mainly because of their own mistakes. They speak of Themistocles, what he did for the Hellenic cause, and what honours were paid him in Sparta.

They take it ill that such outstanding services to Greece should be repaid now with such bitter hostility. They point out that they did not get their empire by force: the Spartans withdrew from the war of liberation, and members of the League begged (δεηθέντων) Athens to assume the leadership. (Writing in his own name, Thucydides later records what perhaps the Athenians were too tactful to say, that as leader Pausanias was intolerable: I 130,2). What then converted a joint patriotic enterprise into an empire? The Athenians are quite clear about it—and entirely innocent: it was the situation itself that compelled them to increase their power: fear of Persia to begin with, then their own τιμή and ὠφελία, national pride and self-interest. Then, they say, Sparta herself became unfriendly and the allies hostile; now, οὐκ ἀσφαλὲς ἔτι ἐδόκει ἀνέντας κινδυνεύειν: "it did not now seem safe to take the risk of letting go". They continue: "We have done nothing out of the ordinary, nothing unnatural: οὐδὲν θαυμαστὸν οὐδ' ἀπὸ τοῦ ἀνθρωπείου τρόπου. We were driven on, κατηναγκάσθημεν, by three of the most powerful motives, δέος, τιμή, ὠφελία: fear, national pride, self-interest. Any city would have done the same, for it is an admitted principle that the strong dominate the weak, and it is universally allowed, πᾶσι ἀνεπίφθονον, that when a state is in danger, it does what is necessary for its security. You Spartans would have done worse than we have, for we have used our power with moderation and liberality."—Since the use of the word κατηναγκάσθημεν, "compelled", has suggested to some that Thucydides held a mechanistic theory of politics, I place on record here a wise remark made to me by one of my early teachers: "A diplomat never 'does' anything; he is always 'compelled to do' it".

And what are we to say of the Athenian speech? That it is Thucydides' defence of Athenian imperialism? That surely would be a little naïve: it is an explanation of the "tyranny" which, on his own statement, was almost universally hated. We can say of it that it is all true—allowing for diplomatic blandness—and all irrelevant: it may be true that any other city would have done the same, and most of them worse, but Thucydides was not such a simpleton as to accept that because Athens had nobly defended Greek liberties in the past, and had become a tyrant-city in what this delegation calls a perfectly normal way, she should now be exempt from the hatred that tyrants normally incur. Sthenelaidas hits this argument on the head with a very blunt instrument when he says that if they were good then and are bad now they should pay double. In the sequence that Thucydides puts before us here—outstanding services to Greece, the grateful recognition of them, preëminence, ambition, self-interest, and fear—there is something vaguely familiar to those who have the advantage of having read *Macbeth.* Perhaps Thucydides read Shakespeare at school when he ought to have been doing Economic History. Another interesting point: it is not mentioned in the speech that in Athens there had been considerable opposition to this imperialist policy.—But then, the Athenians would have had no reason to speak of this in Sparta; no doubt Thucydides will discuss it in its natural place, the *Pentecontaetia.*

But he does not. He tells us, about the allies, what reasons they had for disliking the leadership of Athens more and more, and that they were themselves to blame for the position into which they sank: they were willing to pay tribute rather then render military service to the League (I 99); but of the opposition there was in Athens to at least the extreme imperialism of Pericles, he gives no hint at all. That is to say, once again as always he is quite indifferent to internal politics.

Faced by this refusal of his to tell us what is really important, we may of course blow off steam by telling him what we think of such dereliction of duty, but that will not help us to understand him. Why is he so obstructive? In another branch of scholarship the principle is respected: explain an author from himself. Therefore, before we construct a brilliant explanation from outside the *History*—that, for example, Olorus had carefully kept from his son Thucydides all knowledge of Cimon and of his namesake Thucydides son of Melesias, the opponent of Pericles, doing this for reasons which undoubtedly could be found if we were to look for them—let us consider an explanation deduced from the *History* itself. He regularly speaks of "the Athenians", "the Mytileneans", "the Corinthians", except in cases where dissension reached the pitch of civil war. We know, because he has told us, how he thought about the whole war: such sufferings, παθήματα, had never happened before. But take the Sicilian War, as a conspicuous instance: who chiefly suffered there? Obviously, the Athenians. Why did they suffer? Obviously, because "the Athenians", in Assembly, decided to invade Sicily, and were defeated. The decision had been opposed; Thucydides tells us (for once) that Nicias had spoken strongly against it; but the decision, once taken, was the decision of the Athenians, and with the decision the Athenians had to take the consequences too. In general, Thucydides takes this as his ἀρχή, his starting-point: what this or that city did. Of course he might have started further back; he might have explained, to the best of his knowledge, the reasons for which one view had come to prevail over its rival; but Thucydides was a Hellenic writer. Euripides, in the *Medea*, might have begun further back and written a fascinating scene showing how Jason bargained with Creon about marrying Creon's daughter; but then, Euripides knew what he wanted to say, and he knew that such a scene would only have obscured it. Thucydides also knew what he wanted to say. We may regret that he did not habitually begin further back, but his reason was not unintelligent. For some purposes his notebooks would have been more helpful to us than his *History*—but for others, not.

It is not indeed Thucydides who tells us that the argument used by the Athenians at Sparta was irrelevant, but if we look again at our list of speeches that deal with the Empire we notice this fact: some are made by Athenians, some by the enemy, one and only one by a subject ally, namely the Olympia speech, first part. This, as it happens, goes over the same ground. The Mytileneans also begin with the glory of Salamis and the common enthusiasm of the joint liberators; but as the Athenians in Sparta pleaded fear and self-interest in explanation of their aggression, so do the Mytileneans plead the same in explanation of their revolt. They tell the Peloponnesians assembled at Olympia that so long as Athens was leading independent allies against Persia, Mytilene followed her willingly, but when she began subduing other Greek cities, "we became afraid", *οὐκ ἀδεεῖς ἔτι ἦμεν*. It was clear, they say, that the alliance was a sham, that they were being left independent partly because they were among the most powerful and would naturally be left to the last, partly because their independence was a specious advertisement of Athenian moderation. But their own turn would assuredly come, for with the increase of Athenian power, the very existence of independent allies was bound to become increasingly irksome to Athens.

Both Pindar (*Pythians*, III 20) and Nicias (VI 13,1), seriously warn us not to be *δυσέρωτες τῶν ἀπόντων*, not to indulge in a fatal passion for what we do not have. If accordingly we contemplate what Thucydides actually wrote instead of exhausting our attention on what he left out, it seems clear how he was thinking. These two speeches cover the same ground, but from opposite points of view; they are parallel. If it was "natural", *οὐκ ἀπὸ τοῦ ἀνθρωπείου τρόπου*, for Athens, partly out of fear, to convert a voluntary League into an Empire; if it is "unobjectionable", *πᾶσι ἀνεπίφθονον*, for a state to protect its interests, then it was no less natural and unobjectionable for Mytilene to forestall, if she could, the subjection that she reasonably feared, by revolting when the chance came, and by prudently choosing the moment when revolt would be most perilous to Athens and most likely to succeed. Cleon's rage is answered in advance. And, talking of fear, Thucydides twice gives his opinion that it was fear of the growing power of Athens that chiefly impelled Sparta to declare war (I 23,6; I 88).

Now we may consider what is said or implied about the Empire by Pericles, Cleon, and Diodotus.

Thucydides' admiration for Pericles was evidently as great

as his lack of admiration for Cleon; this is the reason why he has been called the splendid apologist for Periclean imperialism. But we must distinguish. Our text first offers us the remark made by Pericles at II 13,2: "We must keep the allies firmly in hand": τὰ τῶν ξυμμάχων διὰ χειρὸς ἔχειν. He is discussing the conduct of the coming war; no particular comment seems called for, except perhaps the negative one that Pericles does not say anything about the prospect of loyal support from the allies—naturally, since in his third speech he tells the Athenians:

> You cannot enjoy the pride and privileges of empire without also accepting its burdens. Do not imagine that only one thing is at stake, independence or subjection: there is also loss of empire, and the dangers arising from the resentment that empire has created. You cannot give it up, even if at this crisis fear and the desire for a quiet life commend it. By this time you are holding it like a tyranny, which it is thought wrong to seize but dangerous to let go. . . . A state which dares to rule over others is bound to cause offence and incur hatred. (II 63, 1–2; 64,5)

Cleon says:

> You are forgetting that the empire you hold is a tyranny; your subjects resent it, and are always plotting against you. No favours you can do them, to your hurt, will win their compliance; you will maintain your position not through their good will but only through strength. . . . If their revolt was right (ὀρθῶς), you have no business to be ruling them. (III 37,2; 40,4)

What is the difference, here, between the two men? So far as I can see, none at all. Each accepts that the empire is hated by the subject-allies, that like a tyranny it has no foundation except force, and that now Athens dare not let go—as the Athenians had said at Sparta. Cleon does indeed not say it in so many words, but it is implicit throughout his speech, especially when he says (c. 40,4): "If all the same, though it is not right (οὐ προσῆκον), you are determined to rule, then you must punish Mytilene even if it is wrong (παρὰ τὸ εἰκός). Otherwise, give up your empire and go in for moral behaviour".

In other respects, of course, the two men are as different as can be. It was suggested earlier that Thucydides designed the total contrast between Cleon's appeal to anger and Pericles' knowledge that anger leads to grave error. As regards empire, perhaps we may say simply that Pericles is a gentleman and Cleon is not. (I speak, naturally, of Thucydides' presentation of them.) Pericles accepts the hatred and the burden as a challenge, even as a tribute to the greatness of Athens, in the spirit of Pindar's remark, addressed to Hieron of Syracuse: *κρεῖσσον οἰκτιρμοῦ φθόνος*, "Better be hated than pitied". "They cannot complain", he says in the Epitaphios, "that they have unworthy masters" (II 41,3). In his third speech he says, in effect: "Of course it won't last; nothing does. But our achievements and power will never be forgotten" (II 64,3). Cleon has no sense of the glory, but sees nothing but naked domination; Pericles' idea of domination was at least well dressed. There is a measure of truth in his suggestion that the allies have something to put in place of what they have lost; they, in common with others, can freely share in what Athens has created. But if it is on the strength of the Epitaphios that we deem Thucydides to be the admirer of Periclean imperialism, we are using only part of the evidence: the picture that he has constructed, so far, from three points of view, is one of universal detestation; of an admitted tyranny which Athens now dares not abdicate.

> They have tied me to a stake; I cannot fly,
> But, bear-like, I must fight the course.

The difference between what is said by Macbeth and what is said by Pericles and Cleon is that Athens herself, through fear, national pride, and self-interest, tied herself to the stake. Within the pages of the *History* we never see Pericles in a situation where he has to put into practice the policy of "keeping the allies firmly in hand"; things he had done before the war, such as deporting the whole population of Histiaea, are not mentioned and therefore are no evidence for us to use. That he would have been more intelligent about Mytilene than Cleon is certain (in Thucydides' view); he would have been more like Diodotus. But they all have to accept the situation as it is; Thucydides makes that plain. The empire has become a tyranny, and there is no way out. Diodotus rejects as mere folly Cleon's policy of terrorism; he would rely instead on wise and moderate administration. It is clearly the more hopeful and intelligent view; that is all one can say—except that it did not prevail either at Scione or in Melos.

The next discourse on our list is not a speech but a dialogue. Mr M. I. Finley does not include the Melian Dialogue in his anthology of Thucydides; he calls it "a sophistical little piece". It is; that is the reason why Thucydides wrote it. It is as sophistical as Socrates' short lecture on Simonides' poem, which equally no sensible man would include in an anthology of Plato; standing by itself, neither would make much sense. Each makes its point only when we see it in its full context, and respond as the writer expected.

The Mytileneans had said: "Now that the Athenians had the majority of the allies under their control but were dealing with us on equal terms, they were bound to resent the fact that we were on a level with them when the others had yielded" (III 11,1). In the Dialogue the idea is carried one stage further: now the argument is that Athens, in her own interest, cannot afford to allow the Melians, being islanders, to remain neutrals, even friendly ones. First then it is the independence of an ally that is judged to be a sure cause of resentment; now it is the independence of a neutral that is declared to be a cause of insecurity: *τὸ ἀσφαλὲς ἡμῖν διὰ τὸ καταστραφῆναι ἂν παράσχοιτε*, "your subjection would assure our security" (V 97). "Your friendly neutrality would be taken by our subjects to be a sign of weakness in us" (V 95). The word *ὠφελία* recurs: *ἐπ' ὠφελίᾳ τε πάρεσμεν τῆς ἡμετέρας ἀρχῆς* (c. 91,2): "it is in the interests of our empire that we are here".

But this is not the end of it. At VI 18,3 we find Alcibiades declaring: "We cannot possibly estimate, like a housekeeper, how much empire we shall want. We have reached a point where we must both keep all we have and plan the subjection of others, because we run the risk of being ourselves subjected if we do not subdue." A moment later he is saying that victory in Sicily would enable Athens to rule the whole of Greece, and even Carthage is only just over his horizon.

But Alcibiades was just a brilliant but reckless young man? Certainly, but "the Athenians" did choose to follow him rather than the more cautious Nicias, and they had to take the consequences—just as the Trojans, in the *Agamemnon*, had to pay the price for welcoming and not rejecting the bride whom Paris brought home. But in fact Thucydides does not leave us with the impression that the Athenians were stampeded by a reckless young man: he writes a chapter (VI 24) in which he describes their own rosy hopes; and there is still the speech made at Camarina by Euphemus. Hermocrates has gone over familiar ground:

The Ionians and others joined Athens willingly for the sake of taking revenge on Persia, but Athens used any plausible excuse for subduing them to herself; her aim was simply to substitute her own domination for Persia's—and her own rule was worse. Now they are trying by the same means to create a similar empire in the west. Are we Sicilian cities to wait while she takes us over one by one? If you hold aloof because you are jealous and suspicious of Syracuse, you will soon have reason to be sorry for it.

Euphemus answers him. He too begins with the Persian war: this is becoming monotonous. He makes a notably ungenerous reference to the Ionians: they had helped Persia to enslave Greece. His justification for the empire is, first, that by taking it Athens was enabled to secure balance of power with Sparta; second, that the Ionians deserved what they got, and Athens had done more than anyone else to secure Greek liberties; "therefore we deserve our empire" (c. 83,1). We recall, perhaps, the rather different grounds on which Pericles based his assertion that "we deserve to rule". Euphemus goes on (c. VI 83):

It is universally allowed, πᾶσι ἀνεπίφθονον, that a state may secure its own safety. We are here for our own security, and your interests coincide with ours . . . It is from fear, δέος, that we hold our empire there, and from fear that we have come to Sicily; not to subdue anyone, but to prevent anyone from being subdued. . . . We are in Sicily for the sake of our own safety.

We should not say here either, I think, that the spirit of Athens was coarsening. In other ways, yes: Cleon advocated massacre; Pericles, before the war, has been content to confiscate and deport. What Thucydides appears to be suggesting is that empire, from its very nature, can recognise no limits: δέος, τιμή, ὠφελία, fear, prestige, self-interest (or self-help) are still at work; it is impossible to stop, impossible μὴ μειζόνων ὀρέγεσθαι—at least, for such people as the Athenians. He is not exactly condemning Athenian imperialism, certainly not defending it; he is merely explaining what it was, and what were its results—to Athens, as well as to others.

There are two other points to notice in the Camarina debate. Hermocrates appealed for a united front against the invader; Camarina in fact decided to remain neutral. The reason is apparent: Sicily was not united, and Camarina had to decide which would be the worse for her, the victory of Athens, or of Syracuse. The second point is that Euphemus assumes throughout that a cynical self-interest is the only reasonable policy. Before we assume that this is Thucydides' own hard-boiled political philosophy we should remember what is the background of the whole *History:* widespread catastrophe. We should also read what Euphemus actually says (c. 85,1): "Whether in an individual tyrant or in an imperial city, nothing is illogical that is advantageous, and the tie of kinship is nothing unless it can be relied on": ἀνδρὶ τυράννῳ ἢ πόλει ἀρχὴν ἐχούσῃ οὐδὲν ἄλογον ὅτι ξυμφέρον οὐδ' οἰκεῖον ὅτι μὴ πιστόν. It is Euphemus who is hard-boiled: he takes it for granted that an imperial city will behave just like an individual tyrant. We may remind ourselves that Greece had a traditional way of dealing with tyrants. And as for the fear and self-interest which, he alleges, had brought Athens to Sicily, Camarina too considers her self-interest: she remained neutral until she deemed it in her interest to go to the help of the winning side and join Syracuse in the total destruction of the invaders, who had come to Sicily fearing for their security.—We have already asked if Thucydides was capable of a certain grave irony.

This then is what Thucydides has to say, whether directly or "dramatically", about the empire and imperialism, and unless by inadvertence I have overlooked something, he says nothing else. It is true that he is remarkably unforthcoming with information about the way in which Athens managed the empire, but is it really "une figure tronquée"? Is it incomplete? Surely not incomplete; merely unexpected. We ask him our own questions; he is answering his.

We passed over the Melian Dialogue rather lightly. It is indeed a well-worn topic, but not for that reason can an investigation of Thucydides' *poiesis* afford to neglect it.

"Let us have a quiet talk", say the Athenians. "Certainly", say the Melians, "though evidently you have decided already what you are going to do with us"—this being just what the wretched Plataeans had said to the Spartan commissioners (III 53,4).—"Never mind the future: the question is, are you willing to consider the facts of the case, what is before your eyes? (ἐκ τῶν παρόντων καὶ ὧν ὁρᾶτε). We shall make no pretences. As you know, there is no such thing as Justice, except that the strong use their strength, and the weak have to put up with it. Therefore, limit yourselves to τὰ δυνατά, what is possible."—"But there is such a thing as fair dealing. If you abolish it, you may have to pay dearly for it some time, if you run into trouble."—"We are not afraid of *that*. Anyhow, it is our own subjects we fear, not Sparta. One ruling city does not destroy another. Now, we must subjugate you, for two reasons: you would be profitable to us, and we cannot afford to leave you independent any longer, because our subjects take your independence as a sign of our weakness. That we cannot afford; our security demands your subjection."—"But you would only be strengthening the resistance of your enemies."—"The only enemies we fear are our own subjects. And, by the way, do not be misled by false ideas about honour and self-respect; this is no fair fight."—"But do not be too sure; sometimes the luck of war evens things out."—"Hope! An expensive luxury! Do not rely on hope. And as for the gods you mention, experience shows that they are on the side of the big battalions. Do be sensible."

When the Melians have refused to submit, the Athenians say: "What a remarkable people you are! You seem to find what is in the future much clearer than what is before your eyes; what is invisible you already treat as established fact—because it accords with your wishes. You stake everything; you entrust everything to Sparta, luck, and hope. Therefore you will lose everything"—as indeed they did.

A sophistical piece indeed, and if we suppose that Thucydides did not really compose but merely wrote up what was in his notebooks, adding bits like this from time to time, there is no more to be said, except to wonder why he did it, and to point out perhaps that it shows how deeply influenced he was by the new Sophistic. It is, he makes them say, in the nature of things for the strong to dominate the weak; the gods do the same. Foolish of the Melians to trust to Hope, to take any account of the uncertain fortunes of war. Absurd to shut one's eyes to present realities, not to look facts in the face.

"In the same winter the Athenians became eager to subdue Sicily, if they could, with a bigger force than they had sent before, though most of them had no idea how big and populous the island was." Surely the confident sophistry of "the Athenians" in Melos goes ill with such ignorance? Thucydides records that the city of Egesta, desiring Athenian help, deluded the Athenians about their own wealth. The envoys returned with a wonderful report: "It was enticing, but untrue", he says. Nicias put before them, soberly, τὰ πάροντα, "the facts of the situation"; Alcibiades held out other prospects. "These Sicilians, rootless people with no patriotism, torn by faction, will easily be persuaded to welcome Athens. Our navy will guarantee the safety of the army; we shall have the utmost freedom of action, to stay and conquer or to come home, just as we choose." Thereafter we read how city after city closed its gates to them, and how, some eighteen months later, Nicias had to send home his despairing report: "Our ships are rotting, the crews are deserting, many of us are sick; we are not the besiegers now, but the besieged".

Nicias had begged them to safeguard what they had already, *τὰ ὑπάρχοντα σώζειν*; not to incur danger for what was out of sight and in the future, *περὶ τῶν ἀφανῶν καὶ μελλόντων κινδυνεύειν* (c. 9,3); not to be *δυσέρωτας τῶν ἀπόντων*, "to indulge in a fatal passion for what is somewhere else". The language given him by Thucydides is no distant echo of what Thucydides gave to "the Athenians" in Melos. But the Athenians preferred to listen to Alcibiades. "A wild enthusiasm for the expedition came over all", *ἔρως ἐκπλεῦσαι*; and he writes the chapter on the various hopes that were entertained by all classes in Athens. Hoping still to discourage them Nicias proposed an enormous force; the effect was the opposite of what he intended: with a force like that, they thought, nothing could go wrong. Hope did indeed prove to be an expensive luxury.

Thucydides did not much go in for descriptive writing, but he did write a brilliant description of the fleet that assembled in the Piraeus, so impressive, so costly: how the captains poured out from goblets of gold or silver libations to those gods in whom Thucydides himself did not believe; how gaily it raced away as far as Aegina. He tells us that the rowers were paid a drachma a day by the state, and that the captains added more. —Yet with such incomplete figures we are unable to calculate how the expenditure on the fleet compared with the total revenues of the city: because Thucydides had no complete figures and would not guess? I doubt it. Surely he could have got reliable figures from somebody, had he wanted them. He was not thinking of finance, but like this: "It did not look so much like an expeditionary force as like a demonstration of the power and greatness of Athens, and an expression of the most far-reaching hopes". The fleet was carrying with it the pride, the power, and much of the wealth of Athens; that is what was filling the mind of Thucydides, not the precise cost of the expedition. It may be the wrong way in which to write history, but it is the way in which Thucydides thought and wrote it.

At this point we may recall what was said earlier about Athenian naval skill. We extracted all the references made to it in the *History* and set them side-by-side. The last one was: "Their success has betrayed them". What may have seemed improbable then may seem less improbable now that we have set it in its full context. They came, in all their might, to conquer, believing among other things that in this conquest lay their security: they lost all. How did it happen? How did everything go wrong?

Well, who would have expected that the sinister affair of the Hermae should crop up just at this moment; that the brilliant Alcibiades should be implicated; that the Athenians should have the folly to let him sail, one of the commanders, under such a charge, and then recall him for trial; that he should instead desert to Sparta; that the Italian and Sicilian cities would cold-shoulder the Athenian forces so markedly; that the commanders would prove so irresolute; that, with Alcibiades recalled, Lamachus would get himself killed in a skirmish, so that the sole command would devolve on the one most unfitted for it, and that he should fall sick? In one detail Thucydides decidedly does not write like a dramatist: no dramatist would dare invent an eclipse of the moon to crown his catastrophe.

Bad luck? Yes indeed—but then, Thucydides is continually talking about *τὸ ἀσαφὲς τοῦ μέλλοντος*, "the uncertainty of the future", and the need for taking it into one's calculations. At the very outset, I 120,4–5, the Corinthians, irrelevantly, were speaking of the dangers of overconfidence and the risk that the best plans may go astray; more recently the Melians have remarked that sometimes the luck of war evens things out. The hard and confident sophists in Melos were strangely ignorant of some elementary facts; they were building a castle on the sands, and their castle fell down, not in Melos but in Sicily. They were not afraid of retribution from Sparta: it was the anger of the Syracusans that left so many of them to die horribly in the quarries. Thucydides, we are told, was far too modern and intelligent to believe in the gods. Quite so; the difference seems hardly worth talking about.

The story of the Golden Calf seems reasonably apposite here. Moses, descending from Sinai, found the people dancing before a golden calf, "and Moses' anger waxed hot" (Exodus 32:19 ff.). Aaron explained that the people had demanded a new god and had brought their gold to him; "Then I cast it into the fire, and there came out this calf". Marvellous! But Aaron was not telling the truth; the image did not come by chance, even by "divine chance". Earlier in the same chapter we read how Aaron had received the gold "and fashioned it with a graving tool after he had made it a molten calf". We ourselves have been following a long story that begins at Salamis and ends, for the moment, in Sicily: it would be simple-minded to say, of its denouement, "There came out this calf". Someone has done some melting, and has used the graving tool on it. The present writer disclaims all credit, and in support of the disclaimer quotes VII 75,6–7:

Now there was no food left in the camp. Besides this, there was all the degradation. The fact that all were suffering alike—though there is some comfort in the knowledge that one is not alone, but many others are in the same evil case—not even this made it seem easier to bear, especially when they thought of the brilliance and pride of their setting out, and of the humiliation of their ending. This was much the greatest reverse that had ever befallen a Greek army: they had come to enslave others, the end was retreat and the fear that enslavement rather would be their own fate; they had sailed out amid prayers and hymns for victory, they were leaving amid words that spoke only of doom; sailors then, men on foot now, not rowing ships, but bearing heavy armour. Yet all this seemed bearable in comparison with the dangers that still threatened.

"Their success had betrayed them." The great difference between tragedy and pathos is that tragedy links the suffering with its causes. That Thucydides has done.

There remains another big section of the *History* that might repay scrutiny, namely IV–V 25, but as this will involve Thucydides' notorious habit of generalising, we will consider that first.

We all generalise upon occasion, but Thucydides is always doing it. Is it only a habit, or can it be that some of his apparent platitudes are not quite so spasmodic as one might think? Clearly we must distinguish. Phormio, just before the second battle in the Gulf, says to his dispirited men: "When an enemy attacks with superiority in numbers, as ours is doing, he is trusting to his strength rather than to his judgment, but when the inferior force fights though under no compulsion, it is being courageous because it is placing great reliance on its intelligence" (II 89,6). We understand what Thucydides is doing; he is not generalising from force of habit, but putting into Phormio's mouth the kind of reassuring sophism that a commander in his unpromising situation might well make, especially among a race of men who, like the Greeks, did not at once go giddy when confronted with a general idea. Many of the generalisations are of this kind, quite natural in their context—and even here, we might reflect, it was in fact the quick intelligence of an Athenian captain that turned defeat into victory.

But take a different case. The speech attributed to the Corinthians at the second Congress of Sparta is in all respects a perfectly natural one, except that in the middle of it (I 120,3–5) there is a stream of generalisations to this effect: Wise men avoid war if they can, though if they are men of spirit they will fight rather than accept injury; yet they will be willing to make peace again εὖ παράσχον, "when a good opportunity comes".

Success in war will not make them overconfident, nor on the other hand will they put up with aggression for the sake of the charms of peace, knowing that they would lose them for good. The man who presumes upon his successes during a war is foolish. Many a bad plan has succeeded in war, and many a good one has failed; it is easier to make a good plan than to carry it out, because the carrying out is beset with anxiety.

Did the Corinthians say all these things? That is a question we cannot answer. All we can know is that Thucydides wrote them into the speech, and similar ones into other speeches. Why? When they have a direct bearing on the matter in hand, no question arises, of course; those enunciated by the Corinthians have none, but could occur with as much reason in any war-speech. Is it simply a rhetorical habit with Thucydides, or is it possible that these very general observations are a small but purposeful part of his *poiesis?*

As it happens, there is a fairly large group of them that revolve around the same idea, the uncertainty of the future. One speaker after another mentions τὸ ἀσαφές, τὸ ἀστάθμητον, τοῦ μέλλοντος, the obscurity, unpredictability, of the future. With them go, naturally, remarks about the predominating influence of chance, τύχη, or τύχαι, circumstances. To transcribe all of them would be tedious; those I have noted are: I 75,1 (the Athenians on the uncertainty of war); I 84,3 (Archidamus on the same); I 140,1 (Pericles); II 11,4 (Archidamus to his troops); III 42,2 (Diodotus); III 59,1 (the Plataeans); IV 17,5 and 18 (the Spartans in Athens); IV 62,4 and 64,1 (Hermocrates at the Sicilian Congress); V 102 (the Melians); VI 23,3 (Nicias to the Assembly); VI 78,3 (Hermocrates at Camarina). "You never can tell what will happen; chance has the last word": that is the constantly repeated idea—not original, not specially brilliant.

Another fact is just as obvious: in his narrative Thucydides appears never to miss an opportunity of emphasising the unexpected, accidental, even paradoxical way in which events will fall out. The great example is the plague; another is the way in which he handles the Pylos episode, about which many have said that he goes too far in ascribing the turn of events to chance—a criticism that can probably be sustained even without committing the error made by some commentators, that of supposing that the Greek verb ἔτυχε is always translatable by "it chanced that". It is here that he pauses to make a direct comment of his own (IV 12,3), that things had taken a very surprising turn when Athenians, fighters by sea, were fighting with Spartans, landsmen; and the Athenians, on land, and Spartan land at that, were seeking to repel a sea-borne attack of the Spartans. The incident obviously struck deep into his mind.

It is at this point that we may return to our unnamed traveller to Mytilene, whom we have left languishing for so long. Thucydides was bound to mention that the Athenian plan miscarried, yet he might so naturally have written: "The Athenians decided to attack the city on a day of festival, hoping that everyone would be outside the town and they might capture it easily; but the Mytileneans, having received a warning, remained on guard". What he was not bound to do, and what is hardly in his usual manner, is to tell the story of the messenger of whom Gomme well says that he was active as well as fortunate—fortunate because, as it happened, he found at Geraestus a ship just on the point of sailing to Lesbos. Clearly, what impressed Thucydides here was not merely that the plan miscarried, but also the quite unpredictable way in which this happened.

Now, it would be possible but obviously foolish to erect upon all this a theory that Thucydides believed human affairs to be determined entirely or largely by chance—foolish, because of the passages listed above not a few are cast in the form: since this is true, one should act accordingly. The emphasis falls not so much on the obvious fact as on the inferences to be drawn from it. About Pericles, before the outbreak of the war and after the plague, enough was said in a previous chapter; let us take instead Hermocrates, clearly a wise man, in Thucydides' estimation. He says that it is the unpredictable that always has the last word, and goes on: "Just as we are most frequently deceived by it, so too can it be of the greatest possible use to us; for if we all fear it alike, we shall think twice before we attack each other" (Rex Warner's translation). Many a time, he says, a city has attacked in order to avenge an injury, and has been destroyed, or has made war in the hope of gain and has suffered loss instead. The conclusion he draws is that it is prudent to compromise, to be content with less than you think you should have, not to be too eager to avenge a wrong. That is to say, we find scattered through the speeches a dozen or more observations about chance and the obscurity of the future; in the narrative too we find a distinct tendency to emphasise the occurrence of the unforeseeable. There are also the remarks that Thucydides quotes from Pericles and Hermocrates, to indicate that Thucydides did not simply stand and gape at this not very recondite element in human affairs.

We may go a little further. There are other generalisations of no very distant kinship with these: "We are neither made arrogant, *ἐξυβρίζομεν*, by success, nor are we so cast down by failure as other people are" (I 84,2: Archidamus). "Those are strongest, who meet disaster with the least despondency and most resilience" (II 64,6: Pericles). "We are as strong as ever; we simply made a mistake, which can happen to anyone. Therefore you should not think that your present run of success is bound to continue" (IV 18,2–4: the Spartans in Athens). "Success is attained not by wishing for it but by being prudent" (VI 13,1: Nicias to the Assembly), to which Alcibiades makes answer that success comes to a city if it does not remain inactive but follows its own bent (VI 18,1)—which, according to Thucydides, Athens did, on this occasion, though not with much success.

Looking then at this group of generalisations we find a steady preoccupation with one side of human experience: uncertainty, and the folly of over-confidence or of a too easy despair. Thucydides might have written a short essay on the theme; instead, in his usual way, he brings it before our minds dramatically, sometimes in close connexion with the surrounding narrative, sometimes not; but in either case the observations, I suggest, were intended to have a general if not also a particular reference. They are not a rather tiresome series of *dicta* repeated by nearly every speaker in the *History*, as if nobody in Greece at this time could make a political speech without observing that the future is obscure, or as if Thucydides himself thought no speech complete without its due admixture of maxims. Rather, they resemble outcrops of rock which indicate the presence, below the surface, of a continuous stratum; they are part of what Thucydides himself is thinking, and an indication of how he would have his reader think.

It was remarked by the Corinthian delegates with whom this little disquisition began: "The wise man avoids war if he can, and makes peace again when the right time comes". The remark was no indispensable part of his argument, and has no discernible reference to anything that the Corinthians or the Peloponnesians have done or will do; but it is, I suggest, an idea that Thucydides thought or found relevant to this part of his book, where we are on the brink of a long war. If we reflect: "Then how few states are wise! How hard it is to see when the right time *has* come!"—then, I think, we are reading our author as he intended; and it will be neither surprising nor inappropriate if our thoughts turn, for instance, to what the Athenians did after Pylos: "The wise man, knowing how deceptive can be a run of success in a war, will not become excited nor overconfident". Again, we hear nothing about overconfidence and excitement on the Peloponnesian side—but there are two sides in every war (and three sides in some). "Bad plans sometimes succeed and good ones fail, through anxiety": I hesitate to suggest that Thucydides did not write this into his drafts until Brasidas' raid on the Piraeus had been attempted and abandoned; however, it is a case in point. I do suggest that he inserted such remarks not out of platitudinous habit but as a means, a characteristic one, of bringing to the surface considerations that he thought important.

Now, of all the generalisations in which he indulges, the one that seems to have puzzled commentators most is precisely the one which, from this point of view, is among the most effective and illuminating. Cleon is made to say, in the middle of his speech (III 39,3–4) with reference to Mytilene: "They looked at the future in a bold way, entertained hopes that were beyond their strength, although less than their desires . . . A city that suddenly meets with great and unexpected success often inclines toward hybris. For the most part, success that comes *κατὰ λόγον* is more lasting than one that comes *παρὰ δόξαν*, unexpectedly." The phrase *κατὰ λόγον* is commonly taken here to mean "moderate", "reasonable"; however, an established meaning of *λόγος* is "proportion", "ratio", implying two terms of comparison; therefore it seems possible that Cleon, or Thucydides, is thinking of success which comes out of proportion—to what? Out of proportion to what was planned; so to speak, a gift from the gods. It seems possible, though I do not insist on it. But what *εὐπραγία*, "success", "run of good fortune", had come to Mytilene? None that is known to us, and some commentators are worried. On the sentence about hybris Gomme comments: "Doubtless true, but not strictly relevant here; for the only thing unexpected about Mytilene's good fortune was the ill-fortune of Athens (the plague). It is another instance of the love of generalisation making its way into a speech . . . The further explanation of this wisdom [*viz.*, 'Success that comes . . .'] does not improve it".

Thucydides would surely not have used the word *εὐπραγία* of the opportunity which the plague offered to Mytilene, nor of course does Gomme suggest it. But he asked himself the question: "What is the immediate relevance of the generalisation?" Finding none, he concludes that Thucydides is only indulging his well-known habit. We have begun to suspect, however, that some of his generalisations have a general rather than an immediate relevance. Using that assumption let us put the question differently: "Great and unexpected success did not come, so far as we know, to Mytilene, certainly not between the covers of the *History;* did it however come to some other city with which we are concerned?" To this question the answer is automatic: to Athens, very soon, at Pylos—especially (perhaps) as the affair is handled by Thucydides. Let us then look into the matter; not as students of history, trying to make out what happened, and why, but as students of literature and of Thucydides, trying to understand what he wrote.

The Athenian fleet was bound first for Corcyra, then for Sicily; this was the plan. The seizure of Pylos, in Thucydides' account, was quite incidental; the fleet would never have called there but for the storm. It was a bit of opportunism which had astonishing results, entirely παρὰ δόξαν. Its outcome—dismay in Sparta and offers of peace—was certainly δι' ἐλαχίστου ἀπροσδόκητος εὐπραγία, "sudden and unexpected success", and it was a success out of proportion to anything that had been designed or hoped for when (as Thucydides records) Demosthenes, though having no official command, had been given leave "to make use of the fleet, if he wished, against the Peloponnesian coasts" (IV 2,4). The Spartans made proposals of peace: Thucydides does not merely record the fact, as he does when the Athenians tried to make a peace after the plague, but—as if warmly approving of our present line of argument—writes for them a philosophic kind of speech, even prefacing it with a sort of dramatic apology; for as Euripides makes his chorus in the *Medea* begin a mildly ruminative passage (vv. 1081 ff.) by saying: "Of course we are women, but even women, you know, can sometimes talk sense", so the Spartan delegates are made to begin by saying: "It is certainly not our Spartan way to be verbose, but we can be quite articulate when the occasion demands it".

What they say can be described as an extended commentary on the dictum that wise men make peace again when the right moment comes. Their argument is that this is the right time:

the situation has taken a sudden turn very much in favour of Athens, and it would be wise for them to take advantage of the fact, in the knowledge that it will probably change again: "Cities which have had most experience of ups and downs have the best reason to be mistrustful of a run of success (*εὐπραγίαι*), and not to do what most people are foolish enough to do, namely hope for more, and try to get too much (*τοῦ πλέονος ὀρέγονται*), because they have had an unexpected stroke of fortune" (IV 17,4–5). Now is the time to negotiate a peace and to relieve Greece from the miseries of the war (c. 20,2) rather than press on in the hope of dictating a one-sided peace which would leave behind it lasting hatred.

A reasonable historian would have said something here about the terms of peace which Sparta may have had in mind. It is true that matters never reached that point at all, thanks to Cleon; that Thucydides had a rooted objection to guessing, that therefore he could say nothing on that score. This triumphantly explains why he is completely silent about that; it does not however explain why, in these circumstances, he wrote a speech at all. We can understand his silence about that; what we have also to understand is his comparative loquacity about other matters.

So far we have said only what has often been said before. Everyone, I imagine, agrees that in writing this speech Thucydides, in effect, and in his usual manner, is conveying his own reflections on the situation. The Spartans may well have spoken in this vein; if they did not, Thucydides (I think) would have written the speech none the less: it contains *τὰ δέοντα* (I 22,1), "what the situation required".

The narrative continues. Cleon persuades the Athenians to counter the Spartan advances with extravagant demands, including (as Thucydides points out) the cession of territory which Athens had lost before the war began. The Athenians assumed that the Spartans beleagured on Sphacteria could be captured at any moment; therefore "they wanted more" (c. 21,2). Then comes the check on Sphacteria: Cleon denounces the generals, has the command forced on him, and promises to kill or capture the Spartans within twenty days—"a mad promise", says Thucydides; and we should note that he does not say it until he has recorded the fact that the promise was fulfilled (c. 39,3). Then he comments on the immense impression made on the Greeks by the surrender of a Spartan army, and on the corresponding dismay felt in Sparta. He mentions that renewed proposals of peace were made and rejected, and explains that the Athenians "were eager for more", *μειζόνων ὠρέγοντο* (c. 41,4).

There follows at once another Athenian success, against Corinth; then, the next summer, an even greater one, for they captured the off-shore island of Cythera. We are given a vivid picture of the demoralisation that was now paralysing Sparta. Aeginetan prisoners are taken and killed; then comes the pacification in Sicily and the return of the Athenian forces; and Thucydides notes that of the three commanders, two were exiled and one fined, on the charge that they might have conquered the island but had been bribed to withdraw. Then he writes:

> Their present run of good fortune made them believe that nothing could stand in their way, but that they could achieve with equal ease what was possible and what was rather unlikely, whether the forces employed were great or quite inadequate. The reason was the unexpected [? disproportionate] success which had been attending most of their operations, *ἡ παρὰ λόγον εὐπραγία*. This made them think that hope and power were the same thing. (65,4)

Now come the Megarian affair (something of a failure); the double disaster discussed already—the loss of an army in Boeotia and the undermining of the whole position in the north; and finally, the loss of Amphipolis. It is before Amphipolis that we meet Cleon again, and for the last time. Thucydides, whether fairly or not, represents him as being entirely confident of his ability to recapture the city—which is more than his troops were, says Thucydides. The first sentence of V 7,3 is neatly rendered by Rex Warner: "He was in the same confident frame of mind that he had been in at Pylos, where his success had convinced him of his intelligence". He was correspondingly careless: "He thought even that he had made a mistake in not bringing down his siege engines with him: the place was undefended, and he might have captured it" (V 7,4). In an hour or so he was dead; so too were those of his men who had not saved themselves by flight.

Very soon (V 14) Thucydides records that Sparta, for various reasons, was inclined to make peace; so too were the Athenians, "after having been smitten at Delium and again, so soon, at Amphipolis". They had lost the hopeful confidence in their strength through which they had rejected offers of peace when they imagined that their run of success would carry them through to final victory, εὖ παράσχον, "although a favourable opportunity had come". "The Athenians" wanted more; what they got was much less: never again was Amphipolis to be an Athenian possession.

We have now followed Thucydides' narrative of this part of the war, from Pylos to Amphipolis: if one felt the need to make some grave comment upon it, would not this do as well as anything?

> They looked at the future in a bold way and entertained hopes that were beyond their strength, although less than their desires. A city that suddenly meets with great and unexpected success often inclines toward hybris. For the most part, success that comes κατὰ λόγον is more lasting than one that comes παρὰ δόξαν.

If we conceive Thucydides capable of that kind of tragic irony which consists in silently comparing the purposes and hopes of men with the results of their actions, then the irony here certainly does not lose from the fact that the above reflection is put into the mouth, or taken from the mouth, of Cleon—whose speech began with the remark: "I have often wondered if a democracy is capable of running an empire".

Perhaps it will seem unlikely that Thucydides should have written, in the middle of Cleon's speech, a paragraph that does not bear fruit until we are in the middle of the next book; but is the alternative any more likely, that he wrote a paragraph that virtually makes no sense at all?—for we have seen that in the judgment of one of his most sensitive commentators the generalisation is a waste of time and the reference to "success", εὐπραγία, unintelligible. Perhaps it will seem only perverse in Thucydides, if he did try to indicate a serious judgment on the later conduct of the Athenians in this dark and indirect way, when he is ostensibly relating something else, namely what happened to Mytilene. But we have seen already that Thucydides *is* perverse, from our point of view. About these two speeches we say, so easily, that their subject is the fate of Mytilene, and we go on to say that Thucydides is preparing his contrast between the ways of democratic Athens and of Sparta; but when we look into them we find that although the fate of Mytilene is of course the point at issue, Thucydides wanders rather far from that point, and that something like one-third of what is said is indeed concerned with the ways of the Athenian democracy, but only to give us a vivid impression of a democracy which, in Thucydides' view, is barely capable of acting responsibly. It seems almost as unlikely that he should have done this, but I see no means of denying that he did it.

It certainly would be perverse in a writer of (I suppose) any later period if he expected his readers, when they came to the paragraph about success and hybris, to refer it, forward, to what the Athenians did after Pylos, but we should reflect that Thucydides did not use what almost at once became, and has remained, the normal method of discourse in prose: exposition, declaration, argument, steady development. (Even Plato, as we have seen, occasionally departs from it, to the extent of saying things without saying them.) Thucydides' predecessor Herodotus never (I think) composed like this—and for an obvious reason: he was composing, originally at least, with a listening audience in mind; but Thucydides makes a point of saying that he himself was not composing an ἀγώνισμα ἐς τὸ παραχρῆμα, a piece for display, but something to be pondered; and in fact the method of composition exemplified in this last instance of ours is essentially what we have been finding time after time. For instance, he obviously understood the elements of the strategic situation: the commanding position that Athens held in virtue of her control of the sea, and her autocratic position with respect to her allies; also the corresponding weaknesses of the other side. Yet never does he set them forth in the expository manner; the reader is to understand it all as he reads and then rereads, by making his own combination of what is said by the speakers with what happens in the narrative.

As we have said before, it is a question of the response that he was expecting from his readers: once again, we have, as it were, to take the audience into consideration. Anyone who writes a book as serious and as difficult as the *History* is clearly inviting his reader to give him close attention, to collaborate with him. Thucydides does not cite his authorities, or only very rarely: this fact alone, in so responsible a writer, should warn us that he was not expecting readers like ourselves. We discussed the point earlier: he was not expecting the kind of collaboration that we give to a serious historian, but a perceptibly different one; perhaps we may call it less purely intellectual and more imaginative, though neither more nor less responsible and serious. I have remarked elsewhere of the Athenian tragic poets that they avoided interesting complexities of character and plot in order, as it were, that the minds of the audience might be left the more free to concentrate on other aspects of the drama; analogously, Thucydides expects that his readers will take the factual accuracy for granted and will collaborate with him elsewhere: in seizing the significance of these to-and-fro references. The *History*, in fact, is much less bald than the casual modern reader would naturally think. Thus, if I may revert to Cleon's remark—significant of Thucydides' method rather than important in itself: if what was suggested above appears far-fetched and unlikely, the reason may be only that we may be responding in the way that is instinctive in us but not expected by Thucydides. If we find ourselves thinking that (*i*) Thucydides was wrong in not citing his authorities and (*ii*) he was wrong here in writing a paragraph that does not make immediate sense, we should consider if, sometimes, two wrongs do not make a right.

At this point a reasonable question suggests itself: what advantage was gained through writing in this to-and-fro manner? Or was he only trying to be difficult? There seems to be a reasonable answer. It has always been seen that the method is dramatic, but "dramatic", in this connexion, means that what is being presented does not merely go into our heads but also gets under our skin. In the first place, we are being invited to work alongside Thucydides, to draw for ourselves the conclusions that he has drawn but does not formally state—as for example in those first sixty-eight chapters of Book III, so rich and clear in implications of all kinds. Our thoughts are directed by him, of course, or he would have been only a compiler, but they become our own thoughts as well as his because he leaves the final act to us. What we do for ourselves makes the deeper impression. In the true sense of the word, his is an aristocratic art, like the Athenian tragic drama and the other arts of the time. In the second place, his method, the "moving curtain", arrests the attention; it gives the shock of immediacy, it puts us on the spot, πρὸ ὀμμάτων ποιεῖ, as Aristotle more staidly says. Time and again, the forces at work are revealed in action, not stated first and then exemplified, nor contrariwise elicited after the event: the silent succession of the Melian Dialogue and the Sicilian War is only one example out of many. Anybody, of course, can use this method of progressive revelation; its power depends on the quality of mind in the writer who does the revealing.

In short, his *poiesis* was indeed a powerful instrument, designed, naturally, to get down on paper *his* view of the war, and his view is different from the one natural to us; hence our occasional though respectful dissatisfaction with his work, and our occasional misapprehensions. A war, as we said at the outset, is like an iceberg: we look, in the *History*, for the substructure that we know must have been there, in the event; and when we do not find it, or find much less of it than we expect, we are at a loss; though indeed there is more of it than some have realised: I was myself taught at school that Thucydides had no understanding of the importance of sea-power. But the substructure is not missing; it is only different from what we expect. We cited the remark of Mme de Romilly, that Thucydides is interested only in the clash, in the conflict, but we have found him interested in much more than that. Yet "*contre-épopée*" is a suggestive idea. The *Iliad* too is full of fighting and slaughter, and Homer recounts it with exactitude; yet he also has his idea of why it happened, and he tells us: so many brave souls went down to death and the dogs devoured their bodies, because of the insensate quarrel that sprang up between Achilles and Agamemnon, and because of resentment which Achilles vowed he would maintain to the bitter end, but found he could not (XVI 60 ff.). The *History* too is full of fighting and slaughter, and Thucydides, in his exact narrative, keeps it steadily before our eyes. But he keeps other things before our minds.

This is no place to attempt a full survey of the under-water part of Thucydides' structure, though one negative point can be made, and some few others by way of short recapitulation.

The negative point is that Thucydides does not set out to interpret the war from some grand theory, whether political or moral or otherwise philosophical. If he deserves the compliment of being called a "scientific historian"—and if indeed that would be a compliment—it is because he starts with the facts, which he investigated with rigour, and because the general ideas that he puts before us arise out of the facts. For him, as he says plainly and we find difficult to believe, the great fact was the catastrophe, the unparalleled παθήματα, the sufferings, so widespread. Why did it happen? Why did the war and its attendant evils rage for so long? The reason why the *History* is so impressive is, I suggest, that Thucydides thinks upon this neither as a political historian nor a military or economic historian nor as a moralist but simply as a "historian", one who tries to find out, an "enquirer"—though he himself is content to use the word συγγράφειν, "compile". He traces the whole catastrophe, not once but repeatedly, from the glory of Salamis and of the Liberation. As we have seen, he speaks of fear, national pride, self-interest; he indicates that at least the first and third of these began to work also against the Athenians, in Mytilene and in Sparta; he also makes it evident that they are all "natural" motives—and of the nature of men he had no comforting convictions. But lest we begin to talk, with equal grandeur and vagueness, about inexorable laws of historical necessity, we should notice the pungent character-sketch of both the Athenians and the Spartans given by the Corinthians at the first Congress of Sparta—this given not idly; for things would have fallen out differently had not the Athenians been like this and the Spartans like that: the former exceptionally active and ambitious, the latter exceptionally inert and exceptionally bad leaders of any voluntary alliance. The allies too were at fault (he says) in consenting to pay tribute instead of rendering military service. He is not applying a theory but studying the particular case, though believing indeed that the particular partook of the universal to the extent that much the same thing is likely to recur.

All these conditions being given, it was natural that Athens should become a tyrant-city, that her rule should be generally detested, that Sparta should be convinced, sooner or later, that it must be ended, and that when it apparently was ended, by the Sicilian disaster, the whole of Greece should have welcomed the event (VIII 2,1). This, and all that goes with it, is one part of the substructure.

Another we have just alluded to, the strategic situation. As we read on, in the coöperative way that is required of us, especially when we come to the episode of Mytilene, more especially when we read of the demoralisation that came upon Sparta after the loss of Pylos and Cythera, it becomes apparent that in Thucydides' view Athens should have been practically unassailable: the other side could not turn to any account even such a disaster as the plague. Why then did the war drag on, ruinously, for twenty-seven years? There is one pointer in the remark of Pericles: "Do not try to add to your empire during the war. I do not fear the enemy so much as mistakes of yours". Few men, he suggests, have the *οἰκεία ξύνεσις*, the "native intelligence", that he ascribes to Themistocles (I 138,3), or the *γνώμη* and *πρόνοια*, judgment and prudence, that he found in Pericles. Then, so far as Athens is concerned, there are the personal rivalries of leaders, the irresponsibility and mutability of the crowd, the fatal lure of wanting too much, the apparent impossibility of seeing that the right moment has come. To this we have to add the baleful effects of party strife, illustrated from Syracuse, from Boeotia (the Plataean antilogy), above all from Corcyra—where we do well to remember that his subject is not just the war but the whole catastrophe that fell upon Greece and on some part of Barbary too; and as he says (III 82,2), war itself is "a teacher of violence".

But perhaps above all, there is the thought to which he recurs again and again: inevitably, we are always walking into the dark, where chance may have the last word. Not that he, any more than Sophocles, is inclined to throw in his hand at this point, like the later generation that erected altars to Fortune; for we may reasonably suppose that he was impressed with the defiant vindication of reason that he quotes from Pericles, and by the wise observation of Hermocrates that what we all have reason to fear could be turned to our own advantage, if only we would do it; and that conversely he thought little of the cocksure attitude which he attributes to the Athenian delegation in Melos.

Such, or such like, is the interpretation of the *History* at which we arrive once we set aside the expectations aroused in us by our word *history*, and take as our sole guide Thucydides' *poiesis* and his text. Once again, it is a matter of trying to see the work in the perspective in which it was composed. As we come closer to that, we see that the question of historiography and why he so far departed from its normal course does not exist; we see at once why he did not give us more information about the economic and other such aspects of the war. We may still regret it, but at least we can understand it and not look for particular explanations or excuses. For us, this war like any war was a complex political event; for Thucydides it was something rather different. He does treat it as a political event, though not so thoroughly as we would wish—and the reason for that is that he really saw it as a complex human failure, and one which he expected to be repeated, "so long as the nature of man remains what it is"—for he was perhaps the most pessimistic of the Greek writers. If we must, by all means let us say that this is not the way in which to write history, provided that we realise that in saying it we are diminishing the dignity of History itself. When we think of him strictly as a historian, and a very good one in spite of his omissions, we see him as a lonely figure among the ancient historians, with no predecessor and with no real successor either; when we understand where his mind was really engaged, we see him as one of that great company of Athenian writers of the fifth century; different indeed from the tragic poets, but having a similarly wide mental horizon. The range of their minds is not to be grasped if we think in terms of religion, theology, and piety as we understand them, nor of his if we see him as one who is doing his best to be a "historian". The differences between the tragic poets and Thucydides appear wide in proportion as we misunderstand both them and him.

Sometimes, in idle moments, I have toyed with the fancy that Thucydides was present (as he well may have been) at the first performance of the *Tyrannus;* that he was one of a small party that dined, with Sophocles, after the play; that later in the evening, when the libations had been poured, the rest fell silent while these two talked, the old and gracious poet and this grave young officer of the new generation. It is true—or so we believe—that Sophocles' religious faith meant little or nothing to Thucydides; nevertheless they would have understood each other, I think, profoundly, and what they might have said would have been worth listening to.

VII

Shakespeare: *Coriolanus*

ONE OUTCOME of our short study of Thucydides' *poiesis* is the idea that he and the other great Athenian writers of the fifth century have much in common, even though they were poets, he a historian; and they, or at least two of them, faithful to the religious tradition, he one of the new generation that was renouncing it. We may go further: as the three tragic poets had no worthy successors, he had none either. It is as if an epoch had come to an end.

In this final chapter we will first attempt to make a little more precise what it is that these four Athenian writers have in common and—the same thing in reverse—what it is that distinguishes them from their immediate successors. This will not be much more than a bringing together of what has been said in the previous chapters. Then, since no small part of our argument has been that we of the modern world can misapprehend, sometimes gravely, what these fifth-century writers meant, we will ask why that should be so. It might seem that the question is answered broadly if we point to the lapse of more than two millennia and to the differences between the ancient and the modern worlds, but that seems to be not enough. This is where Shakespeare comes in. If it is demonstrable, as I think it is, that we can misapprehend a play of the early seventeenth century A.D. as easily as of the fifth B.C., then the two millennia cannot take all the blame. When we come to *Coriolanus* we shall rely on the same guides as heretofore, the choice and disposition of the material, and the text.

First then, and indeed with diffidence, we try to give a rather more definite from to the general impression of kinship between the tragic poets and the historian. We have already rejected the hypothesis that Thucydides was consciously imitating the poets because they were the only models he had. Rather, he composed like that because he thought like that.

When we contemplate a writer's work, or it may be the work of any artist, a useful question to ask oneself, as it seems to me, is: in his struggle with his material, at what level does his mind became engaged and set to work? For instance, there is Aeschylus and the raw material of the *Persae*. It is a natural and ever-popular guess that he was in some sense commemorating the national victory, but we found on inspection that we cannot maintain this without making three assumptions, none of them credible: (*i*) that his mind, as expressed in this work, was thoroughly commonplace; (*ii*) that his ability to express what he meant was negligible; (*iii*) that the continuity of design which is visible throughout the play got there by accident. We looked at another theory, that he was working as a theologian or philosopher, seeking to lead his audience out of their darkness into his light: we found, I think, that this agrees with the facts of the case not much better. We looked at a third, also popular but much more reasonable, that he was so treating the defeat of the invader as to present a serious moral lesson. But that also was not entirely satisfactory, since it left too much of the play in the air; for the challenging fact in his manipulation of the material is that while so much of the play is unhistorical, much is quite historical, and by that I mean not only that we can trust his account of Salamis, but that also he puts firmly before us, as a historian might, those diverse natural factors that worked against the invader and help to explain his defeat; and these, we had to notice, he associates in an unembarrassed way with the activity of the *theos* or *theoi*. We conclude therefore that his mind was certainly not engaged on the patriotic level nor on that theological level, but that he went right through to the level of thought which I tried to indicate earlier and will not repeat here.

Or we might think for a moment of the *Oresteia*. A few years ago the trilogy was produced in London: one of the leading dramatic critics made a point of this, and seemed to be puzzled by it, that in the scene in which Agamemnon returns, Aeschylus does not make him and Clytemnestra talk at all like a husband and wife who have been separated for ten years. Exactly: this is the level on which we might expect his mind to become engaged, and I am far from suggesting that it is a trivial one and would produce trivial drama. But the mind of Aeschylus was not engaged here at all.

From this point we may turn to Sophocles. It is tempting, and in some degree true, to say of him that he devoted his incomparable dramatic skill to the subtle delineation of characters and of the conflicts that arise between them; but if our analysis of the structure of the *Trachiniae* and the *Tyrannus* has brought us anywhere near the mark—Sophocles' mark—we see that his mind too did not really engage on this level, for the plays, especially the *Trachiniae* and *Ajax*, would have had a very different shape. His mind engaged on something further, on something of which perhaps we can fairly say that it is ultimately of more importance.

Nothing has yet been said about Euripides, partly for the reason that he seems more able to look after himself, now that we have escaped from the delusion that he was a bold freethinker denouncing an outworn religious system, or was a psychologist in drama who studied human passions, especially female ones, or (much more simply) was unable to make reasonable plots. Aristotle, though in other respects he does not manage (*οἰκονομεῖ*) Euripides well, saw at least the essential truth about him, that he was "the most tragic of the poets".

From our present point of view, which is to contemplate him as one of the four great Athenian writers of the century, he is extremely interesting. Where does his mind become engaged? If we are thinking of plays like the *Iphigeneia in Tauris*, *Ion*, *Helen*, the answer must be that his mind came to rest and began to work brilliantly on the level of writing first-rate plays that should be exciting or entertaining or charming or satirical, as the case may be, and on no level deeper than that. But if we ask it with reference to the *Medea* or *Hippolytus* or *Troades* or *Bacchae* or *Hecuba*, then our answer must be substantially the same as when we asked it of Aeschylus and Sophocles: he is not really engaged with his persons—for he will often draw them only schematically or even inconsistently—nor with "theology" and the forms of religion, but with certain permanent and overriding realities, which in his case are also terrifying and disruptive ones. I have already said one apparently foolish thing, that the *Tyrannus* is so true to life; I will now say another, that Euripides' Medea is true to life also; not of course that we may expect to meet a Medea any day when we go shopping, even if it should be in Greek shops, but that excess of passion, overbearing reason and restraint, is for Euripides one of the permanent and disruptive facts of life, like the lust for revenge in the oppressed that he so often thrusts at us—and that this is true. To think of his *Medea* as a powerful study in abnormal psychology would be to miss the point and tragic power of the play entirely; he gives us that in the *Electra* and *Orestes*, but not here.

In these plays then, Euripides is pure fifth-century in this, that what his mind works upon is something that in every sense is real, important, and central. Also in this, that he never gives a moment's thought to what a play ought to be like. (It is at this point that Aristotle becomes unable to keep up with him; he knew what a play should look like, and that it should not look like the *Trojan Women*.) In one sense, all three poets are professional to their fingertips: having decided what they wanted to do, they knew exactly how to do it; as Gomme says of the Greeks in general, ". . . but in their art—put a pen into their hands, or a brush or a chisel, . . . they hardly took a step wrong" (*The Greek Attitude*, p. 162). But they were the opposite of professionals, all three of them, if by the word we mean one who sits down to do the prescribed thing in the perfect way. The dramatic virtuosity that Euripides had at his command might have escaped our notice if we did not possess those elegant plays in which, as it were, he had nothing to do but be elegant; therefore, knowing what he could do in the dexterous management of plot, dialogue, and the rest, we can better assess what he refused to do, as if out of disdain, in what once upon a time were called the ill-made plays. He had little taste for the bogus; all the more are we justified in supposing that what he made corresponds to what he wanted to say, since mere incompetence is ruled out by the other plays.

But such rejection of artificial standards is only a little less notable in Sophocles and Aeschylus. The seven plays of Aeschylus that we have display the utmost variety of style and structure, from the crowded action of the *Eumenides*, with its change of scene from Delphi to Athens, to the *Persae* and *Prometheus*, of which it could be said that they contain almost no action, only speeches; and it would be as obtusely neo-classic to say that he spent his career searching for the ideal dramatic form as to say of Sophocles that he went through a period of duplex plots before he realised that this would not do, pulled himself together, and wrote the *Tyrannus* and *Electra*. In short, all three thought they had something important to say, and devoted their high technical competence solely to the task of saying it effectively.

In at least two other ways they resemble each other. One, obviously, is their avoidance of side-issues, of matters of incidental interest. This does not need much illustration. The chorus of the *Agamemnon* does not sing about the destruction of the fleet; Sophocles does not bring on the body of Antigone or Deianeira; each of them will drop a character like a stone when that character has done its essential job. Euripides does not write a fascinating scene in which Jason negotiates with Creon about marrying his daughter, nor does he trace the mental process by which his ill-used heroines, like Hecuba and Alcmena, turn into vindictive fiends, since all that matters to him is that oppression breeds oppression. Here again his later plays offer an instructive contrast, for in them fresh points of interest arrive on every breeze. (See my *Greek Tragedy*, pp. 318–321.) But of all the tragedies we can say that the poet passes directly to the level on which he is going to think, and takes remarkably little notice of what lies in his path before he gets there.

The other resemblance is a matter that has cropped up several times already, but should be briefly mentioned here. We always say, rightly, that in matters of religion the Greeks knew no such thing as orthodoxy, beyond the proper observance of certain rites, but we do like to impose on the poets doxographical formulations of our own. Where, in the foregoing chapters, I have been contentious, the contention, usually, has been that in our interpreting of the plays, if our formulation, whatever it may be, conflicts with the evident sense of the drama, it is the formulation that is allowed to triumph. As we have said more than once, our own ideas of what constitutes religion or theology or piety are sometimes too rigid or narrow to accommodate the facts of the case, and it seems to be a confession of failure if, in order to work securely within the formulations, we have to assume that the dramatists did not, in the full and natural sense of the term, write dramatically. To my mind, the evidence is clear and consistent. The Religion of the Greeks (in the absence of a guiding orthodoxy) was naturally indeterminate and inconsistent—and we do well to remember that with much else it included the Comic; but if we ask what was the nature of the religious thought found in the tragic poets, I suggest (for the second or third time) that the brief but substantially correct answer is: contemplating how the universe works. Their differences are reconciled in this common conception. The question whether Aeschylus was a monotheist or not has no real substance; it is a *σχιαμαχία*, shadow-boxing. Here too Euripides is in the same tradition, and the old idea that he was denouncing an effete Olympian system was a similar mistaking of shadow for substance. Aphrodite, in the *Danaides* of Aeschylus, was a universal fructifying Power; in the *Hippolytus* of Euripides she is vindictive and ruinous: this does not mean that Aeschylus and Euripides disagreed about Aphrodite; only that they were talking about different things.

This has been an attempt to set down ways of thought and composing which seem to be common to the great Athenian poets of the fifth century, all of whom, as it happens, were tragic dramatists. Certainly there were also the comic dramatists, but I do not see how they would help us in our present enquiry, which is to ask how, if at all, the great Athenian prose writer of the century fits into the picture. Is he recognisably of the same family, or, breaking with the past, is he inaugurating that future in which he had no real successors, or none until we reach Polybius? We must try to avoid the obvious peril of such an enquiry: that of making only formal and verbal points.

A historian of today, if we can conceive that he should undertake to write, as M. I. Finley puts it, the history of an event that still lay in the future, would of course take no less trouble than Thucydides did to ascertain exactly what was happening; he would also ask himself, as did Thucydides, why the war had come about; but he would also investigate with rigour important aspects of the event that Thucydides treats only cursorily or not at all. We need not repeat our list of Thucydides' omissions. The modern would of course also take that wider view that we find in Thucydides: he would inevitably trace the growth of the empire and the strains that it created within the Greek world, and it would not be surprising if at some stage he observed that the war proved to be the most destructive yet known in the ancient world, that virtually it became the first World War of antiquity. But it is with this that the Greek historian begins.

We have spent some time in trying to establish the way in which Thucydides contemplated the event and ordered his material, and my present suggestion is that it is quite different from anything modern, and recognisably akin to the way in which the Athenian tragic poets thought and worked.

In the first place, he did not approach his task like a professional historian: "Herodotus did the Persian Wars; I will do this one". It is surely significant that in the *Pentecontaetia*, in which he is summarising the course of events from where Herodotus left off to where he himself is going to begin, he, Thucydides, such a stickler for chronological accuracy, hardly gives a single date, to say nothing of the fact that here too his omissions are spectacular. In these chapters, I 89–118, he is doing exactly what he says, showing "how the Athenians arrived at the situation in which they had become so powerful", and it does not occur to him to do something else by the way, to turn his eyes occasionally to this side or to that, to set the narrative in a context of the general history of the period. We noted above that he does not even mention that even among the Athenians themselves there was considerable opposition to the policy of imperialism. We should be sympathetic, let us hope, if a modern reader complained of Thucydides that he wrote in blinkers; it would be a mistake, but the perspective in which he writes might give that impression.

Where, at what level, among his mass of material, did his mind become really engaged? Asking that question about the dramatists, we naturally have to deduce the answer from the plays, except when Euripides gives us a direct hint, as in his prologue to the *Hippolytus* or *Troades*. Thucydides tells us: the war was going to be the outstanding event, so far, in known human experience. Therefore, as I hope we have seen, it is at least understandable that as he makes his way through to the level at which he does his thinking, he leaves on one side, as matters not very important, what a modern historian would grapple with first, among which would be, for example, the Megarian decree. This, I say, is understandable—but only if we think of him as a writer of the fifth century, not of the fourth or third, or of any modern date. Although I have not read all the *Antigones* that have ever been written, I should be surprised to learn that any except Sophocles' failed to contrive a tragic or romantic scene for Antigone and Haemon. It is not that Sophocles is indifferent to the love-interest: he writes an ode about it—about the power of Aphrodite. But he writes it at the moment when he has made us feel that Creon's uncomprehending contempt for his son's love toward Antigone is unnatural and must have evil consequences. Not many dramatists could have written a tragic scene for the two lovers more affectingly than Sophocles, but such a scene was not on his chosen path, and he will not write it. It is not that he avoids particulars and deals in generalities; far from it. Nothing could be more sharply particular and personal than the blind hatred that Haemon comes to feel for his father, and tries to satisfy in the cavern when he goes at him with his sword. But surely, it is only because these poets so carefully (or instinctively) exclude everything peripheral, however natural and dramatic it might be, that they succeed in conveying the general through the particular, and with so little generalising discourse. If they wear blinkers, and put blinkers on us, it is in order that we may see the more sharply.

The dramatists are always doing this; we are surely not being fanciful if we say that the historian does it too. We have asserted, perhaps even demonstrated, that for him the War was not simply a complex though definite political event; as he saw it, it was essentially a human experience, and a typical one inasmuch as he expected such experiences to recur. He too, whether consciously or instinctively, leaves on one side (to our dismay) a great deal which, in his judgment, can and must be spared if our attention is not to be dissipated by becoming too deeply engaged in what is only ancillary. Both of him and of the dramatists we may state it as an axiom: the greater excludes the less. In him too there is no scamping of the particulars, where the particulars are necessary: since his subject is war, turmoil, violence, destruction, he will record the details of it with all possible accuracy. This, we may venture to suggest, is the equivalent in his work of the sharp and convincing, though strictly controlled, treatment of character, motive, and situation that we find in the plays. For the purpose of the dramatist it is necessary that the action throughout should, as we say, ring true, for if not, we shall not accept the significance that he sees in it; for Thucydides' purpose it was no less important that his analysis should be firmly based on ascertained fact. Neither he nor they will rely on vague assertions and rhetoric.

But they have in common a more obvious and important fact: their ultimate engagement is with what they think permanent and fundamental. About the poets there is no need to say more in this respect; about Thucydides there is a little more to say.

Should we call his work a political or military or moralising or a philosophic history? When we pass in review, as we have done, what draws and retains his attention, we find it no easier to label his book than it was to docket the religious views of Aeschylus; both of them range too widely for our categories. Perhaps Thucydides was too simple, or we not simple enough. He dwells on what he has found important: the working of fear, prestige, and national self-interest; the "admitted principle" that a state safeguards its own interests; the fact that it is so hard, apparently, to know what one's true interest is; the other general law that the strong will dominate the weak; the lure—a form of hybris—of wanting too much and the difficulty of knowing when εὖ παρέχει, when the right moment has come; overconfidence in success; the baleful results of party strife; the dangers of acting in anger, or for that matter out of despair or out of boundless hopes. Several of these combine to form his judgment that democracy is a perilous form of government unless guided by an exceptional man like Pericles; but there is no indication that he thought the Spartan system any better, or indeed that he had much faith in systems. Sparta produced Brasidas, whom he admired for his courage and moderation, but she also gave the supreme command, at a critical moment, to Alcidas, and even refused to reinforce Brasidas, after his capture of Amphipolis, "partly because of the jealousy of the chief citizens". He left it for the smaller historians of the fourth century to attack or defend democracy. How are we to describe all this? particularly when we add his constant preoccupation with the unpredictable and uncontrollable, his clear understanding of the strategic situation, and—as we can fairly add, thinking of what Pericles said about farmers and cities with no accumulated capital—of the economic situation as well? It is difficult to see how much further a man's reach could go, or how he could more firmly grasp what is important. Surely it is true that here we find the same breadth and penetration, the same desire to reach the essentials, that we find also in the Athenian poets of the time.

As for differences between them, how much weight should we allow to the notorious fact that "Thucydides did not believe in the gods"? Our estimates will vary, according as we attach importance to shadows or to realities. Had Aeschylus or Sophocles expressed in dramatic form the essence of the Melos–Sicily sequence in the *History*, he would have used *theoi*. Thucydides says what they would have said, but without *theoi*. It is only a difference of expression, corresponding to differences of personal temperament, and of the medium; it is nothing radical.

When we add to this a matter that we have sufficiently discussed already, the constructively imaginative response that Thucydides calls for, we can surely say, using Cornford's language, that he and the three poets breathed the same "circumambient atmosphere"; they were of the same "pool". Thucydides' dramatic method was not a copy, nor was it merely an "artistic" way of arranging the material; it was a conscious, or perhaps an instinctive, reliance on pure form instead of on exposition. We find it sometimes in Plato; in any later historian it would be inconceivable. It seems to belong to an age, like the one which the fifth century was bringing to its end, when the intellect and the imagination were in closer contact than they were to be later.

This impression of kinship between Thucydides and the poets

of his time and place can only be strengthened if we look, as best we can, at the tragic poets and the historians of the fourth century. In neither case have we much information; for what was happening to tragedy our best evidence, I think, is to be derived from what Aristotle says or implies in the *Poetics*. (I have discussed the matter in an essay contributed to a forthcoming volume in honour of the late F. J. H. Letters.) Already in antiquity, even as early as Aristophanes' *Frogs*, it was apparent that Euripides and Sophocles had left no worthy successors. The evidence that we can find suggests the reason: it certainly appears that tragedy was now content with a more restricted field of operation—of which fact we probably have a premonition in those later non-tragic plays of Euripides. I take a few points only. Aristotle says (1453A 17 ff.) that the earlier poets called upon a wide range of myths, but now the best plays are made on the stories of a few families only, "whose fate it was to do or suffer fearful things". In his next chapter he explains the phenomenon: the determinant of Tragedy is that it creates Pity and Fear; that requires a pitiful and fearful action, and that in turn requires that kinsman should be on the point of slaying kinsman, whether he actually does it or not; better indeed if he does not, but is prevented by a thrilling, *ἐκπληκτικόν*, discovery; "therefore the poets are compelled to turn to those families among whom this kind of incident occurred". But what can this mean, except that in drama emotionalism is in the ascendant, and mind in retreat? Aristotle virtually says as much when he tells us, in Book XIII, that now the popular kind of play is that in which the good come off well and only the bad suffer, and that the reason is the *ἀσθένεια τῶν θεατρῶν*, "debility of the audiences". We seem to be a long way from Aristotle's own "classical" tragedy, about as far as Rymer and his like were from theirs.

This we should bear in mind if we are tempted to explain the decline of Greek tragedy by saying: "Quite simple: no more tragic poets of genius happened to get born". There was no lack of genius in the fourth century; it simply did not turn to poetry and drama, but to pursuits like philosophy, mathematics, biology, astronomy. We can find a parallel much nearer home.

Nor was genius turning much to history. In history, it seems, there were careful researchers, and there were Xenophon, Ephorus, Theopompus, and the author, whoever he was, of the *Hellenica Oxyrhynchia;* but however competent or incompetent these were as historians, it has never been suggested, I think, that in quality of mind any of them came within miles of Thucydides. That is to say, when we put side by side the best Athenian writers of the fifth century and the best poets and historians of the fourth, we feel that we have moved into a different world; and if we do not wish to think ill of the fourth, we had better confine our serious attention to Plato, Aristotle, and the scientists.

It would not be surprising if in such a case the tragic poets of the fifth century came to be only partly understood. We have little evidence by which to check the surmise, having no fourth-century equivalents of the eighteenth-century men of letters who admired Shakespeare's tragedies so much, understood them so little, and altered them so readily. We know that Euripides was very popular, more so than Sophocles, much more than Aeschylus, but in itself that proves little: Shakespeare also remained popular. Aristotle's solitary remark about the function of the *theoi* in tragedy is not encouraging—that they are a useful dramatic device—and his repeated desire for τὸ φιλάνθρωπον is near enough to the eighteenth-century desire for Natural Justice to arouse grave doubts. The fourth century B.C., like the eighteenth A.D., was an Age of Enlightenment, and seems to have made similar demands on tragic drama: Cordelia must not be allowed to perish in a just cause (as Johnson declared); to show a blameless character falling into ruin is μιαρόν, revolting—which is not true, nor in accordance with the practice of the tragic poets. It is true only if one's horizon has undergone the contraction that is implied in the virtual abolition from tragedy of the *theoi* and the substitution of τὸ φιλάνθρωπον, what is right and proper, for the Dike of the *theoi*, what tends to happen in this world. (It does not seem easy to keep one's mind and observation, at the same time, on the workings both of God's and of Boyle's Law.) The edifying double-ended plot which Aristotle reports now to be in vogue is sentimental, in comparison with the real tragedy of the fifth century; as Johnson said in a different connexion, it represents the triumph of hope over experience. When we combine this with the other fact that Aristotle records, the current search for " strong situations", to which we may add his own declared preference for the "thrilling" solution which avoids τὸ μιαρόν, the shock to our moral sense, a consistent picture emerges: dramatists and audiences alike had lost the wide outlook of the fifth century. What they wanted now was not the typical and permanent, but the exciting individual in an exciting situation; therefore many of the myths used often enough before were now of no use. This being so, it was inevitable that Sophocles and Euripides should have left no real successors. It also seems a natural consequence that Thucydides should have had none; that the best of his should have been diligent enquirers and careful recorders—which indeed he himself had been too. There is no need to be rude about such as these; they were doing honest and valuable work. The great difference is that they were enquiring into what would never happen again, Thucydides into what he rightly thought would.

If it is true, it is certainly interesting, that something of the kind has happened for a second time. That is my excuse for ending this volume with a short study of Shakespeare's tragedy *Coriolanus*. The argument will be that Shakespeare's "meaning", being typical of his own age, soon became and long remained inaccessible, because unfashionable, with the result that one of his most magnificent plays has often been undervalued; further, that our best means of regaining contact with his remote sixteenth-century mind is, again, to look steadily at his *poiesis*. My purpose therefore is to reinforce my own theme rather than to make a contribution to Shakespeare criticism, of which, I confess, I know much less than I might and should.

Ab Iove principium:

The tragedy of *Coriolanus* is one of the most amusing of our author's performances. The old man's merriment in Menenius; the lofty lady's dignity in Volumnia; the bridal modesty in Virgilia; the patrician and military haughtiness in Coriolanus; the plebeian malignity and tribunitian insolence in Brutus and Sicinius, make a very pleasing and interesting variety; and the various revolutions of the hero's fortunes fill the mind with anxious curiosity. There is, perhaps, too much bustle in the first act, and too little in the last.

That is Johnson's *Preface*, quoted entire. Perhaps he wrote it hurriedly; even so, two implicit principles can be discerned: a play is an assemblage of persons who should be interesting, and in this case are; and there is a certain norm, in comparison with which the management of the action can forthwith be judged as good or not good. It is taken for granted that our interest will be mainly engaged with the revolution of the hero's fortunes. That, it seems, continued to be taken for granted. Thus Saintsbury writes, in the *Cambridge History of English Literature*, Vol. V (1910):

Coriolanus is certainly not deficient in variety of incident, or of personage, but every incident and every personage is, in a way, subservient to the hero . . . But he remains one of the noblest figures in Shakespeare, and his nobility is largely the work of Shakespeare himself. What is more, he has provided Shakespeare with the opportunity of working out a "one-man" drama, as, except in inferior specimens like *Timon*, he has done nowhere else.

The play itself inspires some of its critics with respect rather than enthusiasm. Theodore Spencer writes about it with some restraint in his *Shakespeare and the Nature of Man* (pp. 177 ff.):

Coriolanus does not open vistas, like *Antony and Cleopatra;* it closes them. The fact that Coriolanus is what Bradley called "an impossible man" makes the play more claustrophobic than *Macbeth* . . . Nothing that happens to the hero is reflected in external nature, as in *Macbeth* or *Lear*. The play has no cosmology; the gods are mentioned, we feel, when they *are* mentioned, for the sake of local colour, not because they are part of the vision of things.

Spencer therefore calls it a "tight" play. Certainly it contains no blasted heaths or thunderstorms of meteors or ghosts, not even a Fool, but the statement that it lacks "cosmic reverberations" may prove to be interesting rather than true.

On Shakespeare, Granville-Barker is always worth consulting: he knew so much about the theatre. In his *Prefaces* (p. 1), he writes this:

> *Coriolanus* cannot be ranked with the greatest of the tragedies. It lacks their transcendental vitality and metaphysical power . . . The play is notable for its craftsmanship. It is the work of a man who knows what the effect of each stroke will be, and wastes not one of them . . . Was Shakespeare perhaps aware of some ebbing of his imaginative vitality?—well there may have been, after the creation, in about as many years, of *Othello*, *King Lear*, *Antony and Cleopatra*, and *Macbeth*—and did he purposefully choose a subject and characters which he could make the most of by judgment and skill?

Later (p. 172), in a most perceptive passage on the style of the play, he observes that the verse is rarely intense; it is powerful, resonant, compellingly rhythmical. "The words", he says, "are often unmusical in themselves, and they may be crushed into lines like fuel to stoke a furnace"; but "though the verse does not soar, neither does it sag. The play in this respect has not a single weak spot." He calls attention also to the strength and concentration of the structure of the play—but has the critic not fallen into some inconsistency, if he finds the structure powerfully built, the verse often like fuel crushed into a furnace, but the play as a whole lacking somewhat in imaginative vitality and relying rather on judgment and skill? Something seems to have gone wrong somewhere.

Finally, and to much the same effect, I quote from an article written for the New York *Times* by the English critic Mr W. A.

Darlington on the production of the play at Stratford-on-Avon in July, 1959:

Coriolanus is the least likeable of Shakespeare's tragic heroes, because the sin by which he falls is a fierce, intolerant pride. He is that most difficult character—a man undeniably great who is yet not great enough to be humble. No modern audience . . . can readily take to such a man. It is up to the actor, then, to give him an inner quality of nobility that can make him command the respect of the audience in spite of his obstinate hatred of the common people and his flat refusal to accept democratic institutions . . . Later, when Coriolanus leads an enemy against Rome merely to gratify a private grudge against the city, our belief in his fundamental nobility becomes more difficult to sustain.

This approach to the play, like the others, is typically modern and therefore fundamentally un-Shakespearian. It reduces the amplitude of the play to suit the modern (and fourth-century?) idea of tragedy, with its total involvement with the character and sufferings of the central character. "Our belief in his fundamental nobility becomes more difficult to sustain": let it be impossible; what of it? Take another tragedy, the *Persae:* must we say that this fails as a play because we cannot sustain our belief in the fundamental nobility of Xerxes? Aeschylus has no interest at all in Xerxes' nobility, only in the fact that his folly and ambition have been signally punished by the *theoi.* Must we believe in the fundamental nobility of Agamemnon or of Clytemnestra in that other play of Aeschylus'? Or does the *Medea* fail towards its end because we can hardly believe in Medea's nobility when her wild passions are tearing her world to pieces? Plainly, there are more kinds of tragedy than one, and there is little profit in criticising a play for not conforming to one type if in fact it belongs to another.

This, I think, is the reply to another comment that has been made about *Coriolanus*, that the character-drawing, at the critical moment, is deficient. E. E. Stoll, who makes the criticism, says that Shakespeare does not explore the psychological motives whereby Coriolanus resolves to join the Volsces against

Rome; the character-drawing remains *external;* the process of thought is not shown. (Saintsbury makes a similar observation, though not in order to criticise Shakespeare, when he speaks of "that interesting and not very easy character Tullus Aufidius, whose psychical evolution Shakespeare has left in obviously intentional uncertainty".) To Stoll's criticism Granville-Barker makes a sensible answer: in Caius Marcius there *was* no such process; he is not a character who could appropriately be made to *argue* himself into treason, as a Hamlet might; Marcius would do it instinctively. "And what", he adds, "could be more fittingly eloquent at this juncture than thc simple sight—and the shock it must give us—of this haggard and hardly recognisable figure" in Antium, among Rome's enemies?

This is well said; and as for Aufidius, the explanation may be not intentional uncertainty but complete indifference. Perhaps Saintsbury, δυσέρως τῶν ἀπόντων, was looking for what is not there. There is indeed tragedy that turns on internal strife, on the struggle within the soul that leads to the tragic decision, a kind of tragedy in which "external" character-drawing would be useless; but there is also tragedy in which conflicting motives, interior struggle, matter very little, perhaps not at all. Again Xerxes will illustrate the point, or Aeschylus' Orestes. In a tragedy in which man is acting in the presence of the *theoi*, interior character-drawing, though it may be very much to our present taste, might well be not an added merit but a plain excrescence.—But today we seem to have forgotten the *theoi*. Shakespeare had not.

To a Hellenist, one interesting feature of *Coriolanus* is its resemblance to the *Ajax* of Sophocles. It is not easy to think of two characters in drama who are more like each other than Ajax and Caius Marcius: each a magnificent fighter; but proud, convinced of his own worth, dedicated to his own sense of honour, and far too rigid to deal with the demands of life. Further, each play ends with outrage offered to the hero's dead body. The imperiousness of Ajax ends in disaster for him; it calls forth, in the two kings, a response which equally the human condition cannot tolerate; through Odysseus, with his more spacious understanding, the ultimate claims of humanity are satisfied. In *Coriolanus* the outrage is a more transitory one, but it is a similar assault on our feelings of decency—and we may note how Shakespeare brings it to an end: he makes Aufidius begin his last speech with the words "My rage is gone". It was rage, springing from hatred and envy, that produced the horror of a living man planting his foot on the body of a dead one:

> My rage is gone
> And I am struck with sorrow.—Take him up,
> Three of our chiefest soldiers: I'll be one.
> Beat thou the drum that it speak mournfully,
> Trail your steel pikes. Though in this city he
> Hath widowed and unchilded many a one
> Yet he shall have a noble memory.
> Assist.

So do the fires of this furnace die down. Somehow, the comment that Coriolanus is "an impossible man" seems too small. Naturally, we must not allow an investigation of this play to be influenced by its resemblance to an older one; we must attend only to the structure of this one. But it will be interesting, if the resemblance proves to be more than skin-deep.

In another respect the play is interesting to the Hellenist. In our studies of the Greek plays we often have only a sketchy idea of the sources which the poet may have used: here we know, and possess, his unique source, North's translation of Plutarch's *Life*. In several extended passages he followed North so closely as to reproduce his very words with the least possible change; therefore, by taking note of the places where he does not follow Plutarch, especially where he invents details for himself, we have an extra means of making contact with his mind. About the uprising of the plebeians, with which Shakespeare begins the play, what he read in North was this:

There grew a great sedition in the city, because the Senate did favour the rich against the people, who did complain of the sore oppression of the usurers of whom they borrowed money. For those that had little were yet spoiled of that little they had by their creditors for lack of ability to pay the money: who offered their goods to be sold to them that would give most. And such as had little left, their bodies were laid hold on, and they were made their bondsmen, notwithstanding all the wounds and cuts they showed, which they had received in many battels, fighting for defence of their country and commonwealth.

In fact, the background to the tragic story of Coriolanus, as Shakespeare found it in his source, was a straightforward political struggle between the oppressed populace and an oppressive oligarchy, in which the moderate party was overborne by the immoderate hostility of Coriolanus to any kind of concession. In Plutarch, the people act with good sense: their secession to the Mons Sacer—an exemplary form of "strike"—was spontaneous and was carried out with no violence. It had nothing to do with the famine, which (in Plutarch) did not occur until after the Volscian war and in consequence of it; nor was Coriolanus put on his trial for anything said or done at the election, which was now over and done with, but because he had spoken violently in the Senate against the proposal, favoured by many senators, to distribute *gratis* a supply of corn received *gratis* by the State, from Gelon of Syracuse, for the relief of the famine. As for the consulship: at the pre-election the people had favoured Coriolanus out of respect for his valour—and he had shown his wounds in the usual way with no fuss at all; what made them change their minds at the formal election was the unprecedented zeal shown on his behalf by the senators: this turned their good will into envy and indignation, backed by the fear that a Senate dominated by Coriolanus would destroy all their liberties. Malicious tribunes had nothing to do with it. In short, Shakespeare is as anti-historical here as was Aeschylus in the *Persae*. It is true that this *Life* is legend rather than history, but Shakespeare did not know that. On the Day of Judgment each poet must hope for mercy rather than justice.

We may briefly note other changes that he made. In Plutarch's narrative there are no women, until he comes to the supplication of the Roman Ladies near the end. Volumnia is indeed mentioned near the beginning, but only as the mother to whom the son paid outstanding respect. About Aufidius, he scarcely alters the facts, but he disposes them differently: Plutarch does not mention Aufidius and the mutual hatred of the two men until Coriolanus is arrived in Antium, but Shakespeare works this vein from the beginning. Yet there is one significant change even here: the outrage offered by Aufidius to Coriolanus' body is Shakespeare's own invention.

Changes made for obvious dramatic reasons need not concern us—such, for example, as the abridgement of the Volscian campaign fought against Rome under Coriolanus' leadership. In general, when we compare what Shakespeare wrote with what he had read, we may say two things. One is obvious enough: the texture of the play is much richer, much more varied, than of the *Life*. Was it then for the sake of this that Shakespeare deviated so much from Plutarch? Perhaps so—if we are content with Dr Johnson's implied theory of tragic drama. But there is a second point. In Plutarch, apart from the tyranny of the oligarchs (which in any case Shakespeare omits), only Coriolanus himself behaves, politically, with outrageous folly; he is the sole author of his own ruin, a tragic hero indeed. The economy of the play is quite different: we find folly, or worse, almost everywhere: the citizens are weak-headed at home and cowards in the field, except on one notable occasion; their Tribunes are malignant, arrogant, and in the most serious matters of State entirely lacking in judgment (see especially IV 6); and Volumnia is drawn out of the dignified remoteness in which Plutarch left her to become as implacable and contemptuous an enemy of the commons as Coriolanus himself. His major changes all tend in this one direction, for which reason it hardly seems enough to say that he made them for the sake of making his play more dramatic and lifelike.

Our comparison of play with source has perhaps given us a start. I suggest that now we look rather closely at the opening scenes, which ought to lay the foundations of what is to follow in the play; the middle section we will try to deal with in less pedestrian fashion; the final scenes, again, we will examine in some detail, since for some readers they are a little disappointing.

It will be remembered that Johnson thought there was perhaps "too much bustle" in the first Act. Certainly in Scene I Shakespeare covers a lot of ground, and does it swiftly; which fact makes it the more interesting that in one place he moves very slowly. He opens with a scene of violence: *Enter a company of mutinous citizens with staves and clubs and other weapons*. We learn at once that they are starving, full of hatred for the patricians and especially of Caius Marcius, and stupid: "Let's kill him, and we'll have corn at our own price" is not the remark of an intelligent man. Menenius exposes their violence as mere folly; he tells them what we are evidently intended to accept as the truth:

> I tell you, friends, most charitable care
> Have the patricians of you. For your wants,
> Your suffering in this dearth, you may as well
> Strike at the heaven with your staves as lift them
> Against the Roman State, whose course will on
> The way it takes, cracking ten thousand curbs
> Of more strong link asunder than can ever
> Appear in your impediment: for the dearth,
> The gods, not the patricians, make it, and
> Your knees to them, not arms, must help. Alack,
> You are transported by calamity
> Thither where more attends you; and you slander
> The helm o' the State, who care for you like fathers
> When you curse them as enemies.

We have seen how different this is from what Shakespeare found in his source. If we would know why he so altered his "myth", we must read on and find out. And perhaps we may take note of the implied prophecy: "where worse attends you".

This picture of disorder and violence occupies about one-quarter of the scene in which the playwright is going to travel so far; the second quarter, in the circumstances, is remarkable, for vv. 90–160 are a passage that a hard-pressed producer of today might be tempted to prune severely, on the grounds that it advances the action hardly at all. In it, Menenius rehearses the parable of the Belly and the Rebellious Members which Plutarch himself calls an ancient one, and he certainly does it at his leisure. Granville-Barker naturally asks why, observing that "Shakespeare will habitually have swung his main theme into action within half the time or less". His answer is that the slow telling of the tale serves to abate the fury of the citizens, that it gives us a fair view of what they are like before the villainous Tribunes have been able to work on them, and that by holding up the action it emphasises the impetus which it receives when Caius Marcius appears. No doubt—but is that all? In other plays, Granville-Barker says, Shakespeare swings his main theme into action within the first dozen verses or so: perhaps that is exactly what he is doing here too. At all events, having given us a picture of a commonwealth in which the commons, needlessly and uselessly, are threatening violence, Shakespeare detains us for some time with the traditional fable which presents together two important exemplars of Order in nature, the Commonwealth and the human frame:

> The kingly-crownèd head, the vigilant eye,
> The counsellor heart, the arm our soldiers,
> Our steed the leg, the tongue our trumpeter,
> With other muniments and petty helps
> In this our fabric.

Even the uninstructed reader of Shakespeare—the present writer for example—if he is sceptical enough not to suppose that all literature is personal, romantic, or psychological, apprehends easily enough that to Shakespeare, and presumably to his audiences also, the idea of a divinely appointed Order is basic: that "the body politic" was not a tired metaphor, that "the deputy elected by the Lord" was at least a poetic reality. For reassurance the layman can turn to the experts, to Professor L. C. Knights' British Academy Lecture for instance, and learn that it is indeed true; that in Shakespeare there is a living connexion between concepts like Order, Nature, Providence, the peaceful State, the anointed King, Goodness, Fruitfulness, Love.

But if such conceptions—fairly common property in the sixteenth century—occur fairly often in the plays, as they certainly do, then we should ask ourselves at what stage in his composing Shakespeare brought them in. Were they added, as opportunity offered, to plays of which the structure was already complete but for the *lexis*, added simply because Shakespeare could not help thinking, as he wrote? Or were they in his mind from the start, helping to shape the structure itself? The former seems to be commonly assumed. We believe that Shakespeare's design here was to present the tragedy of Caius Marcius Coriolanus: his nobility, his pride, the way in which the one nullifies the other. Believing this, we are inclined to think the present passage incidental. Shakespeare wanted *something* here—something to quieten the Citizens, to mark emphatically the entrance of the hero, to characterise Menenius as the humorous patrician. What that should be was not of the first importance, but since the fable was ready to hand in Plutarch, since its import was familiar, congenial to the poet's own way of thinking, and not irrelevant to the situation, Shakespeare used it—though something quite different might have served his purpose just as well; and when the moment has passed and Caius Marcius is before us on the stage, we give all our attention to him and forget the fable; it has done its work. The alternative is that what the fable adumbrates was in Shakespeare's mind from the beginning, and explains why he remodelled the story as he did, and constructed the plot as he has done. It is a possibility; for the moment we can say no more than that, since we have only just begun looking at the plot.

In the third quarter of the scene we meet, at last, Caius Marcius, the man whom the plebians hate above all the other patricians, and are ready to kill in order that they may lay their hands on the corn which, apparently, is not there. Shakespeare wastes no time in showing how natural their hatred of him is: for the plebeians he expresses a total and violent contempt:

> They say there's corn enough!
> Would the nobility lay aside their ruth
> And let me use my sword, I'd make a quarry
> With thousands of these quarter'd slaves, as high
> As I could pick my lance.

No doubt; but to what end?

Swiftly, we learn, first, that tribunes have been granted to the plebeians, then, that the Volscians are in arms against Rome—news welcome to Marcius partly because the war will give him another opportunity of hunting down Aufidius. The First Senator bids the citizens go home; Marcius bids them follow him—and in these terms:

> Nay, let them follow.
> The Volsces have much corn; take these rats thither
> To gnaw their garners.—Worshipful mutineers,
> Your valour puts well forth; pray, follow.

The stage-direction reads: *Exeunt all but* Brutus *and* Sicinius. *The* Citizens *steal away*. There is no glint of heroism in the Citizens; nor could we expect them to show any, treated like this.

So that for what remains of the scene we are left with the two Tribunes. What kind of men they are appears at once when Sicinius says, of Marcius:

> But I do wonder
> His insolence can brook to be commanded
> Under Cominius—

whereupon their mean little minds cleverly explain why the proud Marcius is willing to serve in the second degree.

Such is the first scene. The second takes us to Corioli. It is a natural bit of dramatic exposition, and it gives us a view of Rome as seen from the outside: struck by famine, mutinous, with the plebeians hating Marcius even more than Aufidius does—and he himself certifies how much that is.

Next, a domestic scene, Volumnia and Valeria in the graceful and ladylike occupation of needlework. The mother is chiding the wife, telling her not to mope just because her husband is at the war. As she goes on with her embroidery she produces talk like: ". . . to a cruel war I sent him. . . . Had I a dozen sons . . ." Virgilia is a "fool" to shrink from blood:

> The breasts of Hecuba
> When she did suckle Hector look'd not lovelier
> Than Hector's forehead when it spit forth blood
> At Grecian swords, contemning.

Why this? Is Shakespeare giving us his idea of what a noble Roman matron was like and inviting us to admire it? But Virgilia too is a noble Roman matron—and a much more natural woman. Perhaps he is doing it in order to explain for us why Marcius is what he is. On the principle that "every incident and personage is, in a way, subservient to the hero", this is what we shall say, and all that we can say; yet had Shakespeare drawn a different Volumnia we should be just as happy, and should explain then that the gentleness of the mother acts wonderfully as a foil, to emphasise the martial sternness of the son. At all events, the poet takes some trouble here to invent a sharp contrast between the two women, equally devoted to Marcius, the one in this way, the other in that; the wife so much concerned for his safety that until he returns she will not leave the house, not even to visit "a good lady that lies in".

And why the butterfly? Valeria—a great Roman lady indeed —admires the embroidery, and charmingly asks Virgilia, "How does your little son?", to which the grandmother replies by saying that "He had rather see the swords and hear a drum than look upon his school-master". Valeria says, Yes, he is just like his father; and relates how she saw him chasing a gilded butterfly for half an hour together until, in a rage, he caught it and tore it to bits. I doubt if Shakespeare intended us to admire this either—and of course none of it is in Plutarch.

If in these three scenes Shakespeare was laying foundations, these are the foundations that he has laid: violence and stupidity among the citizens, combined with a hatred of Marcius which Marcius immediately justifies, with his contempt of the "musty superfluity" of which the coming war may somewhat relieve Rome; malice and meanness in the two Tribunes; and in Volumnia this unwomanly ferocity which in any case is intent only on the glory of her son, not at all on the glory and well-being of the City. Virgilia serves to remind us what true womanliness is, and Menenius of tolerance and good sense in political matters.

For the rest of Act I we are at the war, and quite close to Plutarch. Shakespeare begins, characteristically, with the gay and impulsive wager of his horse that Marcius makes with Titus Lartius: among his equals, Marcius becomes human—and English rather than Roman, as Granville-Barker observed. This, needless to say, is not in Plutarch; nor is the next detail, that when Senators of Corioli appear on the walls, Marcius' first question is:

> Titus Aufidius, is he within your walls?

Shakespeare invents this, and the single combat, and the last scene of the act which ends with Aufidius bitterly resenting his fifth defeat and swearing that nothing, "nor sleep nor sanctuary, Being naked, sick, nor fane nor Capitol", shall lift up their rotten privilege against his hate to Marcius—a hate which (scene 8,4) springs, in him, from nothing but envy, and in Marcius from nothing at all.

Three other incidents are invented, and are worth looking at. First, having given a poor impression of the Roman soldiery, Shakespeare causes Marcius, at Scene 6,65 ff., to inspire them with heroism both by his words and by his example. We see what a magnificent leader he can be, in the field—when he can lay aside his contempt: contrast Scene 5,4 ff. Another of the inventions, inconspicuous indeed but not without its effect, is the incident of the Messenger. This man brings to Cominius the unwelcome news that the Romans before the city have been beaten back, an hour since. Asked why he has been so slow in bringing the news, he explains that he had to evade certain Volscians who lay in his path. At once Marcius arrives to report that the city has been captured.

COMINIUS: Where is that slave
 Which told me they had beat you to your trenches?
 Where is he? Call him hither.
MARCIUS: Let him alone;
 He did inform the truth.

The point is made swiftly and with no emphasis, but we see at once what it is: Marcius will have no injustice done to an innocent man.

The third invention is even more interesting. When he came to the scene in which Marcius refused a personal share of the spoil, Shakespeare read this, in North:

> Only this grace (said he) I crave and beseech you to grant me. Among the Volscians there is an old friend and host of mine, an honest wealthy man and now a prisoner, who living before in great wealth in his own country liveth now a poor prisoner in the hands of his enemies: and yet notwithstanding all this his misery and misfortune, it would do me a great pleasure if I could save him from this one danger, to keep him from being sold as a slave. The soldiers hearing Marcius' words made a marvellous great shout . . .

and though Plutarch does not say it, the clear implication is that the prisoner was released.

That is what he read; this is what he wrote:

CORIOLANUS: The gods begin to mock me. I, that now
Refused most princely gifts, am bound to beg
Of my lord general.
COMINIUS: Take it; 'tis yours. What is't?
COR.: I sometime lay, here in Corioli,
At a poor man's house: he used me kindly.
He cried to me; I saw him prisoner;
But then Aufidius was within my view
And wrath o'erwhelmed my pity: I request you
To give my poor host freedom.
COM.: O, well begg'd!
Were he the butcher of my son, he should
Be free as is the wind.—Deliver him, Titus.
LARTIUS: Marcius, his name?
COR.: By Jupiter, forgot!
I'm weary; yea, my memory is tired.—
Have we no wine here?

Nobody but Shakespeare would have done this. He is not slavishly, or perfunctorily copying his source, because he takes the trouble to convert a rich man into a poor man, and then lets the incident collapse into the negative result that the poor man was not identified and therefore not set free. If we knew nothing about his source, we should be tempted to say that he had found the story there and simply incorporated it without doing anything to make it significant; as it is, we know that he invented it—presumably for some purpose. I confess that I can see only one conceivable reason, and that, not a trivial one: "But then Aufidius was within my view, And wrath o'erwhelmed my pity"; so that a generous and natural impulse came to nothing.

We have looked sufficiently, I think, at Act I. The Citizens, Coriolanus himself, the Tribunes, Volumnia, Aufidius: these are the persons for whom Shakespeare has most bespoken our interest, not counting Menenius, more of a commentator than an actor, and Virgilia, whose role it is to be all that Volumnia is not, in the way of womankind. We will now take note of what

Shakespeare does in the body of the play with each of these separately; it will be one way, and perhaps a convenient one, of setting down the facts.

The Citizens, surely, are "unresisting imbecillity" itself, pliant clay in the hands of the Tribunes; so much so that he who was justly welcomed back to Rome with wild enthusiasm (II 1,194–209,250 ff.) is later—not indeed without some reason—being execrated as a public enemy (III 3, end): "Our enemy is banished! He is gone! Hoo! hoo!" Sicinius thinks it proper to tell them to hoot him out of the city: "Give him deserved vexation": they obey with alacrity:

> Come, come, let's see him out at gates; come, come.—
> The gods preserve our noble tribunes!—Come.

But later (IV 6, end):

> FIRST CITIZEN: For mine own part,
> When I said, banish him, I said, 'twas pity.
> SECOND CIT.: And so did I.
> THIRD CIT.: And so did I; and to say the truth so did very many of us: That we did, we did for the best; and though we willingly consented to his banishment, yet it was against our will.
> COM.: Ye're goodly things, you voices!

Coriolanus too might well say, as he did earlier (III 1,30): "Have I had children's voices?"

Being what they are, they have of course no idea how ignoble are their "noble tribunes". Brutus and Sicinius are drawn as men whose contempt for the commons is no less than that of Coriolanus himself, but the more repulsive inasmuch as it is dressed up by them as its opposite. The fact is too plain to need illustration; the only question is why Shakespeare should have insisted so often on their pride, envy, dishonesty, and "infantlike abilities", as Menenius puts it. The coming tragedy of Coriolanus, one might think, would have been the more impressive had he made enemies of worthier men. But Shakespeare pursues them to the end: he kicks them out of his play in the passage in which their dupes the People have already laid their hands on Brutus, and are swearing that if

> The Roman ladies bring not comfort home,
> They'll give him death by inches.

So does retribution hang over them; but why should Shakespeare have invented it? It seems no necessary part of a tragedy of Coriolanus.

Volumnia: we asked if it was sufficient explanation of the unladylike relish for blood and martial glory given to her by the poet, that it helps to account for the character of Coriolanus. We meet her for the second time when her son returns in triumph: her talk is all of his glory, his many wounds, and of her one hope that remains unfulfilled—though not, she thinks, for long. Of what he has achieved for Rome, not a word.

Our next meeting with her (III 2) is the scene in Coriolanus' house just before the crisis. We learn then, even if we did not know it before, that her contempt for the commons is equal to her son's:

> . . . woollen vassals, things created
> To buy and sell with groats; to show bare heads
> In congregations; to yawn, be still, and wonder
> When one but of my ordinance stood up
> To speak of peace or war.

A moment later:

COR.: Let them hang.
VOL.: Ay, and burn too.

She says (vv. 128 f.):

> Do as thou list.
> Thy valiantness was mine, thou suck'dst it from me;
> But owest thy pride thyself.

That may be so, but another difference between them is made more apparent. She would be politic:

> I would have had you put your power well on
> Before you had worn it out. . . .

> I have a heart as little [?] apt as yours,
> But yet a brain that leads my use of anger
> To better vantage. . . .
>
> I would dissemble with my nature, where
> My fortunes and my friends at stake required
> I should do so in honour.

To him, this is no more than "some harlot's spirit". He promises to speak "mildly", but in fact he cannot speak even sensibly. So that everything goes wrong; he plays straight into the hands of the Tribunes. Therefore we meet her next, with Virgilia and others, taking their leave of him at the city gate (IV i). He says to his mother: Only true nobility can ride out the storms of adversity; you have taught me "precepts that would make invincible the heart that could con them". Very soon we are to see how Coriolanus, so taught, meets his storm. All that Virgilia can say—all that Shakespeare gives her to say during the whole scene—is "O Heavens! O Heavens!" His impatient reply: "Nay, I prithee, woman—" is cut short and overtopped by Volumnia's outburst:

> Now the red pestilence strike all trades in Rome,
> And occupations perish!

Finally, so far as this part of the play goes, there follows the scene in which first she takes the very hide off the noble Tribunes; then, when they have at last escaped her lash, she says:

> I would the gods had nothing else to do
> But to confirm my curses—

which indeed the gods seem on the point of doing, in their own way, when "They'll give him death by inches"—and finally:

> MENENIUS: You've told them home;
> And by my troth you've cause.—You'll sup with me?
> VOL.: Anger's my meat; I'll sup upon myself,
> And so shall starve with feeding. Come, let's go:
> Leave this faint puling, and lament as I do,
> In anger, Juno-like. Come, come, come.
> MEN.: Fie, fie, fie!

Fie, fie! indeed; for what could more vividly express the barrenness of this consuming wrath than: "And so shall starve with feeding"?

How seriously are we to take Shakespeare's *poiesis* here? When next we see Volumnia, "the red pestilence" is indeed about to strike, not "the trades in Rome", for pestilence is not so discriminating, but Rome herself. Coriolanus, apt pupil of his mother, goes into the unknown, whether to prove himself "invincible" or not; time will show. Meanwhile, Shakespeare takes it into his head to write the short scene in which the Volscian spy happens to meet the Roman traitor who is on his way to Antium with news "tending to the good of their adversaries". They surmise that Aufidius will come into his own, now that Rome has lost Coriolanus, and so the two scoundrels make their way cheerfully towards Antium. A moment later we learn where Coriolanus has steered his ship: he too is in Antium.

As for him, perhaps we need not examine in detail what Shakespeare has been doing with him during this part of the play. As he puts a shrewd estimate of the Tribunes into the mouth of Menenius (II 1), so in the scene following he invents two officers who shall talk of Coriolanus: He has so planted his honours and actions in the hearts of the people that they must confess their gratitude, yet he is not one of your great men who, justly, are indifferent to the affections of the multitude: rather, "He seeks their hate with greater devotion than they can render it him".

If we care to be Aristotelian for a moment, we can truly say that here is the great *hamartia* that destroys Coriolanus. As the First Officer says: "That's a brave fellow, but he's vengeance proud, and loves not the common people". Like Ajax, he will have things his own way or not at all; because "the gown of humility" revolts him, he would have an ancient custom abolished. But if we became Aristotelian here, we should have an embarrassing amount of *hamartia* on our hands—in Coriolanus, in the Tribunes, in Volumnia, and in the flabbiness of the Citizens, to say nothing of Aufidius. It is not Coriolanus only who is "an impossible man".

Unless we are paralysed by the desire to believe, all the time, in "the fundamental nobility" of Coriolanus, it is not difficult to see that what is at stake is more than Coriolanus: it is the city itself. "When two authorities are up . . . how soon confusion May enter 'twixt the gap of both" (III 1,109 ff.); "Nothing is done to purpose" (149); "That is the way to lay the city flat" (198 and 204); "Now the good gods forbid that our renowned Rome . . . Should now eat up her own" (291 ff.); "unless . . . our good city cleave in the midst and perish" (III 2,27 f.). There is also Coriolanus' superb:

> I banish you;
> And here remain with your uncertainty.
> (III 3,125)

Later (IV 6,36), Brutus can say, complacently:

> The gods have well prevented it, and Rome
> Sits safe and still without him—

but at once an Aedile comes in: a messenger has arrived, reporting that two Volscian armies have invaded Roman territories. The Aedile's wisdom was to put the man in prison; Brutus', that he should be whipped as well; and all that Menenius can foresee, a little later, is that Rome will be burned down, with the Romans inside it.

This at least makes intelligible most of what we have been recording: Shakespeare has been directing our attention, comprehensively and impartially, to the futility of the Citizens, the meannesses of the Tribunes, and the hatred and contempt shown toward the commons by Coriolanus and Volumnia, and to the people's hatred of them. All this is not only vivid and dramatic but intelligent and necessary as well, if the real theme of the play is the peril to which the city is reduced by the working of these passions. If on the other hand the play is "a one-man drama", then surely Shakespeare is being extravagantly romantic, seriously lacking in a sense of proportion, in making the apparently imminent destruction of a city and all its inhabitants no more than the background for the personal tragedy of one man, however great. Or is it only the inhibiting effect of an addiction to Greek literature that makes one feel uneasy with a criticism which notices insufficient psychical development in the delineation of Coriolanus' character, and does not notice that a city is on the verge of destruction?

But of course we cannot possibly say that Rome, so to speak, is the tragic hero of the play. The death of Coriolanus *is* the climax, and Act V makes it quite clear that Shakespeare's mind is engaged on this and not on the fate of Rome, however prominent that theme may be in the body of the play, and even though it would cogently explain why Shakespeare should have so altered his given material as to create this wide picture of a city full of hatred, contempt, and envy. For we have only to look at Scenes 4 and 5 of Act V. The hypothesis we have just considered would be tenable only if at the end of the play we saw that the patricians and plebeians were becoming reconciled, that harmony and stability were to take the place of discord and insecurity. If we care to exercise our fancy for a moment, we can imagine—merely to see how far it is from Shakespeare's thought—a chastened Coriolanus recalled to Rome as her stout bulwark of defence. In fact, the possibility of his recall is once alluded to by the First Senator, in Scene 5:

> Unshout the noise that banish'd Marcius,
> Repeal him with the welcome of his mother.

Shakespeare was on the verge of inventing a really great and dramatic ending: let the Senate, with the full support of Tribunes and People, solemnly decree the honourable recall of the great hero, and then let the enthusiastic acclamations be suddenly hushed with the news that he has been murdered in Corioli.—But we have seen before that sometimes the greatest dramatists unaccountably miss their way. What he does with

Rome is very different. In the first part of Scene 4 the Romans are trembling with fear; then the great news comes and they are overjoyed at their deliverance. In the very short scene that follows, the Ladies are welcomed as they deserve—and that is all. The stage-directions hereabouts are loud with shoutings and drums and hautboys; there is a Procession, there is a blaze of relief and joy; but obviously, Shakespeare's *mind* is not engaged here; he is merely doing better than Sophocles did when at the end of the *Tyrannus* he forgot to tell us that in fact Thebes was relieved of the plague.

Therefore we find ourselves at a loss. If we put all our money on Coriolanus as the Hero, we have to confess that much of the structure of the play could have been different (as indeed it was, in Plutarch), and that Act V does not really satisfy us. If, with some good evidence, we put it on the fate of Rome, we find that Shakespeare walks away from us, quite uninterested. But if he was a good dramatist, the way out of our *impasse* must be plainly in the text, even if it is badly overgrown with brambles. He was a good dramatist. Let us follow him with close attention, from Coriolanus' arrival in Antium.

The complaint has been made that he has not properly prepared us for it. But he has. We look for psychical development, both in Coriolanus and in Aufidius; what Shakespeare has been putting before us is something, not perhaps more important, but certainly different.

To our astonishment (if we can read the play as if for the first time) Coriolanus is in Antium—and Shakespeare has arranged that it shall be immediately after the scene of the two wretched spies. In him, the "precepts that would make invincible the heart that conn'd them" are apparently compatible with treason. He looks about him:

> A goodly city is this Antium.—City,
> 'Tis I that made thy widows; many an heir
> Of these fair edifices, 'fore my wars,
> Have I heard groan and drop . . .

He muses on the "slippery turns" of the world: friends fast sworn shall, within the hour, on the dissension of a doit, break out to bitterest enmity; so fellest foes shall grow dear friends:

> So with me:
> My birthplace hate I, and my love's upon
> This enemy town . . .

the second part of which is not true; no more true than what Aufidius presently says to him:

> O Marcius, Marcius,
> Each word thou hast spoke hath weeded from my heart
> A root of ancient envy.

Then comes the hyperbolical passage in which he declares, embracing Coriolanus, that he does it with more warmth than when he embraced his newly-wedded wife. But there is no root in this—except, as we soon find, the root of ancient envy.

It has been carefully prepared, though the preparation, not being "psychical" as we require, passes unnoticed or misinterpreted. From the beginning there has been kept before us the insensate hatred which these two men bear each other, and we may call it "insensate" because no reason is given for it, except that for Coriolanus Aufidius is "a lion that I am proud to hunt" (I 1 ,239 f.), while as for Aufidius:

> Not Afric owns a serpent I abhor
> More than the fame I envy.
> (I 8,3 f.)

Never does Shakespeare confer on this hatred a single touch of nobility or chivalry, and this is the hatred which Coriolanus resolved to embrace, when conflicting hatreds had driven him out of Rome. Now, many instances prove that nothing in Shakespeare's philosophy forbade ancient enmity to change to love, but here it is impossible, or if possible, does not happen: in each of the two it springs from his innermost nature, and what is bringing them together is nothing but a common hatred of Rome. No miracle happens; we do not have to wait long before seeing that Aufidius' envy, far from being rooted out, is as strong and poisonous as ever. Menenius is speaking the simple truth when he says (IV 6,71 ff.):

> This is unlikely;
> He and Aufidius can no more atone
> Than violentest contrarieties.

Shakespeare was not much interested, here, in psychical development; someone must have told him that Wrath, Pride, and Envy were among the seven deadly sins, and he is, in his way, passing the news on to us. In retrospect, the words "Wrath o'erwhelmed my pity" gain in significance.

Menenius, in IV 6, is given other things to say which, once we begin to see the level on which Shakespeare is thinking, are a significant preparation for the idea which becomes dominant in Act V: Nature. We are in Rome, where nothing has been heard of Coriolanus since he went out of the gate. The Tribunes are happy: the great enemy of the people has disappeared, and everything goes smoothly. Menenius agrees, in part:

> MEN.: All's well, and might have been much better, if
> He could have temporised.
> SICINIUS: Where is he, hear you?
> MEN.: Nay, I hear nothing: his mother and his wife
> Hear nothing from him.

It is not much; however, we may remember what he said at the gate:

> Come, my sweet wife, my dearest mother, and
> My friends of noble touch; when I am forth,
> Bid me farewell, and smile. I pray you, come.
> While I remain above the ground, you shall
> Hear from me still; and never of me aught
> But what is like me formerly.
> (IV 1,48–53)

Strange, that his sweet wife and dearest mother have heard nothing from him—except that we know what he has done, going to Antium and Aufidius. Is that, perchance, what was like him formerly?

It is not much; only preparation. Later (V 4,12), Sicinius remarks: "He loved his mother dearly". Menenius replies: "So he did me; and he no more remembers his mother now than an eight-year-old horse".

At the gate, Cominius declared, "I'll follow thee a month"; and Menenius:

> If I could shake off but one seven years
> From these old arms and legs, by the good gods,
> I'd with thee every foot.

At the beginning of Act V, we hear how he has treated Cominius: "He would not seem to know me. . . . He was a kind of nothing . . ." Then, with difficulty, Menenius is persuaded to go to him and plead for Rome—Menenius, whom he had called father, who had almost danced for joy when he heard that Coriolanus had sent a letter to him too (II 1). We now have to watch Menenius humiliated first by the Volscian Sentinels, then by Coriolanus, who receives him with one word: "Away!" And he knows what he is doing:

> That we have been familiar,
> Ingrate forgetfulness shall poison, rather
> Than pity note how much. Therefore be gone.
> Mine ears against your suits are stronger than
> Your gates against your force.

Perhaps we wonder if it is possible for a man so to deny all that he had and was part of: if we do, we soon have Shakespeare's answer: "No".

So that Menenius is sent away, with the revealing concession of the letter that Coriolanus had already written for him. As he goes, the First Sentinel says, "A noble fellow, I warrant him"; the Second says: "The worthy fellow is our general: he's the rock, the oak not to be wind-shaken". So thinks Coriolanus too: he had opened up on Menenius by asserting: "Wife, mother, child, I know not"; and he closed by saying to Aufidius:

This man, Aufidius,
Was my beloved in Rome: yet thou behold'st!
AUF.: You keep a constant temper.

But the oak, the rock, has not yet realised what it is he is trying to stand against. Dr Johnson's comment, that there is perhaps too little bustle in this act, makes one wonder what he could have made of Aeschylus' *Prometheus*, or indeed of any other tragedy in which the tension is just below, not on, the surface, and it is evident that the tension is not felt if all we can see is that Coriolanus is one who has gone over to the enemy "merely to gratify a private grudge against the city".

When he sees the Ladies approaching, he says things which have only to be put into words to be seen impossible:

Shall I be tempted to infringe my vow
In the same time 'tis made? I will not! . . .
But out, affection!
All bond and privilege of nature, break!
Let it be virtue to be obstinate.
What is that curtsy worth? or those dove's eyes
Which can make gods forsworn?—I melt, and am not
Of stronger earth than others—

which may remind us of the one wise thing said by Brutus, in this play:

You speak o' the people
As if you were a god to punish, not
A man of their infirmity.

He is like Ajax: he cannot κατ' ἄνθρωπον φρονεῖν, "think as becomes mortal man". Ajax could say to Athena: "Goddess, go help the others; where I stand the battle-line shall not break". He too found—or at least said—that the desolate plea of Tecmessa was too strong for him:

Nothing is firm; the strongest oath is broken,
The stubborn purpose fails. For I was hard

As tempered steel; but now Tecmessa's words
Have softened me, and I have lost my edge.

He too found himself face to face with something much stronger than his own pride and anger: Sophocles expressed it through the imagery of Night always giving place to Day, and Winter to Summer; Shakespeare also has his imagery, hereabouts:

My mother bows,
As if Olympus to a molehill should
In supplication nod; and my young boy
Hath an aspect of intercession which
Great Nature cries *Deny not.*—Let the Volsces
Plough Rome and harrow Italy: I'll never
Be such a gosling to obey instinct, but stand
As if a man were author of himself
And knew no other kin.
VIRG.: My lord and husband!

It does not matter much if Coriolanus is "an impossible man"; what does matter is that he is trying to do the impossible; one or two characters in Greek plays remark that it is impossible to fight the gods—and that is exactly what Coriolanus is trying to do here. A man is not an "eight-year-old horse".

He could assert: "Wife, mother, child, I know not"; but it is not long before he is condemning himself for leaving unsaluted "the most noble mother of the world", and kneels to her, conscious as he does it that it is demanded of him by his own nobility:

Sink, my knee, i' the earth;
Of thy deep duty more impression show
Than those of common sons.

Shakespeare too understood the eloquence of action. We may recall how, when Coriolanus had come back in all his glory from Corioli, he went down on his knee to his mother, and she said: "Nay, my good soldier, up!" It is a reversal of nature indeed when first she bows to him, like Olympus to a molehill, and now kneels to him, "with no softer cushion than the flint"; and she says so:

> I kneel before thee, and unproperly
> Show duty, as mistaken all this while
> Between the child and parent.

But she is encountering her own nemesis. She, who earlier thought it "dishonour" to beg of a son (III 2,124), is forced to do it now; then, she could "mock at death with as big heart as thou": what she cannot mock at is the destruction of Rome by her own son. He also sees that the course of nature is being flouted, and says so in characteristic fashion:

> Then let the pebbles on the angry beach
> Fillip the stars; then let the mutinous winds
> Strike the proud cedars 'gainst the fiery Sun,
> Murdering impossibility, to make
> What cannot be, light work.—

"Words crushed into lines like fuel to stoke a furnace", as Granville-Barker said: Shakespeare himself has almost murdered impossibility in getting these two words into a blank verse. But it is something that Coriolanus cannot do; he is himself murdered.

He fights and fights, but he cannot win. He can say:

> Do not bid me
> Dismiss my soldiers, or capitulate
> Again with Rome's mechanics: tell me not
> Wherein I seem unnatural; desire not
> T' allay my rages and revenges with
> Your colder reasons.

But of course they are not "colder reasons"; they are something much deeper—the "instinct" which he would never be gosling enough to obey.

Not many stage-actions are at once simpler and more charged with tragic meaning than his when, after Volumnia's two long speeches, he moves across and takes his mother's hand. Against the rock, the oak, there have been brought to bear the weakest and strongest forces that exist: the simple realities of the human situation. These conquer where stronger things fail. As Coriolanus himself says:

> All the swords
> In Italy, and her confederate arms,
> Could not have made this peace.

It is strange how these poets—the great ones—seem to repeat each other. There is Achilles, in the *Iliad*. In his rage with Agamemnon, he had sworn to let the Greeks go to destruction, if Agamemnon would not make full amends. The gifts offered in Book IX might look like full amends, but for Achilles they were not humiliating enough. Then, at the beginning of Book XVI, Patroclus comes to him in tears, "like a baby-girl crying to be picked up", as Achilles amiably puts it. But Patroclus tells him that Diomedes, Odysseus, Agamemnon, Eurylochus, all are lying wounded and that the whole army is in desperate straits. In reply, Achilles rehearses once more the story of his wrongs. Then he says: "It was, it seems, impossible: a man cannot maintain his wrath for ever":

> οὐδ' ἄρα πως ἦν
> ἀσπερχὲς κεχολῶσθαι ἐνὶ φρεσίν.

If at this moment Achilles could have escaped from his wrath, things would have fallen out very differently, but it still has him in its grip; so that Patroclus is killed, and a still worse wrath comes upon him, against Hector, even upon Hector's dead body—though each night the gods undo the outrages done to it by Achilles during the day. So Priam comes at last to beg the body for proper burial. He also confronts wrath with the simplest of facts, and they prevail: "Your father, like me, stands on the threshold of ruinous old age, with none to protect him against grasping neighbours. But he lives every day in the hope of seeing you safe home from Troy: of my fifty sons, all are dead; not one is left. Think of your own father and show pity for me; and I deserve the more pity since I have brought myself to do what no man has ever done before me: I have raised to my lips the hand of the man who slew my own son." He is doing, "unproperly", what Volumnia too does, "unproperly". Priam wept bitterly for Hector; Achilles broke down and wept for his father, who now would never see him again, and for Patroclus—whom he had allowed to go to his death because he could not yet escape from his wrath. We may reflect too that the *Iliad*, like this play, and the *Ajax*, *Antigone*, and *Hamlet*, ends with a burial, setting the action in the longest perspective that we can know.

So that Coriolanus takes his mother's hand:

> O mother, mother!
> What have you done? Behold, the heavens do ope,
> The gods look down, and this unnatural scene
> They laugh at. O my mother, mother! O,
> You've won a happy victory for Rome,
> But for your son—believe it, O, believe it—
> Most dangerously you have with him prevailed,
> If not most mortal to him.

It seems hardly enough, to say that the gods are mentioned, when they *are* mentioned, only for the sake of local colour.

Perhaps we should ask: why should it be most mortal to him? He makes a peace humiliating, though welcome, to Rome, gratifying to the Volsces; why should it not rest here? The answer is plain: we should be forgetting Aufidius, and wrath, and envy. Coriolanus, defying all that is natural, embraced enmity, and in that embrace he must remain. In an earlier scene he told how "Wrath o'erwhelmed my pity"; faced with mother, wife, and child, he found that pity—or if not pity at least the inescapable bonds imposed by Nature—overwhelmed, if not his wrath, at least his determination to destroy Rome; now, wrath is to overwhelm him.

We return to the criticism suggested just now, that the play shows some uncertainty of purpose: for a one-man tragedy of Coriolanus, Shakespeare would have done better to follow Plutarch more closely, and not make so much of the follies and vices of the Citizens and the Tribunes, since these bring into too much prominence the peril into which the city itself is brought; yet the impressive theme of a city torn by its own animosities arrives at no satisfactory conclusion.

No doubt it is not incredible that Shakespeare should have fallen into such a structural error; he may have had to write the play quickly. Yet it must have been with deliberation that he so changed and magnified the roles given by Plutarch to the Citizens, the Tribunes, Volumnia, and Aufidius. But since putting forward the criticism we have learned more about the level on which he was thinking; we see now how wide of the mark it is to say that the play has no "cosmic reverberations", that it does not open vistas but closes them. We say such things only because we are not disposed to notice in the play things for which we are not looking, things that do not at once strike us as important—the emphasis laid, again and again, on hatred, envy, pride; behaviour, of one kind or another, that flouts nature, whether Volumnia's very unwomanly observations to the womanly Virgilia, or Coriolanus' desertion of, and determination to destroy, his own city. To such details we like to give an immediate, personal interpretation—and then complain, as in the case of Coriolanus' treason, that it is not properly managed. We may say that "the gods are mentioned, when they *are* mentioned, only for the sake of local colour"; but does that do any kind of justice to this passage in V 4, for example?—

SIC.: The gods be good unto us!
MEN.: No, in such a case the gods will not be good unto us. When we banished him, we respected not them; and he returning to break our necks, they respect not us.

Here at least the gods are more than local colour: they are a power of the same order as that which has in fact just prevented Coriolanus from "returning to break our necks", and that, however, he himself calls "great Nature". When we see that this was Shakespeare's perspective, that his mind was not engaged, as Plutarch's was, on the glaring faults in one man which ruined so much that was noble in him, then we can see the compelling reasons for which Shakespeare rebuilt Plutarch's structure on ampler foundations. His mind was on the passions or vices that are contrary to the harmony of Nature and therefore must work mischief: it is only when we see this that everything in the play comes into focus, makes its proper contribution to the whole, and forms a powerful unity. These vices, and their baleful effects, he exhibits, indifferently, in the city at large and in individuals, for the city is the individual writ large (as Plato thought too, when he began on the *Republic*), and the individual is the city writ small. It is a "political" play not because Shakespeare's imagination was seized with the spectacle of a city tearing itself to pieces—which theme he then forgot to finish off properly. It is "political" in the widest sense of the word: a statement about the relations of man with man, and the laws of Nature, or "the gods", which govern them. When our responses are attuned to the scale on which the tragedy was built, we experience no jolt when, without telling us that Rome now turned to better courses, he brings all the weight of the play to bear on the price that Coriolanus must now pay for *his* flouting of all that is "natural". (A Greek tragic dramatist would probably have left Rome in the air a little earlier.) Conversely, if we see in Rome only the setting for Coriolanus' own tragedy, that too fails to grip us as it should. The same stream of thought continues to the very end, to the rasping scene in which Aufidius, in his envy and hatred, affronts all human feeling by planting his foot on the body; for his wrath, like Achilles', gives way to a more truly "natural" force:

> My rage is gone,
> And I am struck with sorrow.—Take him up;
> Help, three o' the chiefest soldiers; I'll be one.

When study of the *poiesis* has led to such an understanding of the play, as the only one which reasonably accounts for its broad structure and the details, it is agreeable to look back and see that Shakespeare himself virtually said as much at the beginning—except that we were not quite sure whether to listen or not, for he might have included the fable of the Belly merely to quieten the violence of the opening scene, or to help characterise Menenius as the humorous patrician, or to make more impressive, by the delay, the first entrance of the great Caius Marcius. But no; he was doing something perhaps less clever but more serious; he was, in a very natural and easy way, giving an indication of the background to which we should relate the whole action that is to follow—the divinely-ordained harmony, with all that it implies. If we pass this by, then, by Shakespearian standards, the play is not first-rate—beta plus, perhaps; if we do, then let us say, avoiding direct comparisons, that *Coriolanus* is eminently worthy of the company that it keeps in the canon of Shakespeare's tragedies.

We have now done what is, I fear, our best to carry out the programme sketched at the outset, namely to confront Chaos with Aristotle: to take up his doctrine about *poiesis* and see if it works, to see if the way in which a writer first chooses and then arranges his material can do anything to reveal the true unity of his work, and thereby facilitate our contact with his mind and enable us to escape from our own *idées reçues*. The enquiry has been laborious—I hope not unnecessarily so—because there are no reliable short-cuts. How far it has been fruitful is not for me to say.

The reader who has persevered to the end cannot fail to have been struck with a certain sameness: it has been the constant refrain that the writers we have been discussing thought and worked in a perspective different from the one natural to us. It is certainly not a commonplace in critical writing to set side by side for comparison Shakespeare and Thucydides, yet material for such a comparison would not be entirely lacking. Each gives the sharpest attention to the details with which he works, but each passes rather lightly over the middle foreground, as it were, where, as it seems, our own attention most naturally comes to rest. We have just seen that Shakespeare does not always do what we expect: he does not trace the process of thought or emotion that led Coriolanus from Rome to Antium; "the character-drawing is external"; in the last act we try hard to believe in the hero's nobility, and do not notice that Shakespeare is interested in Nature and wrath and envy. In what is surely the same kind of way we are surprised that Thucydides does not tell us enough about finance, internal politics, and so on; but if our analysis has not misled us, the evident fact is that where the mind of any modern historian would be working at full stretch Thucydides' mind is engaged only intermittently, and the region where his mind is continuously active would be visited by the modern only from time to time. In each case, our surprise is surely the same surprise; and at the beginning of this chapter it was argued that Thucydides and the Greek tragic poets too thought in what is recognisably a similar way.

In the face of this, the prudent writer is bound to ask himself if this is a glimpse of the truth, or only a bee in the bonnet. The reader will decide for himself, but if (as I hope) these readings are fairly well grounded on the facts of structure and style and method, then perhaps it is not a mere bee. There is certainly this fact: all the time (if we except Homer) we have been dealing with serious writers whose minds were formed, like those of their audiences, just before a radical change came over the mental outlook of their age; and it is roughly true (for we must not forget Corneille and Racine) that these were the only two periods of European history in which Tragedy has really flourished. Perhaps therefore it is not incredible if they have something important in common. Let us quote Whitehead for a second time; "The specialisation necessary for the development of civilised thought has had an unfortunate effect on the outlook of learned people: as science grew, minds shrank in width of comprehension". And what of the unlearned? We know that superstition began to increase early in the fourth century, and we know that the bourgeois drama of the eighteenth was not so sturdy as the Elizabethan. But we seem to be on the verge of a different enquiry, and this book is long enough already.

Indexes

I. Index of Passages Discussed

II. Index of General Topics